MARKETING FINANCIAL SERVICES

Marketing financial services

Colin McIver and Geoffrey Naylor

With a foreword by Deryk Vander Weyer, Chairman of Barclays Bank UK Limited and, currently, President of The Institute of Bankers

 **The Institute of Bankers**

10 Lombard Street, London EC3V 9AS

First published 1980
Reprinted 1981
Reprinted 1984
Copyright © 1980 The Institute of Bankers
and Colin McIver and Geoffrey Naylor

ISBN 0 85297 054 4 hard covers
      0 85297 055 2 paperback

Prepared by Hobsons Press (Cambridge) Ltd,
Bateman Street, Cambridge CB2 1LZ

Printed in Great Britain by Dramrite Printers Limited.
Southwark, London SE1

Acknowledgments

Grateful acknowledgments are due to two groups of people; those who over the years have helped us learn our craft and those who have helped by providing case study material for Part III of this book. This latter group includes Len Bakewell, Harold Corker, Seymour Fortescue, Mike Jones, John Lawson, Ian Morison, Harold Robson, Graham Savage, Robin Sharpe, Peter Stroudley, Ian Taylor and Colin Trusler. We, and our readers, are in their debt.

We are especially grateful to Ken Bromley and Brian Cox who kindly read through an early typescript and offered us many helpful comments.

The work, and long-suffering patience, of Lynn Lachs and Joyce Cook, our secretaries, deserves our thanks: particularly Lynn who typed (and retyped) the original manuscript.

Finally, we are grateful to the staff of The Institute of Bankers for their willing support and assistance during the preparation of this book.

Colin McIver and Geoffrey Naylor
10 July 1980

Foreword

It has now come to be accepted that marketing is an essential element in the management of a modern bank. For every UK bank, competition – not only from other UK banks but from overseas banks and from other financial service organisations – is intense and grows steadily more professional. The age of specialism in financial services by particular institutions has changed to one where most offer a wide range of services in competition with each other. Thus it has become essential to use all the resources and techniques that marketing can provide. One lesson that I quickly learned when I formed the Marketing Department in my own bank some thirteen years ago, was that marketing has been misunderstood and even resented by practising bankers as simply being advertising and selling and I soon came to appreciate that, for the efficient marketing of the bank's services, a change in internal attitudes was as necessary as acceptance by the customers; and, central to that, was the appreciation by management that the central core of marketing is the establishment of objectives, the defining of a clear strategy and the total management of the marketing mix.

As I have said elsewhere, marketing is 'identifying the most profitable markets now and in the future; assessing the present and future needs of customers; setting business development goals and making plans to meet them; managing the various services and promoting them to achieve the plans'.

As the authors suggest, I might have added 'also adapting to a changing environment in the market.'

The development of the marketing of financial services has not been helped by the fact that most of the very voluminous literature has dealt with the marketing of consumer or industrial products. The priniciples are the same as for the marketing of financial services but the applications are very different and it is, therefore, very valuable to have a new work dealing with the financial services industry.

The merits of this book in my estimation are twofold. First, it is written from the viewpoint of the practising banker by two authors who have been actively involved for a number of years in marketing organisation and procedures in UK banks. Secondly, it is written in plain English rather than the elaborate jargon which can sometimes be found in marketing publications. I believe that not only students of banking but those practising managers who find time to pause in their day-to-day activities and think about marketing as an essential part of their jobs will find this book stimulating.

Deryk Vander Weyer

The Institute of Bankers,
10 Lombard Street, London EC3V 9AS

Contents

Part three   Marketing in action

In this part we move from the general to the particular and describe some of the business development activities now taking place in the London clearing banks which require the application of marketing tools and techniques and an awareness of marketing principles among those involved.

The role of marketing

In this first part we define the role of marketing in management, and describe how the problems of marketing financial services differ from the marketing problems encountered in other industrial sectors.

CHAPTER ONE

Introduction

Introductions are where authors tend to review the whole book and to sum up just why they feel the subject is so important. But readers may not be ready to accept such a view – just as many of us, bankers included, recognise that before you can ask the right question you really need to know the right answer – or at least part of it. So some readers may prefer to skip, or skim, this introduction and return to it when, we hope, some of the right answers will have been noted from later chapters.

For others, we would point out that it is after all customary to start books of a didactic nature by defining terms. When marketing is the subject it is more than usually necessary to do so, because marketing is one of those chameleon words that change their meaning to match their environment. It (whatever it is) may be praised by one individual and damned by another, just because each has a different concept of what he is discussing.

Let us therefore sit in on a discussion between two individuals (both, as it happens, in favour of marketing, having earned their living from it for a number of years) about the Meaning of Marketing. We thought of calling the protagonists Socrates and Alcibiades. But this would be both pretentious and unrealistic since Plato is distinctly *passé* these days. We settled instead for McIver and Naylor, if only because neither is likely to sue for misrepresentation. Moreover, the decision recognises the principle of name registration, to which we shall refer in our chapter on promotion; if we keep up our cross-talk long enough, nobody will be in any doubt about who wrote this book.

Naylor: Normally I'd not bother too much, but in a book on the subject I suppose we had better start by reviewing some of the general definitions of marketing put forward by the various pundits who have preceded us; and then see how far, if at all, they need to be modified, when you come to marketing financial services rather than consumer or capital goods.

McIver: I'm not much of a one myself for definitions either, which seem to me often pretty sterile. Like you I'm much more interested in the way people apply marketing principles or use marketing techniques to make things *happen*. And I've certainly found that the most successful marketers in practice are often the least adept at reciting a textbook definition of it – some indeed would be faintly surprised to be told that what they are doing from common sense is actually marketing. But I agree that if our readers (and we) are to be clear what it is we are talking about, definition is inescapable.

Naylor: Well, then, how about the definition in Philip Kotler's monumental tome on Marketing Management: 'Marketing is the set of human activities directed at facilitating and consummating exchanges'?

McIver: That seems a bit academic for our purpose. I know Kotler says that 'the definition deliberately avoids taking the point of view of either the buyer or the seller', but in this book we have to take the seller's viewpoint. Our readers have a selling responsibility, which no doubt they will exercise with proper concern for the buyer's interest.

Naylor: Well I think the word 'profit' should be included anyway, so how about 'profitable selling'? It adopts the seller's viewpoint the word 'profitable' implies that costs are as much the concern of marketing people as revenues. In other words fitness for purpose rather than the highest quality that can be made. And at least it's brief!

McIver: Yes, but perhaps it's too brief to be helpful. I myself once defined marketing, in another context, as 'the function of co-ordinating and controlling the planning, selling and promotional activities of a commercial enterprise to serve the customer profitably'. I'm not sure that this is adequate in today's banking situation. For instance, can British banks truly be described as commercial enterprises in the purist sense; or do all the regulations to which they are subject, and all the social responsibilities which they accept, mean that they should be properly described as QUACSOS – quasi-commercial service organisations?

Naylor: I would suggest that, rather than assembling a miscellaneous collection of all the innumerable definitions coined by the innumerable marketing *littérateurs,* we adopt the definition propounded by Deryk Weyer of Barclays Bank, one of the first senior bankers in this country to recognise the importance of marketing not just to those members of a bank charged with a selling responsibility, but to the overall direction of the bank. He once wrote that marketing is

1 identifying the most profitable markets now and in the future;
2 assessing the present and future needs of customers;
3 setting business development goals and making plans to meet them;
4 managing the various services and promoting them to achieve the plans.

McIver: That seems to me the kind of flag one could well nail to the mast, not just in banking but in other industries as well. But I think we might suggest, so as to emphasise the constant link between marketing and change which I know he appreciates, an appendix to Deryk Weyer's four points – which might read 'all in the context of a changing environment in the market'. Indeed without marketing, organisations can find their environment changing faster than they are; in effect they could be losing their 'brand share' of the future. But what I particularly like about the Weyer definition is the fact that marketing is clearly identified as a central function of *management* at all levels. It is not down-graded to an optional extra which management buys by the yard from a specialist department down the street, or from outside agencies.

Naylor: As head of a specialist marketing department – down the street – I'm not wholly at ease with that remark. But I see what you are driving at. We need to distinguish, as in practice all the major banks do, between the large and increasingly specific marketing content of the *line manager's* job, and the *staff function* of providing management with specialist marketing services and innovative ideas. The service department's working definition of the marketing function could be quite different from the management definition just quoted. Its functional definition might be as follows.

The marketing services function is to provide all levels and segments of line management with relevant

information about customer attitudes and needs, about legal constraints, about changes in market conditions and about competitive activities as a basis for business development planning and action;

ideas for the development of new products or services or approaches, related to identified customer needs or market conditions;

sales communication material designed to help achieve business development objectives within and outside the organisation;

education of the company's employees in those marketing skills which are necessary for the efficient performance of their jobs.

McIver: In putting forward several definitions of marketing, we are really looking at the same thing from different viewpoints. When you escape from the thin air of linguistics to practical business management you can say that any organisation which sets out to be marketing-oriented will

1　be concerned to study the attitudes and needs of the different categories of customer on whom its business depends;
2　seek to identify those customer needs which it is capable of satisfying from its own or acquirable resources;
3　seek the most cost-effective way of satisfying those needs at a profit to itself;
4　seek to anticipate and react to change;
5　recognise the obligation to observe the moral and legal standards of the community to which it belongs.

Naylor: If the words differ, is that not all part of the essential nature of marketing to which we have already referred? Its concern with change makes it inevitable that it will itself change in emphasis and character over the years. Its sensitivity to the environment means that it must adapt to the situation in which it is operating. Above all, let us not forget that marketing, thank goodness, is by no means an exact science. It will recognise that there is more than one way of reaching the target which management has set.

McIver: I certainly take your point about change. In my thirty-odd years in business I have seen, not only a notable evolution in the understanding of marketing displayed by the average company, but also at any one time some profound contrasts between the under-standing (and performance) of one company compared with another. While there were pre-war examples of classic marketing activities, marketing as I recall was still regarded in the early post-war years as something of an exotic plant imported across the Atlantic along with Coca-Cola. Harvard Business School was the nursery in which it was bred and Theodore Levitt's article on 'Marketing Myopia' its classic exposition. In British business, the manufacturers of con-sumer products were the earliest to accept the basic marketing message that if you want to prosper you must give people what they want: the right product at the right price in the right place at the right time – and promote it – instead of simply toiling to sell them what you happen to make. Marketing research was the most readily and widely accepted aspect of marketing, possibly because managers sincerely wanted to know more about their customers, and, in a world with many links in the distribution chain from producer to consumer, this kind of research was much more reliable than hearsay 'trade' reports; possibly, it seems in moments of cynicism, because market research reports usually contain some items of anecdotal interest, and commissioning them or even reading them doesn't actually commit you to *doing* anything. ('Some people', it has been said, 'use market research as a drunk uses a lamp-post, more for support than illumination.') A more analytical approach to advertis-ing and its attendant activities – consumer and trade promotions, point-of-sale display – was the next major development. Instead of accepting uncritically the blanket statement that it pays to advertise (sometimes it does and sometimes it doesn't), companies, backed and often led by the more progressive advertising agencies, tried to measure the efficiency of the various advertising media available to them and to evaluate the return on their total investment in sales promotional activities.

Naylor: Yes, and part of this development was the introduction of the product manager system, whereby a bright young man was given the responsibility for planning and co-ordinating all the promotional activities designed to maximise the sales and profitability of an individual product or group of products. In theory the early product managers were held to be profit-responsible; in practice, since they seldom had much influence over either the production or the sales function, they could do little more than watch and pray – and, when unduly frustrated, bully the advertising agency, or change jobs! Only after a number of years, and only in the more sophisticated companies, was it eventually accepted that marketing was not just a more organised approach to selling but a vital aspect of building and maintaining a healthy company; an approach which must directly concern top management. Companies, it came to be realised, can survive without their own factories or offices – even at a pinch without their own accountants – but none can survive without customers.

McIver: Right, but it has taken a lot longer for the idea of marketing to gain acceptance among manufacturers of industrial products – if indeed it can yet be said to have gained anything approaching general acceptance. I suppose the reason for this is that the two most readily acceptable aspects of marketing technology, the marketing research which helps you to know your customer better and the advertising and other promotional activities which help you to communicate with him, are less obviously necessary when you have far fewer customers to consider and can deal with the most important of them face-to-face rather than through a chain of intermediaries. Perhaps it is this fact, or at least this illusion, of having a face-to-face relationship with customers which has made the financial institutions so slow to develop the marketing concept. Indeed, looking at the financial services industry from the outside rather than the inside like you, I wonder whether it has yet got beyond the stage of regarding marketing with quizzical scepticism or at best as a rather more organised version of selling.

Naylor: You're generalising too much about an industry as diverse as 'financial services'. In some areas marketing has been well used, mainly in the more narrowly based sectors such as unit trusts. In others it is seen as barely more than an advertising function. I suspect there are a number of other points you would qualify if you weren't generalising so much! But I do agree, there can be a world of difference between a marketing-oriented company and a company with a marketing department.

Marketing as a concept and as a discipline is undeniably a central function of management from the highest level down. Marketing techniques and skills are for the use of management from the lowest level up, and of the specialists – such as market researchers or advertising executives – that one might find in a marketing department. Only when both the concept *and* the skills are present in one organisation can it really be said to be marketing oriented.

It is high time to abandon this contrived dialogue and to shift from generalities to a statement of the particular ways in which the marketing of financial services by banks and other financial institutions differs from current marketing practices in other industries. Marketing is concerned with change and is itself constantly changing. What is said today may not be true tomorrow; and what is true of one institution may not be true of another. Thus there will still have to be generalisations to some extent. But readers will be able, we hope, to discern the kernel of truth in what follows and apply it to their own individual situations.

How does marketing financial services differ from marketing consumer or industrial products and services?

Fiduciary responsibility

A fundamental consideration which must cover the attitude of bank management to marketing and selling can be summed up in the phrase 'fiduciary responsibility'. There has always been a marketing element in banking practice throughout its recorded history, though it may not always have been described by that word. But bankers who persuade their customers to entrust personal or corporate funds to their care or to accept advice on investment on some management matters incur a heavier responsibility than the sellers of candyfloss.

This is not to say that the manufacture of consumer products or the producer of industrial goods or services, or indeed the management of a nationalised service industry, is without responsibility. But the responsibility in these other cases is limited to the fitness of purpose, quality and value for money of the product or service concerned. It is inconvenient but seldom catastrophic if the milk is sour, the refrigerator or telephone breaks down or a manufacturer's raw material shipment is sub-standard. But a banker's failure to discharge his fiduciary responsibility for safeguarding customers' funds or to provide responsible advice on financial matters can bankrupt a company or ruin an individual's life.

For this reason the marketing style of a financial services organisation can never be as uninhibited as that of, let us say, the manufacturer of fast-moving packaged goods. The latter can say, and mean it, that 'this is a marketing company' run by marketing people; and that the production, purchasing and other departments should follow the lead and satisfy the demands of the marketing department. A responsible bank management has to say that marketing skills are important if the bank is to grow and prosper – increasingly important in an increasingly competitive environment – but that other aspects of their profession are equally important.

A corollary of this is that the qualities a bank must seek in its employees are not the same as those that cartoonists would lead us to believe belong to a typical salesman: uncaring aggression at any price. It is true that without sales no company can survive. But the bank manager, dealing with transactions which may fundamentally affect his customer's future, must be more receptive and aware of the possible consequences of a successful 'sale'.

This does not necessarily mean that he will be a less effective salesman (though he may shudder at the notion of being called a salesman); but it does mean that his selling style and the marketing programme which is built around him will be different.

Involvement in national economic policy
In the modified form of capitalism which is characteristic of developed Western nations it would be unrealistic to speak of totally free enterprise. Government economic policies, whether expressed in wages policies, price controls, credit restrictions or other rules and regulations, all make it difficult for company managements to

concentrate on the textbook objective of maximising profits through customer satisfaction.

But the frustration or diversion of commercial objectives in the interest of national economic considerations is an unusually powerful factor in banking. In one year, government decisions on credit controls or interest levels may mean that banks are almost compelled to make large profits, however hard they struggle to avoid it. The next year, a shift in policy may mean that it is desperately difficult to achieve anything approaching the same profit level. This does not of course imply that the word 'profit' should be dropped from the bank marketer's vocabulary; it remains a condition of healthy growth and even survival as an independent organisation. But it does require a more flexible approach to the process of planning, targeting and monitoring marketing activities which will be dealt with later; and it does mean an acceptance of the need to make rapid changes of emphasis in a marketing programme, which is not always easy in a large organisation.

Attracting deposits
A third way in which financial services marketing differs from marketing in other industries is the involvement of marketing not only in the provision of services to customers but in the procurement of the raw material on which most of those services are based. The automobile industry does not have to *persuade* its suppliers to provide it with steel or components – though admittedly it has many other difficulties with suppliers. The banking industry can 'buy' a proportion of its raw material (money) on the money market; but an important proportion of the raw material has to be gained by persuading individuals or corporate organisations to deposit their funds with it. And persuasion is a marketing function.

The fact that the main means of persuasion in attracting deposits is the availability of services – so that the raw material supplier is at the same time a customer – adds a fascinating element of complexity to the truly fascinating business of marketing financial services. Indeed complexity is a predominant feature in this market. It involves some elements of three types of marketing: the industrial, the consumer and the retail level. It requires a range of skills and knowledge which are beyond the compass of any normal man; and it must eventually result in the progressive *segmentation* both of markets and of bank organisations to which we refer later.

The element of industrial marketing
The basic factor which in most cases distinguishes industrial marketing from the other main categories is the sale of the project or services concerned to fewer but (usually) better-informed customers. From this it follows that the element of personal selling as opposed to selling through advertising or other communications media is larger. It also follows that there is both more opportunity and more need for an understanding of the way in which the customer uses the product and of the contribution it makes to the profitability of his own business; and also of the elements in the decision-making process and their effects on the choice of your product or your competitors' – including the motivation of the individuals who contribute to the decision.

The parallel with the corporate sector of the banks' business is close. Acquiring and satisfying a corporate customer requires a range of skills which differs in degree if not in kind from those employed in attracting and satisfying personal customers. These skills range from face-to-face selling ability through the ability to assemble, analyse and interpret data from various sources about a given market and the operations of a given company within that market, to the ability to organise and apply a variety of specialist resources to satisfy the customer's requirements at an acceptable rate of return.

The consumer marketing element
In the early days of bank marketing in the UK much emphasis – possibly too much – was placed on attracting and servicing personal customers. This was understandable since consumer marketing is much the most conspicuous category because of its extensive reliance on media advertising; and it was also the category in which marketing techniques had made the most progress. Moreover, emphasis on personal customers probably assisted the build-up of the banks' image in the corporate sector, since the decision-makers in corporate customers are individuals as well; and their attitudes to banks will inevitably be coloured by their personal experiences.

At the same time the corporate sector is more important to most banks in terms of profit contribution; and it is also more vulnerable to attack from new competition (for instance, the overseas banks which have entered the London market in such numbers during recent years). It may be that more emphasis should have been put on the industrial marketing skills, especially to help overcome the price advantage non-clearing banks can have.

However that may be, the largest proportion of bank staff is concerned with the personal customer; and there are many techniques developed in consumer marketing which can be applied or adapted to the banking scene. They include marketing and attitude research techniques, methods of new product development, 'packaging' and presentation, market segmentation and mass market communications.

Retail marketing
It would be over-dramatising the situation to say that branch banks are in a stage of transition from the equivalent of the headmaster's study – into which customers ventured with apprehension and from which they emerged with relief that the castigation for an illicitly overdrawn account had not been more serious – to a shop which invites them to enter and browse among the available goodies. Security requirements and the heavy investment in vaults and other costly hardware make it unlikely that your average branch bank will ever be as alluring as Harrods or Habitat. However, the proliferation of bank services and the acquisition of related subsidiaries such as insurance or hire purchase companies which look to the branch bank as one of their available sales outlets make it inevitable that branches should be regarded to some degree as financial services shops if not supermarkets. The attempt to develop this logic in the form of the money shop has not been an unqualified success in the UK. But the need and the opportunity remain and a workable formula or formulas will unquestionably be found.

The implication of this is that at least some of the marketing techniques developed by the retail trade will be relevant to the branch banking organisation of the future. One might instance the automated self-service selling forced on the grocery trade by the high cost of labour; and the use of in-store display and merchandising techniques to whet the appetite of the casual shopper (or cheque-casher).

Evaluating customers' marketing skills

The main reason, we suggest, why a banker should have at least an appreciative understanding of marketing techniques used in other industries is that they can be a rich source of ideas that can be adapted and applied in the very different banking environment. But there is another reason which should be considered by those with discretionary lending powers. The lending policies of British banks are traditionally conservative and based on 'the ability to repay' backed whenever possible by tangible security. This is very right and proper, when in the last analysis it is other people's money that is being lent. But British lending policy is more conservative that that of some other countries; and it can provoke either the frivolous reaction that 'they will only lend money to people who don't need it' or the more serious if refutable criticism that bank lending policies are inimical to industrial growth and entrepreneurial initiative. If a combination of pressures should enforce a trend towards the acceptance of higher-risk loans, related less to current assets than to future prospects, the skill to discriminate between profit forecasts which are based on sound marketing planning and those which are the product of wishful thinking could become an even more important part of the bank manager's armoury.

Summary

In this chapter we have

1   discussed various definitions of marketing and agreed that the definition quoted on page 6 was a good description of the marketing function in banking and in most other industries from the *management* viewpoint;

2   made the point that in practice there is another and relevant view of marketing in the *marketing services* departments which see the same function from a different standpoint;

3   said that marketing is greatly concerned with the relationship between a changing environment and the changes in organisational structure and methods required to relate successfully and profitably to that environment;

4   suggested that the marketing of financial services differs in several important particulars from marketing in other industries;

but that many of the marketing techniques and ideas developed in other sectors can be usefully adapted to the increasingly competitive financial services market;

5   suggested that marketing, while it may not be the most important part of a bank manager's skills and responsibilities, must be high on the list; and the complexities of marketing requirements, particularly in a large diversified branch banking organisation, are such that both market segmentation and segmentation of the organisation that serves the market are essential.

Now, how much of this do *you* accept, and how far does it reflect your own experience of the banking scene? You may not agree with everything we have said, but please pause and think about it.

CHAPTER TWO

Marketing in a changing environment

Recognising, reporting and adapting to change

All organisations, unless totally introverted and therefore doomed to suffer the fate of the dinosaur, must be sensitive to the environment and adapt to any relevant changes in it. This is so obvious that it hardly needs to be stated. The trouble is that most individuals and most organisations resist change. It must have been hard for the early mammals to abandon their watery environment and learn to exist on dry land. It is visibly just as difficult for Industrial Man to accept that the job he is doing, or the way he is doing it, is no longer relevant to a rapidly changing economic, social or technological environment.

To bring about change in an organisation, which involves changing the attitudes and behaviour of the people who work in it, is one of the most difficult tasks of the management team, involving all their combined skills.

Management's difficulty is seldom one of needing to take emergency action. Most changes, whether in the market place or in technology, are both predictable and relatively slow; and the process of adapting to change within the organisation is equally slow. The real problems arise from

1 the need for early recognition of impending change that will affect the organisation's activities;
2 getting the timing right. Being too far ahead of your time can have just as serious commercial consequences as being far too late;
3 the difficulties which management, reared and perhaps trained in

calmer times, have in finding the opportunities amid today's crises for thinking about tomorrow and the day after;

4   the reluctance of both customers and employees to change their ways.

Marketing skills, probably embodied in a central department, have a valuable contribution to make in this area. Particular relevant skills are

1   the ability to collect external information through market research and other means, to predict the eventual outcome of emergent changes, and to interpret their significance for the organisation;
2   techniques of planning and co-ordination, relating the speed of internal change – product development, market-related organisation, selling and distribution methods – to the rate of change in external demand and competition;
3   the skills of communication and persuasion needed, first, to bring an understanding of the situation to management and others, and second, to accelerate necessary changes in the attitudes and behaviour of people involved in the company's operations, whether as customers, employees or distributors and agents;
4   techniques for pre-testing possible courses of action or reaction to change, such as market models and test markets.

Changes in customers' characteristics and related needs

The most immediately relevant environmental factor for any organisation is the customer on whose continued approval the organisation's future depends. In almost all cases the *ultimate* customer is some segment of the general public; even the industrial marketer, whose immediate customers are other organisations, is dependent in the end on the ability of those organisations to satisfy the segment of the general public which they serve.

Bankers will instantly recognise the truth of this. Indeed, when they act as lenders to industrial companies, they are one stage further removed from the general public; yet most bankers will still want to know about the ultimate sales so as to judge the soundness of a project. So we make no excuse whatsoever for talking about general marketing principles. Good bankers will see the relevance to banking, even before reading the later chapters in which specific applications of the principles to our industry are described.

For the organisation marketing goods or services (including financial services) to the general public, the changes in personal circumstances and lifestyle which have characterised the last twenty-five years in all countries have opened up many new opportunities while putting a stop to some. The UK with its 56 million population has changed less than most countries of the developed or developing world. The growth both of population and of gross national product has been relatively slow. There has been no obvious revolution in the form of government or in social structure. Industrialisation and urbanisation, the flight from the farm to the factory, from the village to the city, still taking place in many countries, had more or less run their course in Britain before the second world war.

And yet, slow economic growth or not, the income of the average British family has doubled over the quarter century in real terms. Moreover, the cumulative effect of redistributive taxation, strongly supported by the power of organised labour, has resulted in some flattening of the family income pyramid, though the flattening is not as dramatic as some would have wished or others feared. But it does mean that the producers of many products and services, not least financial services, can think in terms of a much wider potential market than they had before.

Home ownership
A wider prosperity and enlarged aspirations have led to a higher level of home ownership and an increased demand for the equipment – furniture, domestic appliances, decorating materials and so on – required to make the home comfortable and beautiful. The marketing opportunities flowing from this include not only the obvious one of making and distributing an immense variety of consumer durables but also such satellite manifestations as home-making and do-it-yourself magazines, to say nothing of the provision of the consumer credit needed to finance purchases that could not be made out of income or savings. And now, with large investments already made in consumer durables, the way people spend their disposable incomes may well start to change; the marketers of consumer credit may have to turn more of their

attention to financing other activities, like holidays, self-education and leisure activities outside the home.

The motor car

After the home the most important of material possessions is the motor car. Widened car ownership again has both direct implications for the manufacturer and the provider of financial services; and indirect repercussions – some good, some bad – for other market sectors. It has created obvious problems for the marketers of public transport systems, railways and bus lines, whose monopoly position has been eroded. But at the same time the increased mobility brought about by widespread car ownership has provided innumerable opportunities for the markets of travel, leisure and other services to be exploited successfully or unsuccessfully according to the marketer's skill in predicting popular demand. Such motor-related manifestations as the drive-in quick food outlet and the drive-in bank have proved a disappointment to their promoters. But the out-of-town supermarket, totally dependent on the car and the parking lot, has flourished where local planning restrictions have been overcome.

Educational opportunity

Wider educational opportunities and changes in the character of employment have gone hand-in-hand to generate new forms of consumer demand. There can be more than one view (and indeed there are many impassioned views) about the practical implications of equal opportunities in education. Against the clearly ethical view that no child should be denied opportunity through an accident of birth or late development is placed the argument that increased opportunity for the under-privileged may reduce opportunity for the well-endowed; and that the outstanding minority, as a purely practical matter, may be more important to a nation's progress than the averageness of the majority. Without taking sides in that argument, the marketing man must conclude that the widening of educational opportunity must inevitably change not only the character of consumer demand but the language of communication with the consumer market. It never was wise to assume that 'the consumer is an ass' who can easily be fooled; it will be even less wise to do so in the future.

Type of job

On the employment front we have said that the flight from the farm to the factory which characterised the industrial revolution was completed in the UK before the last quarter-century. But this does not imply that radical changes in the nature and location of employment are not still going on. There is the major and continuing change from employment in manufacture to employment in the service industries. There is the fact that some 30 per cent of the nation's workforce is now employed by central government, local authorities or public corporations rather than by private industry. Within industry itself (and indeed within the residual but immensely important agricultural sector) there is a progressive shift from the unskilled labourer to the skilled operative in charge of a substantial investment in capital equipment. Different types of job mean different lifestyles and different requirements for goods and services.

The working wife

From the marketing viewpoint a most important change on the employment scene has been the increased proportion of married women (about 50 per cent according to official statistics and probably more unofficially) who take full-time or part-time jobs outside the home. It would be tempting to pursue the sociological sources and ramifications of this development, such as family planning and the women's lib movement. We must confine ourselves to the more mundane marketing implications. The most obvious of these is the impact on manufacturers of demand for packaged foods and other domestic products. The realisation that a wife is not just her husband's better half, but an independent 'purchasing unit' in her own right, has changed marketing thinking in most industries, including financial services.

The additional workload taken on by wives with outside employment does not, in most cases, release them from their so-called housewifely responsibilities. The cooking and cleaning still have to be done, and husbandly co-operation still has not progressed very far beyond giving a hand with the washing up. So there is the need for convenience foods and other devices to ease the domestic burden, linked to the availability of the cash to pay for them. A second marketing implication of some importance is that total family income (particularly if there are also earning children living at home) can in many cases be substantially greater than the income of the family's main earner. At one time market researchers could feel that they had adequately established the socio-economic status of a family by finding out the income of the head of the household (who, in those not-too-far-off days was assumed to be the husband). No longer is this the case; the family's income and decisions on how to spend it can no longer be regarded as a husbandly preserve.

Another consequence of the independent working wife is a boost for the fashion and clothing industries. Independent incomes and more time spent outside the home mean independent personal purchases. Coming closer home to the subject of this book, they can also mean an increased demand by women for personal bank accounts and other financial services. The banks cannot be accused of being backward in this respect, but it is questionable whether the full marketing implications have been recognised and exploited.

The age profile

Yet another aspect of consumer characteristics which must affect the thinking of markets whose products or services are aimed at a specific age segment is the changing age profile of the population. The birthrate bulge of fifteen to twenty years ago makes this a good time for marketers with products designed for the younger generation or with an interest in establishing habits which may last a lifetime, such as the habit of using a bank account. The currently reduced birthrate makes it a correspondingly bad period for manufacturers of baby products. And in due course, as our population gets steadily older, there is a good time coming in the geriatric market. Of course against these general trends one can always expect to find a successful company 'swimming against the tide': the Mothercare chain of shops is a good example. But the flair of individual entrepreneurs in meeting the changing market's needs more effectively and efficiently than their competitors does not invalidate the general trend.

The industrial market

For the industrial market, as for the corporate sector in banking, the direction of change is rather different. Where most consumer markets are expanding, in terms of the number of individuals or families in a position to buy a given consumer product, the number of available customers for the industrial marketer is tending to shrink with the increasing concentration of company ownership. According to one study of the concentration of British industry, the 100 largest British firms in 1935 accounted for 24 per cent of total industrial production; when the 1968 census of production was carried out the 100 largest firms accounted for 42 per cent of total output. It does not always follow that central ownership means centralised buying. But it is certainly true that in many industries, not least financial services, the marketer has fewer but larger targets to aim at; and the process of negotiating a sale with powerful and sophisticated buyers or buying committees becomes a correspondingly more difficult and complex affair. It can become even more complicated when selling to the public sector, where political considerations can be superimposed on normal commercial factors.

Differential rates of growth and profitability between different industrial sectors is another element of change which imposes the need for marketing flexibility on the industrial producer. When a whole industry goes into decline, as the shipping and textile industries have in this country, its suppliers must either decline with it or find new market opportunities, in other industries or overseas, and adapt their products, services, and marketing and management methods accordingly.

A third factor among many others that might be mentioned is the growing power of labour and its involvement in management decisions. As suppliers of new equipment and new techniques to the publishing industry (among many others) have discovered to their cost, it is not enough to convince management of its economic advantages; the labour force and the unions also have to be convinced that it is in their interest to operate the new equipment.

Industrial change also brings with it the necessity for suppliers to be flexible in their choice of location. A chain of retail shops or a network of branch banks may be ideally located when it is first set up. But industrial decline in one area and industrial growth in another will make the distribution less and less ideal as time goes on. The high cost and the personal inconvenience of relocation will sooner or later have to be faced if healthy growth is to continue. And of course, as the UK banks experienced in the 1950s and 1960s, mergers bring marketing problems, especially of image, as well as organisational problems.

Changes in the economy

The fortunes of banks and other financial service institutions are even more closely related to changing economic conditions than those of other industries. Many, if not most, industries have to face the fact that demand for their products will ebb and flow more or less in step with the ups and downs of the economy; if their market forecasting is sound they can do something to mitigate the severity of the swings through planned marketing effort, diversification, the development of counter-cyclical products and so on, despite the growing inflexibility of overheads imposed by conditions of employment and other such factors.

But financial institutions are not only exposed to the winds of economic change; they are also exposed, sometimes to the advantage sometimes to the detriment of their profitability, to the various efforts of governments to control the economy. They must accept directives about which sectors of borrowers shall have priority; about their rate of growth; even sometimes about their pricing policies (i.e. interest rate levels).

Being tied in their basic business to a sluggish and would-be managed economy has forced UK banks to adopt two major marketing initiatives. The first is to place more emphasis than hitherto on development in faster-growing economies overseas; in most banks the international division is the fastest growing part of the organisation. The second initiative is to diversify from the banking base into other financial services like insurance and hire purchase. The ultimate effect, it becomes increasingly apparent, is to convert a relatively simple business of safeguarding and lending money into a much more aggressive multi-national financial services conglomerate, with the need for much greater diversity of management and marketing skills that this involves.

The rising storm of competition

It would be misleading to suggest that the introduction by the government of 'Competition and Credit Control' in 1971 was the watershed dividing the relatively uncompetitive British banking system, which most bankers of mature years elected to join in their salad days, from the increasingly competitive scene which faces them today. Certainly this directive outlawed many previously agreed cartel arrangements and decreed that the clearing banks should compete, and be seen to compete, more vigorously against each other. But competition, even if disguised in a velvet glove, had never really been absent; managers were never uninterested in business development nor displeased at picking up a good account from the rival bank up the street. The real change in the competitive environment has come from the banks' incursions into other financial services sectors and the simultaneous invasion by other financial institutions – including overseas banks setting up in the UK – of what had previously been regarded as the traditional banker's preserve.

Just to summarise the new or enhanced competition which is battling for a share of the British financial services market, there are

1 the 400 or so US and other foreign banks which have opened branches in London and which employ around 30,000 people. In most cases their primary target has been the corporate rather than the personal customer; and their aggressive, often highly professional, marketing methods (helped to some degree by their exclusion from certain requirements imposed on their UK competitors) have necessitated greater professionalism in this sector by the indigenous banks;

2 the fringe banking operations, encouraged by over-liberal banking regulations, are less of a problem now and more of a painful memory. Here today, gone tomorrow; but could they be back again the day after tomorrow in some other guise?;

3 the trustee savings banks, once only a savings medium, now have long-term ambitions to become a real force in personal and corporate banking. They have a number of competitive advantages to build on, including government support, special dispensations on tax, the fact that they are non-profit making, and their solid entrenchment among the traditionally less well-off sections of the population, whose economic importance is steadily growing;

4 the National Giro system has similar aspirations to those of the trustee savings banks, and similar political support. While its present range of services is limited, it does offer services such as cash collection at a cut price; and it does hold out the possibility of harmonisation with the National Savings Bank and its innumerable Post Office outlets;

5 the building societies, again with tax advantages, are very formidable competitors as deposit takers; and they are increasingly
disposed to offer deposit account facilities which come very close
to the banks' current account facilities;
6 the instalment finance companies, many of them owned by banks,
compete both as deposit takers to a limited extent and as providers
of fixed-term or revolving credit to corporate and personal
customers;
7 Unit trusts, investment trusts and especially pension funds are all
managed by people outside the banks, and who offer services
similar to those the banks have traditionally provided;
8 finally, the insurance companies are at the same time major customers of the banks and competitors in the sense that they attract
personal savings and invest them independently of the banking
system.

The pressure of social responsibilities

There is a myth, still embodied in company law and in the utterances
of ultra-conservative economists like Milton Friedman, that the sole
responsibility of company managements is to maximise profits for
their shareholders. If this theory ever could be followed in practice, it
certainly cannot be today. Apart from management's obvious
responsibility to its employees, the growth of consumerism and of
consumerist legislation, together with the pressures from ecologists
and other lobbies, make it plain that social responsibility must play a
large part in corporate thinking. The commercial organisation must
not only earn a profit (for without a profit it cannot survive) but
must also be a good neighbour and a good citizen. It must not, for
the sake of profit, pollute the environment or cause harm to the
individuals or organisations with whom it comes into contact.

It is very difficult to argue with the principle of social responsibility in business or to deny its growing importance as yet another
constraining factor in marketing policy. It can readily be accepted
that profit opportunities must be sacrificed to some extent when
there is an obvious likelihood of serious damage to the public or the
environment. Toxic effluents must be purified, new drugs must be
proved as nearly as possible free of dangerous side-effects, safety
factors must be built into cars and other machinery, even if the

resulting cost cannot be fully recovered in higher prices. Even at the lowest level of enlightened self-interest it is important not to risk public opprobrium and eventually restrictive legislation for the sake of an extra percentage point or two on the profit margin.

The trouble is that the policy decisions which must be made seldom arise in black and white terms. Certainly small profit reductions to avoid great social damage are acceptable. But what if the profit reduction is catastrophic and will throw many employees out of work, while the possible social damage is small? What, as is so often the case, if the social hazard is uncertain and the social benefit obvious – in the case, say, of a new drug which will certainly save many lives but may possibly also cause some deaths?

The decision whether or not to launch a new product or embark on a new investment project is seldom purely a marketing one. But it is a marketing responsibility to investigate and evaluate new development opportunities or to help carry out feasibility studies for new investment projects. When this is the case, consideration of social responsibility, often unquantifiable, must somehow be fed into the calculation with all the other environmental data.

The influence of technological change

Most of the instances of change discussed so far originate outside a company or an industry, and it is marketing's task to help in bringing about the necessary internal changes. With technological change, more often than not, the situation goes into reverse. An industry or company develops more efficient systems or processes, and its marketing people have to find a way of, at worst, reconciling customers to the changes or, at best, generating some positive enthusiasm for them. This can be relatively easy when the changes result in products or services which are demonstrably better or cheaper. For example, the development of transistors, printed circuits and now of silicon chips has revolutionised electronics and converted bulky expensive items into new generations of very much more efficient, more reliable and *cheaper* products.

Economic pressure
But this is not always the case. To take a homely example, centralised production of bread and beer since the war has resulted in

changes in the quality and character of these commodities which not everybody agrees are for the better. Economic pressures in the bakery and brewing industries, made the changes inevitable; but it took a considerable effort to persuade at least a sufficient number of consumers that they were indeed fortunate to be supplied with plastic bread and fizzy beer. And now, with 'real ale' being sought after and small bakers experiencing an upturn in demand, the wheel seems to be coming full cycle. These two examples do represent the marketing principle at work – albeit slowly and belatedly. After all, plastic bread and fizzy beer were certainly not to everyone's liking and there were good marketing opportunities in catering for the variety of tastes, as the resurgence of 'good' bread and 'real' ale shows. Perhaps the economic pressures seemed so overwhelming at the time that these segments of the markets just had to be ignored. But eventually consumers vote with their feet – and a good thing too.

   Similar comments could be made about retail distribution. The revolution in retailing methods from the small personal-service shop to the large self-service supermarket, which started in the food industry and has now spread to other trades, was forced on the industry by rising labour and other costs. Consumers would certainly have had to pay more for their food and other packaged goods if the revolution had not taken place. But it cannot be said to have originated in an irrestible demand from housewives that corner shops should close and supermarkets proliferate. It took considerable skill and capital expenditure by the retail chains involved – aided in this case by the powerful marketing weapon of price – to persuade housewives in sufficient numbers to adopt new shopping habits. Of course some housewives welcomed the new situation; others have yet to change. Such a differential response from different sections of the market is normal and should be acknowledged in any good marketing plan.

The versatile computer

In banking the most important technological development has of course been the increasing versatility of the computer and its various offspring. For the more excitable futurologists this opens up vistas of a cashless and chequeless society just around the corner. Such exchanges as are not handled by computer talking to computer will be effected mostly by credit card; such cash as is required by the old-fashioned and recalcitrant will be obtained from cash dispensers or automated tellers.

Much of this is already feasible. The Bankers Automated Clearing Service Limited now facilitates for processing, distribution and collection of large volumes of payments for more than 2,300 corporate customers as well as for the banks. Such payments include salaries and pensions by automated credit transfer and insurance premiums and mortgage repayments by standing order and by direct debit. The volume of payments processed in this way has grown over a ten-year period to represent about 13 per cent of all non-cash transactions involving banks. The use of credit cards also is growing, though it still accounts for less than 4 per cent of all non-cash transactions by individuals.

But the vision of a utopia when bank employees no longer have to count cash or sort pieces of paper is still a remote one. Despite the availability of automated methods of payment the number of cheques drawn is still increasing and will probably continue to increase at least until the mid 1980s. And despite the increasing use of cheques about 98 per cent of all payments by individuals are still in cash. It will take a very long time before the psychological resistance to accepting an electric impulse in a computer's memory store as an alternative to cash in the hand is finally overcome – to say nothing of the legal considerations, such as proof of payment.

There can be no doubt that the trend towards automated, computerised banking will continue. It would be impossible other-wise to cope with the inexorably growing workload that the banks are experiencing and will continue to experience. But the rate of change will be measured in decades rather than years. The banks cannot move faster than the administrative complications will permit, without risking a catastrophic operational breakdown; it takes at least seven years, for example, to introduce a new automated communications system. Nor can the banks move faster than the customer will accept change, without incurring unjustifiable invest-ment costs. In the US, for example, where enthusiasm for the machine is less restrained, some banks have moved faster in the direction of the automated teller and the semi-automated branch. But there is now some doubt about the charisma of the automatic teller; it seems that even allowing for the undoubted cost savings brought about, it lacks the charm to attract the additional business needed fully to justify the $20,000 – $40,000 investment which it represents. Belated attempts are being made to give it a human face and persuade the public that it is a warm, friendly and instantly obliging creature. Among others the First National Bank of Atlanta has christened its under-utilised Docutel machines Tillie the Teller, painted them red and built a personalised advertising campaign around them. Results are said to have been encouraging.

Problems and opportunities
From the marketing viewpoint the economically essential trend towards automation brings in its train both problems and opportunities. The main problem is the danger of dehumanising the banks' image. The remarkably successful transition to centralised accounting by computer has not been achieved without manifestations of unease on the part of customers who have felt themselves in the grip of a machine even more implacable than the hard-faced banker of fiction. It will take more than Tillie the Teller and a lick of red paint to overcome the public's resistance to dealing on a day-to-day basis with a machine rather than a human being, however harassed. The fact that the machine is almost certainly quicker and less accident-prone is poor compensation for its inability to relax and smile.

Against this there are two potential marketing opportunities of enormous importance to marketing-minded managements. The first is the prospect that increased mechanisation of the routine back-up services, which currently absorb between 60 per cent and 70 per cent of the banks' human and other resources, could release more management and staff time for active involvement in learning about and satisfying the less routine requirements of customers. Planned evolution in this direction will involve progressive organisational changes, the creation of new jobs and redefinition of existing jobs, and a training programme to facilitate the process of readjustment; it will also almost certainly involve reconsidering the location and layout of the banks' premises and branch network. Just how the process of adjustment will work out and how fast the evolution will be is one of the future uncertainties which will make a banking career more than usually exciting during the remaining years of this century.

The second major marketing opportunity lies in the fact that however inhuman Tillie the automated teller may be, she is prepared to work twenty-four hours a day, seven days a week; and she is quite unfussy about where she works. The bank's computer terminal, with whatever facilities are needed from cash dispensing through credit verification to money transfer, is just as comfortable, provided it earns its keep, at a supermarket check-out or in a works canteen as it is on the bank's own premises. This should give the bank's marketers a degree of freedom from the constraints of time and place which can be exploited to give customers an improved level of service at a profit to the bank.

Summary

In this chapter we have said that marketing has an important part to play in the process of adjustment to change, in keeping the organisation and its products or services in step with a constantly, if slowly, changing environment.

Marketing's special contribution is likely to be in the areas of

1 gathering information about the changing environment and predicting the effect of relevant changes on the demands which the organisation should satisfy;
2 planning and co-ordinating the marketing aspects of the changes in organisation, product range or distributive methods that should follow;
3 helping, by the marketing techniques of communication and persuasion, to accelerate necessary changes in the attitudes and behaviour of customers, distributors *and* employees;
4 using pre-testing techniques such as market models and test markets to assess the viability of new projects, before the commitment of major funds;
5 recognising and describing the different needs of different segments of markets served, and how they are evolving.

We have said that the aspects of a changing environment with which marketing is most immediately concerned are *customers'* characteristics and needs.

With personal customers, important areas of change include

family incomes and related lifestyles, more widespread material possessions, equal opportunities in education, changing employment patterns, including more job opportunities for married women, and changing age profiles.

In the corporate sector increased concentration of ownership, growth of the nationalised and semi-nationalised sector, the greater involvement of labour in management decisions and the changing location of industry must all affect the direction of marketing policy.

For banking more than most industries, the changing fortunes of the *economy* and government efforts to control it are a major environmental factor. They have precipitated such marketing policy initiatives as development overseas and diversification into financial services other than mainstream banking.

Increasing *competition* from other banking and quasi-banking institutions is yet another factor requiring more professional and aggressive marketing action on the part of the banks.

Social responsibility is an aspect of market development planning and operations which looms ever larger. Even if managements were disposed to overlook it in the interest of single-minded profit maximisation, they would be prevented by consumerism, the ecological movement and social legislation.

Finally, *technological change* places just as heavy a burden on marketing as on production departments. In banking the computer and its derivatives have revolutionised the mechanics of the industry. Marketing has to ensure that mechanisation does not dehumanise what is, in large measure, a personal service industry.

CHAPTER THREE

Marketing management and organisation

In the very simplest form of commercial organisation, one man setting up in business for himself, there are three essential and *interdependent* functions:

make it – sell it – keep the score.

For 'make it' you can subsititute 'buy it' if the enterprise is a trading one rather than a manufacturing one; or 'create a service' if the new entrepreneur is entering a service industry. The selling function does not necessarily follow the making; in some types of business it is possible to secure an order before starting to make the product, which saves a certain amount of worry if you get the price right and are sure of being paid in the end. The significance of keeping the score can rapidly extend from basic accounting to raising capital and monitoring cash flow, etc. But the principle of interdependence still applies. If one of the three legs of the tripod collapses, so will the enterprise.

But of course in our complicated industrial society things are seldom that simple. There is still room for the one-man entrepreneur and for the first stage of development after the one-man stage, when the production, selling and financial functions are delegated (assuming that the entrepreneur has the none too common capacity to delegate). But in more and more industries nowadays size is essential for success. A one-man aero-engine business is inconceivable; and even the family grocer is being beaten back into the side streets and villages where it does not pay the supermarket chain to pursue him.

For many industries indeed (and banking looks like becoming one of them) a single country is too narrow a base of operation, and multi-national status becomes inevitable. Entrepreneurial Man willy-nilly turns into Organisation Man, and may or may not be happy about the change.

But no matter how large the organisation becomes, no matter how many specialists are bred by the sub-division of functions, the three original legs of the tripod remain essential and inter-dependent. Indeed one of the great problems of professional management, as it struggles to cope with the complications of size, is to make it clear to as many managers as possible throughout the organisation that they are not simply cogs in a great machine but have a responsibility in their respective fields for ensuring the effective co-ordination of the three basic functions. The devices of profit centres, divisionalisation and the like have a part to play in this; and so has marketing.

Marketing in the unitary organisation

Before attempting to generalise about the way marketing management fits into the single, relatively uniform business which we call unitary, it is as well to make two points. The first is that only over the last thirty years has professional marketing gained wide acceptance in this country as an important aspect of management. The rate at which it has been accepted and incorporated in the managerial structure has varied from industry to industry and from company to company. So, for any general statement we make, it will be possible to quote a number of contradictory examples from real life – 'that does not happen in *my* company'.

The second point is the imprecision of nomenclature in the whole field of management organisation, most particularly in marketing management. A marketing manager, as we have already said, may be holding either a line management job or a staff job. Alternatively, most of the essential marketing functions may be handled by a manager carrying some other title: sales manager, commercial manager or general manager. Until you have read an individual's job specification (if he has one) you do not really know whether he is supposed to be doing a marketing management job or not; and until you have analysed the way he spends his working week you do not really know whether he is actually doing the job he is supposed to be doing.

Having admitted at the outset that for almost everything we say the contrary may also be true, we can proceed to some general statements. The first is that the most typical situation in a small or medium-sized company whose management structure is in a state of evolution is that the head of the selling function has been given wider responsibilities and has celebrated them by dropping the title 'sales manager' and adopting that of 'marketing manager'. (In this connection it is significant that the professional body which in 1950 was known as the Incorporated Sales Managers' Association is now known as the Institute of Marketing. And, to add point to this trend, in 1978 a group of senior marketing men came together as the 90th Livery Company in the City of London, the Worshipful Company of Marketors.)

These wider responsibilities derive from the realisation that there is more to selling than disposing of a business's product or service at the best price it will fetch. There is first and foremost the concept of planned *profitability*. Salesmen traditionally and temperamentally love to sell. Only too often, unless there is a proper control system, the triumph of getting a large order can override the necessity of getting the order at a price which will show an adequate profit to the company. To think in terms of profit rather than turnover as the goal requires a change in outlook which is symbolised by the change of title from sales manager to marketing manager. It can also require, particularly when there is a range of products or services to be sold rather than a single line, some addition to the organisation within the erstwhile sales (now marketing) department. This addition may well take the shape of the product manager, responsible among other things for monitoring the profitability of the product or group of products under his charge. More will be said of the product manager's role later.

Another concept which gains in importance with the transition from sales to marketing management is the traditional rule, more honoured in the breach than the observance, that *the customer is king*. This can lead in practice from the relatively uncontroversial idea that the sales function should be expanded to include a market research capability to much more revolutionary conclusions. If and when the sales side gets to the point where its market research enables it to predict with some confidence the level and character of customer demand, the logical conclusion is that production schedules should be the resultant of sales forecasts and product specifications originating in the marketing department. This can seriously upset the balance of power within the traditional production-oriented company, though it certainly will help to ensure its long-term survival.

A third concept that marks the transition from sales management to marketing management, especially in large-scale consumer markets, is the concept of *the marketing mix*. The traditional sales manager's viewpoint is that sales are the result of heroic efforts by the salesmen, backed up by a bit of advertising and sales promotion of one kind or another. The marketing manager recognises the importance of well-directed salesmen in most situations (though quite a lot of selling is done without the intervention of salesmen as such) but recognises that they are only one of many elements to be fitted together in the right proportions. Other elements included within the general description of marketing mix are

1   product specifications;
2   packaging and product presentation;
3   pricing;
4   physical distribution;
5   point of sale display;
6   selling communications including advertising;
7   sales promotions.

A marketing department will need to have the skills, or access to the skills, required to procure all these elements. But above all, the marketing manager must have the flair and breadth of view to co-ordinate them into a single cohesive profit-oriented whole.

The final outcome can be that the marketing manager presides over an organisation along the lines of that illustrated in Fig. 1, linking the established sales force and sales office (themselves probably restructured) to specialist marketing services and a new product management function. (See overleaf).

The product manager

Most readers by now will probably have said to themselves that there's nothing so very original about the much-vaunted marketing concept. It is simply a matter of making commonsensical changes and injecting some additional professionalism to meet the demands

Fig. 1. The marketing manager in a line management role.

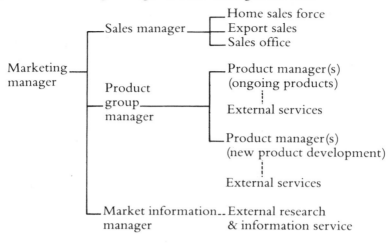

of a changing industrial or commercial situation. We would not dispute that general conclusion.

But there is one quite important and relatively original contribution from the marketing management thinking of the past quarter-century. This is the establishment of the product manager (or project manager) as a key member of the marketing team.

A product manager's, or product group manager's, job specification will probably read more or less as follows:

Reports to   marketing manager.

Main   preparing the annual marketing plan for a desig-
responsibility   nated product or group of products within the
                        context of agreed corporate objectives; ensuring
                        that the volume and profit targets included in the
                        plan are met.

Specific   1 working with the production, financial and sales
responsibility   departments, under the overall direction of the
                          marketing manager, to ensure that the product
                          marketing plan is realistic and that they are
                          committed to its successful execution;

2 preparing and securing management approval for the product marketing plan (the plan should include final and intermediate volume and profit targets together with budgeted marketing expenditure figures);

3 securing continued involvement and support for the agreed plan from the relevant departments (particularly production and sales);

4 briefing and directing the outside agencies (advertising, design, research, etc.) contributing to the execution of the plan;

5 monitoring the progress of results against intermediate targets; investigating the reasons and taking corrective action if results get seriously out of step with targets;

6 monitoring the level of customer satisfaction through attitude research, complaints letters, salesmen's reports and other means;

7 monitoring competitors' activities and recommending any counter-activity that is needed;

8 monitoring the legal framework surrounding his product(s);

9 initiating research or experimental activity aimed at improving the product, customer service or marketing methods;

10 controlling the marketing budget for the product.

Much emphasis is laid in marketing textbooks on the product manager's responsibility for the profitable development of the product or product group assigned to him. He is often described as running his own defined business within the larger business he works for. This is true only up to a point. The product manager certainly has responsibility, on paper at any rate; but he seldom has the power, without which responsibility is something of a fiction. He has some degree of power over the advertising and other outside agencies from whom he commissions work, though even they can usually appeal over his head if they feel he is getting too big for his boots. But he has no power, except the power of persuasion, over the production and sales departments who can make or mar the success of his marketing plan. To some extent it can be said that his role is the mirror-image of the harlot whom Stanley Baldwin accused of exercising power without responsibility down the ages. The product manager, not yet as venerable a figure as the harlot, can be said to enjoy responsibility without power.

Nevertheless there are two very strong arguments in favour of the product manager system. The first is that it provides a framework within which detailed attention can be paid to all the inter-related activities which make for a product's success; it does not ensure success, but it makes it less likely that the product will fail simply because management is too busy to give it the necessary attention. The second argument is that it provides an opportunity for giving the bright young manager an opportunity of experiencing the many-faceted responsibilities of general management in a situation where he cannot do the company irredeemable harm.

In banking, for example, product or brand managers could be in charge of personal lending, of personal resource gathering, of an industry such as petro-chemicals, of import/export financing, and so on. Similarly, in the unit trust industry the brand management technique has been applied to different types of trust within the same 'stable'; and in the insurance business to various kinds of product, even though there are salesmen in the field who are expected to sell the full range of products.

The marketing services manager

So far we have talked about the marketing manager in the context of line management, in situations where he controls the salesforce. But it oftens happens that the evolution of the management organisation takes a different direction, with the sales management function separated from the marketing function; or indeed that there is no national salesforce as such – which is essentially the situation at present in branch banking organisations, though not in other financial services sectors like insurance and hire purchase, or some unit trusts.

In such situations it is more likely that the executive bearing the title of 'marketing manager' will in fact be filling a staff position, reporting perhaps to the sales director, perhaps to the managing director; and his department, though it may be described as the marketing department, would be more accurately called the marketing services department.

In this staff role the marketing manager is likely to be more closely involved with helping management to plot the future course of the organisation (a close link with the corporate planning function is likely), and concerned with current activities only to the extent of providing marketing advice and technical marketing facilities for those line managers who wish to avail themselves of them. The composition and size of his department will depend essentially on the level of demand for the department's services which he generates in line management and on building up a track record which convinces the sceptics that the advice or the services he provides produce useful, – i.e. profit-enhancing – results. (In practical terms the marketing services manager is the equivalent of an internal consultant; if in an excess of enthusiasm he builds up his departmental resources ahead of effective demand he can become a ready target for the next economy drive.)

It is likely, however, that over time some or all of the following functions will accrue to the department:

1   the provision of market information including analyses of 'own company' sales;
2   business and economic forecasting;
3   the marketing aspects of corporate planning;
4   the provision of advertising, sales promotional literature and other sales communications material;
5   the provision of promotional ideas, schemes and packages;
6   the development and testing of new products or new services;
7   feasibility studies, preparatory to entering new markets or market sectors;
8   the marketing aspects of in-company management training.

The typical departmental organisation to which this can lead is illustrated in Fig. 2 overleaf.

The selection and direction of external marketing services

In both our organisation charts (Figs. 1 and 2) describing the 'typical'

Fig. 2. The marketing manager in a service department role.

Marketing services manager
— Promotion, including advertising
— Branch services
— New services development
— Marketing training
— Market research/ economic forecasting/ market statistics

line and staff marketing departments we have indicated that these departments are responsible for selecting and directing various external marketing services, in addition to their internal relationships. These external associations – particularly those with the providers of creative services like advertising agencies and design consultants – require a considerable amount of specialist skill and even diplomacy. Not simply because 'creative people' are involved (the legend that they are difficult and temperamental is much exaggerated) but more because everything that appears in visual or audio-visual form about an organisation or its products contributes to the image of the organisation in a particularly *noticeable* way. Its business practices or the behaviour of its employees in contact with customers or the public actually have just as important an effect. But they are seldom out in the open for *everyone* to see, including other members of the organisation. It has been said that when a banker makes an error everyone tries to cover it up; but advertising is designed to be seen, and an error is very obvious.

So marketing management often has difficult day-to-day decisions to make, in trying at the same time to keep the organisation's 'visible manifestations' in the right key without stultifying the creative skills of the outside services or embarrassing the more conservative members of the organisation. Examples of going too far in both directions are rife in the history of bank marketing and advertising.

The hazards and difficulties of using external marketing services can result in a temptation to build up internal marketing resources so as to handle as much work as possible 'in-house'. This can look like a prudent man's way of playing safe, but it is not in the long run safe at all; advertising, brochures, promotions and other external marketing activities become introverted and stale if they are all produced internally. The judicious marketing manager keeps his department small, but staffed by people of experience and judgment; and he holds his external services to very specific policy briefs, while giving them the maximum freedom of expression within those briefs. Typically, in the UK and in several European banks, very much less than one per cent of staff would be employed in the marketing services described above. In some cases, extra jobs – virtually 'line' functions, such as school banks – may be added to the basic marketing services function and will move the percentage upwards. But of course, many many more members of staff will be carrying out marketing activities as a normal part of their own jobs.

Where does public relations fit in?

We have not attempted so far to fit PR into our marketing organisations, either as an internal or an external service. This is because the term 'public relations' is used almost as loosely as the word 'marketing' itself. In some cases PR is regarded as virtually a form of unpaid advertising – using news releases, press conferences and other devices to seek favourable mentions (or ward off unfavourable mentions) of the organisation and its products in the media. In such cases it may come under the control of the marketing manager or be bought from outside in conjunction with advertising services. At the other extreme its definition may be much wider and cover the whole range of relationships between the organisation and its customers, the general public, government, special-interest groups and society at large. It may also have an interest, alongside the personnel department, in internal attitudes and communications and in the relationships between different groups within the organisation. When this broader definition is given to the PR function (as it is in most large banks) it is likely that the PR department will operate independently from the marketing department, or even have some aspect of the marketing function under its command. (The different roles of PR, and its relationship to the marketing function, are discussed at greater length in Chapters 9 and 10.)

Marketing in the multiple organisation

It is hard enough to be precise about the position of marketing in the unitary organisation. It is even harder in the case of the multiple organisation – a phrase which we use to cover everything from the multi-national conglomerate, through the holding company with a number of specialist divisions or subsidiaries, to the chain of retail shops. Not only are there major differences between one organisation and another within these categories, but any one organisation may oscillate between different organisational structures – swinging, for example, from centralisation to decentralisation and back again – as managements strive to attain the unattainable goal of the ideally managed and effectively dynamic organisation.

We can say, however, that more often than not the multiple organisation will incorporate both staff and line marketing functions at appropriate points in its structure. It is more likely than not that the marketing function or department at headquarters will have a staff role, providing a back-up service for senior management and specialist advice or services, when required, for the operating divisions and subsidiaries. This is a pragmatic manifestation, rather than the result of strongly held theories; it becomes obvious from trial and error that effective marketing requires detailed knowledge both of the geographical area and product category involved and of the character of human and other resources available compared to the competition. A given individual may be an outstanding success at marketing apples in Germany but a total failure (until he has become acclimatised) at marketing oranges in Japan – or at telling the Japanese subsidiary how to do it. He can advise on techniques and principles, he can offer information and ideas, he can transmit central management's policy rulings, but he cannot safely issue detailed instructions on how to do it.

So it is likely that the *executive* marketing function will be positioned as close as possible to the point where the organisation meets the customer. This may be at divisional headquarters or at the level of operating units, or indeed at both levels. And at either of these operational levels it is as likely as not that the line marketing function as we have described it will be exercised by a manager who does not actually carry the title of marketing manager.

An interesting variation on this theme can be found in the case of the multiple retailing organisation. Here there are, in effect, two marketing functions to consider. There is the marketing function of maximising the turnover and profitability of each of the retail outlets in the chain, through location, layout, in-store promotion, local advertising and staff–customer relations, as well as by the total effect of the range of products displayed. And there is the complementary function of merchandising specific product categories in all the outlets by skilful buying, display and sales promotion. The two functions of shop management and merchandise management both demand other skills as well as marketing. But they both contain large marketing ingredients.

Where do financial services organisations fit in?

We must leave it to the individual reader to make up his mind where his own organisation (or the sector of the organisation in which he works) fits into the picture of different types of organisation and evolving organisational structures which we have sketched.

    The range of financial service 'products' to be sold, the method of selling them and the marketing organisation that has evolved to meet identified customer needs are likely to be similar in a given category: for example, UK clearing banks.

    But banks in other countries, merchant banks, hire purchase and insurance companies all have different marketing problems and marketing methods; and even within the UK clearing banks, now that they are so clearly multi-national, multi-service organisations, you will find both staff and line marketing functions, elements both of 'shop management' and of retail merchandising, and both indus-trial and consumer marketing structures operating alongside each other.

    The UK clearing banks, in fact, present a particularly complex problem for marketing organisation, since they are both vertically integrated and exposed to competition at every level.

    There are marketing jobs of various kinds to be done in

1   corporate development planning;

2   attracting deposits, the raw material for a financial services business (most manufacturing organisations can negotiate for their raw materials with a number of rival suppliers all eager to

sell to them; banks must attract their raw material by competitive marketing methods, in the face of other financial institutions - building societies, trustee savings banks, insurance companies and others - all equally keen to lay their hands on available personal and corporate funds, and some of them helped by special tax advantages);

3   building good quality lending;
4   expanding internationally (in competition with financial services institutions in the countries concerned);
5   fighting off competition from foreign banks invading the home market (particularly on the corporate business front);
6   developing new banking services and packages;
7   marketing the products of specialist divisions and subsidiaries (finance houses, insurance brokers, merchant banks, trust companies, etc.);
8   building up the local businesses of branches and regional offices;
9   deciding the best location for new branches or outlets.

Add to the variety of marketing jobs to be done (all of them inter-relating) the fact that the banking industry started to systematise its marketing activities rather later than other industries, and it is scarcely surprising that the rate of change in bank marketing organisation is remarkably fast; this year's organisation chart in any large bank will probably be obsolete five years hence.

Summary

In this chapter we have described in outline how marketing management fits into the organisation of different types of company; and have said that a marketing management *function* will not always carry a marketing manager *title*.

We have said that in the unitary organisation, marketing departments tend to play either a line management role, with responsibility for sales volume and profitability; or a staff role, in which they provide marketing information advice and services to line management.

We have described the 'product management' system as a device which enables managements of multi-product or multi-service companies to ensure that detailed attention is given to the co-ordination of all the elements – production, sales, and finance – which are involved in the success of a specific product or product group.

We have said that the 'multiple' organisation is likely to contain both staff and line marketing management functions or departments at different levels in the organisation; and that the staff functions are more likely to be at the centre and the line functions nearer the interface between company and customer, because of the need for detailed knowledge both of the specific product and of the market place.

We have suggested that the reader should decide for himself whether the financial services organisation (or section of the organisation) in which he works is unitary or multiple; whether the marketing functions he exercises or utilises are 'line' or staff; and which of the many different types of marketing management approach are most appropriate to his particular situation.

We have said, finally, that marketing has a contribution to make to many other functions such as corporate planning, and that the rate of change in the financial services industry is such that this year's organisation chart will probably be obsolete five years hence.

CHAPTER FOUR

The marketing plan

Nobody – not even Cassandra, and she came to a sticky end – can predict the future with any certainty. Even when the direction of change seems clear, the speed of change may yet be uncertain; and a sharp change of direction may be precipitated by a quite unanticipated event. The ability of people, however powerful or managerial their position, to control the behaviour of other people is conspicuously limited. So why does marketing, which claims to deal with the future, with change and with people, make such a big thing out of the marketing *plan?* Surely it is unrealistic even to attempt to produce a detailed plan of action, including a quantified prediction of its results, for the next twelve months, let alone for three, four or five years ahead?

Good questions, which require the thorough answers we hope to give them in this chapter. The short answer is that planning can be valuable or futile, depending on the nature of the plan and the planning procedures, and on the way the plan is integrated into the process of management. It is certainly not unknown for companies to adopt the procedures of planning without accepting its implications, and thus for the marketing plan – *prepared at some considerable cost in executive time* – to become simply a statement of good intentions which is only fit to be buried in some file shortly after publication and disinterred nine months later to provide a basis for next year's essay.

But when planning is taken seriously, the marketing plan can make an essential contribution to the methodical development of a company's business by

1 providing a clear statement of marketing objectives (within the framework of corporate policy) to which every department of the organisation which has accepted the plan is committed;
2 compelling the responsible manager to think through in advance all the assumptions and all the conditions which must be met if the plan is to succeed; and perhaps to face up in time to the realisation that some of the assumptions or conditions are unrealistic;
3 providing a yardstick against which progress will be measured, with provision for appropriate action if achievement is seriously above or below target.

In short, a living, flexible plan for action, about which considerable thought has been given as to how it can best be modified in the light of events, is a vital tool for management. A rigid, ritualistic plan is a waste of time and money. In any large organisation which has accepted the planning principle there will be all sizes and shapes of marketing plans: plans for on-going products and services and for new products or services, plans for increasing business with defined customers or customer segments, group plans, regional plans, divisional plans and unit plans. In theory they should all reflect different aspects of corporate strategy and fit neatly, like pieces in a jigsaw puzzle, into the master plan for the organisation. But even if they fit together neatly at the beginning of the planning period they will begin to reflect the normal untidiness of human affairs before the period is far advanced. Total, inhuman neatness is less important in practice than a level of commitment which will ensure that those plans, or elements of plans, which 'fail' do so for better reasons than managerial inertia.

In enumerating, as we propose to do, the main ingredients of the 'ideal' marketing plan, we risk advocating by implication long, detailed documents which could have diminished impact because busy managers have no time to read them. We should say at the outset that a plan should be no longer than is needed to ensure the right course of action by those involved in implementing it, and to gain acceptance of the reasons for adopting one course of action rather than another. Like bikinis, marketing plans should be brief enough to be interesting but still cover the subject adequately.

Subject headings for the marketing plan

We now turn to the various ideas and topics which everyone who writes a marketing plan should consider, even though he will sometimes write little or nothing under a particular heading. Equally, there will usually be one or more points to be made that are highly specific to any given plan, and obviously these cannot be included here. (For example, the heading 'Distribution methods' obviously needs to be interpreted in a very special way by those who seek to provide a real-time computer-based information retrieval system.)

Conventionally, the first section of a marketing plan is devoted to a description of relevant factors in the market place, a short or long description depending on the amount of explanation required to ensure conviction. The factors which may need to be described are listed below. (Writing the market description for the first time can be a considerable chore, but updating it in subsequent planning periods should not be too difficult.)

1 Overall market characteristics

Total size and value and expected evolution. If it is a growth market, for example, it will look more attractive than if it is static or declining; though a large static market can sometimes offer better opportunities than a small growth one.

Product/market segments. A very important heading. A company which identifies the product or market segment which it is best equipped to supply, and focuses its marketing effort on it, is more likely to succeed than one which looses-off in the general direction of the total market. (We use the words 'product' and 'service' inter-changeably in this chapter, recognising that the range of financial services can extend from a standardised and essentially inflexible 'package', at one extreme, to a completely flexible individual service at the other.)

Relative importance of segments. Obviously, the size of the selected segment should be compatible with the company's strength and sales objectives; and a growth sector is preferable to a declining one.

Seasonal fluctuations. These can be important to profit planning. A product or service with pronounced seasonal peaks – for example, making Christmas toys or providing surrogate Father Christmases for department stores – can raise serious problems of financing stocks or finding alternative uses for the relevant resource in off-peak periods.

Regional differences. If the plan involves, as it should, detailed targeting of individual sales areas or sales offices, an understanding of regional differences and their causes is essential. A demand for the same *per capita* sales or percentage sales increase in every case can be both unjust and demotivating for individuals who know very well how the situation in their territory or catchment area differs from that of their colleagues.

Existing distribution networks. You can have the most delectable product or service in the world to sell, and get nowhere if the channel of distribution to the customer breaks down. The motivation of distributors if you do not own them, the location of outlets if you do, are vital considerations in an effective marketing plan.

2 The position of your products or services in the market

Names of your products and of the leading competitors. Names oddly enough can be important, particularly in the case of a range of competitive products with little but their names and packaging to differentiate them.

Description of products. Obviously if you have a product plus, so much the better. But in most highly competitive markets a clear-cut product advantage is seldom maintained for very long and often carries a penalty in higher production costs. Skilful marketing is more often than not the real reason why one product outsells another.

User benefits. The virtues of a product are often, in the eyes of the beholder, more obvious to the producer than to the customer. It is necessary to be realistic about just what are the advantages *to the user* of your product compared with its competitors.

Positioning of products. In a segmented market a producer may opt to attack the high-priced 'quality' segment of the market, or to go after a share of the lower-priced mass market; or he may decide to have an entrant in each segment.

Alternative packages. The producer of packaged goods will probably need to offer a range of several sizes or flavours. In the same way the producer of financial services will probably want to develop a range of services all satisfying the same basic need; for example, a range of unit trusts may be built around a variety of different investment policies; or institutions may offer a range of saving schemes for shorter or longer periods.

Sales history. Analysis of sales and market shares by units, value, region, package type, etc., as a basis for directing future marketing efforts.

Market gap or problem areas. Identification of areas where product improvement is needed or where there is an opening for a new or modified product.

Planned developments. Any new products or product improvement now on the stocks or under consideration.

3 The company and its competitors

Relative strengths and weaknesses. It is sometimes difficult to be entirely objective about this; your own strengths or your own weaknesses can loom larger than those of your competitors. Evidence from a third party (for instance, a market research company carrying out a sample survey of customers) can be enlightening.

Market shares. Sometimes difficult and expensive to establish exactly. An informed guess may be good enough for the practical purpose of planning marketing tactics.

Marketing methods of competitors. If a competitor is using a different marketing tactic from your own the results should be monitored; it may be an initiative that should be followed, or he may be driving up a dead end.

Expected developments. What is in the wind in the way of new marketing initiatives, pricing policies or product developments?

4 Customers and potential customers

Main customers/customer categories. Description, number, actual and potential value of target customers or customer categories.

Relative importance of individual customer segments. Another aspect of the segmentation of markets and marketing effort which is so important a part of effective marketing.

Customer characteristics, motivation, loyalty, etc. In the financial services industry, which depends so heavily on personal relations, it is especially important to obey the old marketing maxim about knowing your customer; the level of customer loyalty is particularly important, since loyal customers are likely to be the most prolific source of new business.

Purchasing methods and decision making. In an impulse-buying situation, like a self-service grocery store, it is a fairly simple matter to determine what combination of packaging, positioning, labelling, etc., will maximise the chances of a favourable purchasing decision; in the case of the more considered purchase of financial services, particularly by corporate as opposed to individual customers, some understanding of the how, when and where of purchasing decisions, and of the events leading up to them, is more difficult to come by, but is just as important for planning a marketing campaign.

5 Institutional and environmental constraints

Government directives and guidelines. The importance of these in banking and other financial services need not be underlined!

Consumer protection legislation. Increasingly tough in the area of lending, but also present in resource-gathering activities.

Restrictive practices legislation. Again particularly tough in the financial area.

Professional ethics. Sometimes apparently in conflict with restrictive practices legislation, to judge from the periodic government investigations of professional associations.

Labour relations. It cannot be taken for granted that marketing recommendations – for example, for longer opening hours – will be acceptable to the representatives of organised labour, even on an experimental basis.

Tax considerations. In a number of cases a tax advantage may be the major selling point for a financial services package.

Contractual arrangements. Are there any existing contractual requirements which inhibit the penetration of a new market or the launch of a new financial service?

6 Summary of problems and opportunities

The sections of the plan reviewing *relevant* aspects of the market situation are not an end in themselves (though in a ritualistic planning situation they may come to be one). Their purpose is to give background information leading up to a statement of the identified problems and opportunities which the marketing plan sets out to deal with.

As a point of presentation it can be a good idea to relegate the background market data into appendices and plunge the reader straight into a statement of the problems and opportunities created for the company by developing market trends and changes.

The important thing is to state the problem and opportunities as clearly and simply as possible, so as to ensure that those who must approve or implement the plan recognise that it is designed to deal with real-life situations.

7 Marketing objectives

Sales and profit targets. This is at the very core of the whole marketing exercise. There will be other marketing objectives, some of them defensive, some of them designed to improve the long-term health of the organisation at the expense possibly of short-term profits. But they should all be designed to contribute sooner or later to the improvement or greater certainty of profits and turnover (in that order).

Target number and value of purchases. Whether you are aiming for a large number of small purchases or a small number of large purchases has an important bearing on marketing and sales tactics.

Penetration and value of usage. Given the size of the market or its segment, and given the sales target, what is implied about the proportions of potential customers who will choose to use it, at what value? Are these proportions reasonable?

Exports, foreign operations. This will apply only in cases where the foreign operation is managed from the centre. More and more foreign operations are becoming profit centres in their own right, with their own marketing plans.

Enhancement of corporate or product name recognition and reputation. Another marketing objective which has an indirect but often important effect on turnover and profit.

8 Distribution methods

Sales outlets. How will the necessary number of sales outlets, whether owned by the company or independent, be achieved? How will they be made into effective selling outlets, rather than nominal stockists who half the time do not push or display your product?

Agents and associated companies. Should they be involved and how can they be motivated to make the contribution required of them? (In some cases a company with an established distributive network may decide that it is better to provide certain services or look after certain customers direct, in which case the question of agents will not arise.)

9 Pricing policy

Price segments. Which price segment in the market is to be attacked, and why?

Discount structure. What standard or negotiated discounts from the recommended price are envisaged?

Agents' commission, outlets' mark-up. When agents or distributors are used, what will be the gap between the recommended price to the final customer and the net return to the producer?

Average revenue predictions. When the price structure is complicated by quantity discounts, agents' commissions, special offers, and so on, what will be the average revenue per unit sold?

10 The selling plan and sales support activities

Targets for individual areas, salesmen or branch offices. These need both to be calculated theoretically from data about the sales potential of the areas concerned and agreed to in advance by sales management as being fair and reasonable; otherwise the necessary commitment will be lacking.

Relationships with the distribution network. How can the best value be got out of the existing distribution network, whether it consists of the company's own retail outlets or independent distributors? Should only some of the available distribution points be included in the plan on a 'horses for courses' policy? Do the existing distributors (in the company's own outlets or elsewhere) need to be supplemented by others if sales targets are to be achieved? If so, how should they be motivated?

Merchandising through distributive outlets. For example, training and motivating outlet staff, point of purchase display material, leaflets, educational and publicity material, stationery supplies, audio–visual sales promotional devices.

Direct selling to end-users. Should some or all of the potential customers be approached direct rather than through branches, agents or distributors? What should be the method of establishing initial contact with them and generating enquiries? What should be the method of converting enquiries into sales?

Salesforce. Who will be involved in the actual selling? Will this be a full-time job or just a part of their responsibilities? How will they be organised, trained, directed and motivated? What back-up services will they need? How will they be targeted, and what provision will there be for checking results against target? What will be total selling cost, to be set against gross sales revenue?

Sales control and information systems. What provision will be made for management to monitor the performance of individual salesmen, outlets, regions, customer categories and end-products? What provision for salesmen to report back and for their reports to be analysed? What provision for identifying potential customers and keeping track of efforts made to convert them into customers? What provision for an in-flow of relevant information about competitive activity, customer requirements and developments in the market place? What will be the cost of the control and information system to be charged against gross sales revenue?

Sales accounting. What will be the billing procedure? What credit policy and what provision against bad debts? How will customer accounts be kept and how will they be analysed for purposes of market and profit planning? What sales accounting costs should be charged against gross sales revenue?

11 Marketing communications, sales promotion and advertising

Media advertising. How much should be spent on advertising the products or services to be marketed through press, television, posters or other public media? What should be the objective of the advertising? Should it be concentrated on promoting the company name as an 'umbrella' under which the individual services can be marketed? Or should the key services be advertised individually, with the minor services riding on their backs? What should be the advertising message and target audience? Which are the most cost-effective media for conveying the required message to the target audience? What advertising agency or agencies should be used? What form of management control should be imposed to ensure maximum value for money?

Direct mail. How much, if any, of the available marketing funds should be spent on direct mailings to target customers or customer categories? What should be the content of the mailings? How should they be designed to ensure maximum attention and response? What criteria should be used in compiling the mailing list? What provision should be made for evaluating results?

Public relations. Should public relations or editorial publicity techniques be used to help achieve sales targets? What message should be conveyed, how and to whom? What should be the budgeted expenditure and how should results be evaluated?

Special promotions. What types of special promotion – for example, special offers to customers or distributors, conferences, exhibitions, educational courses and seminars – should be included in the marketing communications effort? What will be their objectives, frequency and location? What message will they convey to what target audiences? What will be the budgetary appropriation for them and how will results be evaluated?

Measurement of marketing communications effectiveness. What standards will be used to measure the *overall* effectiveness of the marketing communications effort? What will be the method of measurement – for example, customer attitude and awareness research?

12 Legal considerations

Trade names, patents, etc. Have all possible objections to the use of proposed trade names, or the possibility of patent infringements been cleared?

Forms of contract. Are any proposed contract forms both watertight and within the terms of existing or anticipated legislation?

Consumer protection legislation. Are the products or services to be marketed within both the letter and the spirit of the law? Do the advertising claims that will be made conform with the Code of Advertising Practice?

13 Market information and research

Market information. What provision should be made for providing a continuous in-flow of market information and for presenting it to management in easily usable form?

Market research. What special market investigations are planned, with what objective – for example, discovery of gaps in the market or investigating possible new markets or market segments?

Consumer-attitude research. What provision is to be made for periodically checking consumer needs and habits, their attitude to the company and its products and the extent to which these products satisfy their needs?

New-product testing. What provision is planned for testing new or improved products, services and packages?

Cost-effectiveness. What total market research budget is recommended and how will its spending contribute to long-term profitability?

14 Marketing timetable

Synchronisation. How will the proposed selling and sales promotional activities be linked to product availability so as to ensure maximum impact?

Seasonality. Has the selling and sales promotional plan been timed to exploit seasonal buying peaks?

Build-up. Has sufficient time been allowed for all the preparatory work that is needed before a fully effective marketing plan can swing into action?

15 Marketing budget and revenue forecast

Sales revenue forecast. What will be the total sales revenue before and after commissions to agents, discounts, etc.?

Gross margin. What will be the gross profit on sales after all production costs?

Selling costs. What is the budgeted cost of selling, sales accounting and sales administration?

Marketing communications. What is the budgeted cost of marketing communications, including market research?

Marketing administration. What is the budgeted cost of marketing administration and other marketing overheads?

Net profit. What estimated net profit or contribution to company overheads will result from the efficient implementation of the marketing plan?

Follow-up

So much for the structure of the marketing plan. But the plan, as we keep insisting, is not an end but a beginning. It is only when the plan is implemented and works that it justifies the time, money and effort that went into its composition.

If the plan is to be implemented and have a good chance of succeeding, three things listed below are essential.

1 Securing commitment by all those involved
This means 'selling' the plan both up and down the management line. It needs to be sold up the line to senior management, because the marketing manager or executive who writes the plan is asking for resources of money, material and people to be allocated to its execution, and he is promising that those resources will be productively employed; and, to put it in down-to-earth terms, because it will help him to secure co-operation from departments not under his direct control if he is able to say that the boss is backing the plan.

It is just as important to sell the plan down the line because successful implementation is ultimately in the hands of the men and women in the front line. This applies with particular force to the marketing of financial services, where to a large degree *the service is built around or wrapped up in the person who has direct contact with the customer.* If that person has no confidence in the product he or she is selling, how can the customer be convinced?

2 Plotting and checking progress
We referred earlier to the importance of timing and of having a number of individual and intermediate targets against which progress can be measured. These individual checkpoints may be worked out in the form of a PERT network or critical path analysis (to which we shall refer to later) when the plan is a complicated one; or it may be a simpler matter of a list saying that so and so must have done this or that by such and such a date. But unless the checkpoints exist, and people are constantly nagged to observe them, the best of plans is unlikely to succeed.

3 Providing for change
We have also referred to the need for marketing plans to be flexible and subject to change when unforeseen circumstances arise. The sound principle of flexibility can of course be carried to excess; it is not good practice when things fail to go according to plan simply to revise the plan to conform with the actual outcome. But predicting the future is an uncertain art, and it must be accepted that sometimes assumptions which seemed sound at the time they were made are disproved by events. The financial services environment is more vulnerable than most to invasion by uncontrollable factors like radical changes in government economic policy or the effects of any one of a number of overseas events. When this happens it is pointless to plod on with an unchanged plan as though nothing had happened.

But in saying that provision for change should be implicit in any plan – more so of course in the case of long-term than of short-term plans – we should emphasise the difference between the objectives, the strategic and the tactical aspects of the plan. Objectives may need to be modified or the time-scale of achievement adjusted if developing circumstances make them clearly unrealistic; but they should be abandoned only as a last resort. Strategy, with its roots in long-term policy, should certainly not be changed because of problems which may be only short-term. But tactics – the methods used to achieve objectives within the framework of strategic policy – should be adapted to changing circumstances.

Even tactical changes should not be made lightheartedly; in large organisations, particularly, quite minor changes of direction can be difficult and costly. But a readiness to adapt tactics to suit particular circumstances needs to be built in at all levels of a dynamic marketing organisation. Moreover, it is possible to study the likely consequences of at least limited changes by calculating in advance the sensitivity of the end result to alterations in the assumptions made. For example, it is simple in theory (but perhaps time-consuming in practice) to calculate the effect on bank profits of changes in various interest rates. Such predictive calculations not only forecast the resultant outcomes, they usually also lead to a much clearer insight into the internal relationships in the 'model' or budget or plan being studied.

Finally, wherever possible, and wherever it can be done economically, it is a good idea to build on to the plan some deliberate experiments. Such ploys could include extra advertising in a selected town, area or region and the measurement of its effect; or the use of four or five different direct mailing shots, each to a representative sub-section of the target audience, again measuring results. (One such test in a bank's Access operation revealed a near 3:1 difference in response, with the marketing executive's favoured version doing worst!) Building in such tests is not easy and is seldom willingly accepted by those concerned, but is an excellent way to learn about market behaviour.

Summary

We started this chapter by emphasising the importance of brevity, and ended by writing one of the longest chapters in the book. To make amends we have listed the main headings of the 'model' marketing plan below.

The main headings for a marketing plan
1 Overall market characteristics
2 The position of your products or services in the market
3 The company and its competitors
4 Customers and potential customers
5 Institutional and environmental constraints
6 Summary of problems and opportunities
7 Marketing objectives
8 Distribution methods
9 Pricing policy
10 The selling plan and sales support activities

11 Marketing communications, sales promotion and advertising
12 Legal considerations
13 Market information and research
14 Marketing timetable
15 Marketing budget and revenue forecast

The tools of marketing

In this second part we describe the 'toolkit' of marketing techniques developed initially in consumer and other industries; and suggest how the appropriate tools and techniques can be applied in the marketing environment.

CHAPTER FIVE

The marketing mix

In the first part of this book we concentrated on the management aspects of marketing, describing the elements of the marketing plan and the way marketing management fits in with the general management structure. In this second part we propose to describe the various tools and techniques which the marketing specialist should master and which the general manager should understand and utilise in furthering his marketing objectives.

Before describing the individual tools and techniques we should emphasise that none is very useful or effective in isolation. There is a tendency for established organisations, which embrace the marketing concept in their maturity, to mistake the part for the whole. They fall in love with market research, which has the attraction of providing management with interesting information, but not committing them to doing anything about it; or they embark on a costly advertising campaign without ensuring the executive or sales follow-through which makes the advertising claims credible and converts them into profitable sales. The cost of market research is justified only if it leads to a considered marketing decision, even if the decision is to do nothing. Image-building advertising, when reality is not made to conform to the advertising image, can do positive harm by generating cynicism and disbelief.

It is important, therefore, to think from the outset in terms of the 'marketing mix', the balanced blend of marketing ingredients best calculated to achieve a defined marketing objective as economically as possible. There is no standard all-purpose mix, or even a 'right' mix for a given situation; it is not uncommon to find two organisations pursuing similar objectives in the same market sector allocating their marketing budgets to a quite different mix of ingredients. Table 1 gives a simplified indication of the relative importance likely to be attached to the different marketing mix ingredients in typical situations. But this should not be taken too literally. The most important of marketing skills is not exhaustive knowledge of a single marketing technique, but the ability to devise a cost-effective mix for a given situation with the touch of originality which distinguishes one organisation from its competitors.

The starting point

In the medical field the starting point for compounding a prescription is the diagnosis and definition of objectives. The doctor defines, if he can, the root of the problem facing his patient, decides what changes he needs to bring about in the patient's condition, and prescribes the appropriate combination of treatments. A similar procedure is followed, or should be followed, by the compounder of the marketing mix. With the aid of market research and other sources of market information he will diagnose the problem or opportunity to be dealt with, including definition of the specific market segments needing attention; he will analyse the various changes of attitude and/or behaviour needed to achieve his objective; and from his analysis he will arrive at a first idea of the ingredients which should go into the marketing mix, and an idea of their relative importance in relation to his defined marketing objectives.

Almost always he will find that to do a thorough job on each of the subsidiary objectives will cost considerably more than the value of the whole objective justifies. Then comes the process of deciding where it is feasible to reduce effort or expenditure or to postpone a desirable initiative in favour of some more urgent action. Since the ingredients of an effective marketing mix are inter-dependent it may in the end be better to lower targets or lengthen the time-scale of achievement than to eliminate some marketing element entirely. The latter course could jeopardise the whole plan. In other words, successful marketing is more likely to come from a properly balanced set of activities than from one or two actions carried out intensively.

To take simple examples from branch banking: it would be foolish to have a strong sales drive without adequate back-up in the

Table 1. The marketing mix in typical financial services situations

	Corporate image-building	Regional development	Branch development	International development	New product development	Personal business development	Corporate business development	Business-related services
Preliminary Market research	●	●			●	●		●
Market segmentation			●	●	●		●	
Definition of objectives	●	●	●	●	●	●	●	●
Active ingredients Product/service design					●	●	●	●
Shop/branch design						●		
Pricing					●	●	●	●	●
Selling		●	●	●			●	●
Marketing communications	●	●	●				●	●
PR	●	●		●		●		●
Merchandising			●			●		
Internal communications	●	●	●		●			●
Catalysts Market models					●			
Critical path networks					●			
Accounting controls		●		●		●	●	●
Management information	●	●	●	●	●	●	●	●
Measurement	●	●	●	●	●	●	●	●
Sales/marketing training		●	●			●		●

● = more important for each situation

branch; to have a strong local advertising campaign without adequate follow-up literature (including the inevitable forms); to have smart new premises but poorly motivated staff; to have a great new service to sell but little help in identifying the precise people to whom it will appeal; and so on. How does one achieve the correct balance? By careful analysis of customers' needs as well as our own; by experience; and by an element of creativity which suggests ways in which to bolster weakness without either undue cost or causing a further lack of balance.

The active ingredients

The seven most important active ingredients from which the marketing mix is usually compounded in the financial services market are listed below.

1 Product/service design and packaging

For the man in the street or even the average businessman there is a great sameness about the services offered by competitive financial institutions. Putting together a package of financial services and presenting it in such a way that it catches the interest of the customer segment at which it is aimed is an ingredient in the marketing mix that can do more to create sales than heavy advertising expenditure on an uninteresting or indistinct product. The former is often regarded as 'mere window dressing', but most customers are not experts and they cannot be blamed for wanting the benefits of a product or service explained to them in terms they can readily understand. And bankers should certainly not feel they are reducing the importance of what they may offer, or their own status in offering it, by making their offering as easy as possible for a particular customer-type to understand.

2 Shop/branch design

Most financial services organisations are retailers as well as producers of their services. It is not easy to display a range of financial services (or to display the readiness to help and explain of the people who provide them) in a way that encourages 'shoppers' to come inside; and security requirements make it no easier. Nonetheless, going as far as possible towards making the office or branch attractive to the target customer groups who want to do business face-to-face is an important element in the marketing mix. A marketing-oriented international bank, for example, is likely to have types of branch related to its different target customer segments in its home country and to adapt its branch style to the local environment when it goes abroad.

3 Pricing

Most marketing people would agree that pricing is one of the more crucial ingredients in the marketing mix, with much more to it than the classical economists' theory of the perfect market would imply. It is of course a help, usually, if you can charge less than your competitors for the same quality of product or service and still make an adequate profit. But in market segments where consumers are not very price-conscious it does not necessarily mean that you will sell more. Moreover a relatively high price can be regarded as an indication of quality and attract buyers, particularly when it is allied to effective presentation and promotion. The marketing manager compounding his marketing mix has to regard price as a variable to be traded off against product quality and promotion, rather than as an absolute where the lowest price is the most desirable. Whether he opts for a relatively high price, high-quality product and heavy promotional expenditure or sets his price as low as he can manage (with quality and promotion to match) will depend on the position in the market which he wants to establish for his service or product. If he is aiming for the top segment of the market he will be inclined to price high; if he is aiming for the mass market he will probably, but not necessarily, price low.

4 Selling

For the marketing manager of a manufactured product the cost of the salesforce, or that part of its total cost which is attributable to the product he manages, is a defined expenditure to be included in his total marketing mix. In marketing financial services the face-to-face selling resource is at the same time even more important and rather less easily defined; and it is harder to apportion the total cost of 'multi-purpose' staff fairly between selling and administrative activities. It is more important because the banker or other purveyor of financial services is himself a major part of the service he has to offer.

He has a 'product' in the shape either of specialised access to financial resources or of investment opportunities to match the customer's own resources; but the customer's acceptance of the product's value will be greatly affected, for better or worse, by his confidence in the reliability of the 'salesman's' advice and in his personal probity and expertise. So the personal selling element in the marketing mix will be of crucial importance and will merit more detailed attention from the marketer than it does in, say, the grocery trade, where the product, with its backing of advertising, can be expected to sell itself, once the salesman has ensured that it is properly displayed in the right outlets.

But, important as it is, the selling element is much harder for the financial services marketer to control, because the 'salesmen' are seldom simply salesmen. The corporate business development manager, the manager of a branch bank, or even of an insurance company's branch office, has important administrative responsibilities as well as his selling tasks. These components certainly cannot be neglected, and they may well be a more congenial use of the individual manager's time than what is sometimes thought to be the 'distasteful business of selling'. It is not an easy task for the marketer to activate a reluctant part-time salesman; but unless he solves the problem the rest of his marketing mix will very likely be wasted.

5 Marketing communications
We use this blanket term to cover advertising, direct mail, brochures and all methods of informing or persuading target customers other than face-to-face selling. Some financial services may be sold entirely by such methods. For example, a bank may be able to sell a new credit card to a selected number of its existing customers largely through direct mail; though securing acceptance of the card by hoteliers, shopkeepers and restaurateurs will probably require a personal selling campaign. Or investors in a new unit trust may be solicited primarily by couponed advertising in financial journals or newspapers.

But in the majority of financial services marketing campaigns the marketing communications element – which is sometimes regarded as virtually the whole marketing story – will be only a part of the total marketing mix. And in many cases it will be, or should be, subsidiary to the main thrust of personal selling. The purpose of the advertising, printed literature, demonstration films, exhibitions, conferences and so on will be to make it easier for the personal salesmen to reach the right customer 'prospects' and persuade them to become customers, rather than to do the complete job on their own.

6 Public relations

An important part of the PR function, as we have said before, is to inform target customer groups about the company and help to persuade them to try its products, through means other than paid advertising, direct mail or direct selling. In this capacity it could well be regarded as just another form of marketing communications. However, it also has a wider responsibility for safeguarding and improving the relationship between the organisation and relevant environmental factors, such as government and society at large. Because of this wider responsibility it cannot be regarded as just another marketing tool, and indeed in many financial services organisations its line to senior management is separate from that of marketing. This wider role should not be under-estimated. As one distinguished banker has said, 'Opinion-formers, MPs or journalists, for example, *will* have an opinion. Without information it will be an uninformed opinion. The job of public affairs people is to give the information which enables them to have informed opinions.'

7 Merchandising

In marketing manufactured products through distributors or retail outlets, merchandising is the term used to describe that part of the marketing mix which is allocated to expediting movement of the manufacturer's products *out* of the distributors' shops or other premises. It includes a variety of items, often lumped together under the general heading of 'below the line' expenditure, such as the provision of in-store display material, the organisation of dealer or consumer competitions and other incentives, and reduced price or other special offers. In highly competitive market sectors these items may well account for as much as half the total marketing appropriation.

In relation to the total marketing mix, merchandising can be characterised as an often essential *stimulant,* sometimes dramatic in its effects but ultimately debilitating if over-indulged in. For the packaged goods manufacturer, selling through very powerful multiple retailers in highly competitive market sectors, it is usually an indispensable activity; his product will be squeezed out by more compliant competitors if he does not provide the distributors with a succession of special offers and other merchandising schemes. But he runs the risk, particularly if he is forced to reduce his image-building advertising, that his product eventually will be bought just because it is on special offer this week, not for its intrinsic merits. Once the point is reached where the brand name is meaningless and the product indistinguishable from its competitors, the manufacturer is at the mercy of his distributors, who are free to handle his product – on their terms – or not, as it suits them.

In the financial services industry, where confidence is so important, the use of merchandising techniques borrowed from other industries is a particularly delicate matter. The financial services organisation which operates through a number of branches cannot escape the fact that it has a shopkeeping role, with an ever-widening range of products to sell through its 'shops' and an ever-increasing direct cost per outlet to cover by those sales; it must attract more customers into its shops, and increase its average sales per customer. Any merchandising device which will help to do that deserves serious consideration. On the other hand the long-term value of the financial service packages on offer, so largely dependent on confidence, needs to be considered. The offer of a hamper of groceries or a package holiday in Majorca may bring customers into the money shops and sell the financial services on offer. But will it in the end persuade the customers that the services cannot in themselves be worth very much if such devices are needed to sell them?

The catalysts

We use the term 'catalyst' to denote those elements in the marketing mix which are not 'active'. Unlike the active ingredients discussed above, the catalysts do not have a direct impact on the prospective customers. But they do contribute to our understanding of the marketing process, to our ability to establish sensible and realistic controls, and also to the total effectiveness of the mix. The most important of these 'catalyst' elements are listed below.

1 Market models

Marketing, as a relative latecomer to the field of management sciences, has been somewhat shameless in borrowing useful techniques from other sectors. One such technique is that of 'models', more familiar in the context of operational research. In the marketing context it is used to describe a manipulable representation – based partly on theory and partly on such data as are available – of the economic sector with which the marketer is concerned and of the influences which affect its behaviour. To be of maximum practical use, especially when there are a lot of data, models need to be incorporated in a computer program. Such models can be useful in helping to establish in advance the likely effect on net sales revenue of alternative levels of marketing expenditure and alternative marketing mixes. The technique, which is described more fully in Appendix II, is of practical value only in large markets where a substantial amount of reliable research data already exists. But the logical approach which it implies – trying to think through, if only on a commonsense basis, the likely joint and several effects on an existing market situation of a variety of complementary marketing initiatives – is to be commended to all those concerned with market development planning.

2 Planning networks

Another borrowed technique, this time developed by the wartime necessity to organise the rapid production of new armaments and equipment, is that of network planning, variously described as critical path analysis or PERT (Production Evaluation and Review Technique). This also is described in more detail in Appendix II. Briefly, this technique is based on charting as a sort of elongated Spaghetti Junction the way in which the various elements in a marketing project must fit together, and the deadlines involved at each stage, if the project is to get off the ground on time. It can be as complicated as the complexity of the situation demands. But simple versions can provide a useful discipline in keeping a project up to time and can help to ensure that a planned explosion of marketing activity really explodes instead of going off in a series of splutters.

3 Accounting and management controls

Here we get back from the type of catalyst that is useful on occasions to one that is patently essential for any properly controlled marketing project; but it is one that is frequently neglected. It should be superfluous to argue that, before a marketing project of any importance is launched, provision should be made for regularly checking its progress and its cost; otherwise the marketer will come to resemble the fabled general launching his troops into battle with little hope of seeing them return, or earn a return. Yet every day there are fresh examples in industry of business development projects where costs escalate out of control, or progress grinds to a halt, because nobody in authority is regularly informed of any departures from budgets or time schedules.

4   External measurement
Unlike product development or organisational projects, for which internal controls are usually adequate, marketing projects require the responsible managers to measure the impact of the project on those aspects of the external world that the project is designed to influence. Part of the management control information system, the part most likely to trigger off adjustments to marketing tactics and consequent changes in the marketing mix, has to be data on changes in customer or distributor attitudes and behaviour related to the project. So we come back full circle to market research, which provided the data for initiating the marketing project in the first place and should also provide key data for measuring its progress and ultimate success or failure.

Adapting the marketing mix to the market situation

In the chart at the beginning of this chapter we indicated in very broad terms the elements in the marketing mix which could be considered in a variety of financial service marketing situations. It goes without saying that the actual mix employed must depend initially on the marketing resources controlled by the manager concerned, or available from a central marketing department. In a large structured organisation the discretionary authority and the marketing budget available to the majority of local managers are likely to be limited; more often than not the individual manager will need, within his own sphere of authority, to ride on the back of centralised marketing campaigns initiated by others.

Nevertheless at any level a manager will have at his disposal two essential ingredients: his own capacity to gather and analyse market information, and the proportion of his own time and energy that is not devoted to higher-priority activities. He can clarify in his own mind the objectives of the marketing project on which he is embarking; he can carry out at least basic market research from published data and customer records; and he can analyse the market research so as to identify the market segment on which his efforts can most productively be focused.

As for the active ingredients of the mix, the basic design of the service being marketed may be outside the individual manager's control. But he can at least adapt the way he presents it, in writing or face-to-face, to the individual customer. The layout of the branch or office from which the service is marketed may well be pre-- determined; but the way it is adapted or exploited to draw attention to the service package being marketed, together with any supporting merchandising material, can offer scope for imaginative action. Discretionary power to use the tool of price is probably very limited; but other selling methods and the optimum use of available selling time offer ample scope for individual initiative.

How many of the techniques included under the heading 'Marketing communications' are available to the manager with a marketing problem, who is not a marketing specialist, will vary from situation to situation. Few are likely to command the dis- cretionary budget needed to finance a major advertising campaign. But advertisements in local media, *extending and localising* the message of the main advertising campaign may be feasible; local small-scale conferences can be organised at modest cost; and a direct mail 'campaign' taking the form of a few personal letters to carefully selected individuals may well be more effective than a massive but unselective mail-out. In the same way PR and merchandising activities can be adapted to almost any situation; and the important element of internal communications will apply whenever more than one individual is involved in executing a marketing project.

As for the catalysts, market models and critical path networks, even when simplified, are probably too elaborate for local marketing projects; but the discipline they embody will always help to get one's thinking straight. And making provision for accounting controls and some feedback of management information is essential to the successful management of all projects, as is the principle of measurement. Measurement, in fact, should be inherent in all marketing projects from the outset. (Measurement does not need to be precise for this purpose – a good estimate will do, or even a jotted down guess at a pinch. The important principles are those of feedback and of learning, and both are enhanced if some prior, written-down measure can be compared with a similar measure after the event.) Measure at the beginning the value of the objectives to be pursued; measure the likely cost of attaining them – and abandon the project if the cost is likely to exceed the net return; measure during the course of the operation and at the end of the day to check whether or not your calculations were valid. Ultimately the only sound criterion of a successful marketing project is a measureable surplus of related income over outgo.

Summary

In this chapter we have said that effective marketing must be based on a co-ordinated mix of activities. Reliance on a single unsupported marketing activity, whether it is advertising, personal selling or some other tool, is unlikely to give a good return for the effort and expenditure involved. We have outlined the main tools and techniques likely to be useful in one or other of the many different situations in which financial services are marketed. We have suggested very tentatively the tools which could be most appropriate in the different situations, but have emphasised that the individual manager must make his choice in the light of prevailing circumstances. No marketing rule of thumb is an adequate substitute for the creative thinking of the individual.

Finally, we have pointed out that local managers have the same duties and opportunities, even though 'writ small', as central managers *to get the facts, to plan, and to act.*

CHAPTER SIX

Marketing information

The need for information

'Information is the ever-moving, mighty river on which the marketing craft is floated.' The origin of this pretentious quotation is obscure (we rather think we made it up ourselves). But the principle that a flow of information is essential for a well-managed business will not be unfamiliar to those responsible for managing financial services enterprises. Prudent lending, efficient investment and responsible financial advice all depend on adequate and reliable information.

If marketing information differs from the general information used to manage a business, it is essentially a matter of degree rather than fundamental principles. First of all, marketing is concerned so very much with the future; by the time a marketing decision has been taken and implemented, time will have moved on and circumstances may have changed. So an element of prediction is inherent in all worthwhile marketing information: 'this is the situation today, whence it can be predicted that the situation when the marketing action bites will be. . . '.

Marketing is also concerned more directly with people – people as individuals and people as the decision makers in corporate organisations – and less immediately with figures than are the more technical aspects of financial services. The marketing man is constantly asking himself two questions, 'What are my competitors doing and is it paying off?' and 'Supposing I do *this,* how will my target customers react?' Figures remain of vital importance in establishing the parameters for marketing action, and in measuring the level of success or failure, but always they are the outcome of interaction between people.

It was symptomatic of this difference in priority that when the British clearing banks first embraced the marketing concept their marketing specialists began to ask questions about customers; not just the military formula of name, rank and number, but the more three-dimensional questions, about needs, attitudes and lifestyles, which a financial services organisation should understand if it is to provide a high standard of personal service. In the old days of decentralised and personalised banking it would have been time-consuming but not very difficult to come by the information; it would simply have involved asking the branch managers, most of whom would have spent many years in the same branch, to describe their customers as fully as possible without breaching professional confidences.

But in a more centralised, computerised era it became very much harder to collect and analyse the relevant information. In theory it should have been much easier and much faster; a computer can sort out the predominant characteristics of a very large customer file in a matter of minutes *if* it has been programmed to do so. But the first generation bank computers were programmed in such a way as to deal with the *accounts* of customers rather than the customers as such. Partly because of a commendable reluctance to infringe personal privacy, and partly because nobody had anticipated the questions which could arise in the search to provide a higher standard of service, the personal data which could answer the marketer's questions had not been included.

Schematically, the way the 'moving river' of marketing information relates to marketing activities is illustrated in Fig. 3.

Out of the information, marketing ideas are dredged up; the ideas, if they stand up to rigorous analysis and review, are incorporated in marketing plans; these in turn lead to marketing actions, the results of which are checked against the now possibly changed

Fig. 3.

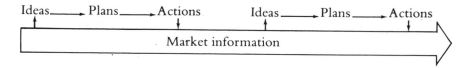

marketing information scene. As a result of this fresh immersion, modified ideas re-emerge, and the cycle begins again.

As a simple, and quite improbable, example let us suppose that information reaches Our Hero, a branch manager, to the effect that old J.B. has left his wife and is setting up home with his secretary. The information gives rise to a number of ideas, some of a marketing nature. Perhaps J.B. will need advice on taxation or financial matters. Or perhaps a personal loan or a bridging loan to deal with his new housing problem. Or a new will appointment could be a possibility. The obvious plan is to write to J.B., or better still find an excuse to go and see him. Action – picking up the telephone – follows almost immediately after the plan.

But then further information emerges. The lady was certainly his secretary, but she is also the daughter of a Greek shipping magnate, so the idea of a personal loan seems inappropriate. But what is her relationship to the shipping business, and indeed how long will her *new* relationship last? A revised plan, to find out whether the bank's corporate finance department is interested in an introduction to the shipping industry, begins to take shape.

The intention of this frivolous example was not to suggest that the type of information needed for marketing purposes is mainly of a gossip column variety. While in any financial services business there will be some customers of sufficient importance to be given extensive individual attention, practical marketing economics require a large measure of generalisation on the personal side of the business. Customers and potential customers will have to be divided into more-or-less homogeneous *segments* for business development purposes.

Basic marketing information is then needed to answer the following questions in relation to each of the financial services being marketed and to each of the catchment areas from which the company hopes to draw its business.

1 What are the characteristics of those segments of the public who
   (a) buy the service from the marketer's company;
   (b) buy it from competitive sources;
   (c) do not buy it?
2 Why do they behave in this way?
3 How satisfied are users with the service provided by the company

and its competitors? Does the service satisfy all or only some of the relevant users' needs? Is it generating repeat or 'once only' business?

4 Which of the customer and non-customer categories are, or are likely to be, the most profitable for the company over a reasonable time-span?

5 What can the company do to encourage customers or potential customers to modify their behaviour to the company's advantage; or prevent them from modifying it to the company's disadvantage?

6 What recent or predictable changes in the situation of customers or potential customers are likely to create new needs which the company can satisfy?

7 What changes in the economic, legislative or social environment are likely to create new problems or opportunities with which the company can assist its customers?

The type of information needed in relation to a corporate customer is similar but rather more complex. It is necessary, or at least desirable, to know about the industry in which he is engaged, its growth trend, its significant features, its dependence on key resources – and whether they are imported or not – about your customer's place in it, about *his* customer relationships, about his corporate structure, about his financial history and prospects. And since the part of a business which counts in the end is not its customers and premises or even its products, but the people who run it, it is important to have as much information as possible about the key people in the business who make the decisions that really matter.

The nature and sources of information

While information is essential for effective marketing it must be recognised that information which involves people and their pre-dicted behaviour can never be either fully comprehensive or wholly reliable. Even those endowed with the rare gift of self-knowledge are seldom certain in advance of how they will react to a particular set of circumstances, or willing to reveal the whole truth to inquisitors. So the seeker after market information has to be satisfied with infor-mation of varying reliability from a number of different sources; and he has to lean heavily on the law of averages, thanks to which it is usually possible to predict not what a single individual will do but how many on average out of a large number will turn left, turn right, or march straight ahead. The danger is that when the proportions are written down in a well-presented document, whether a market research report or a government white paper, the figures may be accepted as the whole truth rather than a reasonable approximation.

Marketing-information sources are customarily divided into two categories: primary and secondary. A secondary source, as the adjective implies, comprises data collected by other people for other purposes. Its great advantage is that it is either free, or a great deal less expensive, than specially commissioned research. For this reason first consideration should always be given to the collection and analysis of relevant secondary information before special studies are commissioned. Its disadvantage is that the information collected in this way, through desk research, seldom answers exactly those questions which the decision-making manager had in mind; and it is not always easy to establish exactly how much reliance should be placed on the figures themselves.

So it is prudent when using secondary information to collect it from as many different sources as possible, and to cross-check. It is prudent also to obtain skilled advice on the degree of reliance which should be placed on the various sources. This is particularly important in the case of research into foreign markets. The need to relate the cost of marketing research to the benefit likely to accrue from it usually leads to a basic dependence on secondary information in the less important markets; and in these markets it takes local knowledge to indicate which of the available facts and figures are relatively reliable and which are quite misleading.

Secondary information sources
The main secondary sources worth investigating in the UK are listed below.

1 *Government statistics.* The publications of the Central Statistical Office and the various government departments provide an increasing variety of information both about economic and industrial trends and about the characteristics, lifestyle and spending habits of the various segments of the population. The sources of the information

should always be checked. Census information for example is entirely reliable within the limits of human error; but there is a lot of published information based on relatively small samples or on voluntary returns from businesses which is accurate enough as a basis for broad commercial policy, but will not support any notions of fine tuning. It is worth checking, incidentally, with the statisticians concerned; quite often they can provide unpublished figures relevant to a particular marketing problem. (HMSO can supply a list of government statistical sources including the topics covered.)

2 *Local authority statistics.* For the manager of a localised business interested in identifying target customers or in finding a suitable site for a new branch, local authority rating lists, electoral registers and development plans are important sources. It is always worthwhile, in the context of forward planning, to establish contact with the local planning department.

3 *Trade associations.* In theory, trade associations should be a valuable source of information for marketers focusing their business development plans on specific industries. But more often than not what they can offer is somewhat disappointing, partly because many do not in fact represent all the firms within the industry they purport to cover, and partly because their statistics are often based on voluntary returns from member companies who are not always as conscientious in their form filling as they might be.

4 *Chambers of commerce or trade.* Some can be very helpful, other less so.

5 *Financial and trade publications.* Again, some can be very informative, others less so; only experience can tell which is which.

6 *Trade directories.* By the nature of things in a mobile economy any trade directory is likely to be somewhat out of date by the time it is published. The best of them can be a useful starting point for listing prospective corporate customers; but they usually need to be supplemented by investigation on the ground: and note carefully whether the firms included have paid to appear. If they have, coverage is likely to be far less complete.

7 *Media research studies.* Many of the studies sponsored and published by media proprietors or television contractors have a wider usefulness in describing the region or population group they serve than the primary intention of the research – to provide reasons for using their advertising facilities – would suggest.

8 *Syndicated market studies.* A number of market studies, for instance those carried out by NEDO working parties, by the Economist Intelligence Unit and by MINTEL, are offered for sale on a subscription basis to companies interested in the market sector covered by the study. These usually state their degree of reliability – where they don't, ask; otherwise, *caveat emptor.*

9 *Economic forecasting services.* Marketers of financial services cannot fail to be as interested in the publications of the economic forecasters as the ancients were in the pronouncements of the Delphic Oracle. But the ancient view that it is not given to mortals to know the future continues to be borne out. Even the most professional of economic forecasts cannot be swallowed whole, but needs to be incorporated as another piece of evidence in the manager's own essential but frustrating task of foreseeing the future of the particular business sectors with which he is concerned.

10 *Other companies' information.* Other companies interested in the same business sector, even friendly competitors, can be a very helpful source of secondary information. This can be particularly true for newcomers to a foreign market, where they are welcomed to the club by their compatriots or existing associates.

11 *Commercial attachés and consular officials.* Again, in foreign markets official national representatives can be exceedingly helpful. It is also not unknown for them to be exceedingly unhelpful.

To anyone who wishes to become more familiar with secondary sources of data, a visit to a good library is a must. Most librarians are only too willing to help and will respond very readily to requests for information – indeed they seem to enjoy the challenge. It is obviously best to pose a question as near to the real core of your quest as possible; even if the answer is not forthcoming you will be sure to get as close to it as the data available will allow; whereas if you ask what you think is as near a question *as is likely to be answerable* you are, of course, substituting your guess for the librarian's years of training and experience.

Primary information sources
The main primary sources of information can be categorised as follows:

1 personal enquiry (the most primary of all);
2 the various types of market research described later in this chapter;
3 the less formal collection of market information from a variety of first-hand sources, best described as market intelligence;
4 advertising research; again, described later in this chapter;
5 analysis of internal records. It is surprising how much information, quite apart from that of a confidential nature, accumulates in the records of a large organisation like a bank and would be exceedingly useful for marketing purposes but is simply never used. And the sampling techniques of market research can be applied to internal records very effectively.

The collection and interpretation of information

The effective use of secondary marketing information sources depends eventually on knowing your sources, being able to assess their reliability, and having some talent for lateral thinking – perceiving a not-always-obvious connection between the data and the profitable business development opportunities which are sought. The collection and interpretation of primary information requires rather more technical skill. There is no reason why the general manager should acquire those skills; but he should be sufficiently aware of them to know what research can and cannot do, to be able to brief the research technicians adequately, and to be able to assess the value of their findings.

Most formal market research falls into one or other of the following five categories:

1   consumer behaviour or attitude research;
2   consumer product acceptance research;   trade research;

3   advertising research;
4   consumer or trade panels.

All of them are exceedingly simple in concept. The researcher simply asks questions (whether in personal interviews, by telephone or by mail) about people's opinions and behaviour, about their habits and experience, about their reactions to samples of new products, about their readership or television viewing habits.

The technical skill is in asking the right people the right questions and producing reliable results at affordable cost. Do you, for example, insist on personal interviews, or do you use the telephone or the post? Personal interviews are expensive, because they involve travel, time and money. Telephone interviews are usually a good deal cheaper, but not everybody has a telephone so you may not reach the poorer groups of the population; and those approached by telephone find it easier to hang up on you than respondents in a fact-to-face interview. Postal surveys are the cheapest of all, but you cannot ask many questions if you want a good response rate; and you are never quite sure whether those who go to the trouble of replying are typical of the whole group to whom the original mailing was addressed, or, when the research is carried out among companies, whether the person who does reply is the best respondent.

Since it is usually impossible to interview everyone who is relevant, practically all formal market research must depend, in order to produce reliable results at affordable cost, on sampling. That this can produce such results derives from the fact, observable by the layman and embodied by the mathematician in algebraic equations, that if you go on choosing units *entirely at random* from a collection of known characteristics your sample after a while will conform very closely to those characteristics. For example, if you pick balls at random from a well-mixed bag filled half with white balls and half with black balls, you may start with a run of whites or blacks, but after you have picked out 100 or so you probably will not have more than fifty-five in either colour; and as you come up to the thousand mark you will very probably be not more than 2 per cent away from a fifty/fifty split. Similarly, if you pick human beings at random out of the total population you will come closer and closer, as the sample gets larger, to reproducing in the sample the characteristics of the total population; not just age, sex and class, but other characteristics such as home ownership or the possession of a bank account. The mathematician's probability theory can tell you how close you are likely to come at different sample sizes. In principle the probable margin of error is reduced only slowly as the sample gets larger; its size is, in fact, in proportion to the square root of the sample size. So it is usually better to be content with a reasonable sample size than to add expensive interviews in the hopeless search for complete accuracy. (The crucial test usually is how small will the smallest sub-group be? For example, if we are interested in bank account holders in the UK more than one in two of adults would qualify; but if we were interested in characteristic ten times as rare then obviously the number we would need to interview to get the same number of 'useful' respondents will be ten times as great. It is this rarity factor which usually determines the basic sample size.)

The main snag in applying pure probability sampling theory to commercial market research arises from the words 'entirely at random'. If you were to pick a sample of, say, 2,000 people to interview out of the entire population of the United Kingodm you could find your interviewers travelling at great cost from one end of these islands to the other, pursuing widely scattered individuals. So for practical purposes it is more usual to concentrate the interviewing through a two-stage sampling technique; first dividing the country into a number of blocks and taking a sample of these blocks, secondly picking a random sample within each block.

When cost is more important, and a calculable standard of precision less essential, market researchers commonly resort to quota sampling. This means giving interviewers a list of individuals to find – so many men, so many women, so many in each age group, so many in each economic group – which roughly corresponds to the breakdown of the total population.

The trouble with the quota-sampling method is that the less conscientious interviewers may stretch the definition of interviewees in order to fit into the required quota; and assessing the reliability of the results is much harder.

But, unhappily, deficiencies in sampling method are not the only cause of unreliability in market research results. An equally important cause derives from the old tag which starts, 'Ask a stupid question. . . '. Stupid questions can take many different forms. They can be quite simply unanswerable, like the traditional 'Have you stopped beating your wife?' conundrum. Or they can be questions to which most people probably do not know the answer, such as, 'What will you be doing at 3.15 p.m. next Thursday fortnight?' Or they can be questions which tempt people to give a misleading answer for reasons of self-respect or prestige, such as, 'How often do you clean your teeth?' Or it can be very easy to prejudice people's answers to the later questions you wish to ask by indicating in the earlier questions what response you are looking for (people have a tendency to give the answer they think will please on a point which doesn't matter greatly to them one way or another). Questionnaire construction, in fact, is just as essential a skill for the professional market researcher – and a working knowledge of it just as essential for those evaluating their work – as sampling technique. (It is usual, indeed it is required by the constitution of the Market Research Society, both to include details of the sample achieved, together with a description of the sampling method, and to attach a copy of the questionnaire to every full report of a market research study.)

The manager in a position to commission a market research study, who wants to get full value and reliable results out of it, should put a lot of thought and effort into briefing the researchers. Only too often researchers are told simply that, for instance, more information is needed on the attitudes and behaviour of school leavers in relation to bank accounts. The result of this is likely to be a report which is comprehensive and largely irrelevant. The manager ends up saying, 'This is interesting, but what in the world do I do about it?' or, 'Well there's not much in all this that we didn't already know.'

If on the other hand the commissioning manager takes the trouble to think through for himself and discuss with the market researchers the hypotheses which he has in mind, and the marketing actions which might result from their confirmation or denial, a far more relevant study is possible: for example, 'We rather think that school leavers find our branches a bit intimidating, and are thinking of doing thus and so to make them seem more welcoming', or, 'We rather think that the parents are the main influence on whether or not, and with what bank, school leavers open an account; if this is so we should direct our promotional effort towards the parents.' Taking the market researchers into your confidence to this extent will enable them to apply their technical skills and experience in a more constructive, practical and profitable way.

Internal information

It has often been said that the best prospects for new business are the customers you already have. This is certainly true when marketing a steadily growing range of financial services. The confidence built on mutually satisfactory (let us hope) relationships is a better launching pad for a new service than cold canvassing or broadscale advertising. Few financial service companies, however disorganised, can fail to know, one way or another, about the characteristics and needs of their more important customers as well as about their financial affairs. But much of the knowledge, as we have said, is likely to be inaccessible – either filed away in widely scattered branch records or locked up in the heads of individual managers and executives. (Of course for individual branch managers this information *is* accessible – his own records are a mine of information which can be of real use. But only if the body of customers is considered as a whole can he expect to see patterns. Customer–by–customer analysis will help him to understand each customer but general marketing guidance can only come from a broader perspective.)

But from the central management's point of view, the great practical problem is how to make the relevant information readily available when it is needed for marketing planning or operational purposes. Logically the first step in overcoming this problem is to have an organised system for reporting and recording marketing information that is relevant either to immediate marketing problems or to problems that may be expected to arise in the future. This requires the facility to analyse sales and customer records in a way which is relevant to future business development, including an organised feedback of information from salesmen and others in contact with customers or prospective customers; and also the ability to relate current information both to past information (so as to establish trends) and to external market data (so as to establish how far the company's own experience is typical of the whole market). This is more easily said than done. In theory a well-planned computer system will make it all possible. But there are practical problems.

The first problem derives from the computer expert's favourite acronym GIGO – meaning garbage in, garbage out. The amount of useful marketing information which can be extracted from a computer system depends firstly on anticipating the questions which management is likely to ask of it and ensuring that the computer staff make it possible to extract the relevant information; and secondly on ensuring that the right information in the right form is fed in in the first place. This in its turn gets back to the human factor; for example, persuading managers and salesmen to overcome their notorious reluctance to fill in standardised forms after sales trips or information-gathering interviews

But, difficult or not, if information is to be interpreted into marketing action, compatibility and availability of marketing information is vital, and completeness an important goal. Given that practically all information is more or less inaccurate, it is dangerous to rely simply on a single piece of information or market study as a basis for an important marketing decision; information from a variety of sources, including the managers' personal experience, should be collected, collated and analysed before a decision is made.

The presentation and use of information

If market information is not well and clearly presented, it probably will not be used by management as a basis for decisions and actions; if it is not used, the cost of collecting and analysing it will have been wasted. But how to ensure, when managers are constantly bombarded with information, only a fraction of which can possibly be absorbed (has anyone ever tried to read every single word in a daily newspaper?), that the research report which you have toiled to compose will be absorbed and used – assuming of course that it has something useful to say?

It is impossible ever to be sure of commanding an audience. A lot depends both on the importance and topicality of the subject matter and on the reputation the report writer has built up for having something worthwhile to say. But there are a number of quite simple rules (summarised in Appendix I) for presenting facts and figures in a written report which should make it quicker and easier for the reader to absorb the gist of it. The essential points are listed here.

1 To remember that your readers are much less interested in your subject matter than you are. So keep it brief. Even the title, like a good advertisement headline, can enliven a report; for example, 'Should we increase prices? Yes' or, 'Three reasons why prices should be increased.'
2 To remember that some readers are even less interested than others. So have a summary section at the beginning. It should always be possible to summarise into a couple of pages the main findings of a report of a score or so pages. The very busy and only marginally interested reader can stop at the end of those pages; the more interested can read on if they choose.
3 To tabulate figures in a format which helps the eye to fasten quickly on the exception. It is the exceptional figures which precipitate action, not the predictable.
4 To illustrate the more significant figures by charts. Most people find it easier to draw conclusions from spatial relationships than from numerical relationships.
5 'Keep it simple, stupid.' Like most other technicians, market research specialists can be exhibitionists and parade their expertise in pretentious jargon. The harassed manager cannot be bothered with this. He is interested simply in what the research means, how reliable it is, and what he should do about it.

A written report is of course not the only way of communicating the results of a research study. A personal presentation, either face-to-face or, if need be, in the form of an audio-visual cassette can be a much more effective way of getting the message across and avoiding misconceptions.

Towards an information system

The effective use of information will always be an active rather than a passive affair. The ideal starting point is for the decision-making manager to analyse marketing problems within his own area of authority, determine what information is needed to solve them and then ask for the information to be produced. The passive receipt of a quantity of unsolicited information may prompt the initiating ideas but is unlikely by itself to provide the complete answer.

However, with the present state of computer technology, there is no insuperable reason why most of the information a manager needs to make marketing decisions should not be available on tap, whether it is current information, historical information, or more hazardous predictions about the future. The essential elements for the ideal information system are

1 the input of reliable and relevant information already discussed;
2 a readily accessible, probably computerised, data bank or storage system;
3 a system of regular reports which enables managers to keep track of the routine information they need for control purposes;
4 an information retrieval system which enables managers to ask specific questions of the central data bank and get prompt replies;
5 a clear picture of the information each individual manager needs or is likely to need in the course of his job.

It is this last element, together of course with cost, which creates the greatest practical problem. The constantly repeated experience of experts trying to devise information systems for large organisations is that managers find it very difficult to specify in advance precisely what information in what form they are likely to need and be able to use. The tendency is either to ask for too much, and then be appalled by the flood of paper which in due course descends on their desks, or to regret, when it is too late, that they have failed to ask for this and this and this. Notoriously, over the whole field of information, the basic problem is not finding the right answers but asking the right questions. Nevertheless, information systems are improving and will continue to improve; cynics might say that there is only too much room for them to do so.

Summary

In this chapter we have said that information about people and companies as a basis for predictions about their future behaviour underlies all effective marketing management; and because information is constantly changing, it needs to be continuous and continuously revised and referred to.

We have divided information sources into two categories, primary and secondary, stressing that data from both sources are almost always no better than approximations; so it is prudent to check the reliability of your sources and to cross-check, whenever possible, against other independent sources.

We have listed the main UK sources of secondary information, saying that this category has the advantage of being inexpensive, but the disadvantage of seldom answering exactly the right questions.

We have also listed the main methods of primary information collection, saying that the reliability of most market research studies depends on the techniques of sampling and questionnaire construction, which involve some professional expertise. But the manager who commissions the studies can contribute greatly to their usefulness by comprehensive briefing and explanation of the expected use of the results.

We have said that the marketing researcher or manager can also do much to ensure the usefulness of his work by putting himself in the place of his readers, and presenting his reports in a way which they will find easy to understand and act on.

We have said, finally, that efficient marketing information *systems,* based on a computerised data bank, are a practical possibility for the medium term, provided that the information users can be induced to anticipate the main categories of information they are likely to need and the form in which they will need it.

CHAPTER SEVEN

The product range

In the early missionary days, when marketing was the new religion which would revolutionise Western industry, its apostles liked to draw black and white contrasts between production-oriented and consumer-oriented companies. The old-fashioned production-oriented manufacturer, they would claim, churned out on his obsolescent machinery whatever product caught his personal fancy, added what he regarded as an adequate profit to his production costs, and then despatched his hard-driven salesmen to foist the results on the consuming public, or suffer the consequences. The virtuous modern consumer-oriented manufacturer would start by ascertaining what consumers want and what they are prepared to pay for it, and would then arrange to produce a range of products to meet those specifications.

Perhaps this exaggerated approach was necessary to get across the point that in the end the customer decides whether the company will flourish or collapse (unless, that is, a benevolent government steps in and elects to preserve it as an ancient monument). But putting the case in such black and white terms now seems rather naive. The fact is that most companies were not born yesterday but have a history, a reputation, substantial resources of capital, expertise and above all people – and an established product range. The product range certainly needs to be constantly modified in the light of changing consumer needs and environmental developments. New products need to be introduced, to ensure maximum customer satisfaction not to say growth for the company. Obsolescent products, which have ceased to pay their way or justify the demands they make on management and selling time, need to be discontinued, often to the great grief of some minority groups inside or outside the company who continue to cherish them. Existing products, which continue to satisfy a basic consumer need but have become a trifle old-fashioned, need to be improved or modernised. But there is no sense at all in the marketing man insisting that an identified consumer need must be satisfied when his company lacks the skills or the resources to do the job, profitably, at least as well as its competitors. Nor, when the company has under-utilised capacity of one kind or another, can he stand aside, saying it is none of his business. Unless a market is found for the idle capacity or, if totally unusable, it is disposed of, it will just be an added burden, increasing the overheads chargeable against the successful products.

Ultimately, of course, it is the marketing man's responsibility to press for change, to identify emerging consumer demands which it is within the company's capacity to satisfy, to protest loudly on the customer's behalf when there is evidence of some remediable dissatisfaction. He must perforce adopt this somewhat unpopular role because he is more closely in touch with the customer's needs than some of his management colleagues. But as a marketing man he should not emulate the over-enthusiastic salesman who is prepared to risk bankruptcy for his company in order to get the order. His task is to achieve a proper balance between customer satisfaction and company profitability, always remembering that governmental consumer protection agencies and other outside bodies are liable to intervene in the buyer-seller relationship. This is not to suggest that customer satisfaction and company profitability cannot go hand in hand – indeed, without the former there will be no long-term profit – but that there can be short-sighted managements, pursuing the proverbial 'quick buck', who preach the antithesis of good marketing practice under the marketing banner.

Of the three main categories of marketing activity related to the product range – developing new products, killing off old products, and modifying existing products – the first is much the most glamorous. But it is also the most costly and the most risky. In most industries, whether manufacturing or service, experienced marketing managers looking back over their careers will be forced to admit that thought and effort spent on the relatively unglamorous activities of product improvement and range extension produced more profit and growth for their companies than fundamental new product development. There are of course situations when the advent of radical new technology makes the last essential; but as a rule organisations are more successful at doing rather better what they already know than at learning entirely new tricks.

In banking, as in other industries, it is the *successful* new ideas that are remembered: cheques long ago; personal loans and unit trusts more recently. Readers will have their own views about which of the many new services launched in the 1970s, following the introduction of Competition and Credit Control, will survive, and for how long. Will credit cards run into the nineties? Will cash dispensers be made obsolete before they have been fully depreciated in banks' books, if society moves more quickly than expected into a low-cash era, helped along by cheap point-of-sale terminals? These sorts of questions can at least be approached rationally. But at what point in the life cycle of tax-related services – for example, those which include life assurance as a means of gaining tax relief – will the law be changed? The 'at a stroke' syndrome for curing our ills is now widely discredited, but the scope for creating change at a stroke remains very wide in the field of tax legislation. Nevertheless marketing must go on, and must attempt to take such facts of life into account. So we turn now to consider some possible approaches to the development of a banking product range.

Analysing the company's product position in relation to its resources and corporate objectives

The logical starting point for any product range policy, whether of product improvement or of new product development, is an analysis of the company's existing product range, including the extent to which it satisfies the company's vision of itself and the degree to which it is adequate as a base for the achievement of long-term corporate objectives. The familiar question, 'What business are we in?', can elicit a different answer from decade to decade in financial services as in other industries. A couple of decades ago the traditional banker's answer to this question might have been to the effect that our business is borrowing and lending money, preferably borrowing long and lending short, with an adequate spread between the two rates. Today the answer would more probably be to the effect that, 'We aim to provide a complete range of financial services and advice to both our personal and our corporate customers and to achieve a sufficient rate of return on capital employed to keep shareholders happy.' At the same time the concept of long-range planning has gained sufficient acceptance for managements to take a view of the size and shape of business to be aimed for in five or ten year's time.

In this situation the product range planner can begin to identify market gaps, areas of customer or potential customer demand which the company is either failing to satisfy at all or satisfying less efficiently than its competitors; and he can begin also to quantify an emergent profit gap, a widening discrepancy between the revenue that can be anticipated from normal growth in the existing product range and the profit targets which management has set for future years. An improved or extended product range, and eventually (if the gaps are very wide) diversification into totally new product areas will almost always be needed, though this is not to deny that the classical routes of extra sales efforts and cost-reduction exercises on existing products will also have their place.

A product development methodology

The starting point for any innovation or product improvement is an idea. But where ideas come from is a mystery that has never been fully explained. Anecdotes of Archimedes leaping out of his bath and rushing naked into the street crying, 'Eureka, I've got it!', or of the apple bouncing off Newton's cranium are all very well. But it is clear that a lot must have gone on – the study of other men's ideas, discussion, creative incubation, exploration of dead ends – before the final illuminating moment arrived. The marketing man whose job requires him to produce successful new product ideas to order cannot afford to wait for inspiration to strike; he must somehow find a way of systematising the creative process.

The first principle in doing that is to recognise that for every good idea which finally makes the grade and earns a profit as a successful new product or product improvement, perhaps 100 have to be investigated and eventually discarded. So it is important at the outset to collect as many constructive ideas from as many different sources as possible, and then to screen out those which do not stand up to serious examination.

Sources of ideas for new or improved products and services

The most frequent external sources for new ideas are listed below (see also Fig. 4 overleaf).

1 Customers (including prospective customers), either making informal suggestions or stimulated by formal market research.
2 Distributors and associated companies. One of the benefits of an international organisation is the opportunity for an exchange of new product ideas between companies serving different markets at different stages of development.
3 Knowledge of government needs. As the largest single employer in most countries the government, with its changing requirements and ample purse, merits special study.
4 Competitors. Allowing a competitor to make the running with a new product, learning from his mistakes, and then launching an improved version is a favourite marketing ploy. But there is of course the risk that if you give him too long a lead you may never catch up.
5 Academic research or other outside technological developments. Formal links with external think-tanks, prepared to work to a client's brief, can introduce a useful element of lateral thinking, free from the constraints of tradition.

Internal sources can include

1 the research and development department, or in a financial services context the specialists in devising new methods of corporate finance, personal savings or insurance schemes and so on, to meet changing economic or fiscal circumstances;
2 the marketing department, whose job it is to monitor customer needs and the market place through the research methods described in the previous chapter;
3 experienced company executives (experience is not necessarily synonymous with conservatism);
4 employee suggestions. Often junior employees, in daily touch with customers, have a closer understanding of customer attitudes and needs than senior managers who have climbed up the promotional ladder into the stratosphere.

Fig. 4. A product development programme.

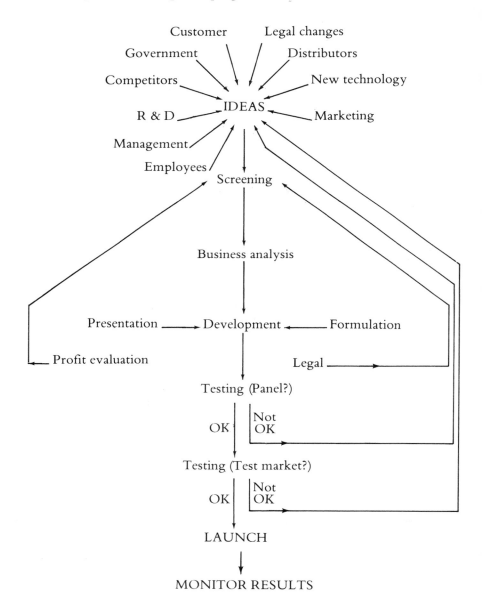

The more communication there is between all these sources, and the more comparison and discussion of ideas, the greater the likelihood of worthwhile innovation. From this viewpoint the device of brainstorming sessions is a useful one. When individuals from a variety of backgrounds and different levels of seniority are brought together and induced by a stimulating chairman to discuss new product ideas without inhibition and without fear of embarrassment if many of their ideas are unworkable, the results can be surprising. A great number of ideas will certainly emerge, and individuals are likely to go away having learned something as well as contributed something, which can be at least a minor amelioration of the ever-present problem of internal communications. But such sessions need to be carefully handled; early criticism will quickly stifle the flow of ideas.

From product idea to product launch

Producing ideas is fun – a slightly more organised version of day-dreaming. Turning the ideas into marketable new products or services is hard work. Very hard work. Success can never be guaranteed, but it is more likely if a nominated individual is assigned the task of making the product or group of products succeed, and if he

1 has the task as a sole or major responsibility, not as an afterthought to other more important charges;
2 has working with him on a part-time basis a multi-disciplinary team of executives who have a talent for innovation (a talent not always associated with a successful record in line management);
3 is empowered to co-opt outside experts on to his team if required;
4 is assured of the continuing interest and backing of senior management, despite the fact that he is presiding over a cost centre rather than a profit centre;
5 is required to work to a realistic but firm programme, timetable and budget.

Starting with the collection of ideas generated by the brain-storming session or any of the other sources described above, the product development manager (as he will usually be called) and his team can expect to go through something like the programme set out below.

1 Screening

If the idea-collecting stages, especially the brainstorming sessions, were conducted in the right uncritical atmosphere, no idea, however harebrained at first glance would have been rejected yet. But primary screening will probably result in the rejection, for perfectly valid and objective reasons, of 80-90 per cent of the ideas processed. Many will duplicate either some existing product or each other. Some will contravene the law. Some will contravene established company policy. Some will be outside the scope of the company's skills or resources. And so on. But don't be too tough at this stage.

2 Business analysis

The next step in the programme will be to subject the surviving ideas to a hypothetical business analysis. What is the size and what are the growth prospects of the market segment into which the new product would be introduced? What are the existing products in the market, and how does the proposed new or improved product compare with them? How formidable is the competition? How would the company bring the product to market? What would be the likely sales volume on the most favourable, least favourable and most likely assumptions? What would be the gross profit contribution? What would be the likely marketing costs? How long would it take for the new or improved product to come into profit? What level of profit?

There would of course be a large element of enlightened guesswork in these calculations, and at this stage the prospective new product should be given the benefit of any reasonable doubt. But if, on the most favourable assumptions, there is no reasonable prospect of the product ever earning an adequate profit it should be abandoned. This is likely to be the fate of at least half the surviving ideas. Too often however an idea is allowed to survive against the evidence for its rejection – for all sorts of reasons, including the mischance that the idea came from a respected senior manager. Equally, the NIH (Not Invented Here) syndrome often causes the premature rejection of ideas. Beware of both motives. Be tough at this stage.

3 The development stage

The product ideas still surviving (possibly 5 per cent of the original number) can then be formally adopted as products under development, each of them endowed with a modest investment budget. Development, whether of a manufactured product or of a service, will normally proceed down two parallel but inter-connected paths. The first could be designated Formulation; in the case of a financial service the precise terms of the proposition to be put to the target customer group, together with the benefit offered. The second could be designated Presentation; meaning the way in which the proposition and benefit are explained to prospective customers, and the supporting literature, contract forms, promotional material and so on. In this stage the details of the 'for real' pricing policy, which is an integral part of any product, will also need to be worked out.

If the project is at all complicated, outside agencies or consultants may well be involved; it will probably be worthwhile in such cases for the project manager to prepare a simple network analysis in order to keep the project in line with target dates. Be realistic.

4 Primary testing

It is more than likely that several of the final short-list of product ideas will drop out in the development stage, either because the market opportunity disappears or because unforeseen practical snags emerge. But there should be at least some which emerge in fully fledged prototype form. These should then be subjected to small-scale testing along market research lines, probably involving exposure to a representative sample or panel of consumers and at the same time exposure to some open-minded salesmen and distributors (or in the case of a clearing bank system, branch managers). It would be unrealistic to overlook the latter, because they can often make constructive suggestions and because a thumbs-down by salesmen and distributors will ensure that a new product flops, however favourably disposed the ultimate consumer may be. Be receptive.

5 Test marketing

For those products which come through the primary testing stage, plus any modification this stage may necessitate, the question then arises: do we introduce it into a test market or do we go immediately into a broadscale launch?

The prudent manager will usually opt for a test market, on the grounds that however thorough and careful your development work and preliminary testing may have been you can never really tell whether a product will sell until you have sold it. Repeatedly. On the other hand, mounting and evaluating a major market test can take up to a year, a year during which you may miss the tide of market opportunity and your competitors will certainly be watching your performance, analysing your product and making their own dispositions. If the product or product improvement is not very revolutionary, nor the investment at risk very high, it may make sense to skip the test marketing stage. Indeed in financial markets it may cost more to carry out a thorough test market operation than a general launch.

But when in doubt play safe and organise a market test. Competitors seldom react as fast as might be feared; and a properly mounted and evaluated market test does have the advantages that (i) it provides insurance at relatively modest cost against a catastrophic failure; (ii) it provides some measure of eventual sales volume and hence of the level of marketing and sales effort which will be justifiable; (iii) the trial run enables you to evaluate and strengthen your marketing and promotional plan; and (iv) all departments of your organisation will get to hear of it, including some who ought perhaps to have known before and who have a contribution to make.

To be of practical value, the test market must be as nearly as possible a microcosm of the final broadscale marketing operation. This means that the starting point should be to write the broadscale plan and then to scale it down to the test area; that the test area should be as representative as possible of the total market, in terms of advertising media and sales outlet availability; and that nothing should be done in the test area which cannot be reproduced on the larger scale (the temptation has to be avoided of getting emotionally involved in the test and making special efforts to ensure its success which cannot subsequently be reproduced). But, again, it is better to err on the side of too much support for the new service or product than to be too sparing. Because then, if it fails, you will be fairly sure that more support would not have made it succeed. For example, if you spend more on advertising than is really affordable nationally and it still fails, you can safely discard it. But if you had spent less would it be correct to discard it?

And finally, with or without a test market, we come to the launch of the new product onto the market. How long has all this taken and how far has a systematic approach eliminated the risk of failure? It is impossible to be specific about timing. It may be a matter only of a few months, or less in the case of a minor product improvement or of a product designed and introduced to meet the special needs of a local office or region. (There is no reason in so multifarious an industry as financial services, with so wide a scatter of branches and so many subsidiary organisations, why every new service should be offered in every location.) At the other extreme it may take a matter of years to plan and implement a major entry into an important new product sector.

The risk of failure can never be entirely eliminated. But a methodical approach along the lines described can improve the odds from, let us say, 20:1 against to 2:1 against success, measured in terms of ultimate profitability. Still, be lucky!

Pruning the product range

We have talked so far mostly about improving existing products and adding new products to the product range. But commonsense, supported by the practical experience of salesmen and managers burdened with an ever-swelling portfolio of products which they are expected to master and market, makes it obvious that too great a clutter of products will clog up the whole system. So provision has to be made for pruning out those which have passed their prime and obstruct the growth of the young and vigorous.

At this point the marketing concept of the 'product life-cycle' should be introduced. This concept, in effect, likens the life-cycle of a product to Shakespeare's seven ages of man, except that only five ages are identified. As illustrated in Fig. 5, the first of them is the period of introduction, when sales volume is low and revenue from the product is insufficient to meet the cost of producing, marketing and administering it. Sometime in its second age, of growth, it should, if all goes well, cross the breakeven line and begin to earn a profit. In the third age, of maturity, profits should be substantial and growth should be continuing. Then comes the fourth age of saturation, when competition multiplies, with increasing pressure on price levels and profit margins. Finally comes the fifth age, of decline,

Fig. 5. The product life-cycle.

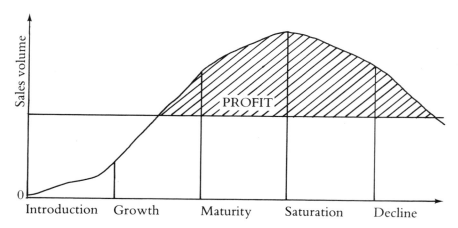

For the sake of clarity, all five phases are shown as being of equal duration: in practice they will be of very different lengths.

when both the sales volume and profit contribution fall drastically and euthanasia or artificial respiration is required to avoid drifting into loss.

That at least is the concept. But there are many variations in the way it works in practice. The life-cycle may be very long, as in the case of a product like Birds Custard which has passed its hundredth birthday; or very short, as in the case of children's toys, which may not survive a single season. And marketing men have come increasingly to realise that the ages of saturation and decline can often be indefinitely postponed by a judicious policy of product improvement. It is very often cheaper, easier and less hazardous, as we have already said, to improve and modernise an existing product than to kill it off and launch a new product in its place.

However, the principle still applies that sooner or later decline is inevitable and the product should be put painlessly to sleep. Some companies provide for this eventuality by having an annual review system, whereby all the products in the range are evaluated and classified in separate groups. One such classification system provides for green-light products with a bright future that merit top priority marketing effort; yellow-light products which are still earning a useful profit but should be watched and probably milked of their profits while they last; and red-light products which have no future but perhaps need to be kept alive for political reasons.

Major diversifications

When the need arises to move into a major new product area, management can elect to follow the road of product development from within (the route followed in the case of the Barclaycard and Access credit cards, born from an original US idea); or it can follow the road of acquisition, adopted by the British clearing banks when they moved into the hire purchase finance industry, and by Midland Bank when it moved into the travel industry through the acquisition of Thomas Cook. The two roads are not of course mutually exclusive. Since the availability of a suitable case for acquisition is a chancy affair, it is no bad idea to develop a product range independently of the acquisition and merge the two if and when the acquisition comes off.

Marketing may or may not be invited to participate in the identification of suitable businesses for acquisition in target industrial sectors. Sometimes the need for speed or secrecy will over-ride the advisability of investigating not simply a company's profit record and physical assets and the calibre of its management before signing a cheque, but also of examining the state of its customer relations and of the product range on which its future depends. But if marketing is invited to participate in the process of evaluation it may well come up with a rather different picture from the financial analysts. A company, for example, with most of its major products in the early stages of their life-cycle will probably have a brighter future than its recent profit record would indicate; contrariwise, a company with most of its products in the stage of maturity or saturation could well be on the verge of a serious downturn in profitability, despite its currently good figures.

Whether a company elects to follow the internal product development road or the acquisition road is largely a matter of temperament and timing. Some companies are bursting with innovative ideas, others have bulging moneybags. The internal development route will probably involve a smaller investment initially, but an increasing one over the years, with a fairly long wait for a substantial return. Acquisition, if all goes well, should assure the acquisitive company of an immediate return on a much larger investment; but the problems, to judge from the success rate of mergers and acquisitions over the post-war years, will then begin to mount up. Either road is a difficult and rocky one, but inescapable if a company is to go on growing, or, indeed, in the long run to survive, for its own traditional services will surely decline, unless updated.

Summary

In this chapter we have stressed the importance of a complete, balanced product range, offering the target customer groups all the financial services they need, so long as it is legal, feasible and profitable for the company to provide them.

We have classified product development activities into the two main categories of product improvement or range extension and the development from scratch of totally new and original products, saying cautiously that the former, though less glamorous, can often provide a better, safer return for a given investment of time, money and effort.

We have said that in both cases the starting point for a product development programme is an idea; or rather a great number of ideas, since many ideas are needed for every one that will work. We have listed a number of different sources for such ideas, and mentioned brainstorming as a useful method for multiplying and improving them.

We have said that a multi-disciplinary product development team, dedicated to the task of turning seminal ideas into profitable products, a methodical development programme and assurance of senior management backing are vital ingredients for success in the product development field. And we have sketched such a programme, progressing from the screening of the original product ideas through a stage of business analysis to a development programme involving formulation on one side and presentation on the other, with due attention to pricing policy. We have then mentioned the need for testing, initially by market research methods and then, if the project is sufficiently important or hazardous, by test marketing before the final launch.

We have also said that in order to avoid clogging up the company's production, marketing and administtative system, provision should be made for reviewing the stage in its life-cycle reached by each of the company's products and disposing of those which have reached a stage of decline from which they cannot be economically revived by product improvement methods.

Finally, we have compared the two alternative methods of major diversification, through internal product development or through acquisition of an existing company with an established product range in the target market sector.

CHAPTER EIGHT

Selling and distribution

Selling services versus selling products

When British banks and other financial institutions emerged from the second world war it was a new and less comfortable world that confronted them. Before the war the market for financial services was small and select on the personal side; and on the corporate side, though competition existed, it was relatively gentlemanly.

After the war the personal side turned from a minority market into a mass market, which could not have been handled without the development of the computer; and the corporate side was exposed to increasingly vigorous competition from overseas banks and other institutions moving into the UK.

Hence the message that has flowed with growing insistence through the management ranks of banks and others: 'Whoever and wherever you are, if you come into contact with the customer at any level, either face-to-face or by telephone or by letter, you are a salesman (nowadays salesperson).'

The message came as no surprise to those who recognised that the banking, insurance and other financial service industries would never have grown and prospered as they have if they had not actively sold their services over the years and centuries; and if a goodly proportion of managers had not been of an expansionist rather than a conservative disposition. But there were also a number of individuals who proclaimed, or muttered, that they had not joined these industries in order to emulate the grocery salesmen; they had aimed for a position of dignity, a measure of power to dispense favours to the rest of the community.

For both groups, and for those with mixed feelings between the two, it was a case of accepting the inevitable. The blurring of boundaries between the specialist financial service institutions, with each beginning to offer more and more of the others' services, together with the arrival of fresh competition from within and from abroad, made it inevitable that more emphasis should be placed on the selling, and in turn therefore the marketing, function. This was particularly so because many of the new arrivals were less inhibited than the entrenched establishment about their selling methods (the Americans for instance seem positively to enjoy selling) and began to make inroads into the more vulnerable sectors of the establishment's business.

Happily for all concerned it rapidly emerged that selling services is a very different affair from selling packaged grocery products; the temperamental characteristics of the banker or actuary, which would probably make him an indifferent soap salesman, can be a positive advantage in his own environment. A salesmanship pundit once said that the qualities required of a good salesman are a judicious blend of empathy and ego-drive. The empathy is required so that he can understand and sympathise with the customer's motivations (including possibly his motive for not wanting to buy the salesman's product on the terms offered); the ego-drive is required so that the salesmen will get his own way in the end and strike a bargain as nearly as possible on his own terms. Clearly the desirable proportions in this blend will vary according to the selling situation and the product.

In financial services, where the product in broad terms is assistance for the customer, whether corporate or personal, to find the resources to further his personal or commercial objectives, or to deploy the resources he has to the best advantage, the requirement for empathy predominates. The customer's needs and motivations are likely to be more complex, and his or her ability to assess alternative courses of action without professional assistance is likely to be more limited, than those of the grocer or housewife making the unmomentous choice between two brands of washing powder. So the salesman must know his customer as well as his product.

Moreover, the sale of a financial service is not based on a fleeting contact between ships that pass in the night and may never meet again. It is either the beginning of, or an episode in, the development of what should be a long-term relationship. In this context winning a transitory advantage by slick or bullying tactics is unlikely to pay off in the long run. For a large element in what the financial service company's representative is selling is himself or herself; and through personality and behaviour they either enhance or diminish the company's corporate reputation. Neither of these last factors implies that the individual should be soft; the element of ego-drive is still required. But a fair bargain, struck in the light of a full understanding of the customer's position, is preferable to a ruthless battle of wits.

In the rest of this chapter we shall be looking at aspects of banking as they relate to, or are similar to, retailing and other service occupations. This may give the reader the impression that the chapter is only of general, non-specific relevance. Not so: our intention is to encourage the reader in the habit of learning from what is common to his industry and others, to make connections across common ground, and to apply to his trade some techniques and practices that have evolved elsewhere.

The selling sandwich

In most of the guide books to effective selling, primary emphasis is put on the actual selling interview, and various mnemonics (most of which we find eminently forgettable) are advanced to ensure a successful outcome. We prefer to think that in financial services the actual selling interview, important as it is, is the filling in the sandwich of which pre-sales activity and post-sales service are the bread and butter; and that the bread and butter is what does most to maximise the success rate resulting both from the immediate sales interview and from subsequent interviews to sell additional services in a developing relationship.

The pre-sales activity is certainly not an unfamiliar concept to the great majority of bank managers, corporate finance managers or insurance representatives. There can be very few who fail to brief themselves in advance of any important interview, whatever its purpose, with such information as is readily available on the customer's or prospective customer's financial situation, likely requirements and previous dealings with the company. When the purpose of the interview is wholly or partly to sell one or more of the company's services, this preliminary briefing should in theory be widened to cover not only past history but reliable information or research-based hypotheses on the individual's or organisation's personality, policies, motivation and objectives. But theory has of course to yield in practice to the practicalities of information availability and affordable cost. If the information system which we sketched in the previous chapter were fully operational, and could be relied on to deliver all the information in a bank's possession instantaneously when and where it is needed, the pre-sales activity would be greatly facilitated. As it is, the individual on the brink of a selling interview, possibly at short notice, has to limit his preparatory work; and even if the notice is not short, he must consider whether the cost of collecting the ideal information file ahead of an interview is justified by the potential benefit to the company which may arise from the interview.

But one thing costs very little: constructive thinking in advance about the sales opportunities which may arise from an interview, or programme of interviews, that is not planned primarily for selling purposes. It is a frequent complaint of branch managers and others that too much of the time they have available for face-to-face interviews is devoted to castigating the bad rather than encouraging the good and, of course, prospective customers. The constructive thinking we suggest should be devoted to preparedness through:

1 recognising, on the basis of such information as is available, that any selling activity should be directed more selectively to customers or prospective customers representing the best business development opportunity for the company (i.e. the admirable principle that all customers are equal in the sight of the company should be modified to the extent that big customers are rather more equal, and entitled to rather more selling time than small customers);

2 refreshing the memory, if not on all the details at least on the key selling points of the services most likely to be relevant to the interviewee's needs. In principle, no interview, except with thoroughly undesirable customers, should be entered on without some idea of the services or additional services which might benefit both company and customer. The ideas may of course be totally wide of the mark, but their discussion can generate new ideas.

The implications of this preparedness principle, which would apply not simply to managers and designated business development officers but to all staff in contact with customers or potential customers, (that is, everyone) can be summarised as follows.

1 The customers and prospective customers within the ambit of the individual manager or staff member should be classified, as far as availability information will permit, into different desirability/probability categories in relation to the major services which the company is anxious to sell (a given individual or company will obviously rank higher in relation to some services than to others).

2 When the desirability/probability rating is high and the prospective return on a successful sale is attractive, more information should be collected about the individuals or categories concerned as a preliminary to positive selling efforts.

3 The information should be pooled among all those likely to have contact with the target customers, either accidentally or on purpose.

4 These company personnel should also be armed with the main selling points for the service or services at issue, recognising that the emphasis to be placed on each of the main points may well differ from one prospective customer to another. (See Table 2).

Concerning the after-sales slice of the sandwich, the main point to be made is that in selling a service, you are selling as a rule not a tangible product which can be inspected and tested, but a promise of future performance. The extent to which that promise is fulfilled will affect not only future sales to the same customer but the attraction of new customers through word-of-mouth recommendation. So part of the sales programme has to be preparatory work to ensure that all the arrangements for delivering the promised service are sound; this means, of course, that those members of the organisation whose role is nominally only administrative are in a very real sense salesmen for the company. The cashier who smiles when she cashes your cheque, the telephonist who keeps coming back to you when the extension you want is busy, instead of leaving you hanging in the air, are both contributing significantly to the total sales effort.

The before-sales preparation and the company's reputation for after-sales service can, as we have said, make the *face-to-face selling interview* very much easier; and the softening up process represented

Table 2. Key steps to gaining and keeping customers

Pre-sale	Selling	After-sales service
Identify key prospect groups/individuals	Explain the benefits to *them* of your own brand of product/ services; often face-to-face but sometimes not	Keep to any promises made
Describe them		Check from time to time that the developing needs of the customers are still being met as fully as possible, offering new services as required
Analyse their needs		
Work out the best fit of *their* needs and *your* services	Ask for business	
Promote yourself/ your services to them		

by media advertising and other forms of marketing communication make it easier still – in some cases (for instance the postal marketing of credit cards) totally eliminating it. But in most cases it is the face-to-face interview at the heart of the sandwich, between the company's representative and the customer or his representative, which makes or mars the sale. And the question arises how far the sometimes rather mechanical selling methods suggested by the sales experts for consumer or industrial product salesmen can be usefully followed by the part-time or full-time salesmen of financial services.

The answer will vary from one individual to another. There is of course always something to be learned from studying the way other people have handled a similar though essentially rather different job. And the rules propounded in most of the sales manuals ('identify the customer benefit', 'describe the product from the customer's point of view', 'anticipate and meet the customer's objections', 'close the interview by clinching the sale') are sensible enough. It would be a mistake to denigrate the contribution which the professional sales trainer can make to sharpening the techniques of those unaccustomed to selling.

On the other hand there is a great variety of different selling situations in the typical financial services organisation, from the specialist selling of a specific service package, possibly with a highly technical content, to the more frequent situation of the generalist manager whose customer interviews are usually only partly of a selling nature and whose task may as often be that of identifying opportunities to pass on to his technical colleagues as of actually completing a sale. The approach cannot be as planned or systematic in the latter case as in the former. Moreover, it has always to be remembered that an important part of selling a service is inspiring confidence in yourself as a key element in that service. From that viewpoint the painful mastery of selling methods and techniques which go against the grain of your own personality may be an obstacle to inspiring confidence; people who are obviously putting on an uncongenial act do not inspire trust. If, for personality or temperamental reasons, a person cannot accept selling as part of his natural self then he ought not to be employed as a salesman. But someone who can, and who is keen to learn, will soon develop his own style – and that, so long as it is based on a proper understanding of the role, is to be welcomed.

The sales management function

At present the role of sales manager, business development manager or marketing manager with an executive selling responsibility is not very frequently found in the financial services industry. This may well change in the future as the selling task becomes more difficult and more specialised. But for the present, management of the sales activity is more likely to be part of the responsibility of a general manager, competing for a share of his attention with a heavy load of administrative, personnel and other functions. This makes it all the more important that the sales management responsibility should be well understood and organised *systematically*.

Sales managers, whether of financial services or of other commodities, must sometimes hanker after the bad old days when life was simple if inglorious. In those not so long ago days the sales manager's task boiled down to appointing a salesman or sales agent for each sales territory, giving him a brief indoctrination course in the virtues of your product range (it was as well not to tell him too much, particularly about your cost structure), equipping him with a bagful of sample biscuits, spanners, insurance policies or whatever, plus a take-it-or-leave-it price list, and waiting for the orders to roll in. If the level of orders was unsatisfactory or if you began to get complaints from customers about the moron or bully boy who was calling on them in your name – or, alternatively, complaints that they never saw your representative – you would have fired the fellow and tried again.

Nowadays, in almost every market E.M. Forster's admonition 'only connect' has been followed only too faithfully. Almost everything in the commercial and industrial world connects with everything else. The sales achieved on any given sales territory or catchment area depend only partly on the efforts of the salesmen or branch manager responsible for that territory. In the first place many of the customers using the product or service in the area will not have the authority to decide which of a number of competitive products or services they will use. That decision will have been made, more and more often as the power and reach of multiple organisations extends, at head office, usually after hard bargaining about terms and about the service to be provided at branch level. The area manager or salesman for the servicing company will in fact contribute to the sale and to the retention of the business by the level of service and follow-through he provides; but he will not always get the credit for it.

In the second place, an important but usually unquantifiable contribution is made to the level of sales by the central, as well as the local, advertising and sales promotional activities of the servicing company. Sometimes this will do no more than open the door for the salesman, and in most cases he will be needed to clinch the sale; but the effort required from him will be increased or diminished according to the weight and effectiveness of advertising support. Sometimes it may make sense to cut down on direct selling effort and expense in order to spend more on sales promotion; sometimes the reverse may be the case. Always there will be an interplay between the two.

Thirdly, it is probable that a proportion of the sales on the territory will be made over the telephone or by post without any direct involvement by the salesmen. A number of organisations, for instance the classified advertisement departments of newspapers, have calculated the relative costs of a telephone call and a physical visit to a prospective customer. They have concluded that when the *purchasing decision* is not a very important one, telephone calls, though less effective individually, are more cost-effective overall. The same can be true of certain types of financial service.

A final factor, complicating the sales manager's task, is the fact that pricing and terms structures have to be more flexible in the buyer's market of today and tomorrow. If not the individual salesmen, at least the area sales manager must have discretion to negotiate on terms; and successful performance has to be measured not simply in sales but in profit contribution.

So sales managers have to think not simply of meeting or beating sales targets through their own efforts and those of the salesmen who report to them, but of the cost-effective deployment of all the selling resources at their disposal, supplemented by the support services on which they can call. They have to think also in terms of allocating a proportion of these selling resources to supporting or following through sales made in other parts of the organisation, and must find a way for accounting satisfactorily for these diversionary activities.

The task of the modern sales manager – or of the area manager or the general manager with selling responsibilities – could be summarised in job specification jargon along the following lines:

1 to identify the potential demand for his company's products or services in the area for which he is responsible;
2 to determine as specifically as possible which of the available customers or customer categories have authority to make their own financial or other purchasing decisions, and which need to be approached through head offices outside the territory;
3 to make the most cost-effective use of the selling resources at his disposal in;
   (a) increasing the level of profitable business with existing customers;
   (b) making selective selling approaches by the most appropriate means at the most appropriate level to prospective new customers likely to be profitable to the organisation;
   (c) following through and servicing the local branches and subsidiaries of customers with head offices outside his territory;
4 to train, direct and motivate personnel under his control who can
   (a) negotiate the sale of existing or new company products and services to new or existing customers;
   (b) identify and report sales opportunities with new or existing

customers;

(c) contribute indirectly to the acquisition and retention of business by the level of service provided;

5 to co-ordinate the selling operations under his control with central sales promotional policies and activities, including the effective use of central sales, service and other specialists;

6 to agree with management quantified sales and profit targets and to monitor progress towards their achievement;

7 to agree with salesmen and others under his control who contribute to the total sales effort individual objectives and targets, and to monitor their achievement.

Like most job specifications this looks fine on paper, but is not so easy in practice. It is only likely to be achieved if the sales manager:

1 works to a version of the marketing plan already described, whether it is written for him or by him;

2 establishes a level of communication with his staff which enables them to understand the part they play as individuals in the total selling effort and equips them to play their part effectively (hence the need for line management involvement in training instead of its segregation in a separate training department);

3 has organised a flow of usable management information reports and statistics which enable him to monitor progress against targets (including any developments which may affect the achievement of targets), both overall and at the level of the individual salesmen and sales support personnel. The latter of course ties in with the various versions of Management by Objectives adopted by a number of large organisations.

For the conscientious sales manager, who may have personal responsibility for large customers and administrative responsibility in addition, there is the ever-present problem of how many tasks can be fitted into a working week. There can be no glib answer to this problem. We can only suggest that the best personal solution may be found somewhere in the triangle represented by personal priorities, delegation and 'systematisation'.

In speaking of *personal priorities* we have in mind that the individual manager should regard himself, together with his salary, expenses and overheads, as a company resource on which he should earn the best return. This means allocating his own time – as much time as he has available after the mandatory tasks have been completed – so as to show the best long-term return to his company. (We say long-term to emphasise the fact that the time spent on staff training, which may show no immediate return, can be more valuable in the long run than time spent on the personal negotiation of a short-term deal.)

By *delegation* we have in mind the observed fact that the most effective personal salesmen are frequently indifferent sales managers; the growth in their value to the company stops abruptly when they reach the limit of their personal selling contacts.

By *systematisation* we have in mind the fact that the computer can be either a good servant or a complete curse, depending on the precision with which its users specify their requirements. The sales manager's task of controlling his patch will be made easier if he insists on getting clear summaries of relevant information. It will be made even harder if he is subjected to a flood of print-outs which he has no time to absorb, analyse and act on.

The sales-effective shop

An additional complication to the highly complicated financial services selling theme is that, unlike most producers, financial services organisations tend to own shops or chains of shops. We do not intend to be derogatory to the marbled halls of the bankers or the glass and steel palaces of the large insurance companies in describing their premises as shops. We want simply to underline the fact that from the marketing viewpoint they are a resource, comparable to any supermarket, on which a sales and profit return should be earned.

This of course does not mean that they should look like supermarkets. The rock on which a financial services business is built is confidence; and too obvious an effort to attract customers, particularly by what look like huckstering methods, may in the long run cheapen the image of the organisation and detract from that essential confidence. But always bearing in mind the corporate image factor, it must be a constant preoccupation of marketing and sales either to attract the maximum number of profitable customers into the shop and/or to service the maximum amount of profitable business out of it. In this, due allowance must be made for the changing climate in which financial organisations find themselves; what was considered appropriate in the 1920s is unlikely to be thought so nowadays. It is not unreasonable therefore to have 'shops' which have moved some way towards a 'supermarket' appearance, except of course where the branch office has a 'Harrodian' rather than a 'Tescovite' customer base.

But how to do it? Most banks and other financial service institutions are established in expensive purpose-built premises which cannot easily be disposed of. So even if an institution wholly subscribes to the principle of cost-effectiveness in its branch development, this has in practice to be diluted by a large element of mend and make do, not least because of the growing tendency of local planning authorities to feel that what they regard as offices have no place in High Street premises. The relatively rapid change achieved by the multiple grocers all over Europe (from chains made up of numerous small shops with a large element of personal service to much less numerous chains of self-service supermarkets and hypermarkets handling a far greater turnover despite their smaller numbers) is unlikely to be duplicated in the financial services market. Changes are taking place, but they are likely to be relatively slow and undramatic. The main factors that have to be considered by management in developing cost-effective shops are listed below.

1 Relating the character, facilities and style of the shop to the type of business and the type of customer for whom it is intended

The branch bank or money shop which is intended to service personal customers will differ increasingly from those branches designed to service principally corporate customers. And, given the conspicuous absence of a classless society, personal customer branches may themselves be designed differentially to appeal to specific economic or social, or other, segments of the public. The racial, as opposed to racialist, branch is needed to provide for cultural and linguistic differences; the women's lib branch is probably not needed but may yet manifest itself.

2 Location

This is a factor which is getting more attention from the marketing-oriented managements of financial institutions than it did in the past.

Not so long ago the dynamic new general manager of a large insurance company proclaimed that within the next twelve months his company would have a representative office in every major town in the land. His loyal lieutenants embarked on a crash programme of new branch openings, to be followed, shortly after his somewhat premature departure from the company, by a less conspicuous but still urgent programme of branch closures, covering the very substantial proportion of new branches which quite clearly had no prospect of ever yielding a return on the investment they represented.

More prudent managements recognise that it is a difficult and expensive matter to find suitable locations for new branches; and that it is wise to preface any final decision on possible locations with a rigorous analysis, aided by market research, of the profit potential in the catchment area of the location concerned.

3 Layout

There are a number of constraints which experts in shop layout must be aware of if they are going to be helpful to organisations marketing financial services. There is the obvious constraint of security, when substantial sums of money are being handled; there is the need to sustain an image of reliability and solidity, which may detract from the welcoming impression which a shop should give; and there is the basic question of the extent to which the organisation actually wants to attract 'store traffic'. It may be policy to do as much business as possible at arm's length and to regard the branch primarily as a servicing unit for those customers who need or prefer an element of personal service.

Nevertheless, there is and will continue to be scope for making the individual branch a more congenial environment for personal shoppers; and an efficient outlet through which to market new or peripheral services. It seems likely that, as financial service organisations become more responsive to market segmentation, there will be a trend away from the standard branch layout to a variety of layouts, adapted to the customer segments (personal or corporate, up-market or mass market) which each branch is intended to serve.

4 In-store merchandising

Whatever the level of 'store traffic', it is clearly a legitimate marketing objective to sell, or make the first step towards selling, as many relevant services as possible to the individuals passing through the branch. Banks and other financial service organisation in the UK have made a lot of progress in the direction of the 'silent salesmen' as represented by an effective display of leaflets and brochures. But with the development of audio-visual and other electronic devices there will be scope for much more effective sales promotional devices than brochures, enabling interested customers to get fuller details of particular services in words and pictures – always remembering the need not to turn branches into bazaars.

5 Staffing

A more important factor than layout, in creating the right environment for a particular customer segment, is staffing. This is a matter not simply of determining what size and character of staff is needed to provide the marketing thrust and service back-up that is required, but how much expenditure on staff is affordable. With well-trained and competent people an increasingly scarce and costly resource, the consideration of cost-effectiveness looms ever larger.

6 Automation

The impact on the financial services industry of the computer, aided and abetted by electronic communications, has already revolutionised branch banking. There is more to come. It is no longer fanciful to foresee a day, not very far ahead, when virtually all routine transactions for which customers now come into branches of banks and other financial service institutions will be handled on a self-service basis through computer terminals, cash dispensers and so on; and human resources will be concentrated on the more useful aspects of dealing with individual customer problems, ensuring that customers are aware of and buy the services they need.

Summary

In this chapter we have said that people involved in selling financial services need a larger element of empathy and a smaller element of ego-drive in their make-up than the salesmen of consumer or industrial products.

We have described the 'selling sandwich' and said that well-organised pre-selling activity and post-selling follow-up are as important as the face-to-face selling interview in the middle of the sandwich, and that they make the interview a great deal easier and more effective.

We have suggested that individuals involved in selling interviews should study the procedures and formulas advanced by experts in this activity, and then throw them away and develop their own selling techniques. We have also stressed the importance of identifying sales opportunities in the course of interviews initiated for other purposes.

We have listed the seven major elements in the sales management function; and we have discussed the extent to which the branch of a bank or other financial institution can be regarded as a shop for selling the institution's various services.

CHAPTER NINE

Marketing communications

The basic definition of 'communicate' is 'to succeed in conveying one's meaning to others'. That is difficult enough in all conscience; people's capacity to misunderstand each other knows no limit. But the marketing man asks more of communication. In his language, successful communication involves not only conveying an understandable message to the audience he is interested in, but getting them to do something about it. Marketing communication involves persuasion, resulting either in some desired action such as buying a particular product or service, or in a change of attitude or behaviour which is likely to lead eventually to the desired action.

The success or failure of the marketing man's communications effort will depend essentially on four inter-related factors:

1 the power of the original message;
2 the clarity and force with which it is expressed;
3 the media through which it is communicated;
4 the level of expenditure.

He can sometimes do very little about the original message, though it will substantially affect the ease of his task. If the message is that the local branch of Bink's Bank is giving away £5 notes it should not be too difficult to get the word around and precipitate action. If the message is that Bink's Bank is best it will be a good deal more difficult to persuade people to change their attitudes, particularly if Bink's Bank is not noticeably superior to its competitors. Occasionally it may be possible to introduce a genuine price advantage, though in financial markets such an advantage will probably be short-lived. But usually the selling message will have to emphasise benefits other than price.

Expressing a message in words or pictures with clarity, precision and persuasiveness, so as to have the maximum impact on the target audience, is one of the essential skills of the specialist marketing man. But the understanding of his fellow beings which is needed is not necessarily confined to the business school graduate or professional advertising man (nor always to be found in these paragons). The effective general manager should also be a good communicator, and he will get better work out of the specialists if he briefs them with clarity and precision.

Nor are the media of communication necessarily confined to those which come automatically to mind in a marketing or advertising context. Television, newspapers, magazines, radio, posters and so on attract most of the attention in marketing treaties and most of the advertising money; and they are undoubtedly efficient means of mass communication. But (as described later) there are other means of getting your story across to your target audience, particularly when it is a numerically small but very specific one. Using a rifle requires more skill than using a sawn off shotgun; but there are many situations in which it is more effective.

In every marketing situation requiring the use of communication (what marketing situation does not require it?) cost-effectiveness should be the watchword. It is not simply a question of getting a message across, nor even of getting a message across in a way which stimulates action; it is necessary to relate the cost of the communication to the benefit accruing to the organisation as a result.

In short, the questions to be asked before any communications activity is undertaken, questions that are sometimes easier to ask than to answer, are the following:

1 Who do we want to reach?
2 What action or change of attitude do we want to bring about?
3 How should the message be framed so as to achieve the maximum impact?
4 What medium, or combination of media, is most cost-effective for conveying the right message to the right people?
5 How much is it worth for us to get the message across?

6 Can we do it for the money?

To put it this way is perhaps to over-simplify what the expert communicators, in common with most experts, have contrived to develop into a highly complicated procedure, liberally sprinkled with its own esoteric jargon. And so far we have talked only of the likely awareness of the communication among the target audiences. Success may depend in part on their ability to afford the product being offered, or on their ability to make good use of it, or on their ethical acceptance of an idea. Perhaps we should look at it all, and the above questions, in more detail.

Identifying the target audience

Two relatively useful marketing in-phrases are 'decision-makers' and 'opinion-formers'. (In banking, obvious examples of these potentates are finance directors, solicitors and accountants.) If you want to persuade people to buy your product or service, or at least to let them know it is available in case they want to come and get it, you need to know the type of individual, family group, small or large organisation which should be interested in buying it (if you follow the best marketing procedures you will have designed it with them in mind); and you need to take a view, whether based on research or experience or commonsense, or a combination of all three, about those who are likely to make or contribute to the purchasing decisions. Then you can address yourself to people as human beings and not simply shout your message from the housetops, hoping that somebody will hear.

Equally, if you suspect that your 'corporate image' is not all it might be and that people are not as anxious to do business with you or work for you as you would wish, you need to decide who are the key people you want to influence, either because their own opinions are important or because they can influence the opinions of others. Once again, if you address yourself to them as human beings, you are more likely to get results than you will by addressing the whole faceless mass of 'the general public'. *It pays to particularise.*

Establishing customer motivation

Especially perhaps in so competitive a field as financial services, which so many people simply take for granted, it is an odds-on bet that your customer will be less interested in buying your product or service than you are in selling it to him. He has many other things on his mind, and many other people prepared to sell him something not very different from what you have to offer. Hence the interest in motivation research as a preliminary to major advertising campaigns. Often the results of such research, based on depth interviews, group discussions and similar attempts to adapt the methods of psychology to commercial ends, are not particularly helpful; seeking to plumb the depths of hidden reasons for this decision or that often results in the revelation that far from being deep-rooted the decision was largely accidental.

But sometimes unexpected reasons do pop up. And usually the exercise is worthwhile, if only because it forces the inevitably self-interested producer to pause and look at his product from the customer viewpoint, asking the crucial question, 'What's in it for *them?' It pays to empathise.*

Designing the message

Manufacturers of branded products have in principle the choice between two different approaches to their marketing communications. They can on the one hand, like the H.J. Heinz Company, place major emphasis on the company's name and fit every product they put on the market into the elastic framework of the Heinz 57 varieties; or they can choose, like Procter & Gamble, to emphasise the brand name and leave it to the small print to reveal that Daz and Tide and Fairy Liquid are all made by the same company. In the same way a chain of retail shops can theoretically choose between promoting the shops as such or promoting the exceptional products or exceptional bargains that can be bought in them. (For some products that are bought only once, establishing a brand name is difficult: consider wedding rings or coffins; though to the trade both *are* branded.)

A financial services organisation, doubling the role of producer and 'shopkeeper', can be said to face the same theoretical choice. It can seek in its marketing communications to build the impression that the customer who wants the best range of financial services should come to one of its 'shops'; or it can promote the main services individually, seeking to communicate in each case with the customer segment which the service in question is designed to satisfy. Of the British clearing banks, for example, Barclays seem to favour the 'umbrella' approach of using the parent name to identify some of its main consumer products (Barclaycard, Barclayloan, Barclaybank); while Nat West tends to promote its individual services or subsidiaries independently.

It is not of course a black and white choice. It is possible to adopt both approaches in separate sales promotional and advertising campaigns, though it is advisable in such cases to make sure that the individual campaigns are compatible in tone and presentation, reinforcing each other rather than clashing. And it is equally possible to combine them in the same campaign; the large preponderance of retail advertising in practice seeks to attract the target segments of the public to the retail outlets by describing a selection of the goods they offer for sale, chosen to enhance the reputation for quality, cheapness or universality that the particular retailer seeks to establish.

Whichever approach or combination of approaches is chosen, the process of designing an effective marketing message starts with a very precise understanding, agreed between the originator and the professional communicator, of the specific news or claim to be conveyed and the general impression about the company and its services which the message should reinforce. Far too many advertisements, brochures and simple selling letters start out with a good idea and then become bloated and shapeless through the well-intentioned addition of superfluous items: 'While we're at it why don't we tell them this and maybe this and perhaps that as well, it won't cost much.' In fact it may well cost you the whole message! *It pays to specialise.*

Getting attention
If the comminicator has won his first battle by keeping the message clear and simple, he has then to apply himself to the problem of catching the target recipient's attention. The communicator who is not face-to-face with his audience in the awe-inspiring environment of the headmaster's study or the bank manager's parlour must fight to gain attention in the midst of a babel of other belligerents. (If you doubt this stop and think, when you fold up your newspaper or turn off your television, just how many of the

advertisements that passed before your eyes you can actually recall in any detail; or chat to a direct mail expert about the huge sense of triumph he experiences when as many as 10 per cent of the recipients respond to his mail-shot.)

Getting attention is not simply a question of shouting louder than the next man, printing your advertisement upside down, introducing a naked lady or some other startling device. What all these may gain in attention they can lose in effectiveness through failing to convince the audience that the advertiser should be taken seriously. Effective attention is more often a matter of tuning in to the recipients' wavelength. People, to put it baldly, pay attention to what interests them. Over forty years ago George Gallup, the doyen of market researchers, undertook a series of studies into the advertisements which caught people's attention, and made the then startling pronouncement that women were more likely to look at illustrations of women and men at illustrations of men; not a question of homosexuality before it became fashionable, but simply of self-identification. (Incidentally, their second choices, it is said, were babies for women and dogs for men.)

On the same principle, if you happen to be suffering from toothache your eye is much more likely to be caught by a feature mentioning this malady than if your teeth are not bothering you; and the chances of your noticing an advertisement for your own company or a competitor are much greater than they would be if these companies meant nothing to you. So the professional communicator seeks first of all to flag his target customers featuring in words or pictures something which he knows or believes to be of lively interest to them.

But interest, once awakened, will not be sustained for long if there is not some immediate indication of a *benefit* for the recipients of the communication. The toothache sufferer will lose interest and patience very rapidly with an advertisement which simply tells him that toothache is a misery; he knows that already. But his interest will be sustained if the advertisement goes on to say not that the advertiser's product can cure the condition (apart from the penalities of being found out, the Code of Advertising Practice forbids exaggerated claims of that nature) but that it will relieve the pain and tide him over until he can get expert help from his dentist. Similarly, an overdraft will not cure a company's fundamental financial weakness, but it can tide it over a bad patch and give it a breathing space in which to take expert advice.

A key benefit is all very well, but why should those on the receiving end of your communication believe you, particularly when there are so many others making much the same claim? This is where the professional communicator starts searching for one of his essential instruments, the *'reason why'*. Is the reason because the old firm has been in business for a long time? Not all that convincing; it could just mean that they have grown lazy and old-fashioned. Or is it because the service is cheap? A convincing reason in some contexts, but suspect in situations where reliability is essential and 'cheap' may be taken as meaning 'cheap and nasty'. Or, 'We have made a special study of this area and know more about it than others.' This can be persuasive, if you can give chapter and verse. Or, 'We have satisfied other customers just like you, so why not you?' Again pretty convincing, so long as the target customer does not number among his friends some of your other customers who were far from satisfied. Or, 'We have some special advantage which others lack', such as the special tax concessions which UK building societies can pass on to some of their depositors. Excellent, if you are fortunate enough to enjoy such special advantages.

The choice of the reason why is crucial, and it cannot be made in isolation from the facts. It is self-defeating for example to advance as a reason for doing business with your company that it is 'friendly and approachable', if your switchboard operator answers rudely and your receptionist never smiles.

The 'product difference' is another tool much sought after by the communicators. How does your company's Home Improvements Loan differ from your competitors' schemes, or, if it is not actually very different, how can it legitimately be made to seem different? It is fairly easy to create a superficial visual difference, particularly if the scheme is presented as a package, complete with brand name, brochures and integrated sales promotion. But to be different only in superficial respects does not get you very far when there is a serious decision to be made by the customer. The problem is to find a product difference (or an image difference for the whole organisation, if the promotional approach is along corporate rather than product lines) which is both genuine and important enough to the reader for it to matter to him.

One school of advertising thought combines the concepts of customer benefit, reason why and product difference into one portmanteau phrase 'the unique selling proposition' (sometimes abbreviated as 'USP'). The essence of this theory, which developed out of the marketing of branded and packaged products, is that the communicator should find a central claim, which describes an important benefit to the user or purchaser of the product that he can find only in this one product. If this ideal combination of circumstances is not available, the recommended recourse is to be the first to fasten on to a claim which others could also well advance, and by constant reiteration identify it with yourself or your product. An example of this theory in action was the dogfood PAL, which was advertised with the slogan 'Prolongs Active Life'. This was not a unique claim. Much the same proposition could have been advanced for other brands of dog food, on the grounds that a dog which is not fed is unlikely to live very long, actively or otherwise. But it became identified with PAL, and not only because the initial letters coincided. 'Players Please', 'Guinness is Good for you' are other examples from an earlier era.

A clear and simple message, an attention-getting device, a customer benefit, a reason why, a product difference – with these you begin to have the makings of an effective advertisement. Whenever feasible, one additional element should be added. This is a clear indication of the action the recipient of the message should take if you have persuaded him that you have something to offer. At one time it was thought undignified for financial services institutions to 'ask for the order'. The result was the practice of so-called 'tombstone advertising', which is still not wholly obsolete. This slightly morbid phrase describes accurately enough advertisements which record the name, address and capital resources of the institution in question, but add nothing else – not even RIP.

It may be that in these more competitive days fashions have swung too far in the direction of importuning the customer to come and buy; but that is a matter of tone and degree. Those on the receiving end of advertisements or other forms of sales promotion are in no doubt that whoever paid for the campaign is anxious to sell a product, a service or an idea. They are unlikely to be surprised or offended if the communication tells them what they should do if they're inclined to buy; whether to fill out a coupon, get in touch with a local manager or agent, or simply send for more information on the subject. Even an institutional campaign, designed for cumulative long-term effect, will not necessarily suffer from an invitation to take some short-term action.

So much for an individual advertisement or series of advertisements. If it is to develop into an effective campaign, two key watchwords need to be observed. The first is *simplicity* and the second is *repetition*. Simplicity has already been mentioned in relation to the message to be conveyed. It applies equally to the way in which the message is expressed. For most people, whether as individuals or as the managers of businesses – not to mention the politicians who supposedly steer our economy – finance is a horribly difficult and complicated subject. The financial services expert, who has spent a lifetime mastering its complexities, can very easily forget that what is now simple to him may be incomprehensible to his customers; and that the technical language he uses, rightly, in communicating with his peers will need to be translated into simpler terms when he seeks to communicate with the uninitiated. So it is wise to keep the language of communication as well as the message simple without being condescending.

For this reason it is as well, when embarking on an advertising or communications campaign, to prepare an agreed 'copy policy' setting out the essential message and the impression which has to be conveyed, in pretty specific terms. This provides a creative discipline which can be invoked, if an accretion of small improvements by individuals anxious to put in their two-pennyworth threatens to obscure the original message and intention of the campaign.

As for repetition, the communicator has to accept that however boring it may be for him to say the same thing over and over again, repetition plays an essential part in getting all but the most dramatic messages into the heads of an audience at least half of whom are only half listening. To avoid losing the attention of those who *are* listening in the first place, it may be advisable to express the message in different ways or through different media. But the gravest mistake in any otherwise effective advertising or sales promotional campaign, a mistake committed over and over again by advertisers worried about becoming bores, is not going on too long, but stopping or changing too soon. It is sometimes said that the advertising agency gets bored with an advertisement before it appears – the advertiser when it appears, the public never – because it is changed before they have even had a chance to read it! *It pays to standardise.*

Picking the right media

The marketing communicator with a defined message to convey and a target customer segment to aim at still has to make the choice of the most appropriate or cost-effective vehicle to carry the message. Depending on the size of his budget and the size and nature of his target, he has a considerable range of media to choose from, each with its special characteristics.

If he has a large budget and is interested in reaching the bulk of the population he may well think first of television, in those countries where commercial television is well established. It is a medium which combines the attention-getting attributes of sound, pictures, colour and movement; and it has repeatedly proved its capacity to stimulate a quick response. But it has its disadvantages in that it cannot easily sustain a long or complicated message which needs serious consideration; one or two basic ideas and a powerful atmosphere is the most that the normal commercial can convey. And it tends to be unselective in the audience it reaches; if your target customer segment is a narrow one you will have to pay for a lot of viewers you do not want in order to reach those you do want to communicate with.

Newspapers, particularly their financial pages, are obviously more selective. Each has its own more-or-less loyal readership, large or small; and each has different editorial characteristics, which can be expected to have some influence on the attitude of readers to the advertisements the pages carry. But they too have their limitations. The press is a difficult medium in which to create a dramatic effect, or to stand out as a financial services advertiser among the welter of competitors' advertising offering similar services in the financial sections of the most frequently used papers.

Magazines, particularly the specialist financial or trade and technical journals, have a still more narrowly defined readership. But advertising in them, though superficially inexpensive, can in fact be costly in proportion to the number of readers. Between these and newspapers it is a choice between expensive rifle shots and cheaper buck shot. You pay your money and you take your aim.

For the advertiser with a geographically restricted catchment area, posters, local radio, cinemas or the local press may be the most economical public media. But because of their nature, most posters can only carry a single headlined message; local radio is about as unselective as television in its audience; cinema-going is a habit which is more or less abandoned after the first flush of youth; and the amount of persuasive weight carried by most local papers is somewhat suspect.

Then there are the less obvious media, like direct mail, a particularly economical way for financial service institutions who must in any case communicate regularly with their customers, to inform customers of a new service or one that is particularly relevant to their individual requirements. (A well-organised financial services institution, with a well-programmed computer, should know enough about its customers not to mail suggestions for will appointments to teenagers, suggestions for dealing with the intricacies of capital transfer tax to struggling newlyweds or offers of piggy banks to captains of industry.) As a means of reaching new customers, direct mail can be relatively costly unless the communication is sufficiently pursuasive and the mailing list sufficiently reliable to produce a 'good' response rate – i.e. one that is cost-effective.

Other media, often lumped together under the heading of 'below-the-line' are the leaflets, pamphlets, explanatory guides and manuals which can be used to support the selling activity on a particular service; point of sale display material, either two-dimensional or three-dimensional (in this electronic age mobile or audio-visual devices are beginning to take over from the humble showcard); the variety of visual or mechanical sales aids which can be used to help the salesmen make a more effective presentation; representation at shows and exhibitions; the sponsorship of cultural or sporting events which with luck and supporting publicity should shed some reflected glory on the sponsor; the organisation of training courses for customers' employees, with mixed educational and promotional motives; and a variety of other devices related wholly or partly to the furtherance of the company's business. How much of such activities can be put under the heading of advertising or promotion and how much should be regarded as a matter of public relations is an arguable question, as indeed is the relationship of the public relations function itself to marketing. (For banks, insurance

companies and other financial services institutions, PR in its broader
sense of creating and maintaining a high level of understanding and
co-operation with all levels of the community from government
downwards, is clearly of the first importance. But in the narrower
sense of securing favourable mention in the media of the organisation, its management and its products, it can also be a valuable
weapon in the armoury of marketing communications.)

How some of the various media listed above might prove useful
is illustrated in Tables 3 and 4. But it should be emphasised that the
choice of media is not just a rule-of-thumb operation, nor can it
safely be left entirely to the advertising agency's computer, which
will tell you with a spurious air of precision that if you use this media
schedule the average member of your target audience will have 7.83
opportunities to see your advertisement; whereas if you use that
schedule, he will have only 6.29 opportunities to see it. The accuracy
of the audience research on which the computer analysis is based is
not always beyond dispute; and, more importantly, the factor of
creative impact – how many of those opportunities are taken and lead
to the desired action – gets left out of the sums. Reading and noting
studies show that it is common for only one in every five of those
who have the opportunity to take it.

Selecting the best medium, or more often combination of
media, to achieve a defined communications objective is as much an
art as a mathematical science. But, whatever the balance, it is
important to pick the particular media which at least reach the target
audience. *It pays to plan.*

Measuring cost-effectiveness

We have already emphasised the importance in principle of making
sure that the results of a marketing communications exercise justify
the cost. But it would be wrong to disguise the fact that converting
principle into practice presents certain difficulties. There are some
forms of advertising, most particularly so-called 'direct response
advertising', where precise measurement is quite easy. If you run an
advertisement inviting people to write in for particulars of a new unit
trust you can use keyed coupons to measure what percentage of the
coupons were returned; and you can go on from there to measure the
proportion of those returning coupons who ended up buying and

Table 3. Communications grid – 1

MESSAGES	AUDIENCES			
	Company staff	Prospective customers	Government	Share-holders
Good to work for	✓			
Profitable				✓
Good products or services		✓		
Socially responsible			✓	

While there will be many messages the company wants to transmit, and many audiences it will want to reach, not every message is equally relevant to each audience.

paying for the product. (Even in that case, of course, the effectiveness of the *offer* rather than the effectiveness of the *advertising* may be the main factor determining response rate. The same principle applies to direct mail advertising. But keyed coupons (i.e. coupons which include an identification of the medium used, its date, etc.) do enable you to compare media, even if none turn out to be effective enough.

But it is very much harder to get any reliable measurement of cost-effectiveness when advertising or other marketing communications activities are only part of a long-term drive to change people's attitudes and behaviour. In such cases it is very difficult both to measure what may be quite a slow rate of change and to disentangle the element which is attributable to the communications effort from all the other contributory factors. The communicator who wants to assess cost-effectiveness has to fall back on inter-mediate measurements such as the proportion of people who can

Table 4. Communications grid – 2. The 'Prospective customers/good products or services' cell enlarged

Messages	Prospective customers			
	Accountants			Others
	in practice	in smaller businesses	in large companies	
We give fast service	Direct mail; advertisements*	Advertisements* PR	Direct mail;telephone calls	etc.
We have standard prices	Not relevant	Advertisements*	Not relevant	etc.
We are friendly and helpful	Diaries	PR	Lunches	etc.

This example is designed simply to suggest that the 'how' of getting a message to a relevant audience can take many forms. The 'hows', or channels of communication, are almost limitless in number.

* Of course different advertisements, different at least in their copy, may well be needed to communicate each message.

recall the advertising message; or the relative standing of his organisation among a target group, where 'standing' is based on several factors such as 'friendliness', 'success', 'social acceptability'; or on the tenor of comments made about his company in the media; or on a number of other surrogate measurements which specialists in communications research will advocate from time to time.

None of these approaches is wholly satisfactory but they are all better than simply hoping for the best.

What it comes down to is that in all but a limited set of circumstances definitive appraisal of cost-effectiveness is impossible. Not only because it is difficult to separate the effect of various strands of the total communications package, but also because some effects take a long time to show through, so the benefits come long after the investment (and every reader of this book will know the difficulties of assessing investments). One must look carefully at all the evidence and try to peer into the future. So too with communications. *It pays to scrutinise.*

Setting budgets

Finally there is the question of what funds to put into an advertising/ promotion/PR/communications programme. Ideally you would set the goals to be reached, work out the cost of reaching them and the total would be your budget. Of course, life is not at all like that, not least because in a competitive world the goalposts keep moving. 'To be as well known as competitor X' may sound all right as an objective; but it is impossible to respond to and plan for if competitor X is himself moving, or planning to move, in directions unknown to you.

In practice, communications budgets are normally set in relation to last year's expenditure (updated for nowadays' inevitable inflation) modified by considerations of 'affordability'. If the computer has to be replaced, advertising may have to be cut, along with other costs, to pay for the replacement. Such a decision may well be absolutely correct. Indeed, even a highly marketing-oriented senior management has to balance a number of demands for resources, and cannot accord an unquestioned priority to the communications function. But given a budget, it is fortunately not all that difficult to sort out how much to allocate to the various elements in the marketing communications programme. What is important is to ensure that all the elements pull in the same direction. *It pays to co-ordinate.*

Who said that?

One of the more irritating outcomes of communications research is for researchers to find a good level of 'recall' for the advertising message but also to find that it is attributed to the wrong company. This happens quite frequently to new entrants to a market dominated by some long-established name; a quite substantial proportion of casual readers attribute the new entrant's advertising, and the new benefits he is offering, to the old-established competitor the newcomer is aiming to dislodge. So whatever other deficiencies your advertisement, brochure or sales letter may have, do make sure that there can be no doubt about the name of your company. Name registration associated with an action-provoking or attitude-changing message is the ideal; but name registration in a vaguely favourable context is better than nothing. After all, it's *your* money. *It pays to be identified.*

Summary

In this chapter we have emphasised the need for the communicator to get quite clear in his mind (and the minds of those working with him) what categories of individuals he wants to reach, what action or change of attitude he wants to bring about, and whether the desired effect, if achieved, will be worth the cost.

We discussed the essential principles of designing the message: keep it simple, attract attention, state a customer benefit, give a reason why, indicate a 'product difference', and whenever possible ask for the order.

We said also that in extending a single advertisement or mailing shot into a campaign it is of primary importance to keep the underlying message clear and to keep on repeating it, though not necessarily in identical words. To ensure continuity of theme it is a good idea to record the basic campaign message in a formal, written 'copy policy'.

We suggested that, because every message will not be equally relevant to every target audience, the use of a 'communications grid' can help to systematise the whole communications programme.

We outlined very briefly the salient characteristics of the main media through which the communicator can choose to convey his message(s). We mentioned the availability of computer-based schedule analysis services, observing that while it is obviously prudent to use all the selling aids to cost-effective media selection that are available, the computer should not be relied on unreservedly to measure the cost-effectiveness of an advertising campaign. Arriving at the optimum mix of media and message involves more than arithmetical analysis. The campaign, we have said, should be evaluated as nearly as possible in terms of *total* effect and *total* benefit.

We added a final word on the importance of name registration, without which any communications expenditure is wasted.

CHAPTER TEN

Internal communications

Of all the topics covered in this book, internal communications is the most likely to evoke the response 'So what? That's commonsense, we do that already', or 'my people do what they're told!' It is probably true that only well-run organisations will already devote considerable thought and effort in this area. But what we mean is that a consistent, structured, well-planned, and above all recipient-oriented communication programme is very, very important. Indeed, we have not attempted to disguise the fact that, although new marketing initiatives are essential if a company wants to grow, or indeed in the long run to survive, the majority of such initiatives fail to achieve fully the objectives their originators had in mind. Whether the failure rate is two out of three or nine out of ten, or some other figure, depends on the stage in their life-cycle at which the initiatives are evaluated and the severity of the criteria used in the evaluation.

In fact formal evaluation is not as frequent as it should be; managers, like doctors, prefer to bury their mistakes. But in many, if not the majority of cases a totally honest evaluation would show that a failure of *internal* communications has been a large contributory factor in the failure of the whole project. The product or service itself may be well designed to meet a customer need, well presented and competitively priced; the external communications may be soundly planned and efficiently executed. But if the various members of the organisation responsible for selling and sales promotion, or the many other necessary support services, do not understand or believe in the product, it will not be as successful as it should be. Nor will an initial success be sustained and built on if there is not continuing provision for reporting progress and sustaining interest among all those involved.

A personal experience in checking the progress of a savings scheme launched by an Irish banking group is typical. The writer approached the cashier in one of the bank's branches enquiring whether he could open a savings account with them (a pretty small account it would have been, given the state of his finances). She was a sweet girl and honest to a fault. 'Oh, I wouldn't lodge it here if I were you,' she said, 'you get a much better rate of interest at the savings bank down the road.' She was of course right. But there were arguments other than the rate offered which were in favour of the bank's scheme, and they had clearly not been effectively communicated to her.

One of the first things a manager at any level should think about, when initiating a scheme either to increase sales of an existing service or to introduce a new service, is the question *who* within the organisation will be in a position to influence its sales for better or for worse; and *how* best to get them wholeheartedly on his side. This is likely to involve communication upwards to superiors (few people are in a position to say as Harry Truman did that 'the buck stops here'); sideways to equals whose co-operation must be secured by persuasion; and downwards to subordinates who must also be convinced by explanation and persuasion, even though a hint of the stick may be visible alongside the carrot.

Communicating upwards

In the plainest terms, if you do not secure the understanding and continuing support of your boss and perhaps of those above him for your project, you will have deprived yourself of an invaluable asset, particularly if the going should get rough. But your boss has a lot more to worry about than you and your goings on. Failure to think through the implications of those two salient facts has damaged the careers of many otherwise bright young men and women.

Yet the implications are so obvious if you put yourself into your boss's shoes. He needs all the help you can give him in making the right decision fast; and he needs assurance that it really is the right decision, so that if he is challenged about it he can feel confident that he knows and can explain what is going on.

Hence the need for communications, whether written, verbal or visual, to be clear, brief and to the point. Winston Churchill's famous request during the second world war, 'Pray tell me on one half sheet of paper', may not always be feasible in a complex situation. But it is an ideal to be aimed at. At least remember that every manager in some degree is fighting a continuous war; and that endless rambling essays, designed to show how thorough and how clever you have been, are likely to backfire.

Bosses have their idiosyncratic methods, which would repay studying. But if you put yourself in the place of your typical general manager or marketing manager (a place that you no doubt aspire to occupy in due course), exposed to the marketing proposals and projects of a lot of bright young men and women, you will probably look for brief but convincing answers to some such list of questions as the following.

1 What is the problem to be solved or objective to be achieved?
2 What do you propose to do?
3 How?
4 Who in the organisation will be expected to do what?
5 How much will it cost?
6 What is the benefit if it succeeds?
7 What are the penalties if it fails?
8 How will you check progress, and keep me informed?
9 What do you want *me* to do now?

The extent to which you as the boss would want to study the evidence or dig into the details of the project would vary, depending on the importance of the project. If the project were a relatively unimportant one, and you had confidence in the bright young male or female, you would probably take it as read. More often, you would either want to ask a few probing questions just to make sure that the bright young male or female *had* collected all the evidence and *had* thought the project through; or you might want the supporting evidence and details to be attached to the proposal in a series of appendices and supplementary documents which you could either read or just skim through. What you would not want is to be forced to plough through pages and pages of blether in order to extract the significant points. What you would look for is a direct simple *solution* to the problem, not an endless account of the problem itself; you have enough of your own. (We go into this topic in more detail in Appendix III.)

Communicating downwards

The days when a boss could say to his subordinate 'Go thou', and he goeth, are long passed in our egalitarian western society. Nowadays if a manager says 'Go thou' too roughly, his subordinate goeth all right, probably to his shop steward to lodge a complaint. How far this is an overdue recognition of the fact that all men (and women) are equal, and how far a brake on efficient management, is immaterial; it is a fact and must be recognised in the way management communications are transmitted down the line. There must be just as much awareness of the need for downstream persuasion and explanation as there is in upwards communication. If not more.

In the marketing context, management communications are likely in most cases to revolve around new devices for marketing existing services, special sales drives and promotions, or the introduction of new or 'repackaged' services. For this the first essential is *'product knowledge'* i.e. the individuals who are being asked to sell, identify opportunities for selling, or simply recommend new products will not get very far unless they understand the benefits of the product or service well enough to be able to explain them clearly to others. In a financial services organisation, whose stock in trade is to have a product available to meet every identifiable customer need in the financial area, this is more easily said than done. It may salve the communicator's conscience to put a full technical description of the new service on paper, and add it as service number 937 in a fat manual. But fat manuals mostly do not get read. So it may seem sensible for a company to segment its selling organisation and to ask individuals to master only a narrow range of services. That can sometimes help, but it is dangerous unless the generalists in the organisation, and those who provide back-up services, are fully aware of more than merely the broad outlines of the services concerned; and are available when they are required.

The best practical solution to an almost insoluble problem is to be as clear and simple as possible in the basic description; to supplement written descriptions when possible with personal briefings, or some form of audio-visual communications as described later in this chapter. Internal spadework of this kind, supplemented by clear guidance on where the individual who gets out of his depth can refer enquiries, will at least reduce the risk that any customer who is spurred to action by the advertising or other promotion for a new service will be met with a blank stare when he tries to buy it.

A second principle in downwards communication is to *secure and sustain the interest* of all those who should understand and act on the communication. This essentially means that the communication should be presented in human terms, related so far as possible to the personal experience of the recipients, and therefore be understandable, and specify the benefits it will generate both for customers and for the organisation. It also means that a single communication will probably not be adequate. A programme of reminders reporting progress, success stories and modifications in the product or marketing plan (if any) can be as important for effective internal communications as for external advertising campaigns.

A third principle is to *be as specific as possible about individual tasks and objectives.* If a manager says vaguely that 'We are confident that we can count on your loyal co-operation in doing your best to publicise and sell this outstanding new service' he will not have much to count at the end of the day. If he says to individuals that 'I am looking for ten enquiries and three firm orders from you each month and will expect a monthly report of your progress against target' he can hope for results.

The fourth principle to consider is that of *motivation.* Why should the individuals down the line do what you ask with any real enthusiasm? At one time salesmen of manufactured products were very directly motivated, since they were remunerated largely or wholly by commission on sales; if they didn't sell they didn't eat. That is no longer the case in most manufacturing companies, since it has been recognised that selling is a complex operation which does not depend solely on the eloquence of the salesmen. Selling on commission would never have been appropriate in a responsible financial services organisation and it is seldom found today (though it is occasionally practised in exceptional or even disreputable circumstances). In general it is very rightly felt that the salesman of financial services should not be encouraged to disregard the welfare of the prospective customer by making it a life-or-death matter for him to conclude the sale.

Of course, being paid will always be important, and reward for effort an acknowledged spur. But if money is not to be the only motivator, what should be added, and in what proportions? Pursuing this question too far would get us into deep water, beyond the scope of marketing, since it relates to an organisation's whole policy of personnel development and remuneration. But money can be a considerable help if the organisation operates some version of Management by Objectives, whereby individuals are set performance goals and have regular meetings with their superiors at which the degree of success achieved in pursuing the goals is discussed, with subsequent repercussions on merit payments or promotion prospects. In the financial services organisation few of the large number of jobs which have some marketing content are concerned purely with selling; so the ranking of selling in the hierarchy of goals specified for the individual may not be particularly high. But provided it is there, and taken seriously, its inclusion in the crucial performance discussions can be an effective motivating factor. On a less formal basis localised competitions can be organised; and if all else fails, a simple 'thank you', a phrase too often forgotten in the large organisation, can work wonders.

Whatever form of motivation is introduced, downward communication is seldom really effective in the marketing context if it is a one-way traffic. However well thought out and well researched a marketing project may be, it is impossible to anticipate all the detailed problems which will arise at the final interface between company and customer; or to foresee the progressive changes which may occur in the ever-changing market place.

So feedback from the front line is of vital importance to the marketing planner or manager who wants to improve his plan of action. Feedback developing into a dialogue, has furthermore, a role in increasing motivation. There will be a better, more imaginative, contribution by those directly concerned with selling if they can feel that their problems are understood and responded to.

Lateral communications

In many marketing organisations, as we said in an earlier chapter, those concerned directly and full-time with marketing are likely to be in a staff rather than a line job. For them effective communication with other managers at roughly the same level is vitally important. A marketing project or package that is no more than a selling proposition will not succeed. It has to be an integrated part of the organisation's operational system. For this purpose the support of line management is certainly essential; but so also is the support of the various service departments. An administrative muddle or a failure in computer programming can kill a project just as effectively as failure to impress the customer.

So the project manager has to think very clearly about the departments or individuals in these areas who need to be not only informed but also persuaded, if not to support the project enthusiastically, at least not to undermine it.

In this aspect of communications, securing and sustaining interest can be even harder than in the upwards/downwards context, since the contribution of effort or readjustment that is required from those involved may offer no obvious reward for them. It is just another chore.

Even so it is very well worthwhile spending time to explain precisely what contribution is needed from the department or individual concerned, the reason why it is needed, and ways in which the practical problems, real or imagined, can be overcome. Networks (see Appendix II) can be very helpful here.

Finally, never forget that the marketing man needs a sense of proportion as well as persuasiveness in his internal communications. Using the squeaky wheel principle (of getting colleagues to yield up the oil of co-operation rather than endure the noise), he should insist on getting the help he needs; but the wheel should not squeak so loudly that it upsets the whole applecart.

The means of internal communication

Organisations in the financial services field are addicted, for obvious reasons, to written communication. Get it in writing and the responsibility for any slip-up can be clearly identified. But (as writers we hate saying it), writing alone is seldom the best way of conveying information or securing action. Teachers and other communicators have long been aware that a combination of the written and spoken word (even the old-fashioned lecturer with his blackboard, indulging in 'chalk and talk') is more effective than either in isolation. If pictures can be added to the written and the spoken word, and if on top of that the pictures move, there is a pretty good chance that even an originally uninvolved audience will get hooked. Hence the increasing interest of the educational system in closed-circuit television and audio-visual cassettes as a reinforcement of the teachers' own efforts to communicate.

There is no need, in a financial services context, to argue the case for electronic communication. With computer terminals and visual display units, the most confirmed addicts of traditional methods have modern technology thrust upon them. But this does not always mean that good use is made of the available range of technological aids in communicating marketing information or stimulating marketing action. There is quite conclusive experimental evidence, for example, that the salient points of, say, a new insurance policy will be more quickly grasped by the company's salesmen if the general manager and underwriter communicate them personally (or as good as personally) via audio-visual cassettes or closed-circuit television. It can be expensive, at least in terms of the initial capital investment; and a supplementary written description will be needed to deal with the small print. But even if the managers concerned are not the greatest of actors, more of the essential points will penetrate and stick.

This is not intended as special pleading for communication by cassette, though undoubtedly this medium will grow until it is superseded by some more modern or economical method, such as audio-visual discs. It is, rather, a plea that those concerned with internal marketing communications should think just as hard about the most cost-effective medium, or combination of media, for the job in hand as they would in planning an external advertising campaign. It is unlikely that the communicators will ever devise anything to beat the face-to-face interview, supplemented by visual aids when appropriate. But the range of available alternatives or supplements is growing all the time.

Towards an information and communications system

It would be easy to say that an organisation cannot have too much marketing information or communicate it too widely. But of course it is only too easy to have overkill in this area as in any other. The productivity of the computer in particular is a constant temptation to inform everybody about everything, and thus ensure that nothing will be assimilated and acted on. So as well as thinking what to communicate to whom and how, it is just as important also to think about what *not* to communicate in order to leave people with some time for thought and action.

This means devising and constantly improving a system whereby an input of information is organised, filtered, stored and then fed out to those who can trigger, initiate or modify action in the light of the information. The number of subject areas covered by the information will increase and the detail diminish as the individual becomes more senior and less specialised. But there should always be provision for more detail to be provided on request.

Establishing such a system can take months or years of work, if it is planned thoroughly enough to include analysis of individual needs, the design of regular forms (for example, salesmen's report forms; consistency of format and regularity of reporting add enormously to the usability of information), and indoctrination in converting information into action. And major changes in organisational structure can leave it all to be done again.

But it is still worth doing.

Summary

In this chapter we have said that effective internal communications are vital, meaning not gossip, not routine exchanges, but purposeful, persuasive, action-oriented communications; and that a breakdown in them is one of the most frequent reasons for the failure of otherwise valid marketing projects.

We have talked about the three directions of communication – upwards, downwards and lateral – emphasising the importance of deciding who needs to be persuaded to do what; and how much information needs to be communicated in what form both to achieve the required short-term action, and to maintain continued interest and support over the long haul.

We have said that although the written word, clearly, sensitively and succinctly written, will retain its importance in internal communications, there are other available media, particularly the proliferating audio-visual devices, which will help in developing an effective internal 'communications mix'.

CHAPTER ELEVEN

The problems of pricing

Of course the price one pays for any product or service is relevant and may even be important. But it is very seldom 'all important'. Indeed cheapness is sometimes seen as a disadvantage by the purchaser. Nevertheless pricing is near the heart of marketing strategy if for no other reason than its direct link to profitability. A scientific approach can be helpful – and we give an example later – but pricing always was, and remains, part of the *art* of marketing.

The generalities are easy. First, price is a very powerful marketing tool. In a now highly competitive but once cartelised market like financial services – where it is difficult to create and sustain either a true 'product plus' or a conspicuous advantage over competitors in the level of service delivered – it is tempting, though dangerous, to regard price as the only effective competitive weapon and to precipitate a price war which in the end benefits nobody.

Second, as every marketing textbook will tell you, price should be based on customer demand as expressed through a market mechanism rather than on the cost of producing the goods or services in question. This is true, but only a half-truth, even in theory. Production costs must come into it since companies which sell their range of products for less than it costs to produce and market them will not survive very long; and companies which charge a great deal more than the cost of efficient production and marketing are simply asking to have their business taken away from them by more realistic competitors. (Even apparent monopolies and theoretically watertight patents are seldom more than a delaying factor, since it is almost always possible to find another way to satisfy a genuine need.)

Third, pricing policy should be flexible, taking particular account of the factors of market segmentation and product life-cycle described earlier in this book. In some market or customer segments, quite clearly, price is a less crucial factor than in others (or, if you like, price elasticity of demand is lower). A marginal 20 per cent added to the price of a Rolls-Royce will probably not bother its fortunate purchasers too much; if anything it may enhance their feeling of superiority to the common herd who cannot afford such prestige symbols. But 20 per cent added to the price of a Ford Cortina, when competitors were holding their prices, could be catastrophic.

In banking we can see a very wide range of price sensitivities, one of the factors that makes banking so interesting. When it comes to buying money from or lending it to large companies which maintain accounts at more than one bank, price is a very sensitive matter. That is one reason why base rates move in line, and why no single bank can stay out of line for long. At the other end of the scale, customer loyalty makes the price of services to individuals a very much less dominant factor in their choice of bank.

Similarly a new product or service, representing a real advance in customer benefit, can command a premium price early in its life-cycle (when costs are high and competitors have not yet caught up); but both price and costs will probably need to be reduced, if and when success attracts serious competition.

The point that a company needs some high profit margin products, not only to provide funds for investment in the future but to offset the products which, for one reason or another, have to be marketed at narrow margins, seems not to have been grasped by the various government bodies which have, from time to time, attempted to regulate prices. They appear to regard price from a moralistic rather than a practical viewpoint. But it is a particularly relevant point in many multi-product industries, including the British banking industry, which for many years has provided its basic personal current account service at or below cost.

The exposure of pricing policies to particularly searching government scrutiny is only one of the factors which makes the specifics of pricing *practice* in the financial services industry very much more difficult than the generalities of pricing theory. There is also the problem that the 'production cost' for an individual service is never an immovable point, fixed beyond all reasonable argument, on which the market price strategist can take his bearings. In an organisation with high overheads (in people, premises and so on) and relatively low variable costs, the way in which those overheads are allocated between the services has a major effect on the 'cost' of an individual service. It can be claimed that the accountancy profession has its 'laws' about the allocation of overheads. But as Lord Brougham said, 'If you would have your laws obeyed, see well that they are God's laws'; and accountants have adjusted their principles too often in recent years to inspire any confidence that they sit on the right hand of God. A new service can look very profitable, marginally profitable or distinctly unprofitable depending on the decision whether to allocate its share of overheads on the basis of variable costs, proportion of turnover or estimated load on executive time, space and so on. Indeed even with an identical set of rules by which the 'allocation' of 'overheads' is decided, the actual charge on Product A can swing simply because of a change in the volume of sales of Product B; for example, home sales can benefit from extra exports. Is this proper? And should it influence the market price?

Moreover, the risk factor looms very much larger in the case of institutions which depend heavily on buying and selling credit, and whose main stock in trade is security, than it does in the case of manufacturing companies whose transactions are over and done with in a short space of time. The unacceptable risk of borrowing short and lending long is drummed into every young banker from the start of his career. The duration as well as the magnitude of risk has to be reflected in the price paid for borrowings or charged for loans. But how to calculate the 'right' price is a question which calls for experienced judgment as well as analysis of all the relevant facts. And of course it is a truism that it is risk-taking, in one form or another, that leads to profit.

But rather than carrying on about the difficulties, it would be more constructive of us to illustrate the ways in which the difficulties have been tackled in the context of the London clearing banks. (There are no absolutes in pricing policy; the problem *has* to be considered in context.)

First of all we should differentiate between those services for which prices are fixed centrally, singly, or in the form of a range of prices, and (as a rule) published; and those for which prices are negotiated individually with the customers concerned. For the main banking services, the position is normally as follows.

Fixed centrally
personal current accounts
deposit accounts
trustee and taxation
factoring
leasing
personal fixed term loans

Negotiated individually
business current accounts
overdrafts
merchant banking
international services
loans (fixed rate or base rate plus)

Pricing a basic service

In the centrally fixed sector, the 'price' charged for personal current accounts is a particularly complex question. It is an area where the competition enjoined by the Bank of England's 1971 document on 'Competition and Credit Control' can be particularly conspicuous, since almost everybody who has dealings, either personal or commercial, with a bank will have a personal current account. For just that reason it can be argued that the current account can legitimately be regarded as a low margin or even loss leader service (comparable to the introductory offers familiar in other markets), provided that the size of the margin either way is quantified and controlled.

But the argument that a keenly priced basic service will generate goodwill and attract new customers to the bank concerned collapses if a significant proportion of account holders feel that they are being discriminated against; and there are wide variations in account usage between the heavy users who take full advantage of most of the available current account services, listed below, and the light users who often are not even aware of the range of services they could call on.

Current account services
cheque cashing facilities
clearing other cheques
standing orders/direct debits
other debit items
credits
statements of account
a cheque guarantee card
a cash card
a credit card
safe custody facilities
a secure home for cash
financial advice
miscellaneous other services

So the marketing strategist is torn between the desire to have a simple price structure, which is easy to administer and to dramatise in advertising and sales promotion; and a reluctance to subsidise the heavy users at the expense of the light users.

In 1973, when competition for current accounts was hotting up, one of the smaller clearing banks resolved to stop playing follow-my-leader and strike out on an independent pricing policy, but to do so only after thorough investigation of the cost implications.

The first step was to ascertain the facts about the use made of current accounts by the bank's customers. Accordingly a sample of accounts was drawn from all of the bank's branches and quantitative data collected on the major variables affecting the cost of account handling:

number of automated credit entries
number of unautomated credit entries
number of automated debit entries
number of unautomated debit entries
average credit balance
minimum balance
debit turnover.

Whenever possible, the totals of and ratios among the key variables were validated against available computer-based 'census'

Table 5. Sensitivity of revenue to changes in the charging basis

SENSITIVITY

	High	Medium	Low
V A R I A B L E S	Charge per unautomated item Notional allowance on average credit balance Interest actually paid on any credit balance – minimum or average	Charge per credit item Level of average credit balance above which all charges are waived	Charge per automated item Level of minimum balance above which all charges are waived Level of charges below which they are waived Notional allowance on minimum credit balance*

* Up to average credit balances of a few hundred pounds

information, to ensure that the sample did not differ significantly from the total customer population.

A price structure model was then made and programmed for use on a computer incorporating the data from the sample, in order to measure the sensitivity of revenue to changes in the charging basis. The outcome was the matrix illustrated in Table 5 (actual figures are omitted).

Armed with factually based estimates of the likely effect on revenue of various charging formulas, the bank's management took the bold initiative of announcing the introduction of 'free banking'. More specifically, existing and new customers were told that if an account was maintained wholly in credit for a charging period (three months) no charge would be levied; otherwise a charge of 6p would be made for each automated item and 8p for each unautomated item, less a notional allowance equal to 5 per cent of the average credit balance, with charges of under 20p being waived.

In the event, the actual cost of the 'free banking' offer fell within the predicted limits and was more than justified by the benefit that accrued to the bank in terms of new customers and favourable publicity.

Pricing a subsidiary service

When the question of introducing a new or substantially redeveloped subsidiary service arises there will be little or no relevant historical data on costings. So the pricing strategist can feel freer to tackle the question along orthodox marketing lines, by first establishing what the optimum marketing price should be and then working back to estimate affordable 'production' and marketing cost figures.

The first step from this starting point is to identify all existing competitive products (your own as well as those of competitors) which offer more or less the same customer benefits and to plot their prices. Unless it is a very unusual market, or one in which very few suppliers operate, there will probably be a range of prices, from the premium-priced services which claim some special or exclusive features down to those which base their sales appeal on a low price.

The second step is to determine approximately where in the hierarchy of prices the new product or service should be positioned, bearing in mind the special features or advantages which should justify its introduction. Consumer research can help to some extent with this. It should be possible to establish by talking to a representative sample of prospective customers – indeed, it already should have been established in the process of product development – how important the special features are, relative to the basic features which are common to most of the competing services. But it is not easy to quantify through this type of research just how much extra the customer would be prepared to pay for the special features. Hypothetical questions along the lines of 'Would you pay x pounds more or y pounds more?' encourage a hypothetical open-handedness which is apt to evaporate when people are invited to put their hands in their pockets in real earnest. So it is prudent, when possible, to set up a test marketing situation where actual packages are sold for actual money.

The third step, which will usually be concurrent with the second rather than following after it, will be to estimate the volume of sales which is achievable at the target price level, and calculate the related costings. There will be two categories of cost to consider: the fixed costs (or more or less fixed) of providing the service, and the variable costs of the raw material required (in the case of financial services this will basically be money), plus the planned expenditure on marketing it. As has been said earlier, the costs of administration and so on are partly factual, in terms of the additional workload on service departments which the new 'product' will generate, partly negotiable to the extent that a marginal costing approach may be agreed when there is under-utilised capacity in the organisation. The cost of money will vary both in direct ratio to sales of the new product and in response to the supply and demand situation for that type of money in the market place. The level of marketing expenditure is the only factor controllable by the marketing planner, and even this only within limits. There is no sense, for example, in settling on an unrealistically low level of sales and sales promotional expenditure simply to try and balance the books.

The fourth step is to juggle the inter-related variables of price, volume and marketing expenditure so as to maximise the net profit accruing to the company. The calculation needs to take into account both the time-scale over which the profit materialises (if there is a long wait, discounting principles will need to be applied) and the possible loss of revenue to other services in the bank's range adjacent to the new 'product'. Whether the calculations are done on a computerised model or on the back of an envelope will depend on the importance of the product and on the availability of data to support the assumptions which have to be made. There is not much point in mounting an elaborate statistical exercise when the amount at risk is not large and most of the relevant assumptions are no better than informed guesses.

In either case a fifth step is essential. If the sums work out, a price is agreed and the product is launched, into a test market or broadscale. The essential step then is to monitor the actual outcome against the assumptions and to take corrective action, whether by reducing the price or increasing the selling and sales promotional pressure, if results fall behind expectations. Since it is a rare experience for things to go according to plan, let alone better than expected, it is a reasonable rule of thumb when hesitating between two prices to pick the higher. It is always easier to reduce the price than to raise it; a high price leaves room for special discounts or deals with major customers; and in any case it is likely that the price will have to be reduced at a later stage in the product's life-cycle.

Pricing off the cuff

Any attempt at a 'scientific' approach to pricing recedes still further into the background in the situations, not all that infrequent in the marketing of financial services, where a responsible manager or business development officer has to negotiate a fee or a charge more or less on the spot. There are usually guidelines or precedents in such cases, but there is still elbow room for the individual concerned to decide on the appropriate figure between the parameters laid down; or to blend two types of arrangement – for example, an overdraft, and a term loan – to produce a weighted average.

It would be easy to say simply that arriving at the right result in such cases is a question of 'experienced judgment' and leave it at that. But without decrying the value of experience or the importance of judgment we would argue that those who get it right most of the time are using instead of a computer their *minds* (in themselves no mean computers, though with less reliable memories) to review the main questions which would be covered more elaborately by a computerised model.

1 What is the range of 'going rates' for this service?
2 What is the approximate cost to the company of providing it?
3 What are the cost sensitivities?
4 What, on previous experience, is the likely risk?
5 How important is this customer's (or this group of customers') business to the company?
6 How important is it to him/them to obtain this service from us?
7 How near the top of the 'going rate' range can I pitch the figure without prompting him/them to shop elsewhere?
8 How great is *his* 'experienced judgment'?

All that this adds up to, you may say, is an admonition to charge what the traffic will bear. Up to a point this is true. So long as banks and insurance companies continue to be commercial organisations they have an obligation to earn sufficient profit to cover their costs, including the costs of retaining their shareholders' funds, provide the safety margin which enables them to back risky ventures and smooth out rough passages, and provide resources for all the other things necessary to ensure the long-term stability of the company. Walking too narrow a tightrope between cost and price will not achieve this.

But there are three factors which would quickly quash any impulse to pitch the price too high. The first is competition; the second is the normal desire to stay in business for the indefinite future, and not to imperil that future for the sake of a quick buck; the third is a deep-seated concern to protect a reputation for probity and fair dealing, which is the most important asset of any financial services organisation.

Summary

In this chapter we have said that the orthodox marketing approach to pricing policy is to start from the end of customer demand (what the customer is prepared to pay for the benefit he receives) rather than from the more traditional end of calculating production costs and adding a 'reasonable' margin for selling costs and profit.

But in practice the question of cost *must* be considered, for the obvious reasons that prices too close to the cost of producing, administering and marketing a company's services will lead to bankruptcy; and prices too far above costs will invite competition to take the business away.

We have described three representative pricing situations, among the many that confront any multi-product financial services organisation and have argued that, although the processes of arriving at the optimum solution may differ, the factors to be considered are much the same.

PART THREE

Marketing in action

In this part we discuss the application of marketing tools to business development problems in different sectors of the financial services market; and describe a number of specific examples of marketing operations carried out by individual banks. We are indebted to the managements of the organisations listed below for providing the material on which examples are based, and for helpful discussions and correspondence.

> *Barclays Bank Limited*
> *Inter-Bank Research Organisation*
> *The Joint Credit Card Company Limited*
> *Lloyds Bank Limited*
> *Midland Bank Limited*
> *National Girobank*
> *National Westminster Bank Limited*
> *Trustee Savings Banks*
> *Williams & Glyn's Bank Limited*
> *Yorkshire Bank Limited*

CHAPTER TWELVE

Adapting the tools to the job

The story is told of Pope Eusebius IV interviewing his newly appointed Florentine architect and setting out on the path he meant to follow by cutting him down to size: 'So this is the little person', said the Pope, 'who would be brave enough to turn the world over on its axis.' 'Just give me a point, Your Holiness,' replied Brunelleschi, 'where I can fix my lever, and I'll show you what I can do.'

The tools of modern marketing, however elaborate and 'scientific', are in the end no more than levers, inert and even dull artifacts when not in use, but capable of producing dynamic results when they have a point where they can be fixed and an agreed direction in which the leverage should be exerted.

In the environment of the financial services groups, which the London clearing banks have in effect become, there is no single point where the marketing lever is fixed, but instead a number of interconnecting points in different arms and at different levels in the organisation, all required to exert leverage in the direction laid down by the corporate plan. Individuals directly or indirectly involved in marketing at any of the points designated by the pontiffs of the banking industry need both a sense of corporate direction and an understanding of the tools that are appropriate to the particular situation.

The marketing department's role as adaptor

Let us then look at the points where the marketing lever is lodged in the domestic marketing department of one of the main clearing

Fig. 6. Structure of a domestic marketing department

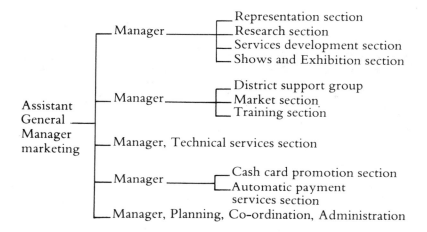

banks. The structure of this central staff department is not put forward as the ultimate ideal to which all banks should aspire. It will no doubt change as the requirements of the market place or management's objectives change; and other clearing banks will have found rather different structural solutions to meet very similar requirements. But it is a good example of one way in which marketing, the identifier and accelerator of change in an organisation, has evolved to meet identified needs.

Under the Assistant General Manager marketing on the non-international side there are five separate divisions (see Fig. 6). The first of these is concerned with identifying opportunities for marketing new services (or repackaging existing services) and with the outlets through which the bank's services are offered to the customer. It includes four sections: Representation, Research, Services development, and Shows and Exhibitions.

The *Representation section* is concerned with the outlets through which the bank's services are sold from the viewpoint, not only of suitability, but of profitability. (It is often said that, overall, Britain has more branch banks than it can afford, but it is not an easy decision for any one bank to pull out of an over-banked locality and cede the ground to its competitors.)

The work undertaken by the section is described as follows.

Surveys for regions and districts to assist in decision making for opening, relocating or closing branches. Studies and reports on different types of representation. Liaison with the bank's working party in its work on the branch network.

The work undertaken by the *Research section* is described as follows.

Accumulates and analyses facts related to the financial practices and needs of people. Identifies the characteristics of customers and non-customers and the bank's penetration of the various markets for its services. Develops information about the possible needs of customers and potential customers and evaluates the potential of new services and changes to existing services. Monitors progress and results of special projects and pilot exercises. Monitors competition and provides reports for general management Undertakes research for other parts of the group.

The work of the *Services development section* is described as follows.

Investigates for feasibility ideas for new non-technical services, improvements to existing services; identifies market demand and, in co-operation with other parts of the group, develops proposals for approval. Conducts pilot exercises and develops new services to the point of launch. Responsible for communicating to the group, through the Services Guide, current details of all services. Agrees copy and the distribution of new and revised sheets. Responsible for maintaining the guide in an up-to-date condition and for improving its format and content.

The section's responsibility for the Services Guide brings it up against a basic problem which is shared by all the clearing banks. They all have the advantage of a national chain of retail outlets, offset by the disadvantage that the 'products' which have to be sold through those outlets comprise a very long and varied list of personal and business services. Few of them are suitable for the self-service sales methods which have saved the bacon, so to speak, of the grocery trade. So the manager of the branch bank and his staff have the problem of determining which service fits which customer, and vice versa. Moreover, they have to do this in addition to a variety of other duties, in relation to a range of services and a list of customers whom it is impossible to know individually in great depth.

Some ways in which this problem is tackled are described in a later chapter. A well-organised Services Guide is one part of the answer, particularly if it does not simply describe the services but also describes the type of customer problem the service is designed to meet and the specialist back-up available within the group to deal with the knottier problems.

The *Shows and Exhibitions section* deals with a specialist aspect of representation. It is 'responsible for bank representation at agricultural shows, exhibitions and conferences; it administers bank sponsorships'. (Sponsorship of sporting, cultural or other events is in theory one of the more subtle methods available to a bank which wants to create a distinctive image for itself in an industry where all cats tend to be grey in the dark. But in practice, unless a sponsorship is administered with a fair degree of enlightened self-interest, it can degenerate into a costly charity.)

The second major division of the bank's marketing department has the vital responsibility for maintaining the constructive link between the staff marketing function and the executive marketing activities of line management. Without such a link, backed by mutual understanding and respect, the most inspired of marketing initiatives will end in futility. This division comprises three sections: a District support group, a Market section and a Training section.

The *District support group* is the immediate link with line management, liaising with the marketing managers in the field, one of whom reports to the local directors in each of the bank's thirty-five districts.

The *District support group* is responsible for advising and assisting in the preparation of branch and district marketing plans. Assists in implementation of the bank's plans by supporting branch effort and co-ordinating marketing campaigns through district marketing managers.

The *Market section* carries into practice the principle of market segmentation by concentrating on the implementation through the branch network of business development campaigns directed at defined customer segments (such as the under-twenty-fives). It 'prepares and manages campaigns directed at clearly defined segments of the personal market. Ensures that trust company marketing activity is co-ordinated with the bank's planned key tasks and objectives'.

The *Training section* provides a less immediate but in the long run equally important link with line management – or should do so if its input to staff training succeeds in convincing the managers of the future that marketing is an essential and rewarding part of their jobs. The Training section is described as

responsible for marketing training for all levels of staff either by running courses or by providing material for use in districts or at staff training centres. Provides a speaker, or trains a leader, to utilise prepared material and visual aids.

A third division has only one section, *Technical services,* but embodies a fundamental marketing principle (which many industrial companies have never accepted) that the sole commercial justification for technological development is to provide a better bargain for the customer and a better profit for the producer. There is no escaping technological progress and innovation, from atomic energy through to the computer and the microchip; but its application in the banking context can waste a lot of money unless somebody asks fairly early in the proceedings 'What do we do with it; where's the return coming from?'

The Technical services section is set up to answer this question and if possible to start from the concept of human need rather than the technological device. Its stated objective is

to consider the needs of the personal banking market in the 1980s and 1990s and to examine whether different services and standards of service should be offered, and if so by what method or methods. To examine the profitability of down-market accounts, the future development of debit cards, point-of-sale terminals, autoteller equipment and the magnetic striping of plastics. To conduct small-scale experiments using technical, automated systems, to monitor their progress and make recommendations for future development.

A fourth division with two sections deals with two aspects of automation already in existence, one related to personal customers and the other to corporate customers.

The *Cash card promotion section* deals with automated cash withdrawals (alias Tillie the Teller, mentioned in an earlier chapter). The section is

responsible for co-ordination of present and future agreed cash card service, the siting of cash dispensers and promotion of the service. Co-ordinates the phased withdrawal of obsolescent machines.

The other section looks after *Automated payment services* for large customers. It has two sub-sections, and

deals directly with customers of the bank who use computers and provides a continuing support service. BACS Liaison Section promotes the facilities of Bankers' Automated Clearing Services Limited in the electronic trans- mission of Bank Giro Credits and Debits. Bank Data Service markets a range of computer facilities to larger customers of the bank.

The fifth division need not be described at length, since adminis- tration is always with us. It is

responsible for co-ordination of the department's work programme, its administration and the development of an annual marketing plan setting out a programme of action designed to support line management at all levels in the achievement of agreed key task targets and levels of performance.

Other marketing functions

Readers who recall earlier parts of this book may observe that this line-up of staff marketing activities, extensive as it is, still leaves some notable gaps. Whatever became of advertising, one of the conspicuous marketing levers? How about international marketing, a major growth area for large companies, financial or otherwise, based in the relatively static British economy? How about all the sub- sidiaries and associated financial services, like insurance and hire purchase?

The short answer is that a British clearing bank, in the process of becoming a financial services group, is a very large organisation. In such a large organisation manageability, or ensuring that a man's responsibility should not exceed his grasp, has to take precedence over textbook tidiness. In this particular bank, as in all the other clearing banks, the international marketing function is recognised to be substantially different from the domestic function and is organisationally separated from it. The advertising function is a central one, serving both the domestic and the international side of the business but independent of both. Other sectors of the business, like the hire purchase company and the credit card activity, have their separate marketing units, liaising closely with but not directed by the central department.

There are, in fact, many different points where the marketing lever is fixed and has the opportunity to show what it can do. But none of the points is wholly independent of the others. The individual should be able to measure the results of his own exertions; but the results will certainly be disappointing if he does not secure the support and understanding of all the other departments and divisions affected by his activities.

The communications watchwords 'only connect' lie at the heart of all effective management. They apply, even more vitally than elsewhere, to the relationship between the marketing technician and the line manager. A marketing services department that fails to use its arts of communication and persuasion to ensure that theory is converted into practice by the action men becomes purely ornamental, and dispensable. A line manager who fails to make use of the appropriate marketing tools, when they are needed, will reduce his own effectiveness. They must connect. But each must recognise the true role of the other and not trespass.

One practical point is made by several managers who have won their spurs (or acquired their scars) in the battle to establish marketing as a cost-effective contributor to a bank's growth and profitability. The point is that *credibility* is all-important. Unless a marketing department and its members can convince line management that the information, advice or sales promotional support they offer is relevant and useful, very little will actually happen as a result of their efforts. Building credibility in an environment where organised marketing is a relatively novel concept takes time; in the long run it can only be achieved through performance, helpfulness and demonstrable success. But the rate at which credibility grows can be accelerated if the department is largely staffed, or at least stiffened, by bankers turned marketers rather than marketing people (who, of course, are also needed) trying to convince their line management 'customers' that they fully understand the banking scene.

The links between users and tools

The description in this chapter of one bank's domestic marketing department, with its multifarious activities, does not imply that in an ideal world (ideal for marketing specialists) the line manager with a marketing problem or requirement will automatically send for the marketing department. In this example, as in other banks, the domestic marketing department is far from having a monopoly of the supply of marketing services or marketing ideas. Other departments look after specific aspects of marketing or specific sectors of the bank's operation; more importantly, a great many managers throughout the organisation, who would not claim any special marketing expertise, handle marketing activities very effectively, either on their own or with the help of outside service organisations. An internal marketing department or galaxy of departments cannot and should not do more than handle or contribute to major development projects, provide back-up services and cultivate a seedbed for new projects or new methods which will grow to maturity in other hands.

So let us look at the marketing levers which are, or could be, useful to a couple of different executive management groups, without any implication that they should necessarily shop for them only at the marketing department supermarket. First, the management at the centre, and then in the wholesale area.

1 Central management

In the orderly world of management theory, senior management has the Olympian role of planning the future of the business five or ten years ahead; and checking to make sure that their past plans are duly achieving fruition. In the real world, with all its mostly unpleasant surprises, all levels of management tend to get sucked into the time-consuming business of coping with today's crises; shaping the future has to be crammed into the odd corners of available time. Nowhere is this more true than in banking, whose central position in the economy means that it is affected by almost every major development, economic, political or technological, anywhere in the world.

Nevertheless shaping the future, and contriving the internal changes it involves, remains a major responsibility of senior management. The main marketing techniques which can help in discharging that responsibility are set out below.

Market information and research. You cannot plan for the future without a clear understanding of what is currently happening and a reasoned identification of those current trends which are likely to affect the future.

Prediction. The time taken for any management decision to achieve its full effect obviously varies greatly according to circumstances. But all positive decisions have one thing in common: they take much longer than expected to achieve the expected results. Even apparently simple decisions like closing one branch and opening another, or discontinuing an old service and launching a new one, turn out not to be quite that simple after all. So the hazardous skill of prediction is required in relation both to the environment (a special preoccupation of marketing) which the product of the management decision will face months or years ahead, and to the repercussions of the decision itself on the organisation.

The marketing plan(s). In some companies, particularly manufacturers of consumer products, the annual marketing plan can become the fulcrum on which the whole conduct of the business is based. In banking the corporate plan takes precedence and the marketing plan or plans (usually the latter) simply describe and cost the marketing action needed to implement individual parts of the corporate plan.

Customer services development. One such part of the plan will be the development of new customer services, with which the Services development section of the marketing department described above is concerned. Needless to say, marketing is not by any means the only department involved, nor does it carry the sole responsibility for development; but its privileged detachment from day-to-day pre-occupations and its access to information about trends in the environment and in consumer requirements, should enable it to make an important contribution.

Development of sales and service outlets. The questions 'What shall we sell' and 'Where shall we sell it?' present themselves as Siamese twins to any senior management planning for the future. In the banking context, plans for service development are inseparable from plans for the branch network and other sales/service outlets – including such equipment as computer terminals in non-bank premises – with which the Representation section in our example is concerned. Once again marketing is only one of the various levers available to management; but its ability to give a reasoned and research-based answer (not invariably, it must be admitted, a wholly accurate answer) to the vital question 'How will the customer react?' should make its contribution of special importance.

Humanising technology. We have already touched on the major dilemma facing managements, that businesses cannot survive without the support of modern technology but at the same time men and machines do not always get on too well together. Customers would rather converse with a person than a computer; employees often resent seeing a machine doing much better and much faster a part of the job they have spent a lifetime mastering. In our example the marketing unit which concerns itself with this dilemma is somewhat confusingly described as Technical services. Marketing men are seldom technicians, though they do need to understand the potential and the limitations of the technology affecting their industry. But their skills in attitude research and in the arts of persuasive communication will help determine the time and effort involved in persuading customers to accept the inevitable invasions of technology, perhaps even to enjoy them.

Persuasive communication. In our example and in most other clearing banks the advertising and PR functions, though usually considered a marketing preserve, are not handled by the marketing department. The responsibility for communicating with customers and potential customers, other than *viva voce,* is divided roughly between 'above the line' and 'below the line' activities. Advertising in published media is the responsibility of one department; manuals, brochures and other printed information are handled by another, which will usually also handle internal sales promotional communications – essential if a business development decision by senior management is to be implemented effectively. Such a division is undoubtedly a disadvantage, making the desirable co-ordination of all forms of communication aimed at various sectors of the market (and other groups who can influence events in the market) more difficult, but may be deemed necessary for reasons of internal management control.

Marketing and sales training. The training contribution required from marketing, either directly or through the training department, is another consequence of the changing role of the banks. As the banks widen their range of services, they come face to face with ever-widening circles of competitors. They must inevitably change their sales policies from essentially reactive to positively (though responsibly) aggressive, and, just as inevitably, both the skills and the attitudes of individuals in contact with the customer must also change. Formal training and refresher training is one element in this process of change, an element that can be significant or insignificant, depending on how well it is done, and on what degree of support it receives from top management.

2 The wholesale market
The most competitive market in banking nowadays is the so-called wholesale market: selling a range of financial services to large and medium-sized companies, including other financial institutions. It is highly competitive, for the obvious reason that it is accessible to international competition. Overseas banks moving into the UK market can sell their services to large UK companies without investing in the costly infrastructure of premises and people that is needed to enter the retail market. And of course the same applies to UK banks developing overseas.

More and more, as the banks adopt the principle of market segmentation, the responsibility for wholesale marketing is being disentangled from the responsibility for handling personal and small business customers. From being a substantial part of most branch managers' responsibilities, depending on the geographical location of the branch, the 'wholesale' sales and servicing activity tends to move further up the line towards regional offices and head offices. Corporate business development groups are emerging as specialist cells at these levels, with their own targets stated in terms both of increased share of business with existing customers and of new customers to be approached.

In this wholesale sector the marketing role, as in industrial marketing, is more one of close support for the sales function than of trail-blazing. The marketing unit is likely to be embedded in the selling organisation – which itself will be selling partly direct and partly through intermediaries in the branch network – and the relevance of the eight marketing levers set out above will vary accordingly:

Information. The first lever, information, will be of great importance. Corporate business development executives and others responsible for dealing with the financial directors of customers and prospective customers need to be fully informed both on the commercial affairs of the company itself and on the commercial and economic environment in which it is operating; otherwise they will not be able to sustain a discussion on equal terms, let alone sell a proposition tailored to meet the needs of the company concerned.

Prediction. The prediction of future commercial relationships with specific companies or groups of companies, while still difficult, is rather less complicated than 'global prediction', because it is more directly related to sales forecasting. Predicted changes in the commercial and economic environment will certainly affect customers' requirements for borrowing and other financial services; and government restrictions on lending will affect the bank's ability to satisfy what demand there is. But to some extent at least the achievement of sales targets is controllable by the sales organisation.

The marketing plan. This will also be more of a sales plan, and as such less dependent on specialist marketing skills.

Customer services development. This is likely to be a good deal more important than it is in the retail market. More corporate customers require tailor-made service packages rather than standard services.

Sales and service outlets. The development of these, again, is much more relevant to the retail than to the wholesale scene. The customer's own office serves as well as the banker's parlour – usually better in fact – for sales or servicing meetings.

Humanising technology. Again, this is less important in the corporate sector; industrial management has already come to terms with the computer and will not be unhappy if some of the customer service dialogue is between their computer and the bank's rather than between expensive and fallible human beings.

Persuasive communication. This is of course just as necessary in the wholesale as in the retail sector. But marketing's contribution will be more in the form of training in selling techniques and sales aids for the face-to-face salesmen than of mass media advertising. There is not much point in spending large sums on press or television advertising if your target customers can be listed and visited individually. But visual or audio-visual sales aids, and the organisation of formal presentations or seminars, may well reinforce the effectiveness of the face-to-face salesmen sufficiently to justify their cost.

Marketing and sales training. This is still important, but redefined as sales training with a marketing flavour. But it is more appropriate for the training to come from the sales expert than from the marketing expert.

There are, of course, executive management groups other than 'central' and 'wholesale'. But, as will already be apparent, the same set of levers will be available to, and should be applied by, the management of, say, the retail area or specialist services. The length and strength required of each lever will differ, but skilled managers will willingly discuss with their marketing colleagues the design of an appropriate set. Some of the aspects of such discussions are briefly mentioned below. What is essential in all cases is that there is a clear understanding by all the parties involved of the *structure* of the problem. In other words, it is essential at the outset that someone has an architect's, rather than a bricklayer's, eye-view of what is being aimed at before work starts. And that the plans are available to and understood by all those involved.

The retail market

For the professional marketer the retail sector is perhaps the most fascinating, though not necessarily the greatest contributor to the bank's profits. It comprehends both the process of developing and promoting a range of products for sale through the bank's chain of retail shops, and the business develoment activities of the individual branch within its own catchment area. The two are indissolubly wedded. With few exceptions (for example, unit trust shares and other financial products that can also be sold by direct mail) the products cannot succeed without the co-operation of the branches; and the branches need the products – including the basic banking services – to develop their local business. In principle, our eight marketing levers can be useful at both the central and the local levels. In each case the manager or other executive responsible for the operation will need to decide how much time and money should be invested in marketing tools, considering the anticipated return from the individual business development operations to which they relate.

Marketing international and specialist services

The same principle applies to each of the specialist services which a banking group has to offer its customers. Some individual or individuals within the complex organisation of the group will be responsible for the profitable development of that business sector or service. The marketing tools are available either within the group's own organisation or from outside suppliers of marketing services. But they all, from information to training, cost money. It is up to the profit-responsible manager to decide which tools to use and to ensure, at least in rough and ready fashion, that each contributes more to the success of the total operation than it costs.

CHAPTER THIRTEEN

The banks' organisation related to marketing

Some years ago, when bank advertisers were more concerned to construct a favourable image for themselves than to identify specific customer benefits, one of the UK clearing banks ran a campaign stating, beneath a picture of a spreading chestnut tree, that 'our roots are our branches'. Just what their customers were expected to do about this interesting arboreal curiosity was not stated. But the phrase did encapsulate what has proved something of a dilemma for bank managements and their marketing advisers.

Certainly a bank's branches do provide the bank, through its local depositors, with a valuable source of funds for the roots (or centre) to absorb and use elsewhere; and they do provide a base on which to erect a variety of personal services for customers. Unhappily, handling a customer's personal account is often in itself an unprofitable exercise; and there is little question that, adding together all the branches of all the banks, this country is over-banked. In an age of high mobility and high labour costs it makes little economic sense that every town centre should boast three or four branch banks, each offering a complete range of nearly identical services. The banking industry, like the grocery industry twenty years ago, is being forced to the conclusion that it has inherited from the past too many of the wrong kinds of shops in the wrong places.

It is, of course, impracticable to deal with this situation in the somewhat ruthless fashion adopted by the grocery trade, which in effect faced the public with the accomplished fact that their local, personal service store was closed and they had no choice but to make off to the nearest self-service supermarket. The banks are in a different position, believing themselves to have a very special responsibility both to their customers and to their employees. Moreover, a branch bank represents a substantial capital investment that is not readily convertible to other uses; and abandoning a site means losing at least some business, both to competitive banks and to other types of competitor like the building societies. Rapid changes in organisational structure are unlikely.

Nevertheless, it is clear that social and economic factors, together with the banks' changing concept of their commercial role, will necessitate evolutionary changes both in the organisational structure of the large banking group and in the characteristics of the individual branch (or banker–customer interface). Technical developments in electronics will facilitate and accelerate the changes; already many of the banking services required by both personal and corporate customers can be provided just as readily (and sometimes more conveniently) by a computer terminal as by the costly concatenation of counters, cashiers, strongroom and bandit-proof screen.

In all the major UK banks, marketing departments are involved in the analysis and prediction of future market requirements and in setting up controlled experiments designed to assist senior management in answering such questions as:

How far should we segment our organisational structure to allow for specialist outlets or specialist individuals dealing with different customer categories?

How can we achieve the best compromise between the efficiency of electronic banking and the humanity of personal relationships with customers?

In what locations are existing branches superfluous, and in what locations do new branches need to be opened?

What alternative methods of servicing and communicating with customers should be considered?

How can the whole complicated organisation be controlled and co-ordinated, while leaving room for individual initiative?

Much of what individual banks are doing or planning in these respects must remain confidential. But here are some examples which we have been allowed to quote.

A branch opening strategy

For most of the major clearing banks the reorganisation of branch structure is likely to involve more closures of branches, that do not contribute to the bank's profitability or provide an irreplaceable service for customers, than new branch openings. One of the smaller British banking groups, however, is still in the enviable position of having nowhere to go but up, being still unrepresented in many population centres, some very large. It has set itself the task of opening four or five new branches a year in such centres, with the proviso that each new branch will be allowed only a limited payout period before making a positive contribution to the group's profits.

A methodical market-oriented procedure has been adopted in deciding where the new branches should be located and in giving the appointed manager and his staff a flying start towards the achievement of agreed business targets. The procedure involves three levels of activity:

1 market research to identify the most appropriate centres in which to seek premises;
2 formulation of a branch operational model and data input in order to appraise each investment proposition individually;
3 training and assisting branch management in the new branches to prepare and implement branch business development plans.

The first requirement for the market researchers was to screen over 100 population centres, which had been nominated as potentially suitable for new branches, and to put them in order of priority. The most obvious criterion to use was a purely quantitative one, the number of individuals and businesses located in the catchment area under consideration. But at the outset a niggling question was raised: 'Is bigger really better in the banking context?' Research was instituted into the bank's own experience of new-branch progress, comparing large towns with small towns. The results were reassuring to those who did not share the fashionable view that small is beautiful. It may be so in social terms; but in this case it was found that on every measurable commercial basis bigger was significantly better. Moreover it was possible to determine from the research an approximate breakpoint where small and unprofitable changed into big and profitable.

But of course quantitive data alone could be misleading and needed to be supplemented by qualitative information. As a starting point in this direction a broad sample of the bank's line management was asked to identify those features of a population centre which were most likely to form an attractive base for a new branch. Each factor mentioned (values for which could be discovered by desk research) was weighted according to the importance attached to it by respondents and the consistency of response. From the answers, weighted in this way, nine factors stood out, including the number of professional practices in the area, the size and nature of the industrial base, and the socio-economic characteristics of the residential districts.

These nine factors were used to screen the centres originally identified on a population basis, producing a numerical score for each centre. The seventy top-scoring centres were then visited by the researchers in order to supplement the impersonal statistical findings of desk research by a more human understanding of current and future activities in the areas concerned. The visits revolved around discussions with the town planners. We reproduce the heads of discussion in detail, since they may be a useful checklist for any branch management anxious to ensure that no business development opportunities are missed through lack of information about the immediate environment. The researchers were instructed to plan their visits and reports as set out below.

1 Visit

Before seeing planner   Obtain town map if not on file (but not town guide; planner may supply one free).

Establish where the following are in relation to each other:

industrial, retail, professional areas;

major retail outlets;
car parks;
pedestrian traffic flows;
competitive premises (please make note of special
features; for example, off-centre, how many floors,
car park, reception suite).

Remember place and street names that will assist
discussions with planner.

With the planner	Confirm where the various sectors are.

With the planner

Confirm where the various sectors are.
Discuss the sphere of influence of the town,
personal and industrial.
Also sphere of influence of other towns around,
employment and shopping.
Ask about communications, pedestrianisation,
one-way streets, etc.
Industrial: industries represented, major companies
and reliance on these, location and size of industrial
estates, size of individual units, type of industry on
estates, list of companies (if possible), government
grants?
Retail: agree central area, latest turnover figures.
Developments: for industrial, office, and retail;
check for growth figures over last few years as well
as current future developments; establish firmness
and time-scale for future ones.
Discuss planner's attitude to banks in the central
area and establish where we would be welcome.
Get a map showing ownership of premises (if
planner has one).

After seeing the planner

Go and see the industrial estates; are all sites taken,
is it simply warehousing, local site of major
national company?
Get a feel for the town's activity/prosperity;
numbers of people about, full car parks, usage of
banks and numbers of tills, are cars modern and
good quality, any empty premises, vacancies in
local employment office/local paper, etc.

2 Report

Restrict its length to two sides if possible. Usual format is:

> brief introduction;
> desk research;
> on-site research (does it confirm desk research?) split by personal, professional, retail, industrial, with dynamics of each; site within town (if town meets requirements); suggest area within which we should seek premises;
> conclusions.

At the end of the research stage recommendations were drawn up for each population centre identifying, where appropriate, the district within each town where premises should be sought. On the basis of these recommendations a shopping list for the bank's property department was agreed with the management and written into the bank's corporate plan. The shopping list is periodically updated.

Formulation of model and data input for individual propositions

It is now generally recognised that the use of statistical models, based on past experience, to predict the future results of alternative courses of action can help to eliminate the wilder flights of human error; but it is certainly not a foolproof procedure, whereby you can feed in your data, push the button, close your eyes and wait for the right answer to emerge. This would require the unlikely combination of perfect identification of all the factors affecting the outcome and perfect accuracy in calculating their relative importance, as well as pre-supposing an unchanging environment in which all those relationships remained constant. In the case we are at present reviewing, the bank's marketing department has constructed a cost/revenue model, which is in a state of constant change and improvement, and probably always will be. The model is designed to incorporate probable income, on the basis of perceived market potential, and projected costs, once specific premises have been identified and secured.

The procedure of feeding the collected market and other data into the model and analysing the computer print-out 'highlights', says the bank, the question whether the proposition will meet the bank's established investment criteria within the timescale laid down. 'Highlights', not guarantees, since banking, despite all appearances to the contrary, is in the end a risk-taking activity.

New-branch marketing activity

Once the decision has been taken to go ahead, the bank's marketing department works closely with the management team of the new branch to make as sure as possible that the inevitably fallible revenue projections are attained or exceeded. Areas of collaboration include

1 learning about the marketing opportunities available within the branch's catchment area;
2 joint formulation of the launch and follow-up publicity campaign;
3 collating calling lists for prospective customers;
4 agreeing a programme of promotional support, such as seminars and local sponsorships.

Enhancing the personal factor in an electronic scene

A fundamental dilemma facing the marketer of all but the most basic of financial services is the fact that on the one hand the customer at any level is looking for a *personal* service, a relationship with an individual or group of individuals whom he can know and trust; but on the other hand the requirements for providing the service efficiently and economically are inimical to the personal relationship. Mechanisation and computerisation are inevitable if costs are to be kept within reasonable bounds, but customers seldom enjoy corresponding with a computer; adequate security is obligatory when handling cash in an increasingly violent society, but the bandit-proof screen does not encourage warm personal relationships; size is an important element in providing a full range of national and international services for mobile customers in a shrinking world, but this means that the bank's staff too must be mobile as they rise in their profession; thus local relationships are often short-lived.

One of the London clearing banks, adapting an idea pioneered in

North America, has sought to counteract the trend towards depersonalisation by instituting in some of its larger branches a cadre of 'personal bankers', with the slogan, 'You want advice. There's a queue at the counter. The manager's busy. Now you can ask for your *personal* banker.' The personal bankers, most of them young and extroverted, are given specialised training, with the help of video-tapes which enable them to see themselves as others will see them, in the physical and psychological techniques of personal communi-cation. Customers attracted by the scheme (or indeed by the personal banker) are provided with a card, similar to but differentiated from a cheque or credit card, with the name, business address and telephone number of the designated personal banker.

It is emphasised in the promotional literature that the service is free and that

1 the personal banker is not a substitute for the manager, but can act as a sort of casualty clearing station dealing with the simpler problems and preparing the way for an interview with the manager when there are weightier matters to discuss;
2 the personal banker can deal with routine matters like ordering a new cheque book or changing a banker's order; and can obtain professional advice, related to the individual customer's personal situation, on such matters as insurance and investment (if the personal banker gets out of his or her depth the customer will be referred to the appropriate specialist);
3 there is no need to make appointments for personal interviews, and minor matters can be cleared by telephone.

That this service represents a logical marketing solution to a deep-seated problem is unquestionable. Whether or not it will prove to be cost-effective in achieving the two objectives of restoring a personal relationship between bank and customer and enabling branch managers to make more effective use of their limited time remains to be seen. The scheme is still regarded as a test and its results are being monitored. At present most of the workload of the personal bankers seems to relate to the more routine services like checking account balances and obtaining new cheque books. Its value will be confirmed if and when the personal bankers are successful in persuading their customers to make more extensive use of the bank's facilities in such forms as personal loans, insurance or endowment policies, will appointments, travellers' cheques and foreign currency.

Another marketing initiative of the same bank, again drawing on American experience, is still in the planning stage. If practical problems such as the usual concern about security can be overcome the intention is to set up in an experimental branch a banking hall laid out like an open plan office. In place of the traditional long counter there will be square mini-counters dotted about, each with up to four cashiers. These 'module' counters will carry only small amounts of cash which will be paid out through a special dispenser linked to a time-lock safe. Cash paid in will be transferred by pneumatic tube (modern technology paying appropriate tribute to Mr Kipps) to a central high-security area.

It may or may not work. But it is a practical example of the marketing principle of converting a logical concept into a prototype model which can be tested and improved if it shows promise or liquidated if it does not perform. Before the era of scientific marketing the principle was described as 'suck it and see'.

Putting the computer in its place

The reverse side of the coin for the same bank (and, of course, for its competitors) is using the new facilities made available through the rapid development of computer technology in a way that will improve both the level of customer service and the bank's profitability.

Currently the most conspicuous manifestation of electronic banking is the Automated Teller Machine, which as every schoolboy old enough to have a bank account knows enables him to withdraw up to £50 or £100, depending on his solvency, without joining the queue at the teller's counter or (in the case of ATMs outside bank premises) going into the branch at all. The key which unlocks the bank's cash store is of course a plastic card with a magnetic stripe recording the individual customer's account particulars; and the ATM itself is either connected by a dedicated telecommunications link to the bank's central computer, or has its own mini-computer to record details of transactions.

By the end of 1979 the four major clearing banks had installed between them over 1,000 ATMs, and a further 600 were scheduled for installation in 1980. Curiously, the bank with the largest number of installations had elected at the outset to site most of its machines inside branches, so forfeiting the customer benefit of being able to withdraw cash outside banking hours. This bank has now joined its competitors in preferring an outside wall of branches.

The development of ATMs, in which the UK is well ahead of other European countries, is an interesting example of marketing working hand in glove with technology. Acceptance of ATMs as a useful addition to banking facilities has not taken place overnight. As long ago as 1967 the English clearing banks started to instal an earlier generation of mechanical cash dispensers. These were the so-called 'ten-pounders', which provided card holders with what now seems the pitifully inadequate sum of £10 and then swallowed their cards, to regurgitate and return them after an appropriate interval.

Major investment in these now obsolete devices got under way in 1969, partly to offset the effects of the banks' joint decision in that year to close branches on Saturdays. The ten-pounders were not a success. One major bank calculated after eight years of operation that only one in thirty of their personal customers were active card-holders; and even they generally regarded the service simply as an emergency means of obtaining cash. This bank concluded, with the benefit of hindsight, that failure in this case had been a lucky escape. Retrospective calculations indicated that two £10 withdrawals through the ten-pounders would have cost the bank 34p more to handle than the average £20 cheque encashment across their counters.

However, the need remained for an alternative method of obtaining cash outside banking hours, or when bank counters were congested by a volume of business that has doubled over the past ten years. So in 1973 the computer systems and O & M people of one bank started to look around for a successor to the mechanical cash dispenser. After exhaustive testing of six prototype machines the bank decided to purchase forty ATMs; most of these were installed by the end of 1975 either inside branches or, in two or three cases, in remote sites such as a department store and the head office of a large insurance company.

But this time management was determined not to risk the same costly mistakes as had been made in the past and a working party was formed, chaired by the head of marketing and including represen-tatives from management services, inspection, property, and the credit card division. The working party was required to advise management on the future utilisation of ATMs and on a long-term strategy for automated cashier equipment. The establishment of objectives and a cost benefit analysis were major priorities.

Excluding such imponderables, it was concluded that, once an ATM had built up to its target workload, it would save the bank 7.9p per encashment, compared with cashing a cheque over the counter; it would also produce lesser savings on the cost of statement requests and balance enquiries which the ATM could readily be programmed to accept. But, conversely, any deposits accepted by the ATM, instead of over the counter, would cost the bank an extra 12p, which makes it less than surprising that few ATMs now offer this facility.

It remained to determine what was the number of encashments required for an ATM, once installed, to break even (a function of the ATM's siting, of the number of card-holders and the use made by them of their cards) and to ensure that the breakeven point was reached as soon as possible after installation.

The breakeven point at that time turned out to be 1,130 encashments a week for ATMs installed inside or outside branches, 2,800 encashments a week for ATMs installed at a remote workplace site, and 3,365 encashments a week for ATMs installed at a remote public site. Since it was also easier to secure staff involvement in servicing ATMs installed at the branch, workplace and public sites were given a low priority.

It also very rapidly, and unsurprisingly, emerged that a through-the-wall ATM attracted more business than one installed inside a branch. So the inside versus outside question was settled. But what type of branch? Analysis of encashment levels for the pilot installations by type of branch indicated that university branches had come closest to breakeven with an average of 905 encashments a week. Branches in major shopping areas averaged 706 encashments a week, suburban shopping areas 477 and commercial centres 446. A rag-bag category, including areas with high industrial workforces, tourist and entertainment centres and residential suburbs, brought up the rear with an average of 263 encashments a week. The obvious conclusion was that the shopping centres of towns with a population over 50,000 and university towns should be given top priority in the allocation of ATMs; a site which combined both characteristics should be a winner. (As the bank's marketing department had confidently expected, the usage of all ATMs has risen substantially since this paragraph was written.)

As regards the issue of cards, the Consumer Credit Act, which prohibits amongst other things the unsolicited mailing of credit tokens, precluded the type of inertia selling which in some cases characterised the early days of credit cards; and the bank was in any case reluctant to impose a relatively expensive item on customers who might make little use of it. So mailing shots were despatched to lists of customers selected by branch managers in the same catchment area. The mailing shot included a personal letter from the branch manager and an application form; it was accompanied by an explanatory leaflet describing the service and featuring the claim: 'Now we're open for business even when we're closed.' Responses to this invitation were good, up to 50 per cent at machine branches and up to 35 per cent at catchment area branches. The combination of initial selection by the manager with the customer's freedom of choice has produced an adequate level of usage per card, an average of 10.9 withdrawals a year and still climbing after the first eighteen months.

The story of ATMs is still no more than half told. Soon a magnetic stripe will be incorporated on the bank's credit cards, making cash advances available to card-holders through the ATM. They can be made to perform other tricks if there is sufficient demand; for example, in Japan ATMs have been fitted with passbook readers and printers to produce statements. And, according to a German banking pundit, the true economies of these systems, with really large user-frequency, will only be realised when the system is organised on a pool basis, involving several banks – as is now being developed in Belgiam.

CHAPTER FOURTEEN

Planned business development

Ultimately a bank's business development plan will derive from the corporate strategy laid down by top management. It is top management's responsibility, aided by inputs from the various departments, including marketing, to answer such ticklish questions as the following.

1   What shape of business do we want in five, ten or fifteen years' time?
2   Where are the future profits coming from?
3   What are likely to be future consumer needs?
4   What resources and organisational structure do we require to satisfy them?

The corporate plan resulting from their deliberations may well deal separately with what are increasingly four separate streams in the complex organisation of the banking group: corporate business, personal business, international, and specialist financial services.

When the broad policy-framework has been established, the detailed work of developing the new services or securing the new customers needed to achieve corporate objectives has to be tackled. Depending on the nature of each project, marketing is likely to have a major, or at least a contributory, role to play in the early conceptual and planning stages; and, when necessary, a continuing support role in the subsequent stages of implementation. Reference is made in later chapters to the marketing role in the international and specialist service areas. In this chapter we describe some typical examples in the personal and corporate sectors.

Students and school leavers

All the London clearing banks are clearly agreed on one point; that in the personal customer sector it makes sense to catch them young. The reason is quite simply the clear evidence from market research that, once banked, people tend to stay with the same bank for life; and the future earning expectancy of teenagers must be greater on average than that of those who acquire the banking habit late in life.

It also makes obvious sense to aim selectively for young customers who are likely to reach the higher income brackets and make full use of banking services rather than adhere to a weekly income and expenditure pattern.

The result was that in the early 1970s, when banks were becoming more openly competitive, a significant proportion of the competition was focused on student accounts. Initially competition took what now seems the rather simplistic form of offering and advertising modest material incentives to the 200,000 or so school leavers who proceed each year to higher education. The incentive gifts took such forms as clipboards, plastic briefcases, ballpoint pens and book tokens. This left various questions unanswered. For example, is an eighteen–year–old, who is intelligent enough to qualify for higher education, really going to be impressed by the offer of a plastic briefcase? How important is it to provide students during their formative years as bank customers with tailor-made services, even at a loss, which will help to build long–term loyalty? And are the 500,000 school leavers who start work each year, including 100,000 who enter a salaried occupation, so much less likely to succeed in life that they should be forgotten?

All the banks have researched these problems and made their individual decisions on appropriate marketing action. One of them, at least, concluded that their marketing plan should comprehend both market segments, the school leavers who go straight to work and those who go on to college; and that incentive gifts did not do justice to the student segment. This bank was also realistic in accepting that factors which no marketing action could change have a major influence on school leavers' choice of bank. These influences include the bank in which the parents maintain an account, the location and convenience of the closest branch bank, and, in the case of those going to work, the bank used by their employers. With these factors predominating, competitive advertising and sales promotion directed at school leavers cannot be expected to achieve more than a few percentage points shift in market share.

This bank's basic marketing decision was to opt out of the incentive gifts activity and to offer instead the inducements to school leavers and students set out below. (Not all of those listed were part of the initial package; some were added later as part of the normal marketing practice of revising and extending a product range in the light of experience and changing market needs.)

School leavers

1 A cheque account conducted free of charge for the first year provided it is maintained in credit and opened either before leaving school or within three months of leaving.
2 For minors, a special cheque guarantee card until they reach eighteen years. This is issued subject to a satisfactorily conducted account being maintained for six months and upon the holders being in regular employment.

Students

1 A free-of-charges account, which could, by prior arrangement only, be overdrawn up to £50. Interest is charged on money borrowed.
2 A student cash card, which is an identity card enabling the student to cash cheques up to £20 per day at any UK branch of the bank. If the student is at least 18 years old and in receipt of a UK Local Education Authority Grant, he is offered a Barclay card.
3 'Student business officers', members of staff, generally in their mid twenties, situated in branches near colleges. They are specially trained to understand and be able to solve students' financial problems. Students are encouraged to deal with their student business officer rather than the branch manager.
4 If students require financial assistance the bank will normally advance up to £100 by way of overdraft, provided this is for the usual necessities of student life. Repayment is normally made from a holiday job or a grant cheque at the start of the next term.
5 In order to help with their budgeting students receive a statement automatically halfway through each term.
6 Students (provided they are over eighteen and their account has

been maintained satisfactorily) are offered a credit card after six months.

7 Students opening an account at branches close to their colleges are automatically issued with a cash card. This enables them to draw cash from automatic teller machines twenty-four hours a day.

8 On graduation student customers are offered a loan of up to £500 in order to help them become established in a job. The purpose of the loan is to buy clothing, a deposit on accommodation, a season ticket, etc. The loan is contingent on their passing their finals and obtaining a firm job offer. The loan is at a preferential rate of interest and repayable over one year, starting after three months.

So much for the 'product'; how about the promotion? Media advertising is of course directed at the two market segments. Because the size of the budget which can be afforded for a relatively small, though important, market segment is limited, media advertising is concentrated in two-month bursts: for the school leavers when their final term ends, in June/July; for the students when their first term is about to begin, in August/September.

But an important part of the marketing effort, linked to the media advertising (all members of staff are given copies of the advertisement), is the sales promotional activity at branch level. What this includes is set out below.

For school leavers

1 Branch staff giving talks about banking to children in schools during their final year, supported by specially made films. (These talks are, of course, designed to inform the children about the help any branch will give them with their financial planning when they leave school, rather than to 'sell' a particular bank.)

2 Visits by parties of school children to their local branch after hours.

3 Mailings to parents included with bank statements.

4 Direct approaches to parents by branch managers.

5 Poster displays in branches.

6 Local press advertising.

7 Local commercial radio advertising.

8 Publicity brochures.

For students

1 Attendance at fresher fairs on first day of term, with stand unit, posters, etc.
2 Promotion by posters and promotional material within branches close to university campuses.
3 Advertisements in college handbooks.
4 Mailings to freshers before they arrive at college, using lists supplied by colleges.

A facility exists for students to open accounts at branches close to the colleges they will be attending by making arrangements in advance through branches near their homes or by completion of press coupons.

Part of the student marketing effort is directed towards retaining accounts once they have been won. Individual activities include

1 a mailing to freshers to educate them in budgeting and running a bank account;
2 an open evening at their local branch during the first term so that they can get to know the staff and their student business officer;
3 on graduation a mailing and posters offering the special graduation loan and encouraging students to make arrangements for the transfer of their cheque account when they leave college.

Is the marketing campaign cost-effective?

Like any professional marketing department, the department responsible for the school leaver and student campaigns has taken steps to measure results, in terms both of the marginal accounts gained and of the cost of servicing the accounts as well as the promotional expenditure. Market share figures for the school leaver accounts are confidential, but published figures for student accounts indicate a small but useful increase in the bank's share after it embarked on the new marketing policy. Overall, the cost of retaining let alone building market share of school leaver and student accounts is felt to be well justified in terms of immediate results as well as long-term benefits.

Credit assessment on personal loans

Historically, one of the fundamental problems confronting a bank with a large lending operation is to appraise efficiently the risk element of new loan applications. Until very recent times, banks have tended to rely on subjective evaluation by their branch managers to assess individual applicants. There are a number of difficulties with this approach, not the least of which are that constant training is necessary and that it is extremely difficult to communicate the necessary expertise.

There have been wide-ranging arguments and discussions about whether lending is an art or a science, but this is of little use to the practical banker and the arguments tend to be both academic and irrelevant. Even though for many years the lending function has tended to be considered as an art form, this does not preclude the application of scientific processes. However, such processes must be shown in practice to improve the quality of decisions made in determining risk; and at the same time middle management must be convinced that a more systematic approach to the evaluation of risk can have a significant effect on the profitability of lending.

In 1972 one of the major clearing banks concluded that a credit assessment system could be helpful in improving the quality of personal lending decisions. Some form of systemisation or streamlining was urgently needed because of the rapid growth of this market sector. At the time of going to press, this particular bank can expect to sanction some 300,000 new personal loans annually.

There was an immediate snag at the outset of the project. It was established that the existing personal loan application form not only failed to ask for sufficient information for the development of an objective system, but it also failed to provide adequate market information. Accordingly, priority was given to the design, approval and introduction of a new personal loan application form.

Subsequently, statisticians began collecting data for the construction of an assessment system. A provisional system, based on an analysis of questionnaires, was produced in 1973 for use in conjunction with the new personal loan application form, and it was agreed that a sample of branches should assess copies of applications after lending decisions had been taken in the normal way.

An assessment working party was formed during September

1973 to monitor the progress of the provisional system and to consider further developments in credit rating. The reaction of branches involved in the trial was generally favourable towards the system, which involved branches in using the services of a credit reference agency for applications where the current account had been open for less than a year. About 10 per cent of the credit register searches yielded adverse information, usually in the form of a county court judgment, previously unknown to the branch.

The greatly improved quality of information about good and bad accounts led to the production in 1976 of a more efficient system. The new system was introduced for unsecured personal loans, again in conjunction with credit register searches for applicants whose current accounts had been open less than a year.

The full details of the method are confidential to the bank concerned, and indeed change from time to time as accumulating experience makes more accurate evaluation possible. It is no secret that the following personal factors are taken into account:

employer's business;
duration of employment with present employer;
frequency of payment of income;
method of payment;
residential status;
number of years at present address;
number of years with account at this bank;
purpose of loan;
method of repayment (for comparison with the information supplied on level of income and method of its payment);
security (not an overriding factor; the provision of adequate security would take the application out of the unsecured loan category).

In the introductory stages considerable freedom was given to managers to override the system, though there was a requirement from the outset that all personal loans should be processed or scrutinised except in very unusual circumstances. This enabled managers to accommodate customers whose rating was unsatisfactory, but who were known to them personally as individuals of the utmost integrity.

In such cases managers were left with the obligation to justify their decision if it should prove subsequently that their confidence was misplaced. Further experience has tended to increase the bank's branch and central management's confidence in the reliability of the adopted system.

The benefit to the bank

It is important to recognise that no system of assessment is perfect in the sense that all bad accounts can be eliminated without rejecting any good accounts. However, with a credit assessment system based on objectivity, management have a choice over the levels of bad debts they are prepared to accept and the profitability they can expect to achieve, subject to government policy. This choice may be effected simply and quickly by altering the minimum acceptance score. Credit policy itself can also be implemented more efficiently, for instance, by moving the minimum acceptance assessment up or down in order to achieve a fall or rise in the volume of lending by a pre-determined amount, whilst maintaining the highest quality of lending consistent with the overall volume.

Given the impossibility of achieving perfection, success can be claimed on the more mundane level of lending performance. As efficiency has increased, with successive improvements in the system giving better quality of information, bad debt provisions and irregular payments have begun to decline in number, while the overall growth in new personal loans sanctioned has continued, subject only to credit policy directives.

To claim success for a system on the strength of a slight improvement in bad debt experience would, however, be to miss the point. The real gain which emerges from its use for the sanction of personal loans is the potential saving in branch managerial time. In such a high volume/small lending market (the upper limit for a single unsecured loan has been set at £2,000) delegation of decision-making responsibility is imperative. The system provides for reference back to managerial level of doubtful cases and refusals, and it makes such delegation practical with two clear benefits:

1 it frees managers for other duties; the potential saving in managerial time is estimated at around 100,000 man-hours a year,

or over 60 full-time managers.

2 it gives younger members of staff lending experience and the opportunity to help customers when they most need help.

Marketing home improvement loans

Still in the same field of personal loans, another bank has provided information on the development and launch programme for their home improvement loan scheme. Development of the scheme started, like most planned marketing projects, with analyses of consumer needs and of the competition.

The consumer need

Three factors combined to create a presumption that there would be a lively interest in home improvement among householders. First, the inconvenience and expense of moving house persuaded many people to adopt the alternative of enlarging their homes by building extensions. Secondly, heating-conservation and energy-saving schemes prompted by the government encouraged many house-holders to install double glazing, cavity wall insulation and loft insulation; a great deal of publicity was given to these measures together with positive advice on the best means of going about them. Thirdly, many householders were installing central heating and taking complementary insulation measures at the same time.

There are 17.5 million dwelling units in this country, and it was estimated that 5 per cent of them were owned by the bank's customers. Further research revealed that 35,000 customers would be likely to build extensions in any one year and a similar number would install central heating. Many would do both at the same time.

The average cost of building an extension in the base year (1974–75) was £1,500; for the installation of central heating the average was £700 plus the cost of any structural alterations. Because of inflation these figures were increasing steadily year by year, giving impetus for such work to be done sooner rather than later, and clearly motivating customers to take advantage of a new loan scheme designed to provide finance for these purposes.

The competition

Other clearing banks also provided finance for home improvements, using flat-rate loan schemes. Finance houses had various schemes to finance the installation of central heating and home improvements, but usually charged higher rates of interest. And building societies also provided funds for house extensions.

Sales volume forecast

The full potential of the new loan scheme could have required the provision of approximately £60 million per annum. The market for cavity wall insulation and double glazing was not well documented and the figure assumes that some 10 per cent of the bank's customers who install central heating and build home extensions would spend an additional sum on insulation and double glazing.

Not all customers would, however, finance improvements using bank finance but 30–40 per cent might well do so and the impact of a new loan scheme could eventually require the provision of approximately £20–25 million per annum.

The product

The amount of loan required would obviously depend on the precise amount of improvement a customer decided to carry out. Those involved in building home extensions would clearly require considerably more than those simply installing central heating or carrying out home insulation. Customers involved in both schemes would require a proportionately higher sum.

With this in mind it was decided that loans would be offered within the range of £1,000 minimum to £5,000 maximum with repayments up to a maximum period of five years, depending on the customer's ability to repay from his available financial resources and available income. Interest would be charged on a flat-rate basis for the period of the loan so that customers would know the precise extent of their monthly commitment. A feature of the scheme could be the provision of free life cover.

If repayments fell six months in arrears, demand for full payment would be made and arrangements put in hand to realise the security given to the bank.

Specially designed stationery would be prepared and a new leaflet printed to explain the loan scheme to potential borrowers. The leaflet was designed to attract the interest of what was recognised to be a very important section of customers, those who own their own homes.

Marketing planning

A project controller was appointed at the very first stage of the scheme to co-ordinate all phases of the operation. A clear flow chart, specifically detailing development areas and time-scales as far as possible, was constructed to provide clear objectives for those involved in the launching of the new scheme.

An action plan was created to cover the following points:

1 approval for the operational details;
2 a detailed procedure plan for other head office departments involved;
3 careful consideration of the requirements of computer accounting;
4 careful consideration of any parts of the scheme affected by the Consumer Credit Act 1974;
5 design of the promotional leaflet;
6 calculation of interest tables and tables to cover refunds in the event of early repayment;
7 major policy decisions – for example, free life cover;
8 consideration of interest rates for secured and unsecured lending if they are to be split;
9 promotional activity – design of display material;
10 clear branch instructions to be prepared and circulated to the appropriate head office departments for their opinions;
11 printing and distribution of leaflets and application forms;
12 branches notified of changes in branch operational instructions and rules;
13 advertising arranged on television and in the press;
14 a form designed to provide feedback from branches.

Communications to branches

Branches were given clear and precise operational instructions. This was done by a circular preceded by a letter from the Chief General Manager outlining the new scheme and communicating the policy decisions of the executive. The circular included

1 a description of the scheme;
2 a description of the potential customers who would find it attractive;
3 instructions for the completion of the application form;

4 the procedure for opening the account;
5 reference to the interest tables and the amount of monthly repayment;
6 instructions on how to record interest in branch records;
7 realisation procedures in the event of a customer defaulting;
8 the method of dealing with arrears of repayments;
9 a point of reference for enquiries;
10 how staff applications should be dealt with;
11 amendments to branch operating instructions;
12 amendments to book of instructions.

Launch activities

These involved the preparation of media advertising and of publicity material for use in branches. Branches received leaflets describing the main features of the scheme; they incorporated details of interest rates and the precise amounts to be charged. (The wording of the leaflets had to be checked to ensure that it conformed with the terms of the Consumer Credit Act.) Branch managers were told to make approaches to potential interested customers, and clear instructions were given them on how to promote the scheme.

The outcome

The scheme was a success. The first year's sales forecast was exceeded by a factor of five, the second by a factor of seven. To forestall the cynics who may remark that this was evidently a case of bad forecasting, the bank's marketing manager comments that 'The most important element in the whole process was our timing – we launched during a time of rapidly rising house prices and managed to catch the growing market for home improvement. This fact dominates all others in the creation of the scheme and underlines the basic marketing principle of riding a rising market – by design or (as often happens) by accident.' In this case the scheme eventually went on to generate a loan portfolio well in excess of the original estimate.

Corporate customers

Developing or consolidating business with large corporate customers requires a rather different marketing approach. The banks have to understand their individual needs and systems and the way the bank fits into the picture, how it can provide a tailor-made service or improve an existing service to meet the customer's individual needs. This often requires a collaborative investigation, involving both bank and customer.

An example of such an investigation was a study carried out in 1978 by the Inter-Bank Research Organisation, a multi-disciplinary organisation set up in 1968 by the London and Scottish clearing banks to study and research matters of common interest. The study related to the banking requirements of local authorities – important customers for the banks both as big collectors of funds through the rates system and equally as big spenders. The immediate subject of investigation was the principles and practice of collecting regular payments. The Southend Borough Council made the study possible by providing information on the methods and costs involved in collecting rates.

It was agreed at the outset that four main factors needed to be considered in determining the most satisfactory method of rate collection. These were

1 the needs of the ratepayers (who elect and can unseat the council);
2 the council's cash flow;
3 the payment processing costs;
4 the level of bank charges, reflecting the workload on the bank concerned.

The ratepayers' requirements
What the ratepayer wants, short of not having to pay rates at all, is convenience and flexibility in the method of payment, in the frequency of payment, and in the locations where payments can be made. Like most consumers, in fact, the ratepayer wants a choice.

This clearly conflicts with at least the immediate interests of the local authority. Offering a choice is inconvenient and expensive to the extent that it attracts more overheads. However, in the case of Southend there was a wide range of choice among the following payment methods:

bank Giro credits (credit transfers);
cash;
cheque;

direct debiting system;
National Girobank transfers;
postal or money orders;
standing orders.

Ratepayers who do not have a bank account can pay by cash, postal or money order. Bank account holders can pay by cheque, by standing order or by the direct debiting system. (At the time of the study 66 per cent of ratepayers had bank current accounts, compared with only 50 per cent of all heads of households.)

As regards frequency, ratepayers are given the choice between paying once a year or in two, four or ten instalments spread over the year. Those who pay by direct debit are given the additional option of paying in twelve monthly instalments, because, for reasons which became clear during the course of the study, this method of payment is favoured by the council.

As regards location, ratepayers have the choice of paying direct to the civic centre offices, by post, at post offices by National Giro in-payment forms, or at bank branches by bank Giro credits.

The council's cash flow management

Managing the cash flow of rate collection involves a delicate balance between trying to get the monies into the account as quickly as possible and keeping the level of service to ratepayers as high as possible. It is clearly important that the internally generated delays in cash flow must be minimised and that wherever possible the external delays, those caused by the ratepayers and the banking system, must be reduced. Any delay costs money and may mean that money has to be borrowed to cover the council's outgoings. In order to determine what frequency of payment would come closest to meeting the requirements both of the ratepayers' domestic economies and of the council's cash flow management, IBRO started by analysing existing payments methods and frequencies. It emerged that 50 per cent of the bank current account holders were paying their rates in two instalments, and 36 per cent in ten or twelve instalments a year; the most frequent method of payment was by cheque in the case of the six-monthly instalments, and by standing order or direct debit in the case of the ten or twelve instalment payments. Those without bank accounts followed much the same frequency pattern, but the great majority of payments took the form of cash.

The next step was to use discounted cash flow methods in calculating the net present value of a notional £200 annual rates payment, when made in one payment at the beginning of the year, in six-monthly or three-monthly instalments and in ten or twelve instalments. On this calculation the annual payment method, adopted by only about 10 per cent of ratepayers, was worth about 2 per cent more to the council than the more popular payments methods, after giving the ratepayer a 2 per cent cash discount. But six-monthly or three-monthly payments were worth less than 1 per cent more to the council than ten or twelve instalments per year. This was before taking into account internally or externally generated delays in getting the cash into the council's bank account.

The period between the payment falling due and the payment actually being made varies considerably, depending on the means and frequency of payment. Standing order and direct debit payments are generally initiated on the due date. But with payments by cheque or cash, and other means where there is some discretion when payment is made, there is usually some delay; for half-yearly and quarterly payments the delay averages two weeks and for instalment payments of 10 per year it averages one week.

In addition to this form of delay there were time lags between the customer paying and the payment being banked; and between the payment being banked and the funds becoming available to the council. The former can add one to three days in the case of payments by cheque, postal order or cash; the latter can add a further two to three days with all methods of payment, the notable exception being direct debits which are debited and credited to the appropriate accounts on the specified date. Taking these additional delays into account it emerged from the study that monthly payments by direct debit produce a cash flow equal to or better than six-monthly or three-monthly or ten payments per year by cash or cheque; or than ten payments per year by standing order; and only 0.5 per cent worse than six-monthly or three-monthly payments by standing order.

Processing payments
When analysed, the processing of rates payments, like any other instalment payments, breaks down into three activities:

identifying each payment;
reconciling payments due with payments received;
follow-up procedures.

All of them are subject to human error. Identification is made difficult when the ratepayer forgets to quote his assessment number or when the assessment number is quoted incorrectly on Giro credits or standing orders. Reconciliation is time-consuming; particularly in the case of standing order payments and payments by cash or cheque which have to be processed individually in order to identify what each is for and who it is from, and hence to produce a list of payments due but not made. Follow-up procedures are awkward and cumbersome, especially when there is difficulty in being quite certain that the ratepayer has not paid. The normal procedure is, first, to wait until it is certain that payment has not been made, then to send out a final demand, then to wait again for a response and, finally, if necessary, to start legal proceedings.

Processing costs and efficiency vary considerably in relation both to the range of choice between payments methods and frequencies which the ratepayer is offered and to the options selected. The wider the choice, the higher the processing cost and the risk of error. But there is no doubt that the direct debiting system comes closest of all to minimising cost and error. The risk of an incorrect assessment number being quoted is much reduced when a council itself gives the numbers. Reconciliation is much quicker and simpler, since the direct debiting system works on an exception basis, giving details only of those payments that are not received. Follow-up procedures can be initiated sooner and with greater confidence that the innocent will not be persecuted.

Bank charges

These are of course a matter for individual negotiation between each local authority and its bank. So IBRO is cautious about claiming that encouraging ratepayers to adopt the direct debit method of payment is bound to reduce the charges that form an important part of the cost of collecting rates. But the report does go so far as to say that 'on average, the item charge to local authorities for direct debits is less than for all other bank payment media'.

Establishing the facts is of course only the beginning of the marketing story. It still remains for the bank to assess the profitability; for branch managers to convince their customers, the local authority, that a shift in this direction will benefit them, and for the local authority to persuade its ratepayers that there is a benefit to them in a regular monthly payment which can be written into the family budget and then forgotten. But an understanding of the facts, an identification of the best course of action for all concerned, makes persuasion that much easier.

CHAPTER FIFTEEN

Marketing at regional and branch levels

Everything we have said so far will, we hope, lead to the conclusion that the essential marketing functions in a branch banking system are to bring the customers in, to devise services which meet their needs (while earning the bank some profits) and to link the appropriate service to the appropriate customer. Successful accomplishment of this three-point objective is greatly assisted if there is effective co-operation and mutual understanding between branch management and the bank's central marketing services.

Bringing the customers in

We describe here one example of an analytical approach to the basic problem of attracting customers with the help of marketing tools. The starting point was the adaptation to banking of well-established marketing theory about the way in which people make purchasing decisions. The precise nature of decision-making varies, of course, from market to market; the way in which customers choose a particular bank differs in detail from the way in which they choose a television set. But the general model of consumer decision-making, based on market research in a number of different fields, can be applied in its essentials as much to the decision to open a bank account as to the decision to buy a television set.

The model of even an apparently simple and rapid purchasing (or repeat purchasing) decision is in fact quite a complex one. It usually proceeds sequentially and involves, among others, the following elements:

awareness, knowledge and established attitudes;
stimulus to purchase (or repurchase);
search behaviour;
purchase behaviour;
post-purchase behaviour (customer loyalty, etc.).

All these factors, according to accepted marketing theory, are inter-related and are involved to a greater or lesser extent, consciously or subconsciously, in every purchase decision. For example, awareness and knowledge about banking in general and individual banks in particular lead to the development of attitudes and preferences. The degree to which consumers are prepared to enter into active search behaviour, comparing and contrasting individual banks, will also have a direct influence on attitude formation. An individual, clearly, must feel the need to have a bank account before he or she will open one; so a specific stimulus will be needed to trigger the 'purchase behaviour'. Once an individual becomes a customer of a particular bank, the key consideration will be continued customer loyalty. And so on, in as great a complexity of inter-relationships as you care to cope with.

The bank in question decided to use the basic tools of market research to obtain information from customers and potential customers about their attitudes to and use of the bank and its competitors. The following techniques were used:

1 group discussions;
2 individual depth interviews (particularly useful in 'sensitive' areas such as banking);
3 large-scale sample surveys.

The research findings helped to illuminate the background factors in the model which the bank would have to deal with in looking for effective purchasing stimuli in its particular situation. Some of the basic findings are set out below.

Awareness and attitudes
In all sectors of the public, awareness of the major banks is high: 80 per cent of people can recognise the names of at least five banks. There is little perceived difference between banks. A large number of

people feel that banks are unapproachable and 'superior'. Banks are seen as being safe places for keeping money, efficient and at the forefront technologically.

Search behaviour
Very few potential customers go to the trouble of actively visiting and comparing individual banks before choosing one to open an account with. They tend to solicit the views of relatives and friends and act on their advice.

Stimulus to purchase
The act of opening an account is usually triggered by a change of income or expenditure patterns. For example, many people leaving school open an account; others come under pressure from employers who wish to change methods of wages payment.

Post-purchase behaviour
Once a person joins a bank, inertia creates a great deal of customer loyalty. On the whole people change banks only when they move to another district, amalgamate accounts on marriage, or are very actively dissatisfied.

The specific market 'purchasing stimuli' devised by the bank's marketing department will not be universally applicable, since each bank's competitive situation is peculiar to itself. But it will be generally true that the areas where marketing action can be taken are those of promotion, services development and branch support or selling. The bank's comments on each of these areas are set out below.

Promotion
Among the major banks high awareness means they are virtually household names. However, with a small bank great efforts are made to get the name across to the public. This is a marketing starting point. It appears that people do feel all banks are fairly acceptable provided they have heard of them. The lack of perceived difference between banks creates a situation whereby market share correlates with distribution. Marketing opportunities do exist for banks which can differentiate themselves along some dimension of universal value. Again, small banks have been more successful at this than the

larger ones. The absence of active search behaviour and reliance on word-of-mouth recommendation means that banks have to provide a high standard of service to customers so that favourable recommendations will be encouraged.

Services development
The major bank services of money transmission, saving and lending are well-established and are likely to remain unchanged. However, much innovation can be expected in the manner these services are delivered in order to maximise speed and quality of service. Development in the field of automatic cash dispensers and new queuing systems are examples. This increases customer loyalty and encourages favourable word-of-mouth recommendation of the bank to potential new customers.

Selling
Aspects of consumer behaviour make the branch manager a key influence on people's decisions. As stated, preferences for individual banks are not strongly formed, therefore a manager with an active selling approach is unlikely to encounter resistance from consumers on the grounds that they prefer another bank. An active selling approach is likely to be amply rewarded.

In this particular case the research was handled centrally and the marketing initiative came from the top. But it would not have been successful without co-operation at the level of the individual branch. And there is no reason why the initiative should not come from the branch level, backed by appropriate local market research – which can be much more specific than a national survey.

Branch marketing activity plans

Another, rather larger, banking group has provided an example of a systematic approach to business development at branch level, starting with some pump-priming by the central marketing department and growing from that into a systematic procedure for branch managements to work out their own marketing plans, supported if necessary by central marketing.

The central marketing department started the ball rolling by organising a trial run in seven branches, specially selected to provide a broad spectrum of experience. The declared objectives of this exercise were

1 to increase branch profits through more business customers and professional practices;
2 to develop a standard approach to achieving, sustaining and developing such an increase.

What was done
Research was undertaken at each branch to assess any significant strengths or weaknesses in the structure of the branch's business. This involved studying the twenty-five largest corporate accounts and a sample of personal accounts. Any opportunities or limitations arising from the branch's layout, its physical impact and its personnel were also noted. At the same time the branch's catchment area was studied in detail in order to identify specific potential customers and local opportunities.

The results
Between thirty and sixty corporate business development prospects were identified in each branch area, and basic company data were provided for each. The branch manager was also given details of local professional practices, suggestions for any modifications in branch layout or organisation related to business development, and ideas on the most effective methods of increasing the bank's business with existing customers and of approaching prospective customers.

Broadening the approach

Having read the marketing department's reports on the seven 'trial' branches, the regional banking divisions nominated a further eighty-four branches which they considered to have suitable capacity and potential to benefit from the marketing activity plans approach. In this wider context the marketing department, which had also learnt something from the pilot exercise, felt that it should be possible to reduce the time spent on each branch by about 50 per cent and still retain the more important elements. The method of working adopted at this second stage was to spend one week of research prior to a branch visit lasting only a day or so, and to complete each branch report within three weeks of its commencement. Time spent at the branch analysing branch records, and perhaps disrupting the normal flow of business, was reduced by relying more heavily on the identification of potential corporate customers through reference books held centrally, together with local sources of information and any contacts the branch manager might have. The resulting reports in most cases identified roughly forty prospects and made specific suggestions to the branch manager concerned of the best way of approaching them.

Longer-term developments

Since the initial pump-priming exercises were carried out the major responsibility for initiating local business development activity has shifted from the marketing department to the branches. Each branch is encouraged to set up its own business development programme. This is likely to include a shortlist of between six and ten corporate prospects as well as in-branch promotions, exhibitions, and other more generalised schemes for attracting new customers. The marketing department provides back-up information and material on request, such as annual reports and data sheets for the identified corporate prospects, and advertisements, display material or literature for the localised promotions.

In developing their own marketing activity plans the branches are advised to make use of the standard reference sources described below, as well as any specific publications produced by local organisations.

Dun & Bradstreet Register
The Dun & Bradstreet Ltd. reference agency produces a list of companies for which it has had to provide a credit rating. These are listed according to their town of domicile, and the information provided includes address, trade, date of formation, nominal and issued capital, and name of bankers.

Kompass Register
This is a compilation of company information produced in association with the Confederation of British Industry. It provides a

detailed breakdown of products and services, with a key indicating which companies in the UK provide them, and also a geographically ordered list of the companies included in the products breakdown, by county and then by town. The number of companies included is fewer than in the *Dun & Bradstreet Register* but, for many of the companies listed, more detailed information is available, such as number of employees, names of directors and senior executives, location and a description of the nature of the company's business.

Key British Enterprises (KBE)
Another Dun & Bradstreet publication, this time with companies listed in alphabetical sequence only; the information contained is similar to that found in the *Kompass Register*.

Who Owns Whom
Yet another Dun & Bradstreet publication, this lists every UK parent company in alphabetical order together with their subsidiaries, and then lists subsidiaries in alphabetical order giving the names of their parent companies.

Solicitors Diary & Directory
Lists all solicitors' practices and individual members situated, firstly, in London and then in other English and Welsh towns; this publication also lists barristers at law.

Institute of Chartered Accountants in England and Wales: List of Members and Firms
Lists all members alphabetically, members in practice and firms alphabetically, and then members in practice and firms by towns, with London split into postal districts.

Marketing council rent payments through National Girobank

It is easy to drift into a tacit acceptance that the only commercial banks in the UK are the familiar High Street names. Not so. In many aspects of their work the clearing banks have a direct competitor with no less than 21,000 branches. It trades under the name of National Girobank and the 21,000 branches are of course the local post offices up and down the country.

National Giro, as it was then termed, opened in 1968 as a money transmission service and as a provider of simple banking service, primarily for the 50–60 per cent of the adult population then without a current bank account. The National Giro service was based on a single centre, at which all accounts would be maintained, and to which all transaction documents would be sent and processed direct from customers, from over 21,000 post offices and from the banks. The main transactions were transfers (between accounts), in-payments (payments made at post offices by non-customers to customers' accounts) and out-payments (cheques).

In the three years preceding opening and in the early days of the service being operational almost all the organisation's management and staff resources were devoted to establishing the service. What marketing effort was available was used to achieve some level of awareness and involvement through direct contact with potential users and media advertising.

Identifying a market segment and its specific needs
Market segmentation and the design of specific facilities for specific users began to be developed in the early 1970s and has progressively evolved ever since.

Local authorities were among the earliest organisations to be approached because they represented a significant sector in money transmission operations. It was in that sector that particular needs and opportunities became apparent in rent collection.

There are about 5 million publicly owned houses in the United Kingdom, with each tenant paying rent at frequent intervals to his local authority. Methods of rent collection are many and varied but the two most popular methods were the use of outdoor rent collectors and rent collection offices strategically positioned on council housing estates. Both these services have inherent disadvantages.

First, with the increasing crime rate, there was the growing danger of moving cash, either on the person of individuals or from the local offices. Second, wives were increasingly taking up full-time employment and the proportion of abortive calls by the rent collector had increased, especially in the south of England and most especially in London. Third, the national building programme for council houses had reached such proportions that the provision of a convenient network of 'owned' collection offices was becoming more expensive, and few councils could afford to provide full coverage.

Developing a 'product' to meet customer need

Discussions between National Girobank and some of the major local authorities, in particular with the Greater London Council, resulted in the development of a 'product' to meet the specific needs of housing departments. It soon became clear that the in-payment service, with some minor modifications, would provide a solution. The elements of the service were as follows.

1 Specially printed stationery, personalised to each tenant, showing the local authority's Giro account number and the tenancy reference number, was issued in book form to each tenant. This book showed the conditions of tenancy and replaced the rent book. To enable the tenant to advise the local authority of any repairs, etc., a tear-out pre-paid postcard was also provided within the book.
2 On rent day the tenant would pay his rent in cash over a post office counter. The counter clerk would detach the rent counterfoil from the book, date-stamp the remaining stub as a receipt and, at the end of the day the counterfoils were sent to Girobank, Bootle, where they would be used as input documents for posting to the local authority's account. Afterwards, a statement of account, showing payments in tenancy reference number order, together with the counterfoils, would be despatched to the local authority, who would use this information for updating their records.
3 A refinement of this service was the issue of the statement of account in magnetic tape form, for direct input to the local authority's computer, and the in-payment documents which had been previously microfilmed were destroyed.

Pilot operations to establish 'product effectiveness'

Test marketing to a few local authorities showed that there was considerable interest in this idea and, as a result, seminars were organised to cover all the United Kingdom. Afterwards, by reviewing the specific needs of a large number of housing departments, Girobank was able to develop other versions of the service which matched more precisely the existing collection services' requirements.

Long-term market development
Continuing sales pressure, through a mixture of direct selling and mailing and selective media advertising, has produced a market growth rate that would content any marketing director. As Table 6 shows, Girobank is now used by 160 local authorities and has become the largest rent collector in the UK, with an annual rent roll of £40 million.

Table 6. Growth of Girobank's rent collection service

	Local authorities using service (no.)	Total rents collected (£m)
1972	2	0.5
1973	35	5
1974	56	14
1975	85	18
1976	118	27
1977	129	30
1978	139	36
1979	160	40

Marketing home insurance through the trustee savings banks

The TSB is another conspicuous exception to the easy assumption that UK branch banking is synonymous with the familiar English and Scottish High Street names. Those with a taste for history will recall that the trustee savings banks were founded in Scotland in the early nineteenth century to provide a small savings medium at a time when the qualifying deposit of £10 for opening a joint stock bank account represented roughly one year's earnings for the average working man.

For many years the local trustee savings banks were virtually quasi-state savings banks dependent for a significant part of their investment income on a national Fund for the Banks for Savings, and substantially controlled by the National Debt Commissioners. But in 1973 the Page Committee to Review National Savings recommended that the TSBs, now co-ordinated by a Trustee Savings Banks Control Board, should be allowed to become a 'third force' in the banking world, provided that they could reduce their numbers from the then figure of seventy-three to less than twenty. In 1976, by which time the number of banks had been reduced to nineteen with a combined total of 1,655 branches, the Trustee Savings Bank Act enabled the organisation – which could best be described as a federation of banks – to compete for business with the other commercial banking chains.

One of the market segments which TSB management selected from the outset as a suitable target for their branch network and customer base was consumer credit. Home improvement loans, bridging finance and mortgages quickly followed – from which home-related insurance services were a short and logical step.

Life assurance presented few problems. The TSBs already marketed a mortgage protection plan through their unit trust and insurance subsidiary, the TSB Trust Company. Low-cost and full with-profits endowment contracts were comparatively simple additions to the product range for an established life assurance company.

Home insurance presented an opportunity of a different kind because the TSBs had little experience at that time of the direct marketing of high volume non-life insurance as a product in its own right.

The potential of the TSBs' eight-million customer base for insurance to cover buildings *and* contents had, of course, been recognised, and entry into the mortgage market provided the incentive to develop the product.

The development process fell into distinct stages as enumerated below.

1 Research

A considerable amount of research is available on home occupation, and from data relating to the banks' customer base, total market size and sales volumes were estimated, as a base for profit and expense forecasts.

The evaluation of products already on the market, including analysis of weaknesses, strengths, special features and, of course, price, was invaluable in the construction of a product specification.

Since the Trust Company had no power to underwrite non-life insurance, it was clear that the scheme would have to be under-written by another insurance company. Criteria for the selection of a suitable company were

nationwide representation to support a nationally known bank; absolute security;

willingness to consider the TSBs' specific requirements on their merits – many insurers were eliminated because of entrenched opposition to any change to their standard practice;

systems compatibility;

willingness to share development costs;

satisfactory terms.

2 Construction of product specification

Evaluation of available products, application of qualitative and attitudinal enquiries, and experience of the business, helped the writing of the outline product specifications. It was necessary to reconcile customer needs with those of the banks staffs who would be expected to sell the product. Fortunately, from the outset, it was clear that *simplicity* was a common feature. Customers, to begin with, complained of difficulty in understanding insurance. In particular, in a period of rapidly rising prices, the accepted basis of calculating sums insured attracted much criticism. People could not understand why property with a market value of, say, £30,000, had an insurance (replacement) value of £50,000, and why under-insurance penalties should apply to the insurance for £30,000.

Simplicity was also essential to busy bank staffs who do not have the time to acquire the specialised knowledge of an insurance broker. Without support at branches, the contract just would not sell.

The search for simplicity virtually defined the product, which was designed

to be sold in branches, by branch staff, who could explain in a few words what pages of brochures failed to make clear;

to provide straightforward 'standard' cover at a reasonable price; 'all risks' extensions were deliberately avoided as they would complicate training and could provoke resistance to the product;

to provide prompt settlement of claims, indicating a 'new for old' basis wherever possible.

Features of the product which followed naturally from the above included

a tabulation of minimum sums insured and premiums, based on careful research of costs of buildings and contents of various types and sizes of property in different regions;
the simplest of procedures, which enabled a policy to be issued on the spot;

premiums paid by unspecified amount direct debit mandate, to facilitate indexation; indexation preserves the purchasing power of the cover for the customer, and of the value of premiums for the bank; and direct debiting helps with retention of renewal business;

all administration, other than sale and issue of policy, handled by TSB Trust Company or insurers;

a simple brochure which drew attention to the way claims were paid; i.e. what the product *did* for the customer, rather than what the product *was*.

3 Negotiation of the contract
A shortlist of insurance companies was drawn up for final negotiations.

Earlier indifference by some companies was now translated into enthusiasm for a product which, it was clear from the research already described, could be sold in large volumes, of high quality, at low cost.

Satisfactory agreement was reached on remuneration and profit and cost sharing, product specifications, price and systems.

4 The launch

Throughout the development stages, reference had been made to representatives of regional bank marketing departments to ensure that the features of the product remained acceptable.

Procedure standards were prepared, together with attractive descriptive material for branch staffs, and delivered, with the relevant stationery, well in advance of the launch date.

The product was sufficiently novel to justify a press conference, and very considerable editorial space was given to the product by all sections of the press. Launch advertising was not, therefore, required – indicating the value of a planned press contact programme.

5 Maintaining sales

Most products have a 'life' during which sales decline from a peak; sales of TSB home insurance, however, are still increasing due to a mix of advertising, direct mail, and motivational and informative material directed at bank staffs. Business reports are produced at regular intervals for regional marketing managers to monitor the progress of their business development plans. Press interest in the product continues, and every opportunity is taken to obtain editorial coverage.

6 The 'cybernetic loop'

After research, development and launch, comes a review of results, which may lead to changes in the product.

The launch of TSB home insurance is regarded as successful because

sales (independent of associated mortgage business) are increasing after a good start;

new customers have been attracted to the bank by this product, and remain prospects for further cross-selling;

the product is applicable to all but a handful of the properties and customers for which it was designed;

pricing and calculation of minimum sums insured are broadly correct; 10 per cent of customers require more than the minimum cover;

procedures have proved to be simple;

the potential market for buildings insurance (free of mortgages) has been established at approximately 30 per cent of the total market by number of policies issued;

a demand for extensions of cover indicates that bank staffs have absorbed the product information more quickly than expected;

informed trade press comment has acknowledged that this development pointed the probable course of such business in future.

But of course, there are some features for which corrective action is necessary. These include

uneven geographic distribution of sales;
the need for further simplification of some wordings;
the need to streamline premium collection processes.

And so the cybernetic loop continues, spiralling upwards to the next change of market conditions and the next change of marketing tactics.

CHAPTER SIXTEEN

Marketing specialist services

It would be an exaggeration (or would it?) to say that the perceived role of the UK clearing banker has changed fundamentally over the past thirty years. In the immediate post-war years he was still basically a provider of 'conventional' banking services. He could advise at least some of his customers on any aspect of their financial affairs about which they chose to consult him. But he did not seek to provide all the corporate customers' financial services requirements; or to look after all the private customers' financial affairs from the cradle (or at least from school leaving age) to the grave and after. Now that the banker has become an employee of an expanding financial services conglomerate, consciously competing not just with other banks but also with a variety of different financial services organisations, he has to retain his integrity as an objective adviser to his customers; but at the same time he has an obligation to be fully informed about the non-banking or para-banking services which his organisation can provide, and, other things being equal, to steer his customers towards his own group's services rather than those offered by competitors. Ideally the customer should benefit from having his financial needs considered in the round; the banker should benefit from having a range of resources with which to satisfy those needs; and those responsible for marketing the various specialist services under the group's aegis should benefit from the link with the traditional banking system.

It is not our intention in this chapter to describe the marketing activities of each of the specialist departments or subsidiaries which are clustered together in the typical banking group. Insurance services, merchant banking, hire purchase, leasing, factoring, trustee services all tend to be separate profit centres with their individual marketing problems and objectives, but within defined corporate goals.

How far they should market their services direct, and how far through branches of the clearing banks with which they are associated, is a question which the responsible managers have to decide in the light of individual circumstances. Rather than attempt a superficial description of each situation, we propose to describe, first, a specialist service, the Access credit card, which was launched jointly by all but one of the clearing bank groups, and was more dependent for its success than other specialist services on close co-operation with the banking side; and, second, a farm loan service, which was launched by one of the major clearing banks independently of its branch network.

Access pre-launch marketing activities

We have emphasised in the various parts of this book that the success of any marketing operation is largely dependent on the preparatory work that is done before the new product or service is launched, in market research, the definition of marketing strategy, detailed pre-planning and preparation of the required back-up services. The launch of the Access card was no exception to this rule.

Market research and analysis
The first plastic cards in the UK were T & E (Travel and Entertainment) cards. The first well-known name, Diners, was launched in 1963, followed by American Express which entered the UK market in 1966. Neither offered credit, though some customers took it.

The first UK credit card with an extended credit facility was Barclaycard, which was launched by Barclays Bank in June 1966 with an initial base of 1 million card-holders and 30,000 retail outlets. (Barclays Bank, in fact, naturalised in the UK the blue, white and gold card scheme of Bank Americard, now called VISA worldwide.)

Throughout the 1960s the other clearing banks were studying the market and observing Barclaycard's mounting progress.

By about 1970, the five key factors listed below were emerging from the market studies.

1 Barclaycard had begun to penetrate the current accounts of the other banks; just under 20 per cent (250,000) of the card-holders did not bank with Barclays.
2 Research showed a clear profit potential for a scheme with as many card-holders as Barclaycard.
3 Market research indicated strong resistance among retailers to each bank introducing its own credit card scheme.
4 There would be significant economies of scale if the banks were to enter the market on some kind of a joint basis.
5 Finally, the other banks took the view that there was room in the UK market for only *two viable* general-purpose cards.

As a result a somewhat unusual event occurred. Lloyds, Midland and National Westminster Banks, who are in competition with each other, formed a joint working party to examine the possibilities of launching a common credit card. In 1971 a joint press release was issued by these banks, stating that they would launch such a card in September or October 1972; and that a common service company would be formed, which is now known as The Joint Credit Card Company. Before the launch Williams & Glyn's Bank also joined the Access set-up.

The basic marketing tasks
With this commitment there were four basic marketing tasks to be accomplished during the pre-launch period:

1 to recruit 3 million card-holders;
2 to recruit 60,000 retail outlets;
3 to create the advertising and promotional platform and pro-gramme for the launch;
4 to select a name for the new credit card (Access was chosen after duly diligent research).

Just as important as the four marketing tasks was the task of establishing the necessary computer operation facilities. This went on in parallel with the marketing activities.

Advertising and promotion
All the appropriate media for delivering persuasive messages to

potential or existing customers, such as press advertising, leaflets and direct mail were considered, as also were the point-of-sale support materials, such as display material in shops.

What had to be recognised was that the new card-holders in most cases would have had no previous experience of using a credit card; so their knowledge and acceptance of the benefits to be gained from intelligent use of the card would be low. The prime task of the advertising and promotion would be to encourage use both of the card itself and of the extended credit facility which it represented.

Analysis of the consumer research, supplemented by creative imagination, suggested that the intangible concepts of instant finance and flexible repayment could be made more tangible when expressed in terms of the things that people want and of when they want them.

Things have a value over and above their intrinsic worth – the value which is conferred on them by being available at a particular time; they can be more valuable at certain times than at others – what was called 'the time utility of money'. A refrigerator, for example, tends to be more valuable in summer than in winter, and a family holiday is more valuable when the children are on holiday from school than two months later. And winter clothes must be bought in good time, even if, say, a car repair bill arises suddenly.

The new credit card, it was concluded, could provide access to things when they are needed, when they are most valuable. From this, and involving the name of the new credit card, came the launch slogan 'Access takes the waiting out of wanting.'

Execution of the marketing plan

While the basic thinking was being done on the advertising and promotional approach and on the name of the new card, preparatory work was being done in the two recruitment areas: card-holders and retailers.

Card-holder recruitment
This was carried out in four stages.

1 The Access department sent each branch of the collaborating banks selection criteria for new card-holders with a suggested target figure.

2 Each branch supplied a list of potential card-holders, with proposed credit limits assigned to each name.
3 The bank's Access department analysed these lists and made the final decision on which current account customers should be offered an Access card.
4 After the basic advertising theme had been agreed, an introductory mailing kit was created and assembled, to include the new credit card. The objectives of this mailing were
  (a) to provide the necessary explanatory details of the new service to the card-holder;
  (b) to encourage use of the new facility through the 'Access takes the waiting out of wanting' theme.

Retail recruitment
This essential task was entrusted to a brand new salesforce set up by the Joint Credit Card Company Ltd. Because Access was going to be a financial service offered by the banks to their customers, it was decided to recruit the salesforce from bank staff. An establishment of 145 salesmen and sales managers was agreed on.

By January 1972, nine months before the launch date to which the original three banks had publicly committed themselves, the salesforce was ready to go.

Outcome of the launch phase
One month before the stated launch date the target of 60,000 retail outlets had been exceeded; 70,000 had been signed up. The final figure could have been still higher, but the retail recruitment programme was stopped at this point, for fear that the computer operations centre would not be able to cope with the volume of business generated by a larger retail base.

The target of 3 million card-holders was also exceeded by half a million. Moreover, the initial use of the card, thanks to the way in which the concept had been sold, was considerably higher than had been expected.

Access – the follow-up

So far so good. But just as important as a successful launch in any marketing operation (if not more so), are the various follow-up stages, including adjustment to changes in

> the economic environment;
> government restrictions on credit cards;
> increased understanding and experience of the credit card industry.

Four phases, in retrospect, were important.

1　The launch period 1972–73

The banks, as it turned out, were lucky in the period chosen to launch the Access card. It coincided with the height of the Barber boom, when consumer financial confidence, expenditure and demand were at a record level. The white-collar section of the public at which Access was aimed (60 per cent of card-holders are ABC1s, who represent around one third of the general population) was in a receptive mood to be told of the availability of instant finance for large purchases, linked to the flexible repayment facility. And it was appropriate that the advertisements should be deliberately designed to appear luxurious, featuring high-value merchandise.

2　The post-launch period 1974–76

Towards the end of 1973 the Barber boom collapsed. In November the government announced an emergency budget which had the basic objective of reducing the money supply. The most directly significant elements of this budget for the credit card industry were the imposition of two restrictions to become effective on 1 January 1974. These were:

> 15 per cent minimum repayment on the amount owing on each statement (up from the initial 5 per cent), with a minimum repayment of £15 (up from £5);

> £30 maximum cash advance; down from the open flexibility of the launch agreement.

This change of climate and legislation meant that the very successful launch campaign had to be abandoned. The only property of the credit card that could be promoted in the new circumstances was its convenience as a method of payment. Only very minor emphasis could be given to the flexible repayment feature.

The level of advertising expenditure was substantially reduced. It was not expected that the campaigns would have the same impact as the launch campaign. But in retrospect it appears that the advertising was less effective than it might have been, even allowing for the reduced expenditure, because of the lack of singlemindedness: three different campaigns in as many years are more likely to confuse than to penetrate the public consciousness.

3 The readjustment period 1977–78.

Towards the end of 1976 the attitude of the government and the Bank of England towards *responsible* promotion of the major purchase facility offered by the credit card showed signs of softening. In the changed circumstances a new campaign was devised to illustrate the fact that an extended credit facility, if used responsibly, could bring tangible economic benefits.

The advertisements illustrated the cost of high-value merchandise and showed that, including the interest charge on repayments spread over six, nine or twelve months, there could be significant savings for card-holders using the credit facility to make a cash purchase. The campaign was supported by yet another slogan 'Access makes the most of your money.'

By the end of 1977 inflation was declining and wage increases were resulting in the first real gain in consumer buying-power since the Barber boom. Restrictions on money supply were relaxed and, in the April 1978 budget, credit card restrictions were lifted. Once again there was a new economic situation, requiring a new promotional approach. As there was new market research information indicating that through ignorance or timidity, many card-holders were not getting the full benefit of the facilities the card represented, the campaign consisted of advertisements with dramatic illustrations such as a birdcage with an Access card on the perch, captioned 'If you let it out will it fly away with you?' The campaign's basic aim, to reduce card-holders' fear of using the card, was underwritten by the slogan 'Use Access to make the most of your money.'

4 A new approach – 1979 onwards

There is always a danger that advertising which illustrates a fear in order to allay it will simply enhance it. In 1979, with yet another change in the economic climate, and with inflation once again gathering momentum and consumers uncertain how to react to the combination of reduced direct taxation and increased taxation on purchases, the Access marketing team took the view that while the fear certainly existed, a more positive and reassuring approach to allaying it was preferable. Following a change of advertising agency, another cartoon character was developed, this time a friendly Mr Access discussing with Mr Money the advantages of using Access and the convenient method of payment.

Developments on the sales side

While the marketing and promotional side was trying to adjust to changing economic circumstances, the Access salesforce was able to follow a rather more consistent course. For the salesmen the year following the launch, 1973, was something of an anticlimax. The intensive recruitment effort of the previous year was replaced by a predominantly servicing role, and the lion's share of salesmen's time in 1973 was spent in calling back on retail outlets signed up in the previous year as a servicing, consolidation and public relations exercise. Call sheets were completed which sought retailer reaction to questions about the efficiency of the Access service, whether retailers were happy with the level of business transacted, and so on. Display material was replaced where necessary and any problems in the operation of the system relating to sales voucher stocks, the imprinting machines and so on, were dealt with.

In 1974 a start was made with broadening the retail base for Access into less obvious sectors. A special services section of the salesforce was set up to expand credit card activity in the rapidly growing mail order market; to research, approach and recruit the major insurance underwriters; and to develop Access business in the holiday and travel trades.

Since 1974 other 'non-standard' service industries have been recruited, such as rating authorities, water boards, home fuel distributors, the professional services, opticians, dentists, and others; and the salesforce has been required to absorb an increasing range of retailer/service product knowledge, as well as developing tailor-made sales approaches for the very varied categories of 'buyer'.

By 1979 the salesforce had settled down to a role which involved not simply servicing the collaborating retailers but stimulating them to more positive efforts on behalf of Access. Staff training sessions are organised for retailers and specific trade promotions are undertaken, featuring both card-holder and retailer incentives. Town centre events are organised, including window display competitions, and personalised promotions have been arranged with individual retailer chains. How far these activities contribute to increased use of Access cards is difficult to quantify; but there can be no doubt that, when combined with regular calling on the more important outlets, they help to maintain an active interest in the scheme.

Forecasting Access turnover

The Joint Credit Card Company's marketing department has been exceptionally successful in the difficult task of forecasting turnover. The starting point for their work was the premise that aggregate card-holder expenditure must relate to national expenditure patterns. So consumer expenditure forecasts, to the extent that they are reliable, should be translatable into Access turnover forecasts.

A theoretical problem in relating Access turnover to consumer spending arose from the much more rapid growth rate of the Access population. This was dealt with by ignoring the very small UK population growth and adjusting the Access data by the number of card-holders who used their Access cards each month. Various comparisons were tried by simple graph-plotting techniques and as a result the following historical relationship was identified:

$$T/O \div DA \div H = K$$

Where:

T/O = Turnover for quarter (sales *plus* cash advances *less* returns).

DA = Total for three months of the number of 'debit actives' – i.e. persons who used their Access card counted month by month.

H = Henley Centre for Forecasting's estimate of consumer spending. (This is essentially the same measure as the CSO 'Consumer Expenditure' series; except that it is not subject to such large revisions, and also is foreast by the Centre for the future twelve–eighteen months ahead.)

K   = A factor which, if the relationship is to be useful, should be constant from quarter to quarter.

From this historical relationship the forecasting model shown below was arrived at. The model of course can only respond to changes in consumer spending and is bound to deviate significantly when external factors (for example, changes in VAT) intervene to upset the spending pattern. Apart from such occasions, forecasts derived from the model have proved generally accurate, as shown in Table 7.

Forecasting model

$$H \times Kn \times DAE = T/O\ ESTIMATE$$

Where:

H   = Henley estimate for consumer spending.

Kn   = The 'K' factor from the historical relationship (as in the foregoing) averaged for the same quarter of each year to give four separate 'K' factors, one for each quarter.

DAE = Debit active estimate (based on a seasonally adjusted linear regression method which has been shown to be reliable).

T/O ESTIMATE   = Estimate of turnover, in a quarter.

In 1980 the model is used by the marketing division of the Joint Credit Card Company Ltd., both for forecasting Access turnover and for sales targeting purposes. With inflation once again rapidly increasing, the basic calculation is done on deflated turnover and consumer spending, and then reflated according to the most likely projection for inflation. And of course, having discovered this 'law', it becomes possible to calculate retrospectively the effect of various events (such as the relaxing of restrictions in 1978) and thus to learn more about the environment in which Access operates, with a consequent improvement in management control.

Table 7. Forcast turnover less actual turnover as a percentage of actual

Quarters	1975	1976	1977	1978	1979
I	−0.3	−1.7	+0.7	+2.0	+3.4
II	−4.3*	+0.9	+2.8	−4.5†	−10.0*
III	+1.8	−1.4	−0.3	−7.5†	−3.2
IV	−1.3	−1.6	+3.8	+1.8	−7.1
Total‡	−1.0	−1.0	+1.9	−1.1	− 4.8

* Advance notice was given of increases in VAT
† Repayment restrictions were lifted
‡ i.e. the weighted average of the four quarters

Marketing loans to farmers

A much simpler example of marketing a specialist service was the programme developed by one of the large clearing banks in 1978-79 for marketing farm loans. This was not in essence a new or unique 'product' (all banks as a rule look favourably on loan applications from farmers, an exceptionally credit-worthy section of the community). But the way the loan facility was presented and marketed was a departure from the traditional practice of leaving it mainly to branch managers to identify and satisfy the loan requirements of their farmer customers.

Pre-launch activities
The project originated in the autumn of 1978, when the bank's agricultural office discussed with the marketing department the need for a readily accessible source of finance for farmers and growers. In the new spirit of inter-bank competition, the finance should be made available, it was felt, to the customers of other banks as well as those of the originating bank; and the facility should be brought actively to the attention of farmers, instead of waiting for the farmers to apply.

Development of the product idea

Putting together the agricultural office's knowledge of farmers' needs and the marketing department's promotional expertise, it was agreed that the main features of the new product should be *simplicity* and *flexibility*.

With these basic requirements in mind it was decided to take a leaf out of the book of the finance companies in their hire purchase dealings with garages and make the country's major agricultural merchants sales agents for the loan product. They would benefit by having a line of credit to offer their customers and also by getting immediate cash once a deal had been completed; the farmers would have the benefit of being able to buy when they needed to, on the best terms, without waiting for the cash to accumulate.

Loans from £500 upwards would be made available through merchants for the purchase of

> fertiliser, seed and agrichemicals;
> dairy and other stock requirements including feed;
> horticultural requirements;
> farm and horticultural equipment;
> tillage and general machinery;
> related storage buildings;
> fuels;
> livestock;
> contractors' services.

The loans would be unsecured, subject to approval by the bank's agricultural managers, and a flexible repayment programme could be worked out over a period of up to three years to suit the cash flow of the individual agricultural or horticultural business.

The product was christened NatWest GrowCash.

Development of terms and conditions

Bank marketers know only too well that a new financial services product is doomed to failure unless the terms are at least as good as those offered by competitors, and conform with the bank's own policies; and the internal administrative arrangements have been thought through and organised. So, before the terms and conditions of the loan proposition were finalised, competitive offerings were analysed and internal policies and procedures worked out with those who would be responsible for the approval of loan applications and the processing of repayments.

It was agreed that farmers should be given the option of repayment over a period of up to three years either by equal monthly or quarterly instalments or by fixed sums at irregular intervals, specified by the farmer in advance. The farmer would be given the choice of three different interest rates:

$1\frac{1}{4}$ per cent per month fixed for the whole of the agreed period if repayments made monthly (commencing the month after delivery of goods);

$1\frac{1}{2}$ per cent per month fixed for the whole of the agreed period if repayments made quarterly or at irregular intervals;

3 per cent over base rate per annum, fluctuating with the market, with either monthly, quarterly or irregular repayments.

An application form was designed, incorporating a direct debit mandate, for the merchant's farming customers to fill out. This gave basic information about the farming or horticultural activity for which the loan was required, and of the purchases on which the money would be spent, in sufficient detail to enable the bank's agricultural office to process the application. A proposal form was designed for leasing and lease purchase, the methods by which GrowCash finances the acquisition of heavy machinery and buildings. And a simple form-letter was provided for the merchant to forward applications to the bank, giving any supporting information about his trading experience with the customer concerned.

The market launch
This featured a teaser campaign in the farming press, directed at merchants and farmers, announcing 'NatWest GrowCash, financial ground to grow on' as a forthcoming service to be offered by the bank. At the same time a short-term twenty-five-man salesforce, comprising five bank staff and twenty professional salesmen, was recruited and given two days' indoctrination in the product before being despatched in the following month to call on selected

agricultural merchants in the country. The salesmen were equipped with sales kits, including application forms, explanatory leaflets, copies of the advertising and point of sale display material.

In October, when the salesmen were on the road, the main advertising began. This was based on double-page colour spreads in the farming press, describing the highlights of 'NatWest GrowCash, a new financial service designed specifically for farmers and growers', and urging readers either to see their merchant about the scheme or write for a free copy of the descriptive brochure.

Additional promotional activities included representation at the Smithfield show and a press party organised by the bank's public affairs department.

The outcome
Two months after the launch the bank will say only that early results are most encouraging and that provision is being made for follow-up support. This is likely to include a small permanent service team of bank people, working out of the agricultural office and making business development calls on co-operating merchants. The bank's branch managers will be kept informed of developments, and, who knows, may pick up some new customers.

CHAPTER SEVENTEEN

Marketing internationally

Trade, it is commonly said, follows the flag. And close on the heels of trade follows the need for banking services. Historically, British banking had a unique and eagerly accepted opportunity to market financial services not only in the quarter of the globe that was coloured red but in parts of the world like South America which were opened up with British capital.

Needless to say times have changed. British banking retains an enviable reputation internationally and the invisible income from financial services contributes handsomely to our balance of payments. But, as the Union Jack is hauled down in one territory after another, and the UK's share of international trade continues to shrink, the game is no longer cricket but what the Americans would describe as 'another ball game'. No longer is international banking a relatively comfortable business of providing facilities for expansionist British firms and teaching the locals the rules of the game through overseas offices and correspondent banks. It is on the contrary a fiercely competitive business in which the British banker, operating from the base of a shaky economy has few competitive advantages apart from his inherited reputation and professional skills.

That these skills were in need of some readjustment was brought home to the industry over the last twenty years when international banks from all over the world dramatically increased their hitherto modest establishment of offices and branches in the UK and embarked on aggressive selling policies to win a share of the financial services market. In the personal market they have not been particularly successful, apart from those which aimed primarily for an ethnic clientele. The experiment in money shops, for example, tried by one or two of the American banks was far from being a conspicuous success.

However, in the corporate market, which was the primary target of most of them, the combination of very positive selling, highly competitive rates and the claim of special advantages on their home ground has seen results that are almost as painful for the British banker as the comparable efforts of overseas car manufacturers are for the British automobile industry. Some 30 per cent of corporate loans in the UK are now made by foreign banks.

There had to be a counter-attack if British-based banking was to continue as a growth industry. The counter-attack has been two-pronged. The first prong has been the defensive one of concentrating sales and marketing effort in the UK on the customer categories most at risk through the creation of corporate finance departments, specialist sales teams, and so on. This appears to have succeeded in holding the foreign banks' share of UK corporate business at the 30 per cent level.

The second prong has been to carry the battle into the enemy's camp by using more selective and aggressive business development methods overseas to gain a larger share not simply of British-originated international business but of the business that was open to bids by allcomers. This too has been successful, to the extent that the international divisions are the fastest growing sectors of the main British banks; and that British banking overall leads in, for example, the highly competitive Euro-currency market.

It must be confessed that the tools and techniques of marketing have not as yet been used as extensively on the international side as in domestic banking. This may be partly because the techniques developed in the marketing of consumer products are more obviously relevant to personal than to corporate banking (just as marketing has made less progress among industrial manufacturers than among the producers of consumer goods). In part, perhaps, it can be attributed to the evident need for an entrepreneurial approach and decisiveness in the international sector, which appears to be (though need not be in reality) inconsistent with the more methodical approach favoured by the marketing man. However this may be, the value of the marketing capability on the international side, adapted to the special conditions which prevail in that sector, is increasingly accepted. Here, for example, is the way a marketing department has taken shape in one of the Big Four clearing banks, which at one time was less committed than some of the others to international development.

As must always be the case with a staff department, the international marketing department was set up as a support to the main streams of line management; its ultimate success will depend more on the relationship it establishes with them than on the quantity and quality of marketing documents to which it gives birth.

The most important streams it has to support are

1 the market managers responsible for developing business in designated parts of the world through overseas branches and correspondent banks;
2 the international offices or units responsible for handling the international business (other than routine transactions) of domestic banking customers at regional level;
3 the international finance executives responsible for selling the services of the international division direct to large UK companies (both customers and non-customers of the domestic bank). This of course involves close liaison with the corporate finance division of the domestic bank, and cannot ignore the larger branches with customers having potential international business.

In order to support these activities the division has set up six inter-connected sections:

> market information
> market research
> market analysis
> marketing plans
> product development
> market development.

Unlike some of its competitors this international marketing division disposes of its own advertising budget; and it is also very actively involved in training international finance executives and others in effective selling and other marketing techniques.

It should be emphasised that this organisational structure

describes the chosen solution of one particular international division at a particular stage in its development. Other banks have adopted different solutions to deal with very similar problems; and it is by no means improbable that this bank also will change its marketing organisation as the market environment and the needs of line managers within the organisation evolve. There is no ideal organisational structure that will serve for all time.

Let us now turn our attention to a further three examples, provided by another bank, of the way marketing has sought, successfully or unsuccessfully, to meet the needs of line management as part of a total management developing strategy.

Using overseas market research

The first example is in fact that rarity among published case histories; not a success story but a failure story. It describes an unsuccessful attempt to utilise the results of external market research and translate them into specific business strategies for an international bank.

Background

Professional market research is used extensively by companies involved in the manufacture and marketing of industrial and consumer products. These firms either employ their own staff to undertake research or commission specialist independent research organisations to do the fieldwork and analysis for them. The reports from market research are used to determine the relative strength of a particular product *vis-à-vis* competitors, or to assess the attitudes of existing or potential customers.

The picture for the financial services industry is somewhat different. External market research *is* used by banks and other financial institutions involved in *personal* finance (bank accounts, credit payments, investments and insurance), because they need to sample the habits and perceptions of large groups of people across all social and economic classifications. In the area of *corporate* or wholesale banking the number of customers is much smaller and the type of relationship very different.

Example

The bank in question wished to expand its marketing efforts in North America. Market research was proposed as a useful source of relevant data to aid the development of strategy for this key market.

The bank had an established market presence in North America with offices in New York and several other key locations in the United States and Canada. Relationships existed with several major US multi-national companies, but the level of business was modest and the majority of it involved routine foreign exchange transactions and short-term finance. It was part of the bank's declared objectives to increase penetration amongst US multi-nationals in respect of its medium-term lending and specialist financial advisory services. If there was shown to be a potential market for a non-US bank to offer these types of services to US multi-nationals on a *worldwide basis* it would clearly be worthwhile to make the necessary investment in staff and marketing support activities as part of an expansion of North American business. This would enable the bank to market its specialised services more aggressively.

The market

US multi-national companies represent a particularly attractive and growing business target for all major banks. With their world-wide basis of operations they demand a sophisticated level of service from their banks which often involves a willingness to be innovative in introducing new financing techniques to match the growth of the customer's business in both value and complexity.

Market research available

The type of research most applicable to this market is the 'multi-client study'. As its name implies it is research carried out on behalf of more than one client. In the United States several research companies offer these services to financial institutions. In this particular example the organisation offered not only the results of its comprehensive interviews with senior financial executives of over 300 major US multi-nationals, but consultancy time with the bank to interpret the research more specifically for future marketing strategy.

Claimed benefits of the research

In selling their services, the market research company stressed the following major benefits:

1 an objective report on the bank's market share and competitive position in banking with the American multi-nationals, including year-to-year trend data;
2 knowledge of how the multi-nationals view over sixty competitor banks who service their needs;
3 information on how many of the companies interviewed would expect to add the bank to the list of banks they use for international services; and, equally important, how many are anticipating adding competitor banks;
4 knowledge of how the executives of multi-national companies evaluate the bank *and all other major banks;* with this bank-by-bank information the client bank could sharpen its competitive strategy for this major market.

Response of the bank

Executives of the bank were favourably impressed by the staff of the research company and the claimed benefits resulting from participation. Enthusiasm was shared equally between the US-based staff and the London-based functions dealing with the specialised lending and advisory services. The types of companies being inter-viewed were just those to whom the bank wished to market these services; many were either existing customers or target solicitations. If there were any doubts they centred on the practical uses to which the information could be applied. But the bank was willing to test the water.

Problems arise

In the four months that elapsed between agreement by the bank to participate in the research and presentation of the results, difficulties ensued.

First, there was pressure on the marketing department to produce recommendations regarding business development in North

America. The market research findings were clearly crucial to an evaluation of the market and assessment of the bank's competitive position.

The second difficulty was that the research findings were delayed by over a month.

Reaction to the research

The research reports duly arrived in the form of two weighty volumes of analysis and comment. While it was possible to isolate rapidly references to particular banks, it would take some time to evaluate the data against existing information on progress in North America.

Questions were immediately asked by senior management as to the evidence in the research about the demand for particular services amongst particular companies, and it became clear to the marketing department that too much was being expected from this type of study. Because of the desire to 'sell' this kind of research within the bank, too little emphasis was placed on the limitations of such studies. Although the 'multi-client study' technique offers a cost-effective way of participating in a complex, large-scale investigation involving some 500 hours of interviewing, it is not flexible in permitting individual banks to introduce their own choice of questions to be asked. The questionnaire design is dictated by the research organisation, and clients purchase the report as written. Therefore, the questions asked at senior level within the bank could not be answered from the research data. Because the research was late in arriving it failed to contribute to an urgent review of strategy for business development in North America. This led, almost inevitably, to a reluctance to utilise the follow-up consultancy which would have benefited both the bank and the research company and which had already been paid for.

An opportunity for a specific piece of external market research to prove the value of such expenditure had been lost due to over-expectation and an unfortunate time constraint on information input.

Lessons to be learned

Very often there is more to be learned from a failure than from a success. In this case, the bank's main conclusions were as follows.

1 The marketing department should ensure that the senior management of the bank who approve the expenditure on this type of research are more fully briefed as to the limitations as well as the benefits of multi-client studies. This would avoid there being too great an expectation, with consequent disappointment when two fat volumes of data do not answer everyone's questions.

2 Research such as this is only worthwhile if there is a commitment at the highest level within the bank not only to paying for desirable information but to incorporating the results into overall marketing strategy. True benefit will only accrue to the bank if outside research is valued as part of a more detailed analysis of the market place and especially competitor activity. Having this data on a 'nice to know what we already know' basis is wasted money and effort.

3 Working with market research consultants to interpret the findings of the report for *the particular bank* demands that the management of the bank take the consultants into their confidence and discuss with them alternative strategies in the light of the information available.

Implementing the key customer concept

The second example is of interest because the principle it sets out is widely applicable.

'So far as I am concerned all customers are equally important to me' is a fine-sounding statement that falls not infrequently from managers' lips. But it is no way to run a business. The harsh fact is that even very large businesses are usually dependent for a high proportion of their revenue on a small proportion of their customers; and it would be folly not to allocate to those customers the amount of selling and servicing effort which their importance merits. Hence the familiar marketing concept of the key customer list. This example describes how the concept was applied in an international banking context.

Background

The concept of 'key customers' has been operative within this particular international bank for the last five years. During that time it has been refined and an information system has been created to support the marketing objectives.

Why is the concept needed?

At the local branch level overseas of a major international bank it is a relatively straightforward matter for *local* management to order their priorities amongst *local* organisations with which they have or wish to have a banking relationship. It is reflected in greater frequency of contact, with specific visits to discuss prospects and financing needs. The local branch manager can justify the efforts made by his staff in terms of loans on the books; and of the contribution made towards both the total of accounts held and also towards profits for the bank.

But what happens when the approach for help comes not direct from a prominent local company, but via another branch of the bank which has a good relationship with a major multi-national corporation? This corporation wishes to avail itself of local finance in a country where at present it has only a small operation which has not come to the notice of the original branch of the bank. Although the bank is naturally anxious to pursue such business there is the distinct possibility of a conflict of loyalties. The local branch will be reluctant to commit scarce funds in the form of local currency to a previously unknown borrower; they would prefer to keep these scarce funds for valued local customers. The executive handling the headquarters account of the multi-national will obviously think very differently. Who is correct? Should such conflicts require the intervention of senior regional or head office management to arbitrate between competing customer demands?

One answer which works for many international banks is the key customer concept. This is as much a philosophy of approach as it is a marketing technique. It involves building into the responses of marketing officers an awareness of the significance which *the bank as a whole* attaches to major international clients, who may be dominant in some markets, modestly represented in others, and still altogether without a presence in some countries.

How does it work in practice?

In the example under discussion the approach to the operation of a key customer system was communicated widely throughout the bank by means of a detailed memorandum. Some extracts are given below.

Selection of names for key customer status

The selection was made by the banking directors, meeting as the marketing committee; they have chosen the names from the lists of target customers submitted by the divisions with the following criteria in mind:

1 customers with a high potential for increasing low-risk profitable business over the next few years at least;
2 customers needing a broad range of services which we can provide competitively;
3 customers growing in activities in those areas where we are expanding our business; for example, Middle East, Far East, North America;
4 customers with growing requirements for specific services which we are emphasising.

Priority throughout the bank

It is logical that if priority is given at parent company level to key customers, so it must be given at all other divisional, circuit and branch levels. The objectives of a careful selection of a small number of names for business development will not be attained unless all concerned make a special effort to attend to banking opportunities, correspondence, contact and evaluation reports on these names. It follows that there is an implication that branches will have on occasions to commit scarce currency or scarce executive time to key customers. The question of scarce country exposure will sometimes also arise. These matters are being further examined in head office but the following guidelines will assist now:

1 we should endeavour to meet all requests from key customers at least to the level they can expect from our competitors;
2 if there is conflict with any other claim on these resources, the key customer will normally be preferred;
3 we should try to satisfy the customer's needs from other friendly sources if we cannot fill them ourselves, with, whenever possible, some benefit to the bank;
4 when we must decline to help, every effort must be made to ensure the customer willingly accepts our failure to supply the service, and a report with explanations must be sent on the business declined to the controlling division with copies to head office.

It is emphasised that the list is a 'live' one and names may be dropped and new names added by decision of the marketing committee if, after a period, targets are achieved or results are not as expected. It is not however anticipated that the total number of key customers will be appreciably increased.

It is important that full information is collected centrally on current activities of the bank with these names, together with other general information to aid ultimate selection by the marketing committee of names for special key customer treatment.

We are anxious to ensure that other customers, major and minor, are not 'downgraded' by this exercise. All target customers are, by definition, vital to the bank's future, and, since the bank must increase the volume of its customer business over the coming years, the continuing selection process will be pointing to the *best potential* in a vast number of possible international customers. What is therefore now being requested is no diminution of efforts towards our international customers in general, rather a special emphasis on a small number of prime targets.

Organisation and training for overseas business development

It is a marketing axiom that the secret of successful marketing is to have 'the right product in the right place at the right time'. In the people 'business' of banking, it is equally important to have the right people (with the right training and expertise) in the right place at the right time. This third example describes how the same international bank, which already had overseas representation in over forty countries, and a reservoir of in-house expertise and close contact with other financial institutions in its London headquarters, went about expanding its specialised medium-term lending and financial advisory services to governments and major corporations worldwide.

The approach taken

The systematic approach, developed by the bank over a period of two years, involved three elements:

1 building on existing branch structure overseas;

2 improving knowledge of overseas staff in respect of the specialist services offered by the bank;

3 placing specialist bankers overseas (in certain circumstances).

Details of the three elements

1 Existing branch structure overseas

The initial response to the problem was to expand the services available within the *existing* branch structure of the bank in the main countries overseas. This was achieved by having the head office specialist bankers play the role of *advisers* to local bank branch management. This route was chosen in preference to the setting up of a parallel team of specialists in each major locality under some such title as 'international banking services' or 'merchant banking services'. The major advantages of this approach were that

it built on existing strengths and local market knowledge;

it enhanced the range of services marketed by existing staff (as a by-product it also enhanced the *status* of local personnel);

it avoided costly duplication of physical and financial resources.

2 Improving the knowledge of overseas staff

This particular bank recognised only too well that in order to improve marketing *to customers* it was essential to improve *internal* marketing amongst its own executives. In other words it needed to train its overseas staff in new concepts and types of services. The strategy of advising local staff was supported by formal training programmes to bring non-specialist calling officers and senior branch management up to date with the latest techniques in, for example, the financing of capital projects and trade financing. The sums involved in these transactions regularly exceed £100 million for a single deal, somewhat outside the range of normal corporation banking. The second major topic at these training courses, usually held in London and lasting for about a week, was the respective roles of the specialist and line management in marketing specialised international banking services. The position taken can be summarised as follows.

(a) Role of the 'man in the field'
(i) Identification of business opportunities;
(ii) initial customer contact to obtain more details;
(iii) decision on when to alert specialist in head office in London;
(iv) maintenance of continuity in any subsequent negotiations between customer and specialist bankers;
(v) follow-up negotiations in an attempt to obtain ancillary business for the local branch;
(vi) monitor results.

(b) Role of head office specialist
(i) Contribute to practical training of local personnel in basic details of specialist services currently available;
(ii) keep local management informed of *international* developments which may affect their area/customers;
(iii) respond quickly to indications of specific business opportunities;
(iv) be willing to visit local market to follow up positive leads;
(v) involve local staff in any negotiations with customers or potential customers; not only as a courtesy, but as a means of educating them and providing for further introductions to similar business opportunities;
(vi) follow up visits with firm proposals to local customer;
(vii) maintain contact with local branch to ensure smooth running of negotiations and adequate follow-up.

3 Placing specialist bankers overseas
Despite the basic philosophies outlined in headings (a) and (b) above, there were certain key areas overseas for this bank where it was appropriate to place a specialist banker on detachment from head office in London, *but* still reporting within the branch network so as to maximise internal co-operation.

The main justifications for this expensive exercise in limited 'decentralisation' were

(a) need to operate effectively in geographic time-zones remote from easy day-to-day contact with London (for example, California, Singapore);
(b) intensity of competition from local bank and other international

banks with on–the–spot representation;
(c) evidence of significant potential for specialist banking services.

Such overseas specialist personnel obviously made the tasks of the organisation under headings 1 and 2 above that much easier by being a focal point for information and marketing activity.

CHAPTER EIGHTEEN

The bank of the future

When peering into the future of an industry it is usual, and useful, to start by picking out the various factors which can be expected to have significant influences on it. For this chapter, eight such factors have been selected (illustrated diagrammatically in Fig. 7) and each of them will be discussed separately. To do this is, of course, to over-simplify, since changes in one factor may well have a bearing on the direction or intensity of changes in another. But this is a book about marketing, not futurology, and in this chapter we discuss only a selection of those changes which could have a major impact on the structure and practices of banks. Moreover, we have confined our vision to the UK – the opportunities and pressures in markets overseas will significantly widen the range of options available to the banks.

We also have refrained from progressing to the second stage of prophecy, which is deducing from an analysis of influential factors the likely future shape of organisations within the industry. We leave this to the reader for two reasons. First, we would undoubtedly be wrong – a fate that is anathema to the authors of a textbook. Second, in any competitive situation the policies adopted by one organ-isation, in reaction to a given set of circumstances, are likely to differ in material respects from those adopted by another very similar organisation. Both solutions, in their different ways, may be right; but they will be different.

The eight factors chosen as relevant to future bank structures and practices are those that seem most important to us. Readers no doubt will not only think of others, but also have their own views on the changes likely in the eight. Furthermore, some key areas (for

Fig. 7. Eight factors affecting the future of UK banks

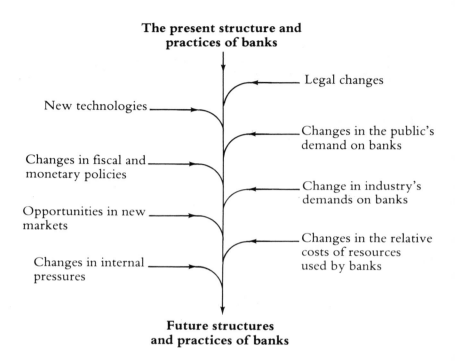

example, decisions within the EEC and its associated authorities) will influence many of our factors, but are not themselves discussed explicitly here. So the 'model' is not very comprehensive, but it will serve to structure our thinking about the future; it can be thought of as a sketch map of where we are going, but not as a detailed ordnance survey of the area.

We can now examine each of these influences in turn. We will assume that the present structure and practices of the banking industry are sufficiently well-known to readers not to need any great elaboration here. It is in essence an industry which consists of multi-product companies (with all the pricing and cross-subsidy problems that this brings); the industry has a large degree of vertical integration, especially in the domestic sector; has a quite exceptional range of customers and 'order size', from junior savers to multi-national corporations; is subject to a large degree of control (or, as some see it, interference) from central government; but nevertheless has intense competition from within the industry, including competition from government-aided companies and other institutions which enjoy preferences of one sort or another. Above all it is an industry of giants; little independent banks disappeared generations ago.

Legal changes

The current trend towards greater consumer protection, if continued, seems unlikely to alter the structure much, though it obviously will affect banking practices. Just as the Consumer Credit Act imposes constraints on where small loans may be discussed (thereby in general limiting *a* branch to *the* branch – to the exclusion of the golf course) so it seems likely that the consumerist movement will increasingly place upon all institutions rules needed to discipline only a very few. More rules and regulations, in other words, at the individual level.

Not that this kind of development need worry major banks very much. Such rules are designed to protect consumers from over-aggressive organisations, and the big banks are rarely that, at least so far as personal customers are concerned. But there will be a need to appraise proposed legislation very carefully; the Consumer Credit Act very nearly led to overdrafts becoming illegal, a development prevented only by intense activity rather late in the day. So, certainly, tomorrow's domestic bankers will have to operate within, and formally comply with, tighter legal constraints. But these are unlikely to cause much of a change in personal banking practice.

Macro-legalities are however likely to change structures. That different requirements produce vastly different banking systems is obvious. Just what major changes the EEC will produce in the long term are very difficult to foresee. In the shorter term the UK will come under increasing pressure to conform more closely to European systems.

To indicate what this could possibly mean, here are a few fairly random examples of some differences in a few European countries.

Belgium
Commercial banks are obliged to invest a specified proportion of their deposits in government securities; consequently bonds account for an unusually large proportion of their balance sheets.

It is common practice for banks to issue a statement every day there is a transaction on an account; if the statement is posted the customer pays a charge to offset mailing costs.

France
Since 1967 wages and salaries of more than a specific amount have had to be paid by cheque; this has resulted in a large increase in the total number of bank accounts.

The rapid growth of leasing in France in the late 1960s and early 1970s reflected the fact that this form of finance was exempt from credit restrictions.

French commercial banks find it very difficult to break into the agricultural lending market because subsidised credit can be disbursed only by the Credit Agricole.

By contrast, French banks have been able to expand their term lending more than banks in many other countries because of the existence of special refinancing facilities.

Italy
Commercial banks have been legally prohibited from engaging in term lending; consequently such finance is provided by other institutions.

There are controls on the opening of new bank branches, and certain banks are confined to operating in particular regions; this has resulted in an ossified branch banking structure.

Italian banks are obliged to invest a specified proportion of their deposits in various designated public sector securities; because these securities are low-yielding, the banks have unusually wide margins between their deposit and lending rates to make up the shortfall in net income.

All bank accounts are interest-bearing, including what we in the UK call current accounts.

Netherlands
Controls in 1961 and 1965 severely limited the expansion of all credit

except that backed by long-term deposits; as a result Dutch commercial banks had to make great efforts to attract savings deposits, almost doubling their share of an expanding market between 1965 and 1977.

In 1970 the government intervened to prevent financial institutions paying too high a rate of interest on personal current accounts. (In certain other continental countries the payment of *any* interest on current accounts is expressly forbidden.)

Of course it is always possible that in the UK the political situation will some day result in legislation to bring under central control further sections of the industry, despite the fact that research conducted for the Committee of London Clearing Bankers in 1976–77 showed very clearly that bank nationalisation was firmly rejected by an overwhelming proportion of bank customers and of the population as a whole.

What changes *could* pressures to conform to these legal or political developments cause? Some of the more obvious possibilities include the further separation of personal from non-personal banking facilities; a limitation on the number of branches allowed to institutions not directly controlled by central government; a limitation on the size of the balance sheet of any private banking institution.

What one would *like* to see is perhaps irrelevant. But it would be beneficial if ways could be found to channel funds into very small enterprises. Who knows, perhaps a movement based on local effort, with due benefits to the locality, will emerge, just as the early building societies did. (It is no coincidence that so many of the 300 or so building societies have 'town' names.)

New technologies

Obviously computers come under this heading. To those who would argue that they are, in the early eighties hardly 'new', we would reply, 'You ain't seen nothing yet.' Only now are computers growing out of their data processing role and into the more potent control mode, where the decisions they 'take' will conform to rules determined by central as opposed to local management. It is very likely that inter-active systems will soon provide tight guidance to branches in response to branch-originated questions, never failing to recall relevant data and never using out-of-date information; perfect memories and perfect 'forgetories', too. Thus junior staff at branches, or even customers themselves, will be able to call up for assistance and be routed by way of simple questions to optimal, fully up-to-date, solutions.

Properly constructed systems will be very powerful. For example, if each question allows four pre-set answers then only five questions can divide the whole field of possible enquiry into a thousand parts and five more into over a million. (The GPO Prestel system gives several examples of information retrieval by this means.) On-line cash dispensing terminals, many of which offer much more than cash itself, are merely the tip of this development.

With the growth of home terminals, capable of transferring information to each other, the future of personal branch banking begins to look very different. Already credit cards mean that painful interviews with branch managers to negotiate an overdraft can be avoided. Will paperwork dwindle away, and across-the-counter selling to personal customers be replaced by other methods of communication? For example, Continental Illinois uses direct mail techniques very successfully. With only three offices in the US which accept retail deposits – but with 100 offices round the world – they are in the same league as the UK's 'Big Four'.

But branch banks will survive, not in such great numbers perhaps, because of three needs: the need to recruit new customers, the need to deal with physical things such as wills or securities which customers may want to see at short notice, and the need to service non-personal business. Cash dispensers are all very well, but bulk cash receivers (from shops, etc.) are a different matter.

So branches will remain, but with very different working arrangements. At least one clearer is already testing magnetically encoded personal 'cards' for use at counters. The data encoded are all that is necessary to identify the customer and the account. This approach obviously opens up the possibility for the cashier to slip the card into a special reader, type in the amount (and whether a debit or credit transaction) and make or receive the payment. The data would go directly to the central computer via a 'back office terminal'; no paperwork except a receipt for the customer. With similar terminals in shops the structure of banking so far as money transmission services goes would be radically changed.

Providing financial services to industry and commerce is a different matter. But it is not difficult to imagine a greater concentration of experts in regional or large town centres to which businessmen would go (as they do now, for example, to medical specialists) or who would visit businesses (as do other technical salesmen).

For personal customers a service rather similar to a television rental service may be common, with computer terminals instead of television sets. These terminals will be capable of retrieving, assessing and directing information, for information is in essence what cheques, standing orders, etc., really provide. Cash there will be, but along the lines of the Co-operative Bank nowadays, available from shop sites which do not provide today's range of services, and from a multitude of cash dispensers located in places of great convenience to banks' customers: free-standing units in car parks, railway stations, and so on.

Looking not much further ahead, it is possible that eventually everyone will carry his own miniature computer with him, the size perhaps of a matchbox. Such devices will be able to communicate with each other or with shop-based terminals, thereby effecting inter-personal and person-to-shop financial (and other) transactions. By plugging them into special units at home credits could be entered into their memories for the next day's use. What role would be left then for much of today's personal banking business?

And non-personal banking could easily develop along similar lines. Already computer to computer dialogues take place with the computers based miles apart and under separate ownership. It would be technically a trivial matter (though far from trivial in its effects on banks) for such computers to address each other and form a 'clearing house'. After all, BACS does something closely similar now, but in future why move the magnetic tapes around?

You do not like the sound of our brave new world, dominated by the infallible and inflexible machine? You are worried about the security task, when anybody who may contrive to gain unauthorised access to a computer's data store can rapidly acquire a wealth of sensitive information? You are concerned that the whole system may come to a shuddering halt in case of sabotage or operative strikes?

There is certainly cause for concern. The saving grace is that the machine is an obedient beast. It will not do more (or less) than it is programmed to do. It is up to the human being, its master, to foresee the hazards and guard against them. If the transition to mechanised banking (which is inevitable) is handled skilfully and imaginatively the mechanical bankers will be confined to the boring, repetitive and time-consuming aspects of the business. And the human banker's time will be liberated for the more constructive functions of business development and customer service.

Changes in the public's demands on banks

Of course these changes will sometimes trail and, sometimes, lead technological changes. The less traditional services of banks, for example, have been given increased support over the past couple of decades and there is no reason to suppose this kind of emphasis will not continue. In addition, new services can easily be introduced. Indeed, in service industries, innovation is usually very much cheaper than in manufacturing, and can be very much quicker.

   In the main, changes caused by the customers' demands are likely to be evolutionary rather than revolutionary. But could we see a rapidly increasing consumerist demand for new types of financial service; together with not only a greater disclosure of methods but also more and more formalised systems which presume that the consumer is right unless he can be proved not to be? Such demands will come from both official and unofficial sources and will, for example, want to know, and influence, the reasons why different institutions use different weights in credit scoring systems; will want a greater variety of loan/repayment methods; more open information especially on records kept and exchanged with other organisations; and so on. None of this need present any major problems to properly run institutions. Indeed many have already moved a good way in this direction. What will be new is the exposure to the public gaze of more junior management levels and a need to be seen at all times to be acting in tune with the prevailing social philosophy.

   Such openness, in which more information is available to more people, will lead to sharper competition and more change, a situation which will open up avenues for new competitors, making it necessary for banks and others to respond quickly to customer-generated pressures.

Changes in industry's demands on banks

What is true for pressures from the public is even more relevant in the case of commercial organisations. Banks have responded extensively to the developing needs of industry, especially perhaps of exporters, in the past. In the field of financial services this will inevitably continue. But in money transmission it will become increasingly easy for major – and not so major – organisations to find complementary partners with which to swap funds on a counter-cyclical basis: ice-cream manufacturers with electric-blanket makers for three or six months; heavy with light industry for two or three years. Certainly such 'direct selling' has been developed in other industries to the advantage of the partners and to the disadvantage of the now-excluded middleman. If such swap arrangements do develop to any reasonable extent they will certainly affect the role and structure of the banking industry substantially.

Already newer transmission systems, both domestic (BACS; credit cards) and international (SWIFT), are having an impact on bank procedures. But all remain under the banks' umbrella. If, however, efficient separate systems emerge, their effect could be massive. There are, of course, examples where alternative systems have failed to live up to their protagonists' high hopes. But there always have been many failures in advance of success; it is just that we remember the successes.

Changes in fiscal and monetary policies

Here it is perhaps more difficult to foresee likely changes and their effect on banks. To the extent that changes in policies have an 'even-handed' influence, that they do not in fact (whatever the intention) favour one section of the general finance industry more than another, their consequences will be slower. But if one section is more favoured than another which is in close competition, change will be rapid, for money moves easily.

By the same reasoning, sharp, radical changes will be likely to produce rapid results. Anyone who lived through the late sixties and early seventies, and who worked then in the banking industry, will know how sudden and how sweeping the effects can be of major shifts in policy. No model of the future pattern of banking should fail to incorporate the possibility of such changes occurring again.

This is not the place to discuss what changes *ought* to be made in fiscal or monetary policies. But as an example of the effect of a possible change, consider what might happen if building societies were exposed fully to equal competition. Suppose they not merely lost the spirit of protection, which led to banks being prohibited from offering more than 9.5 per cent interest to depositors for a period in the mid seventies while societies were free to offer what rate they liked; but also the privilege of the composite rate of tax under which they can offer higher effective net rates of return to taxpayers at the expense of those who pay no tax, but who nevertheless deposit funds with them.

The effect surely would be to divert a significant proportion of savings back into banks, thus increasing the funds available for lending to industry. It is, obviously, a highly political decision whether society's savings should be devoted first to home ownership or whether industry should have priority. (In the latter event, standards of housing could be improved out of the additional wealth created, especially at the lower end which building societies do not reach.) But the present trend is for more and more resources to be devoted to home ownership which is doubly subsidised: once by non-taxpayers, who accept the return offered to them by building societies which is lower than they can get elsewhere, and once by taxpayers, since most mortgage repayments qualify for tax relief. Were this bias to be reversed the effect on banks, and industry, would be dramatic.

Opportunities in new markets

It is very likely that banks will seek to exploit markets which are either new to them, or new altogether, over the next couple of decades or so. Readers will have their own views about which existing markets banks should enter, and no doubt their own ideas on the possible new markets the future will bring. But, rather than speculate on what these could be, it is better to discuss the criteria by which the question 'To enter or not to enter?' may well be decided.

It is likely that one criterion will be that any existing markets to be entered must be national, or even international, in scope rather than local. It is also likely that they will need to be serviced by skilled men. This is not to deny the existence of skilled women, but merely to recognise that the great majority of male employees of banks will still be employed by them in the 1990s, whereas most women employed in banks today will have left. Thus any reduction in 'manpower' needs (and here 'man' *does* embrace 'woman') is likely to come about throughout a lower recruitment rate of women. Other criteria are likely to include rejection of manufacturing as being too far from present management style and know-how, and preference for services that can be charged on a fee basis so as to bring some counter-balance to the banks' generally interest-related profits due to the 'endowment element' in their resource mix.

New opportunities, new that is to everyone, can arise out of legal changes or from other stimuli. Similar criteria would be applied to these, but perhaps with less rigour, since there is widespread evidence that being first in a new market is an advantage. So there would be a trade-off between the market being less than perfect from the banks' point of view and their getting into it before any other industry.

Although we have said that we would not speculate about possible new markets, it is tempting to suggest a few. Matching people to jobs could be one; in other words, using the accepted wisdom that bank managers are shrewd judges of character to supplement with personal interviews a computerised matching system to identify possible candidates. This could use the national networks of branches (all of which already are used to computer terminals) to reduce the time needed to arrange interviews; and would mean that a larger number of candidates could be 'screened' quickly to yield a shortlist for the employer to deal with. Another possible market would be reservation systems covering the matching of people not to jobs but to some of their other needs; for example, new homes, hotels, holidays, theatre seats, cross-channel ferries, and so on. There is no doubt whatsoever that the technology exists to allow such a massive matching system to operate efficiently nationally; the question is whether established methods would be cheaper (or sufficiently entrenched) and so be able to stave off new entrants to 'their' market.

But for markets that are wholly new these potential restrictions cannot apply, and opportunities will undoubtedly present themselves. Banks, however, because of their size and financial resources, have the option of waiting and buying their way in when the highest failure rates have passed. This seems the most likely route.

Changes in the relative costs of resources used by banks

This factor, referring as it does to internal costs, might be thought to be irrelevant to marketing people. Not so. Marketing is about profit, and it is obvious that the right mix of services must be offered to the right markets if the resources available to banks are to be used profitably. Certain changes in internal costs have in the past led companies to withdraw products; one task for marketing people is to attempt to foresee how predictable cost changes can open up new opportunities. (We should mention, however, that sometimes these changes are more apparent that real. New years, and particularly new accountants, are likely to herald new procedures for the 'allocation' of indirect costs. Such new allocation 'rules' can swing products or services sharply from apparent profit to apparent loss, and vice versa.)

The most obvious trend in costs for most organisations of any size is the relative collapse in the price of 'units of computer power' (i.e. the computer plus all its associated add-ons) and the soaring costs of labour. For computers the pattern has been that over the last quarter century the costs for processors have fallen to less than 1 per cent of their former level, while for storage the drop has been even more dramatic, down to around 0.25 per cent. Over the same period bulk has been reduced, so that today in a given sized room it is possible to accommodate data storage facilities some 12,000 times larger than before. These trends are continuing.

We have already outlined some of the likely consequences of the growth in computer availability and power, and these figures show why we could argue earlier in this chapter that progress will continue to be rapid. It is not only *possible* to do new things, it can also be worthwhile in cost terms.

The real cost of human labour has moved, less spectacularly, in the opposite direction. Compared with twenty-five years ago, the average British worker today can expect to earn for an hour's work 50 per cent more of the representative basket of goods included in the retail price index. From the employer's viewpoint the cost of a unit of human labour is now 150 per cent of its cost twenty-five years ago, while the cost of a unit of computer power is less than 1 per cent of its former level.

The moral has to be that human resources should not be wasted on doing the routine tasks which a computer can do better and more cheaply, but should rather be employed on work requiring higher intelligence, imagination and flexibility. The opportunities ahead for more efficient organisations and more rewarding jobs are limitless, provided that people are willing to be flexible and adaptive rather than rigid and backward-looking.

Changes in internal pressures

This last of our selected 'factors for change' includes such things as developments in the attitudes and behaviour of staff towards their jobs, changes in top management's view of their own responsibilities, possible changes in the internal structures of institutions, and perhaps changes in the basis of remuneration.

The attitudes and behaviour of staff are of course evolving and reacting to other changes all the time. But the next few years will see greater changes than ever previously, and the dichotomy between two basic approaches to change – resistance or acceptance – will be highlighted. Jobs will change, some will disappear, others will be enriched. (We sometimes wonder whether job 'enrichment' is not a middle-class concept which not everyone shares. Many cases can be found in which workers prefer very simple tasks and resist the extra complexities that job enrichment entails. But bankers tend to be more willing and able to accept middle-class mores and so perhaps the concept *is* valid here.) Very few jobs will become more boring; the drudgery will be removed by the 'chip'. So staff will be rather more likely to accept job changes, and the retraining and redeployment this involves, than to resist them. Some will not, of course, but in the main, banks should have a relatively easy time, at least in the early years, in introducing this kind of change. Cash dispensers relieve counter pressure and are OK. But will they still be OK later on, when they can be seen to be not simply relieving but replacing counter staff? As it happens, most staff affected in the early stages will be younger females (this is a factual, not a sexist statement) whose lengths of service tend to be under five years – so natural turnover will give the flexibility needed. Male staff will see more than one change in their working lives, however, and will undoubtedly want more and more to be consulted, and to be given more opportunities and time to share in decision-making as it affects their jobs.

Top management's attitude to these staff pressures are more difficult to forecast. Why? Because such pressures are only one of a whole set of pressures that bear upon the management of any company. There always has to be some ordering of priorities among the set – workpeople, customers, shareholders, local communities, society in general, as well as those special causes which crop up from time to time such as 'the environment'. Students of banking history will be well aware of the hierarchy of priorities practised by earlier generations of bankers, which with hindsight seemed to put staff only just below customers but well below shareholders (often the bankers themselves) although well above the community. Not so today. Less so tomorrow. With an equal gift of hindsight, and advice from an encirclement of experts, tomorrow's top management will be more ready for change than ever before. Which pressure group will succeed and for how long will vary from year to year. So marketing men will need to be alert to keep the interests of customers well to the fore.

Internal structures will be evolving and changing, too. We have already discussed how bank branches may be affected. Will regions and areas disappear, to be replaced by segmentation based on personal versus corporate business? Shall we see a 'brand management' concept emerge with a team of people responsible for the profits of individual services? Shall we see more worker participation in all levels? The answers to all these questions is yes. We shall see them all, in different organisations at different times, because the better control systems which will be available will enable top management to supervise properly a whole variety of structures and not lose that control when the structure changes. In other words the computer (yes, again) will be able to store, and to marshal in appropriate fashion, all the basic data necessary to run the business in a rapidly changing world. 'Cybernetics rules, OK?' will undoubtedly appear on executive washroom walls.

And it can safely be predicted that the remuneration of individuals will become much more closely related to performance, for managers in future as for typists and clerks today, simply because the facilities for measurement will be more readily available. Naturally, companies which accept the challenge of measurability will tend to attract the better people, who will be paid at their own level and not at the average level. Such companies, equally naturally, will prosper; and it is in the nature of competition that others will not.

And so on. Not forgetting such well-publicised probabilities as the trend towards shorter working days/weeks/years/lives, and the dispersion of large groups of office workers, whose basic 'product' is information, a product which will be handled quite differently thanks to, well, yes, again, the computer.

What we have attempted in this chapter is to indicate a possible approach to prediction, an approach which has shown how some of the predicted effects can arise from more than one 'factor for change'. To that extent some predictions can be considered more likely than others. None should be thought of as 'certainties' but rather, as we have said, as the outcome of this particular approach. No reader will have expected a definitive blueprint of how one bank is planning for the future; such documents are closely guarded, and rarely seen even inside the organisation. Rather what has been discussed is how a start can be made towards your own personal blueprint by separating major areas of influence and considering how these may operate in the future. It would be easy to complicate our diagram (Fig. 7) to show interactions between the factors; and indeed any serious attempt at forecasting would not only do this but would also quantify the factors more precisely than we have. But whatever approach is used, and despite the possibility of 'wobble' in any of the figures used to forecast the future, one thing is certainly clear. It is going to be different; for many it will be exciting; and since dealing with change is at the heart of marketing, for good marketers it is going to be rewarding.

Appendices

Uses and abuses of statistics

Introduction

Many people regard statistics either with awe or with disdain. Such attitudes often stem, like many other ailments, from poor feeding. Everyone who uses statistics to aid an argument has an overriding duty to make certain that their content, presentation, source and purpose is as adequate and as appropriate as possible to the needs of his readers. Data should never be served raw. Obviously no single set of data will be equally suitable for all the uses to which it may be put, any more than even the most precise single set of accounts can answer all the questions a manager may ask about a business. To make your statistics more digestible to your readers there are some worthwhile guidelines; but you should be prepared to discard them whenever you have a good reason to do so; they are not rules but *guidelines*. This brief section is not trying to teach you statistics. If you want to learn that science the Institute of Statisticians can help and can examine you. Rather, this appendix summarises many years of writing, and even more of reading, reports; and many years of studying how figures can best be presented.

There are a number of aspects to consider. For what purpose are the data being quoted? How precise need the figures be? (Not how accurate; that is a different subject and is discussed later.) What standards are there – theoretical or derived in some other way – against which data can be judged? Are graphs useful? Is there a 'right' way to lay out a table of numbers? And so on.

Purpose

Sometimes figures are included in a report simply because the author

Table 8. Sales and stock cover over five years

	Stock	Sales	Stock cover*
5 years ago	297	1,978	7.81
4	360	2,314	8.09
3	414	1,762	12.22
2	349	2,018	8.99
Last year	308	2,133	7.51

* Year end stock divided by sales in previous twelve months multiplied by fifty-two

wants to show everyone that he has 'done the work', and because in any case, the figures 'ought to be recorded somewhere'. If this is your reason at least be polite enough to put the data in an appendix – do not clutter up the main report with them. Better, leave them in the filing cabinet and merely indicate their availability in the report.

For example, if the accounts of a company over a number of years are being analysed, then separate small tables, dealing, say, with liquidity relationships, or sales to stocks ratios, should be used (see Table 8).

There are aspects of Table 8, however, that are unsatisfactory and which are discussed below. Readers are invited to draw up their own versions of the simplest way of illustrating the changes in stock cover over the period.

If data are required in the course of a report they should be used in a strictly controlled manner. It is far better to have several small tables than one large one; it is far better to relate tables strictly to the point being made with no redundant or superfluous information included; it is far better to use one table to support or to make one point at a time; better to do these simple things than to put all the data into one table and, in effect, tell your readers to 'sort it out for yourselves'. It is the undoubted responsibility of the author to do the work of sorting, grading, classifying and interpreting the data he uses.

Precision

Too frequently statistical data are given to a much greater level of precision than is needed to support the point being made. It is necessary, though, to draw a distinction here between statistics used for managerial control purposes and decision making, on the one hand, and accounting and 'working data' on the other. The latter group may well need very precise numbers; the former rarely needs more than two digits.

What is precision and what is accuracy? Consider a group of children asked to measure the length of a table. The average measurement given was 5.4913 feet. This is obviously a precise figure, but we cannot say whether it is accurate or not unless we actually know the length of the table. It would be just as precise — that is, to a level of around one in 10,000 — if the children had stated 5.4913 miles as their average. That we 'know' to be inaccurate.

Obviously figures we use should be as accurate as necessary: 'around three or four' may be quite accurate enough, but not if a different decision would be reached if the figure *were* three rather than four. Equally obviously figures we use should only be as precise as necessary: 'five and a half feet' would be quite precise enough for the average of the children's measurements.

Can you now improve Table 8?

Standards

If your doctor told you your hæmoglobin count was a bit below ten would you be happy, worried, or dead? The answer, as it happens, depends on your sex. Most women could be happy; while many men might be a little worried. But most people would not know how to react because they would now know what standard to use as a basis for their judgment.

So, too, in presenting data in a banking context. Beware of assuming that your readers will know the appropriate standard. Better to add just a line to give the 'expected' value than to risk the reader missing the whole point of the table.

But what is an 'expected' value? There are three possibilities. First, one derived from general experience. Often this will be the 'average' of previous measurements, but may not always be very precisely quantified: for example, 'Brighter than the brightest star', or as is implied in a statement such as 'You have put too much salt in', or 'It is a rather high rate of interest.' Second, one given by law or laid down by some authority. For example, 'Average contents forty-eight matches', or '70 per cent proof', or 'A reserve assets ratio of

12.5 per cent.' Third, one based on theory, which of course in practice will usually be based on, or derived from, numerous observations. For example, the expected price of a fixed-interest security, or of a conversion loan stock, or the speed at which an object falls to the ground.

Of course it is essential to use the correct standard of whichever type is appropriate; using the wrong one is worse than not using one at all.

Setting out a table

There are a few simple 'rules' which can help make statistics more digestible when presented in a table. They do not have to be followed slavishly; indeed they cannot be, because sometimes they are contradictory. But when you break them, do so consciously, trading off the specific advantage you foresee against the general experience the rules embody.

To start with, figures which are 'expected' to be similar should appear beneath one another. There are two reasons for this. First, if a series of numbers is read across the page, your eye sees the least significant digit of one number followed by the most significant digit of the next. So there is a see-saw effect to the importance of the numbers your eye scans. Second, it is easier to see changes when the numbers are underneath each other. Try writing out a few 3 digit numbers; each, say, one third bigger than its predecessor. This 'rule', then, implies that with time-series data the years (or months or weeks) should go down the page and not across. (Yes, it is true that such a layout will take up more space sometimes than running across the page, but that is a small price to pay for giving readers an easier task in understanding the figures.)

Another good rule is to not use numbers with more than two, or possibly three, digits. Not of course in your calculations, but in statistics presented to management. It is unusual, to say the least, for managers to take decisions based on figures that differ by only 1 per cent or thereabouts. So a table like, for example, Table 9, is much easier to understand than one like Table 10, even though in Table 9 the actual earnings are 'wrong' in the sense that the result of multiplying £57 million by 1.2 per cent is 684 and not 700. The sacrifice of not being able to check the author's arithmetic (not a great sacrifice, since if you cannot trust his arithmetic should you trust anything?) is much more than offset by the greater ease of being able to grasp the pattern of the figures. Try yourself to re-arrange data you deal with in this way and you will quickly realise the benefits. Note that in Table 9 suitable units have been chosen, and that in the earnings columns this has meant using three digits rather than two, but that the third is zero. Again, try for yourself the effect of entering the third digit and see what difference if any, it makes. The budget column is, of course, the 'standard'.

Table 9.

	Loans (£m)	Margin (%)	Earnings in £000	
			Actual	Budget
5 years ago	57	1.2	700	760
4	66	1.3	850	830
3	71	1.2	880	880
2	65	1.3	870	900
Last year	82	1.2	980	950

Table 10.

	Last year	2 years ago	3 years ago	4 years ago	5 years ago
Loans	£82,231,522	£64,892,464	£71,055,367	£65,698,223	£57,311,576
Margin	1.193%	1.337%	1.244%	1.297%	1.215%
Earnings	£981,022	£867,612	£883,929	£852,106	£696,336

Graphs and other pictures

Graphs, pie-charts and other pictures can be excellent devices for showing simple relationships between two, or possibly three, measures. Note that it is the relationship that needs to be simple, not the measures themselves. For example, a graph showing both a set of observations and a theoretical prediction based on a very complex theory will, if the 'fit' is good, show a simple relationship.

But the very simplicity of graphs and other pictorial representations can lead to difficulties. Graphs which have 'unusual' scales

Fig. 8.

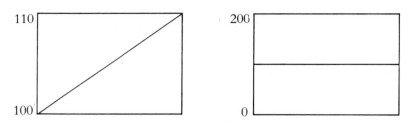

can give a quite false impression. Compare the visual effect of the same data drawn to two different scales, as illustrated, for example, in Fig. 8.

Using pie-charts to illustrate change poses a possible ambiguity: is it the area, or is it the radius that is the proper dimension to reflect the true change in the total? In Fig. 9, for example, it is obvious that the *shares* represented in A and B for factors 1, 2 and 3 have changed and that the total has as well. But has the total doubled in size – in

Fig. 9.

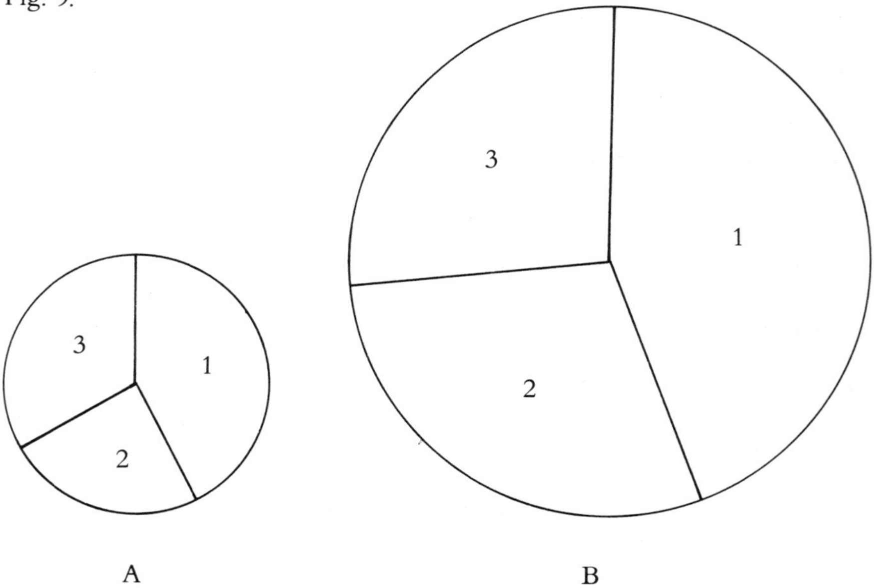

A   B

proportion to the two radii or quadrupled in size – in proportion the two areas? It is rare, but not unknown, for a graphical method to be better than a well-produced table. Bearing in mind the ways in which ambiguities or even misleading impressions can arise from using such techniques, it is as well to take special care.

Summary
Fitness of purpose is the keynote in using statistical data. Different purposes require different techniques. But perhaps the overriding requirement is that each and every presenter of statistics should be aware of the needs of his customers; not an inappropriate attitude to propound in a book on marketing. Beware the trap of assuming your readers will have appropriate 'standards' or benchmarks clearly in their minds; it is better to remind them what the standards are than to risk misleading them.

Business models

Introduction

Models are a representation of the real world, made to a level of accuracy and precision relevant to their purpose. Some models are made to very high standards indeed, perhaps out of sheer pride or enjoyment in their creation, perhaps because they are to be used to test ideas that in the real world will become very expensive (for example, wind tunnel models of new aircraft). The same principles apply to business models, which can range in complexity from the economic system models we read about (the Treasury model or the London Business School model, for example) to very simple types whose greatest use perhaps is purely as an aid to thinking about a particular problem. This latter kind may well be couched wholly in logical terms and have no arithmetical capabilities at all.

Of course, no model can be as 'real' as the real thing – any more than a model train can carry people. (If they do, then they are small trains and not models.) Indeed some models used in forecasting may be virtually unreal all the time, in the sense that actions are taken to avoid their forecasts. But here we will discuss simpler models, and indicate some areas in which they are useful.

Sensitivities

One of the most interesting uses of business models is in predicting the effect of given changes in various elements in the model. To take a very simple example, consider a loan from a bank. By how much should the lending rate rise to offset a given rise in the cost of money? (Here, 'to offset' means that total profit from the loan will stay constant.) Obviously, aside from agreeing what measure of the 'cost of money' to take, the answer depends on what proportion of total cost the money costs represent. For a loan of several million pounds the relationship will be near to 1:1, so that the lending rate should move almost in step with money costs to leave absolute profit unchanged.

But in small loans the inevitable administration and other non-money costs will be a significant proportion of total costs and will lead to a dampening of the effect of changes in money costs. The 'model' could be written as

Revenue = Profit + Administration costs + Money costs

and to take an arithmetical example or two, suppose P = £10, A = £10, M = £80, then revenue will be £100; i.e.

$$100 = 10 + 10 + 80.$$

Now suppose there is a 12.5 per cent increase in the cost of money. By how much must R rise if P is to stay at £10? Well, we know A will stay constant because we *defined* it as 'non-money' costs, so we will have $R = 10 + 10 + 90$ (i.e. 110) and so R must rise by 10 per cent to offset a 12.5 per cent rise in the cost of money. Readers should consider other arithmetical examples such as administration costs of £20 or £1, and also changes other than 12.5 per cent in the cost of money. It will then be possible to draw graphs showing a whole family of lines if the resulting change in R is plotted against given changes in M, with one line for each value of A. And, of course, you will now be able to estimate the required change in R for *any* change in M once you know the value of A. (Just to check for a given change in M, what change in R is required to keep P = 10 when A = 0? This is what is called a limiting case, since A cannot be negative and is therefore at its lowest limit.) Readers will already be arguing that in real life other factors need to be taken into account. For example, there will probably be *some* extra administration costs when interest rate changes have to be applied to an existing loan. So we cannot say that A will stay constant. But any such *increase* in A will occur if rates go *down* just as much as if they go up. So we cannot say A is linked to M, but would have to complicate the model in some other way. This process of gradually making the model more and more like the real world is typical of the modeller's art. But it is not always easy.

A more complex model can be illustrated by the following (it is part of a model development by the marketing group at Williams &

Glyn's Bank, and we are grateful to the bank for permission to use it here). It concerns the revenue which might be expected from the personal current accounts of the bank for various tariffs of charges, and is a good example of how predictions may never be right because people may decide to change the way they use their current accounts as a result of any change in the tariff. And while it is true that market research might be able to estimate the likely size of any such change in use, the cost of the research was judged to be more than the extra precision was worth. The extract from the model is

$$R_j = F + N_{aj}. C_a + N_{uj}. C_u + T_j.t - a.B_j$$

This somewhat frightening equation simply says that tariff revenue from the jth account (a mathematical way of saying for any given account) is equal to the sum of five elements. The first is a fixed charge, F, which because there is no suffix, j, will be the same for all accounts. The second is a charge related to the number of automated items, N_{aj} passed through this account, multiplied by a charge for automated items, C_a. The third is the same as the second but is based on the number of unautomated items, N_{uj} for this jth account and a charge C_u which we can make equal to or different from C_a, the charge for each automated item. Then the fourth element in this revenue model is a turnover charge where T is the total debit turnover and t the rate of charge. In practice, both F and t were set at zero, in other words there is no fixed charge per year on an account and there is no turnover charge for Williams & Glyn's personal customers. But both concepts were included in the model and possible values investigated. The final element is the allowance given on the average credit balance B_j on this account at the rate a, where a might be, for example, 5 per cent or 10 per cent per annum, or indeed any other value. Since this allowance is notional (that is, it can be used only to offset charges that would otherwise be incurred) the model also contained a 'constraint' that caused R_j to be given the value NIL whenever $a.B_j$ was greater than the total of the first four elements.

We can now ask this model about sensitivities. For this we would program a computer with this model and tell it to print as an output the total value of R_j for all values of F, C_a, C_u, t and a that we have set. Then, of course, if we change C_a by, say, 1p we will know how many thousands of pounds difference this single change will make to total revenue (provided that we have also given the computer all the values of N_a, N_u, T and B for every account). In practice, those values would probably be available for only a sample of accounts and the total suitably adjusted, but this would be a fully acceptable approach. And in practice, the computer would probably print only the total revenue and not the detail for each account.

Again, students are urged to do the simple arithmetic to calculate R for a few accounts, setting the charging factors F, C_a, C_u, t and a at say 0, 8p, 15p, 0 and 10 per cent per annum and choosing values for N_a, N_u, T and B to represent their view of how, say, typical students, housewives and businessmen use their personal accounts.

A well-known example of a model is, of course, a business budget and the budgetary control system which goes with it. Data have to be collected and analysed, and then certain predictions can be made. But it is unusual for the relationships which exist among parts of the business (and which therefore should be reflected in their budgets) to be stated explicitly. A budget is usually merely a frozen image, so to speak, of the organisation at one moment of time. But flexible budgets are better models because variations between the original budget and the real-world performance can be better understood, and proper adjustments made, as they arise.

Flow models
Some models have time as an essential ingredient. Consider a very simple model of a market into which a new sweetener is to be introduced which has zero calories, like saccharin, but which does not have the aftertaste some people believe saccharin has. The market consists of people who use saccharin, those who use sugar, and those who use neither and possibly some who use both (ignored in Fig. 10). The question is, 'From which group, or groups, will the user of the new product be drawn?' Diagrammatically, it can be presented as in Fig. 10. overleaf.

The likely flows of users of the new product (along the lines *a*, *b* and *c*) can be estimated by market research. But why bother? The reason, of course, is because the *promotional* appeal will be different to each group (in the words of Chapter 9, there are three audiences and each needs a separate message). For example, present saccharin users will need no more than reassurance about the calorie value but

Fig. 10.

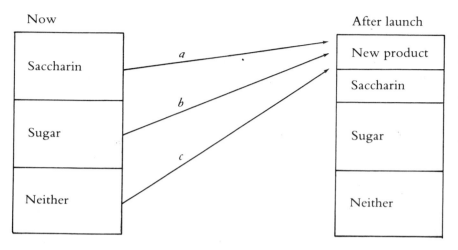

will have to be persuaded about the lack of aftertaste; for sugar users the message may well need to feature the slimming aspect more; and so on. In this example we have perhaps been over-simple; but the point is that such an approach can greatly assist at the thinking and planning stage.

A better-known model of this type is a network, in which various activities, some of which must precede others but not all, can be shown diagrammatically in a way which highlights the logical time relationships of all the activities. Networks have been widely adopted and have proved their value in many industries, for example in the construction of a major building, ship or refinery. They are also of use in planning the launch of a new product or service. Indeed, a network is virtually essential in any situation which has too many elements to carry in one's head, all of which must come together on time for a successful outcome, especially if there are sub-stages each of which must be completed on time if the project as a whole is not to be delayed. (The PERT concept referred to in chapter 5 is a very sophisticated example of such a network.)

As a simple example of a network consider Sunday lunch. It is important to have everything ready at the same time, and to do this some activities must be carried out in parallel with others. On the other hand, you cannot carve the meat until it has been cooked. So a

Fig. 11.

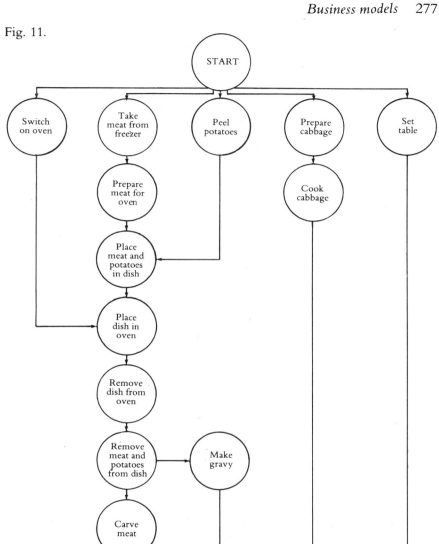

simple meal network could look like that represented in Fig. 11, with five separate routes to start along and four routes which lead to lunch being ready.

It will be immediately obvious that the lapse of time between some of these 'events' is very different from that between others. For example, only fifteen minutes need elapse between preparing the cabbage and serving it; but, if the meat is to be tender, several hours must elapse between taking it from the deep freeze and even starting to cook it. So an obvious development would be to add times to the diagram; and this is exactly what most users of networks do. But networks have a use as an aid to structural thinking even when no times are included.

Decision trees

This type of model, as its name suggests, is designed to show up all the possible decisions which are (theoretically) available. (Often, however, it would not be very practical to show them all.)

The likelihood of any given outcome of a series of decisions can be estimated if probabilities can be assigned to each intermediate step. Consider a very simple example of deciding whether to go out with a particular set of friends this evening, as represented in Fig. 12.

Now, if each Yes/No split is a fifty/fifty chance then you can see that there is only one chance in eight (12.5 per cent) that you will go out and an 87.5 per cent chance that you will be staying at home to revise. Of course, most decision trees are much more complex than this, both in having many more decisions to be taken and in each decision having more than two possible outcomes. Moreover, a typical situation to be modelled in this way will contain costs and pay-offs. For example, 'Shall I spend £1,000 and go abroad to try and sell to this overseas customer?' with the probability of making a sale – any sale – being, say, 70 per cent if you do but only 40 per cent if you do not. If we now add in the idea that the size of the sale will probably be different in both cases, and the make-up – and therefore profitability of the sale – will also be different, we already have a tree of some complexity. If we modify all these outcomes by whether competitors behave in one way or another it becomes obvious that, without some device to structure our thinking, it will be very difficult indeed to be even fairly sure that all the possibilities have been considered, let alone that the optimum decision has been made.

Fig. 12.

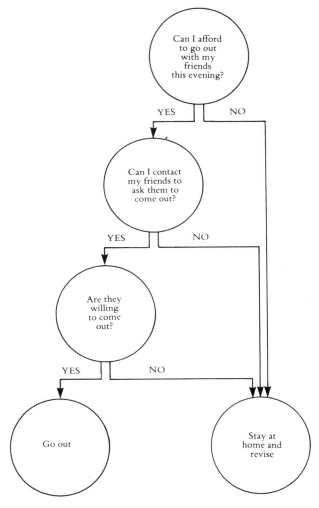

Just how you establish the probabilities (which we assumed to be 50 per cent in every case in the example above) is a topic which we can barely touch on here. In some cases previous experience will be available as a guide; where no guidance is available it is possible to insert guesses and see what changes in them produce a different 'most likely' outcome.

We are thus again considering 'sensitivities', and can see that this concept is a very useful one in marketing management, indeed in management of any kind.

Communicating

A topic as broad as 'communicating' cannot be covered adequately in a mere appendix. After all, some people study the subject for a lifetime and many books have been written about both the science and the art of communication. Nevertheless, telling other people is so central to marketing that we decided to set down some of the more basic principles we have learnt during our combined half-century or more of experience. And the first must be that even these basic principles can be ignored at times.

Brevity is a virtue – and we have more to say about it later – but it can be carried too far. One of our secretaries, many years ago, asked to write to decline a sales approach, typed 'Dear Sir, No, Yours faithfully'. On the other hand, when, just after the war, the Ministry of Transport was giving consideration to digging an underpass in London from one side of the Strand to the other opposite Charing Cross railway station, they received, so the story goes, a market research report which said simply '15.8 seconds'. They were happy with this because they had worked out that, using the proposed underpass, pedestrians would take about forty seconds to get from one side of the road to the other. Very sensibly they asked a famous market research company to observe the mass of commuters and time them crossing the Strand. The result, an average of nearly sixteen seconds, convinced them that no one in a hurry to catch his train home would bother to use the underpass. But that such brevity is acceptable is rare. (Of course the market research report probably included some lengthy appendices, but these must have been largely ignored.)

To return to the more general scene, good communication can

be judged against four criteria: clarity, credence, relevance and action. There are things to be said about each.

Clarity

Roget's Thesaurus links 'clarity' with ideas embodied in words like 'elegance', 'simplicity' and 'intelligibility.' We would add 'brevity' wherever possible. Learning to be clear in one's communications need not be a slow process. It is important to start with a sharply focused idea of the *structure* of your message, and to announce it in advance – just as we have announced that the structure of this section would be based on the four elements of clarity, credence, relevance and action. It is a good idea, too, to summarise from time to time just whereabouts in the argument one has reached, though in brief reports this obviously is unnecessary.

Clarity will be enhanced if more than one 'channel of communication' can be used. Pictures as well as words; tables as well as prose; listening as well as looking, are all improvements. Face-to-face communication can involve facial expressions, gestures and interruptions, all of which can aid communication. Indeed, the instant feedback in face-to-face situations is a very important aspect since it enables the 'transmitter' to judge whether the 'receiver' is 'tuned in' or not. Thus, written communications are not as good as telephone conversations, which are not as good as face-to-face dialogue, in making sure one is being correctly understood; but the written form does of course have other benefits; it is a record, for example.

In writing it is useful to keep sentences short. It is useful to avoid long words. It can be useful to use jargon; i.e. expressions which are clearly understood by experts but not necessarily by others. And it can be helpful to keep to a familiar pattern of reporting or presenting information. Above all, it is worthwhile to keep clearly in mind just who will be the reader that you are seeking to influence, persuade or inspire.

Credence

Roget links 'credence' with 'believability', with 'reasonable' and with 'expected', among other words. It is the idea of expectation which is most relevant for us. If your readers have a frame of reference against which to set the new information then its significance and its credibility can be more readily assessed. An obvious example is to be found in management accounting where the budget is the framework against which to set the period's actual results.

Where no such framework exists you must provide one, unless you are certain that normal business experience will be sufficient: but the responsibility is yours. So err on the right side and state clearly what you would have expected as well as giving the latest information. Remember your boss will be even busier than you are, and you should do everything possible to allow him to understand *and judge* what you are telling him. Much too often matters which are of great importance to a subordinate, and which may be one of only two or three projects which he is handling are of much less importance – and one of dozens of responsibilities – to his manager. Good reports, oral or written, recognise this fact and start with a friendly reminder of the previous position.

So far, then, we have suggested that a report should be brief whenever possible, clearly and simply presented always, and contain sufficient points of reference to allow its significance and credibility to be properly assessed.

Relevance

This third aspect has to be considered in two dimensions: not only the obvious one, of excluding extraneous matter while including information necessary for the decisions required, but also time. Roget again: 'relevance' is associated with 'fitness for purpose' and 'in context'.

It is never easy to decide on the first dimension. What is necessary to one member of your target audience may well appear superfluous to another. But appendices can properly be used to meet this point. What is important is that matter relevant to the decision to be made should not be omitted. Models can help in this, by revealing the structure of the problem and the possible solutions. Moreover, as outlined in Appendix II, models will often reveal the sensitivity of any proposed solution to variations in the assumptions made. Obviously more attention should then be given to those factors which have high sensitivities: those with the greatest likely impact on the correctness of the action put forward.

Similarly, networks which include estimates of the costs and times required to accomplish the various intermediate tasks can help to ensure that proper authorisations are obtained at the right moments in the development of a project.

Action.

Every report made, oral or written, should have a purpose. At one extreme it may simply be to reassure its audience that all is well, or simply to go towards the building of a data base on which future decisions will draw. In these cases you can expect them to be heard or read, their relevance and accuracy assessed, and then they will be 'filed away'. But at the other extreme they will call for action of a more influential and more immediate kind.

With such 'action now' reports it is essential that they contain a firm recommendation as to what that action should be, and by when the decision to take it should be made. Roget's Thesaurus links 'action' to 'battle' and to 'energy', and it is certainly true that it is often necessary to fight with vigour for the decisions you want. So make it as easy as possible for those who decide. Keep reports of this kind short, with the key elements of the problem defined, with the possible options outlined, and the recommended solution clearly stated, costed and timed. Put less-immediately needed information into appendices.

And end with the polite question, 'Do you agree, please?' That way you are likely to get decisions faster; and in a rapidly changing world that could be a real competitive gain.

Reading list

Part one

These books should be read by students wanting to consolidate their understanding of bank marketing principles and practices.

Marketing for the Bank Executive
Editors: Berry & Capaldine
Published by: Leviathan House, 1974
A good textbook, edited jointly by a professor of marketing and a bank president, which reviews US banks' marketing activities.

Bank Marketing
Authors: Hodges & Tillman
Published by: Wesley, 1968
A series of case studies from a variety of US banks, covering a wide range of their marketing activities in America.

Cambridge Seminar Papers, 'The Marketing of Bank Services'
Published by: The Institute of Bankers, 1971
It is what it says it is, a collection of papers written by specialists.

Marketing Management, Analysis, Planning and Control
Author: Kotler
Published by: Prentice-Hall, 1976
A widely used and recommended textbook which covers marketing generally, not financial marketing.

Marketing for Bankers
Authors: Berry and Donnelly
Published by: American Bankers Association, 1975
A sister book which describes marketing in a US banking context. It has a bibliography of American marketing books.

Part two

This group of books should be read by those wishing to extend their grasp of marketing, particularly those who can interpret general principles and apply them to financial marketing problems.

Marketing for Profit
Author: Hardy
Published by: Longman, 1971
A good general introduction to what marketing is all about.

The Fundamentals and Practice of Marketing
Author: Wilmshurst
Published by: Heinemann, 1978
A basic textbook which describes the various elements of marketing and how they fit together.

Compelling Selling
Author: Lund
Published by: MacMillan, 1974
A very worthwhile read; written in an easy style enlivened by a free-flowing use of conversation snippets.

Marketing Research: Text and Cases
Authors: Boyd, Westfall & Stasch
Published by: Irwin, 1977
Now in its fourth edition, this successful textbook covers both the theory and the practice of marketing research.

Basic Marketing: A managerial approach
Author: McCarthy
Published by: Irwin, 1978
The title says it all: a recommended textbook for those who intend to spend some time in marketing departments.

Manual of Public Relations
Authors: Bowman & Ellis
Published by: Heinemann, 1977
A practical book of real value to those who aspire to higher management, by two skilled practitioners.

Part three

These books deal with topics relevant to modern marketing management, but their usefulness is wider. Every manager will benefit from studying them.

A Guide to the Writing of Business Letters
Published by: BACIE, 1973
Eighteen pages of reading that will influence thousands of pages of your writing, for the better.

Data Reduction
Author: Ehrenberg
Published by: John Wiley & Sons, 1978
370 pages of numerate commonsense (and some mathematics) distilled from years of experience and many experiments, of relevance to marketing people and to others.

An Introduction to Critical Path Analysis
Author: Lockyer
Published by: Pitman, 1969
A classic in which the product more than lives up to its packaging; the title is becomingly modest.

How Full Could Your Hotel or Restaurant Really Be?
Authors: Hotel & Catering EDC
Published by: NEDO 1970
These forty pages should be read and translated into banking terms, by every ambitious branch banker but they may be difficult to obtain.

Facts from Figures
Author: Moroney
Published by: Penguin, 1951 (and frequently re-printed since)
Statistical techniques explained simply but critically. An obvious bargain for budding statisticians.

Manwatching
Author: Morris
Published by: Jonathan Cape, 1977
A fascinating study of man's – and woman's – patterns of non-verbal communication.

Index

Games

for
Juniors

Second edition

Jim Hall

A & C Black • London

First published 1995 by
A & C Black Publishers Ltd
37 Soho Square, London W1D 3QZ

Second edition 2004
Reprinted 1998, 2001
First edition 1995

ISBN 0 7136 6674 9

A CIP catalogue record for this book
is available from the British Library.

Cover illustration by Eleanor King
Cover design by James Watson

Note Whilst every effort has been made to ensure that the content of this book is as technically
accurate as possible, neither the author nor the publishers can accept responsibility for any
injury or loss sustained as a result of the use of this material.

A & C Black uses paper produced with elemental chlorine-free pulp,
harvested from managed sustainable forests.

Printed and bound in Great Britain by Bookcraft, Bath.

Contents

Introduction

The near total disappearance of out-of-school play – due to hours spent watching television and videos, playing computer games, traffic increase, reported attacks on children and parental concern when children are out of sight – means that regular and vigorous physical lessons where girls and boys move, share, play and learn together, are more important than ever if our children are to achieve anything like their potential physical, social, emotional and intellectual development.

Primary school physical education lessons are doubly rewarding. First of all, they satisfy the natural biological need for movement in growing, naturally active children, providing pleasure, satisfaction and a healthy outlet for restless, surplus energy. The sense of wellbeing and achievement inspired by enjoyable activity can enhance the quality of school life and childhood. Secondly, the wide range of skills practised and learned will be remembered by the body for a great many years, giving continued pleasure and potentially a lifelong involvement in enjoyable, sociable and healthy physical activities.

Games in the fresh air should make strong and almost continuous use of large muscle groups, particularly the legs, making big demands on the heart and lungs, and promoting normal, healthy growth and physical development.

Games provide unique opportunities for social development through working co-operatively and competitively with others, through showing self-control and unselfishness, and through developing a capacity and desire for fair play and good sporting attitudes.

The following lesson plans and notes aim to help teachers and schools with a wide variety of material for lesson content, development and progression. The lessons take account of the nature of the weather, with lively running or invasion games throughout the winter, and the less vigorous net/wall and striking/ fielding games during warmer months. Each lesson is repeated three or four times to allow plenty of time for the planning, the practising and improving, and the evaluating which are the essential elements in good practice in the National Curriculum (NC).

Games equipment

The lesson plans in this book assume that schools have, or are planning to have, the following items of equipment: 30 large balls; 30 hockey sticks; 30 small balls; 6 playground hockey balls; 6 rugby balls; 6 20-cm foam balls; 2 sets netball apparatus; 8 marker cones; playground chalk; 30 short-tennis rackets; 30 outdoor short-tennis balls; 15 playbats; 30 skipping ropes; 6 7-m skipping ropes for group skipping and to make 'nets' when tied between netball posts or chairs; 15 1-m hoops; 6 relay batons; 6 rubber quoits; 6 bean bags; 1 set stoolball apparatus; 1 set Kwik Cricket apparatus.

Games in the playground

All the lessons in this book are planned for the school playground where most primary and middle school games teaching now takes place. Precious time spent travelling to a field; the high cost of coach travel; a wet, muddy surface for much of the year; the need for expensive footwear; and a playing surface on which it is difficult to practise the variety of activities and small-sided games we are required to offer, have all combined to make the school's own playground the setting for the games programme in most schools in preference to a playing field.

Each rectangular third of the netball court is clearly marked with painted lines that should last for several years; these thirds are an ideal size for the three different games which are the climax of each lesson. It is recommended that schools have a line painted from end line to end line, in a different colour to ensure that the netball court is not affected. The extra line means that each rectangle is sub-divided into two halves. The line can be the centre line for games across each third and a useful, definite marking for those games where, for example, you may want to limit defenders or attackers to their own halves. The line can also be a 'net' for summer term games of short-tennis, quoits or volleyball.

Lesson Length

The following lessons are broken down within 30 and 45 minute sessions. Where a school allocates the recommended two hours per week for physical education, it is usually timetabled as a 1 hour games lesson, and half hour lessons for gymnastic activities and dance. If a teacher feels strongly that he or she would like the class to have a movement lesson on as many days of the week as possible, the games hour can become two 30 minute lessons, giving the children an activity lesson on four days per week.

When the games lesson is of the typical 60 minutes duration often after lunch or the afternoon .break, the time spent arriving in the classroom and then changing usually means a lesson of about 45 minutes, particularly if the children need to be dressed, ready to go home at the end of the day.

It must be emphasised that the most important part of the lesson is the final group practices and small-sided games which should never be cut short. The teacher needs to count back on his or her watch to check the time at which this main part of the lesson is due to begin, and ensure that it does begin promptly or even early.

The playground 'classroom' and safety

At the very beginning of each year the class must be made aware that the extent of their outdoor 'classroom' or teaching space is the netball court. They must always remain within its outer lines while taking part in the practices which make up the beginning and middle parts of the lesson.

When all members of the class are so contained the teacher can easily see and be seen, be totally in control, and not need to raise and strain his or her voice by shouting to be heard over great distances.

If the school has only one netball court, each of the three games, practices or activities of the final part of the lesson is accommodated in one of the marked thirds of the court. If the school has a second court, a part or the whole of this court can be used to provide more space where it seems sensible, such as in the warming-up activities, the skills practices, and for one of the more lively running games.

When asked, children say that a game appeals to them when 'it is fun to play; is always going; is exciting; has lots of action, nobody is left standing doing nothing; and when the rules prevent quarrels, let the game run smoothly with all having a turn, and prevent rough, foul play.'

Another appealing quality of good games lessons that the children might have included is 'accident free, safe activity'. A teacher's checklist of safe practices will include:

- sensible, safe clothing with no watches, jewellery, rings, long trousers that catch heels, or unbunched hair that impedes vision

- good supervision by the teacher whose circulation, mainly on the outside looking in, means that the majority of the class can be seen at all times, with few behind his or her back

- good teaching which aims to develop skilful, well controlled, safe movement

- good behaviour with a tradition of quiet tongues and feet, and instant responses to instructions

- an awareness of danger points such as fences, walls, sheds, seats, or steps into buildings. These must be avoided by the fast moving, dodging and chasing children who must be trained to remain inside the lines of the netball courts.

Classification of games

In planning an all year round games programme, and to satisfy NC requirements, it is necessary to understand the three groupings into which games can be divided.

Group 1 Invasion or running games

Skills: throwing or striking; catching or collecting; carrying or propelling.

In invasion games such as football, netball, hockey, basketball, rugby and lacrosse, two equal teams compete and the playing area is shared. Players try to advance the ball, eventually to aim to score a goal.

The throwing or striking is used to interpass to unmarked team-mates who are in a better position than yourself. Catching or collecting are the skills used to receive a pass, ideally after moving into a space. The carrying or propelling is a second method of advancing the ball, either when there is no team-mate to pass to, when space permits, or when there is a scoring opportunity.

Invasion games, with their possibility of continuous action, are popular and include our best known and most frequently played winter games. They are exciting and vigorous because of the element of chasing and being chased by opponents who share the same playing area with you.

However, running games are difficult to play well because of the need to outwit close marking opponents and to co-operate with team-mates in passing and receiving to advance self and ball towards the opponents' goal – a combination of skills calling for a large measure of social and intellectual maturity in addition to physical skill of quite a high level.

Modifications of invasion/running games must be used to keep the number of players per team down to 2 to 5 at the most. A small area needing little territorial advancement of players is essential. The scoring act has to be simple, such as arriving on the goal line with the ball in your possession. A variety of ways to score is recommended to open up the game and prevent the defenders dominating. In touch rugby, for example, the scoring act could include placing the ball down over the opponents' end line as usual, or passing to a team-mate standing on the line, or bouncing the ball in one of two hoops in the corners of the opponents' half.

Running games can be played all year round and are the only type included, outdoors in mid-winter, in extremely cold conditions, because of their continuous running and vigorous nature.

Group 2 Net/wall games

Skills: striking and aiming as in games such as short-tennis, tennis, volleyball, quoits and badminton.

The 'net' can simply be a painted or chalk line marked on the playground, long skipping ropes tied between netball posts or chairs, or a light net tied between posts or chairs.

Net games are the least complicated of the three types of games and they are the only group where you are not restricted to using a ball. Shuttlecocks, quoits, bean bags as well as balls can be the objects struck, thrown or aimed over the net or line. The court is small with the two teams on separate areas with the minimum of distraction. Teamwork is simple and 'singles' can be played. Little time is wasted and long rallies of continuous play can be engaged in with the ball, quoit, bean bag or shuttlecock being easily reached by the receiver. The target to aim at beyond the net is a generously large one.

Games can be modified easily to allow, say, one bounce of the ball on the court before making a return strike in volleyball, or two bounces in tennis.

Because of their more static, less vigorous nature, net games are more suitable for warmer weather from late spring until autumn.

For most primary schools, the net/wall group of games is limited to net games because they do not have a games wall adjacent to where games are taught. Where there is such a wall, children can play by themselves, or with or against a partner, kicking, heading, throwing, batting or striking with hockey stick, hand or racket. After the rebound the children can:

- control the ball, then send it off again
- return the ball, first time
- have alternate strikes
- keep the strike to see how long a rally each can achieve, before letting partner take over
- play competitively to try to make partner miss the return.

Children, individually, with or against a partner, can also be challenged to 'invent a game or practice for two players and one ball at a wall. What is your main rule? How do you score? How is your game re-started after a score?'

A painted line at about waist height can serve as a net to encourage even more accurate aiming or sending.

Group 3 Striking/fielding games

Skills: striking, bowling, throwing, catching, collecting, aiming.

In games such as cricket, rounders and stoolball, the one or two players batting are wholly concerned with striking and they compete against all of the fielding side who are concerned with bowling, throwing, catching, fielding, aiming and collecting the ball.

The striking of the ball is similar to the striking in net games but made more difficult because the ball usually approaches the batting player more quickly, either through the air directly or after bouncing up from the ground.

Fielders require a wide range of skills to catch or collect all varieties of approaching balls, fast, slow, high, on ground, bouncing unpredictably, coming towards you, or moving at an angle to catcher or fielder. In addition, the fielding side has to master the varied roles of bowler, wicket-keeper, backstop and fielder close to or far from the batter.

Unfortunately, with young, inexpert children where the batting is poor, weak or erratic, the whole game becomes stagnant, inactive, boring and unphysical with little action to keep the fielding side interested, busy and excited.

Batting games should be played in small groups of 3, 4 or 5 where 'tip-and-run' or 'non-stop-cricket' is used to stimulate action among the whole group who continuously change over the roles of bowler, batter, backstop and fielder.

Children can be asked to devise ways of developing their small groups in cricket or rounders-type games to introduce other ways to score, and be 'out', and of alternating the different duties.

Batting games with their potential for inactivity, particularly among the young and inexperienced, are more suitable for warmer weather during late spring, summer and early autumn.

(15-a-side rounders, often with the teacher bowling, which abounds during the summer term, is the antithesis of all that good physical education stands for. It is neither physical nor educational.)

NC Requirements for Games

Key Stage 2: the main features

'The government believes that two hours of physical activity a week, including the National Curriculum for physical education, and extra-curricular activities, should be an aspiration for all schools. This applies to all stages.'

Programme of Study

Pupils should be taught to:

a play and make up small-sided and modified competitive net, striking/fielding and invasion games

b use skills and tactics and apply basic principles suitable for attacking and defending

c work with others to organise and keep the games going.

Attainment Target

Pupils should be able to demonstrate that they can:

a select and use skills, actions and ideas appropriately, applying them with co-ordination and control

b when performing, draw on what they know about tactics and strategy

c compare and comment on skills and ideas used in own work by modifying and refining skills and techniques.

Main NC Headings when considering progression and expectation

- **Planning**, with pupils being challenged to think ahead carefully about their intended responses.

- **Performing and improving performance** expressed in safe, focused, hard work by attentive pupils who continually aim for a more skilful and confident performance.

- **Linking actions** smoothly and safely, using space sensibly, and able to remember and repeat the whole sequence successfully from its start right through to its controlled finish.

- **Reflecting and making judgements** to help pupils progress and improve, as they plan again, adapting and altering as required, guided by their own and others' comments and judgements.

Achievement and progression

One way of assessing how pupils are progressing is by referring to the main requirements within the NC, under the following three headings;

Planning

Performing and participating in a thoughtful, well organised way is the result of good planning which takes place before and during performance. Subsequent performances will be influenced by the planning that also takes place after reflecting on the success or otherwise of the activity. Where planning standards are considered to be satisfactory, there is evidence of: **(a)** thinking ahead to visualise the finished action; **(b)** good judgements and decisions being made; **(c)** good understanding of what is required; **(d)** originality and variety through trying own ideas; **(e)** consideration for others, sharing space and equipment well; **(f)** positive qualities such as enthusiasm, wholeheartedness and the capacity for working and practising hard to achieve.

Performing and improving performance

We are fortunate in physical education because of the visual nature of the activities. It is easy to see, note and remember how pupils perform, demonstrating skill and versatility. Where standards of performing are satisfactory there is evidence of: **(a)** neatness, accuracy and 'correctness'; **(b)** skilfulness and versatility; **(c)** consistency and the ability to remember and repeat; **(d)** appropriateness of responses and safe, successful outcomes; **(e)** originality of solutions; **(f)** ability to do more than one thing at a time, linking a series of actions with increasing fluency, accuracy, control and skill; **(g)** adaptability and ability to make sudden adjustments as needed; **(h)** pleasure from participation; **(i)** a clear understanding of what was required.

Evaluating/reflecting

Evaluation is intended to inform further planning and preparation by helping both performers and spectators with guidance and ideas for altering, adapting, extending and improving performances. Where standards in evaluating are satisfactory pupils are able to: **(a)** observe accurately; **(b)** identify the parts of a performance which they liked; **(c)** pick out the main features being demonstrated; **(d)** make comparisons between two performances; **(e)** reflect on the accuracy of the work; **(f)** comment on the quality of the movement, using simple terms; **(g)** suggest ways in which the work might be improved; **(h)** express pleasure in a performance.

Lesson Plan – 30–45 minutes

WARM-UP AND FOOTWORK PRACTICES - 4–6 minutes

1 Show me your best and quietest running, with bent arms going straight forward and back, and knees lifting and pushing well forward.

2 Keep running. When I call a number, make a circle, hands joined with that number of people, as quickly as you can. Let's see who is not in a circle or last to join one. (3! 2! 4!; intersperse numbers with good running.)

SKILL PRACTICES: PLAYBATS OR RACKETS; SMALL BALLS - 8–12 minutes

Individual practices

1 Walking with ball balanced on bat or racket.

2 Walking, striking gently and catching ball on bat or racket. Can you do this gently and rotate wrist each time to produce a forehand and a backhand position?

3 Strike up, let bounce; strike up higher, let bounce; strike up even higher, let bounce.

Partner practices

1 Walk beside your partner, one of you with ball balanced on bat or racket. Can you transfer ball to other bat or racket?

2 Four metres apart, bowl slowly underarm to bounce for partner to hit back for an easy catch by bowler.

GROUP PRACTICES AND SMALL-SIDED GAMES - 18–27 minutes

1 Bat, racket or hand tennis over rope 'net'. Co-operate with partner in striking ball gently just short of partner for easy return. Keep your best score. If this is too difficult, one can throw gently for other to strike.

2 One hoop each.
Place hoop on ground. Show me how you can use it for balancing activities. Pick up hoop and show me how you can use it on the move. Bowling? Throwing and catching? Skipping?

3 One bean bag among 3.
2 v 1, where the '2s', about 3 metres apart, interpass to outwit the '1s'. Emphasise 'Pass and move sideways'; 'Fake to pass; hold; then pass'; 'Hands forward in ready position to receive bean bag.'

Lesson Notes • 4–5 Lessons Development

Lesson's main emphases

a The NC general requirement that pupils should be taught to be physically active and respond readily to instructions.

b Safe practice in dress; immediate responses; sharing space co-operatively; and remembering that games are meant to be good fun, to teach us worthwhile skills and help us physically, not cause us hurt or accident.

Equipment 30 small bat shapes or rackets, and 30 small balls; 10 hoops; 3 bean bags; 1 long rope as a 'net'.

TEACHING POINTS

Footwork practices

Emphasise that in good running you do not follow anyone, and you do not continually run anti-clockwise where everyone follows everyone. (Very common in primary schools.) Stop class occasionally anyway to practise responding immediately to a command. Ask them to move 1 or 2 steps away from anyone near them, to be seen standing in their own space. In good, quiet running, we lift our heels and knees, and we run on straight lines, not curving around, following others.

Individual practices

1 Racket is held quite high at about midchest height so that you can have a good look at the ball while balancing it.

2 Use the wrist to move the bat or racket to propel the ball, not the elbow or the shoulder which would give too strong a strike. 'Forehand' means palm up; 'backhand' means knuckles up.

3 Practise the striking up to bounce on the spot, then on the move when ready. Once again, use wrist action and 'feel' how much is needed for the different heights.

Partner practices

1 Demonstrate with good couples who transfer ball from bat to bat slowly, near eye level, on the move, with wrists doing the work.

2 'Bowl low and slow' for easy returns and catches. six each, then change duties. Bowl to partner's forehand side for easier return.

GROUP PRACTICES AND SMALL-SIDED GAMES

1 Tennis over low 'net' made by tying long skipping ropes between netball posts or chairs. Use hand, bat or racket as necessary to ensure success and allow reasonable rallies to be achieved.

2 Hoop balance: walk forward, back, sideways or on hands and feet. Try skipping with hoop swinging side to side by 1-hand action.

3 '1' can be passive, not trying to intercept, if class is inexperienced in 'outwitting' an enthusiastic, chasing defender. Change the '1' over often.

Lesson Plan – 30–45 minutes

WARM-UP AND FOOTWORK PRACTICES - 4–6 minutes

1 Run freely and quietly, visiting all parts of our playground classroom. Use side steps or direction changes to avoid others coming towards you.

2 All-against-all-tag. Count how many others you touch and count how often you are touched. Be gentle with your touching. No hard, dangerous pushing.

SKILL PRACTICES: LARGE BALLS - 8–12 minutes

Individual practices

1 Walk, throwing and catching the ball above head height with both hands.

2 Walk, bouncing ball with fingertips, with left and right hands, and with changes of direction and speed.

Partner practices

Throw ball to one side of partner who is moving into space to receive it. Pass; then move into a space to receive when partner is ready to pass.

INVENT A SKILLS PRACTICE IN 2s - 3–5 minutes

Can you and your partner invent a practice to develop the habit of running into a space, ready to receive a pass, and the habit of always looking for someone moving before making your pass?

(For example, catcher develops a signal to use before running into a space. Point with 1 hand, then go in that direction, or run with 1 hand upstretched as target for passer to aim at.)

GROUP PRACTICES AND SMALL-SIDED GAMES - 15–22 minutes

1 Large ball among 4.
2 v 2 in half area, with attackers having 3 'lives' to score on opponents' line. Decide the scoring system, how to advance the ball, and the main rule. Change over after 3 attacks or 'lives'.

2 1 bat, 1 ball among 4.
Non-stop-cricket in half of area.

3 Skipping rope each.
Practise, revise, show me how well you can skip. Quiet, slow, with little hand action. Keep going, as a group, for 1 minute, showing good variety, e.g. on the spot and moving; feet together or one after the other; in different directions.

Lesson Notes • 4–5 Lessons Development

Lesson's main emphases

a The NC requirement to improve the skills of sending and receiving a ball, and to make up and play their own practices.

b Appreciating how much we need and depend on a partner or a small group to provide the unexpected and the unpredicted which are elements that give games their attraction and their potential for excitement.

Equipment 30 large balls; 2 bats, small balls, cones or wickets; 10 skipping ropes.

TEACHING POINTS

Footwork practices

1 Visit all parts of our playground classroom – the ends, sides, corners and the middle. Look out for and avoid other runners.

2 In all-against-all-tag, or 'it', stop the game every 12 seconds or so to calm them down, re-assert control, and to check on 'Which good chasers caught 5 or more? Which good dodgers were not touched at all?' Demonstrate with a good dodger being pursued.

Individual practices

1 Practise on the move to keep class warm and to give games-like conditions as we continually work among and keep aware of other movers. Catch with both hands and grab ball in to yourself, securely, carefully watching ball the whole time.

2 Fingertip dribbling, as in basketball, is a good way of 'travelling with a ball'. Emphasise 'use your wrists strongly, not your elbows or your shoulders, as you dribble the ball, and practise changing hands, height and speeds, for variety.'

Partner practices

'Pass, then move! Give, then go!' will be said continually so that the passer comes to expect the previous thrower to be moving into a space to be available for the next pass.

INVENT A SKILLS PRACTICE

Planning, performing and reflecting on the practice you and your partner have worked together to create, helps to make you more thoughtful participants and better observers generally.

GROUP PRACTICES AND SMALL-SIDED GAMES

1 In 2-versus-2, you can score by touching ball on line, by passing to a partner on the line, by making 3 good passes, etc. A 'life' is lost when the opponents steal the ball from the attackers.

2 In non-stop-cricket, the batter must run round cone and back every time a hit is made. All change duties often for variety. Rules to get batter 'out' in various ways should develop by mutual agreement.

3 Encourage 'can your whole group plan and demonstrate a good variety within your non-stop skipping? Use eyes as well as legs.'

Lesson Plan – 30–45 minutes

WARM-UP AND FOOTWORK PRACTICES - 4–6 minutes

1 Run quietly and well without following anyone. Show me slow running when near others or in a corner, and sprint running when there is plenty of space.

2 Tag, with 6 chasers wearing bands, who can catch you if you are within the lines. You can 'hide' on any line. When caught, put on a band and become a chaser.

SKILL PRACTICES: LARGE BALLS - 8–12 minutes

Individual practices

1 All dribble, slowly, football fashion. Listen for my 'Stop!' when you will bring your ball under control as quickly as possible, with foot on top of ball. 'Stop!'

2 Do the same again, feeling which part or parts of your feet can dribble the ball with most control. Stop!

3 Push the ball gently a couple of metres ahead of you, then run to control it, and repeat. Use dribbling taps to take you into a space.

Partner practices

1 Shadow dribbling, with the leader dribbling to a certain pattern for the following partner to copy. Leader changes over after about 3 repetitions of the pattern.

2 Four metres apart, pass to your partner who has moved to a space in which to receive your pass. Receive on count 1; move ball forward ready for pass on count 2 (watching for partner's move); pass on count 3; then move to a space to receive on count 4.

INVENT A SKILLS PRACTICE IN 2s - 3–5 minutes

Can you and your partner invent a practice or game to develop the skills of dribbling, passing or receiving that we have been doing? (For example, 8 metres apart with a line in between, one dribbles 4 metres to line, passes to stationary partner, then returns to own starting line as partner repeats the activity.)

GROUP PRACTICES AND SMALL-SIDED GAMES - 15–22 minutes

1 Dribbling-tag, large ball each.
All try to score points by touching other football dribblers. Control ball while tagging.

2 Large ball among 4, 2 v 2.
Attackers score by bouncing ball in 1 of 2 hoops in the corners. Half pitch area. After 3 attacks, change duties. Decide on main rule.

3 Large ball between 2.
Including chest and bounce passing, show me ways to send ball accurately to your partner (e.g. kick, head, throw, volley).

Lesson Notes • 4–5 Lessons Development

Lesson's main emphases

a The NC requirement to improve the skills of sending, receiving and travelling with a ball, and making up and playing their own games or practices.

b An awareness of the need for all to work hard to make our lessons into 'scenes of busy activity' as we move into winter and colder weather. We want maximum, vigorous physical participation and a minimum of 'dead spots' when no-one is working.

Equipment 30 large balls; coloured bands; 4 hoops.

TEACHING POINTS

Footwork practices

1 Changing running speed is also an excellent dodge in games to evade a close marking opponent.

2 In tag, where you cannot be caught on a line, the class will probably agree a reasonable time limit (about 5 seconds) for those 'refugees' who linger on their lines unsportingly.

Individual practices

1 Ask class to look at a good group and tell you which part or parts of the feet being used seem to work most successfully, both for 'travelling with the ball' and for quick control.

2 Encourage them to practise with left and right feet.

3 Push it into a space where you won't impede others or be impeded in your followup run to regain control.

Partner practices

1 In shadow dribbling, the performer has to remember the sequence to repeat it. The follower has to recognise the 2 or 3 parts concerned to be able to repeat them in the right order.

2 'Pass and move. Give and go. Pass and move into a space' will be heard over and over again in games lessons and teaching. It is hoped that the 'give and go' pattern becomes an ingrained habit. A passer is expected to move into a new space to be ready for a return throw.

GROUP PRACTICES AND SMALL-SIDED GAMES

1 In dribbling-tag, do not allow chasers to leave their ball and tag someone. Gentle tags. No rough pushing.

2 In 2-versus-2, the game is one way only, half pitch, with same team having 3 'lives' or attacks, then becoming the defenders. Send the ball to your partner in a variety of ways – straight chest to chest, bounce, after a fake – then move to a new space to help. In deciding their main rule, emphasise that the rule aims to keep the game fair for both teams, and to keep the game flowing. In cold weather, running side by side, passing rugby style, is good for keeping you warm.

Lesson Plan – 30–45 minutes

WARM-UP AND FOOTWORK PRACTICES - 4–6 minutes

1 Follow-the-leader, walking, running and jumping over lines. When you think you can repeat your partner's sequence, ask to become the new leader.

2 In pairs, marker shadows dodger. On 'Stop!' both freeze to see who is the winner; the dodger clear, or marker still within touching distance. Change over.

SKILL PRACTICES: LARGE BALLS - 8–12 minutes

Individual practices

1 Run, ball held low, like a rugby player. Run with arms swinging naturally from side to side. making fake passes to each side.

2 When I call 'Change!' put your ball down on the ground with a rugby-try scoring action, and run and pick up another ball. Use two hands for both actions. (Teacher can add to the fun of this practice by removing some of the balls so that not all succeed in finding one to pick up.)

Partner practices

1 Run side by side, passing rugby style, sideways to your partner. Pass across the leg nearer to your partner and just ahead of him, so that he runs on to the ball.

2 One of you stands still while the other runs round in a circle about 3 metres away. The still partner throws in front of the running partner who carries the ball a few strides before passing the ball back. Change duties often.

INVENT A SKILLS PRACTICE IN 2s - 3–5 minutes

Half of class still have a ball. Can anyone invent a game that uses carrying the ball and dodging to avoid being touched? (For example, those without try to touch a ball being carried to gain one – having a ball is good. Or those with ball could touch someone without who then must take it – not having a ball is good.)

GROUP PRACTICES AND SMALL-SIDED GAMES - 15–22 minutes

1 Rugby-touch, 4 v 4, large ball among 8.
Score by passing to team-mate catcher near opponents' line or by touching down on end line.

2 Invent a game, 1 v 1, large ball between 2.
Using part of line and 1 ball, invent a football dribbling game. Decide main rule.

3 10 hockey sticks, 7 balls.
Three pupils, with stick but no ball, try to take one from the dribbling 7.

Lesson Notes • 4–5 Lessons Development

Lesson's main emphases

a The NC general requirement to make appropriate decisions quickly and plan their responses.

b Using the leg muscles vigorously in invasion or running games and practices which are appropriate in winter to warm us and keep us warm. In addition, good responses and excellent behaviour become even more important to ensure that the lesson is seldom stopped.

Equipment 30 large balls, including as many rugby balls as possible; 10 hockey sticks and 7 small balls (playground hockey type if available).

TEACHING POINTS

Footwork practices

1 In follow-the-leader, aim to be so good that you and your partner can almost perform in unison, stepping together.

2 In dodge-and-mark, encourage, coach and demonstrate good dodges, fakes of head or shoulders, and direction changes. Discourage high speed, dangerous sprints by dodgers. Be very firm against the cheating, commonplace in this game, by those who do not stop immediately you shout 'Stop!'

Individual practices

1 A fake pass is one that looks as if it is going to happen but doesn't.

2 The 'Change!' balls practice is good fun, calls for a quick response, and is an excellent rugby practice.

Partner practices

Aim to give your partner an easy two-handed catch to run on to by aiming just in front of his chest. Turn your upper body right round to face the target, letting both arms follow through towards the target as you pass the ball.

INVENT A SKILLS PRACTICE OR SIMPLE GAME

One of the class, particularly if he has invented the game suggested, can shout 'Change!' to change the aim of the game from having to not having a ball in your possession.

GROUP PRACTICES AND SMALL-SIDED GAMES

1 In rugby-touch, the choice of scoring ideas produces more goals. The teams can be challenged to add to these. Teams must agree how to re-start after a score, and one main rule to keep the game fair to both teams.

2 In 1 1 dribbling to score at a line, decide how to score, how to restrict the defender, how to re-start, and the one main rule. The defender might be required to stay within a metre of the line.

3 Teacher will spend much time with the hockey group, teaching the correct, safe way to hold stick low and in front at all times.

Lesson Plan – 30–45 minutes

WARM-UP AND FOOTWORK PRACTICES - 4–6 minutes

1 Jogging is an easy, quiet form of running, with arms hanging low and heels not as high as in normal running. Practise easy jogging at a speed you think you can easily keep going for 2 minutes.

2 10-points-tag, all against all. All have 10 points to start with. Each time someone touches you, you lose a point. (N.b. gentle touching. No pushing. Check who has the most points left and who caught the most, after 12-15 second game.)

SKILL PRACTICES: HOCKEY STICKS AND SMALL BATS - 8–12 minutes

Individual practices

1 Run, with stick in right hand by side like a suitcase. Hold stick in the middle, flat side to left and head pointing forward.

2 When I call 'Change!' place left hand on top of stick, leaving right hand where it is. Carry in front, head of stick near ground as if about to receive a ball. Keep running. (Change between '1' and '2', several times.)

3 With your ball now, keep the flat side of the stick forward and slightly to the right.

Push the ball gently in front of you, along a straight line.

Partner practices

1 Your partner is 3 metres away. Dribble round your partner and back to your starting place. Push ball to partner who repeats the practice.

2 Walk side by side, gently sending ball in front of each other.

GROUP PRACTICES AND SMALL-SIDED GAMES - 18–27 minutes

1 Hockey stick and ball each.
Walk with ball 'glued' to stick. When you see a space about 2-3 metres ahead push pass ball into the space. Run after ball and repeat. Emphasise low stick in front of you at all times. No high follow-through.

2 Large ball among 4, 2 v 2, half pitch.
Attackers try to score, rugby style, by usual touch down over opponents' line, by a pass to partner on line, or into one or more hoops which can be additional scoring systems. When touched by defender, you must pass the ball.

3 Large ball between 2.
Allowing one bounce on the ground in between hits, keep your best score in juggling the ball to keep it up and bouncing, using foot, thigh or head. A sort of football-tennis on the spot.

Lesson Notes • 4–5 Lessons Development

Lesson's main emphases

a The NC requirement to play fairly, compete honestly and demonstrate good sporting behaviour.

b 'Keeping going', as in our jogging start, and in our near non-stop lesson. This is something children do not experience sufficiently often, according to a survey by Exeter University.

Heart health is always an aim of a good, vigorous physical education lesson, particularly now, when children's sedentary lifestyles are so lacking in vigorous play and exercise.

Equipment 30 hockey sticks and small balls; 7 large balls.

TEACHING POINTS

Footwork practices

1 Find, feel, and almost hear your own rhythm in your jogging. 'Jog, jog, jog, jog; 1, 2, 3, 4.' There is little forward body lean. Hands and heels are low and 'easy'.

2 In 10-points-tag, encourage good dodges with head and shoulder fakes, quick changes of direction and changes of speed.

Individual practices

1 This carry of the stick by your side is safe, unlike running and waving stick about, and easily comes to hand to play the ball.

2 Stick is carried low and in front when ball is being played or has been played. Side carry alternates safely with forward carry.

3 Straight line push forward is done by placing the stick behind the ball then giving it a push. There is no long, dangerous, out of sight backswing.

Partner practices

1 Walk and dribble to start with, passing partner with your left shoulder. Send ball to partner by placing stick behind ball, then pushing, not hitting or slapping it.

2 Side by side, dribble for 3 or 4 touches, then place stick down at back of ball and push it just ahead of partner who keeps moving forward to receive it easily. Turn and pass to other side.

GROUP PRACTICES AND SMALL-SIDED GAMES

1 More time for individual hockey dribble and push ahead practice to reinforce, adapt and improve the earlier attempts.

2 Half pitch, 2 2, rugby-touch games require good co-operation between the attackers and skilful, accurate passing. The touch by the defender must be gentle with no dangerous pushing. To keep the game interesting with lots of scoring opportunities, other ideas for scoring are always being looked for.

3 Both players must keep 'on their toes' to be able to move quickly to where the next bounce is going to happen. Players can agree to alternate hits or to a little, individual rally, then 'Over to you, partner.'

Lesson Plan – 30–45 minutes

WARM-UP AND FOOTWORK PRACTICES - 4–6 minutes

1 All in half of third of netball court. Using changes of speed and direction, and running on the spot, try to share this small area without bumping. Go slowly when crowded, faster when room.

2 Dodge and mark to one end of area so defenders stay 'in line' between partner and target line to impede progress. Change duties often. Defenders keep feet apart, hips low for 'boxer's shuffle' sideways and backwards.

SKILL PRACTICES: LARGE BALLS - 8–12 minutes

Partner practices

1 3 metres apart, chest pass to partner with both hands and then move sideways into a space to receive the return pass.

2 Bounce pass to partner, moving to new space for return pass. Aim to bounce ball about 1 metre in front of partner.

3 Fake a pass one way, then chest or bounce pass to partner the other way.

Small group practices in 3s

1 2 versus 1 passing where the '1' is passive, keeping between the '2', but not trying to intercept. Change over '1' often.

2 3s, team passing where the person with the ball passes to a team-mate who has just moved, or better, signalled and moved into a space about 3 metres from ball-handler.

INVENT A SKILLS PRACTICE OR SIMPLE GAME IN 3s - 3–5 minutes

Can you invent a game with 1 ball to improve and develop the skill of passing and moving? (e.g. each has a number 1, 2, or 3. Ball passed 1 to 2 to 3 to 1 to 2 to 3. Next receiver has to call his number, signal low before running to a space if bounce pass wanted or with high arm for a chest pass. Fakes can be added before run to a space.

GROUP PRACTICES AND SMALL-SIDED GAMES - 15–22 minutes

1 Hoop-ball, 2 v 1, half pitch.
Attackers score by bouncing ball in one of defenders' hoops. 3 'lives' or attacks each, then change duties.

2 2 v 1, hockey stick, 1 ball.
'2s' try to pass to each other. '1' is passive, simply trying to keep between the other 2.

3 Invent a game, large ball, 1 v 1 at a line. Attacker tries to cross line, dribbling by hand or foot. What is main rule? How is goalkeeper restricted? How many attacks each?

Lesson Notes • 4–5 Lessons Development

Lesson's main emphases

a The NC requirements to explore and understand principles of defence in invasion games and sustain energetic activity.

b Working hard as a team defence with good body positioning and footwork to frustrate the attacking team. The opponents will find it hard to score if you keep 'in line' at all times.

Equipment 15 large balls; 10 hockey sticks; 3 playground-hockey balls; 4 hoops.

TEACHING POINTS

Footwork practices

1 Neat footwork and quick reactions are needed to prevent bumps.

2 Pairs can play across thirds, line to line, with attacker trying to pass defender to arrive on target line. In the low, defensive 'shuffle', feet never cross or come together.

Partner practices

1 We 'pass and move into a space' because that is the way to advance yourself and the ball in invasion/running games, and to keep warm in winter, with constant movement.

2 The bounce pass is used to push ball under the arms of a close marking defender, particularly one who is taller than you.

3 A fake, dummy or decoy pass can be made by moving head, foot or shoulders and ball in one direction, stopping suddenly without throwing, then passing the other way as an unexpected move.

Small group practices

1 In 2-versus-1, the passive '1' is still very lively, moving fast to keep between the passers, forcing them to move sideways and forward to be open to receive a pass.

2 In team passing in 3s, you will not receive a pass if you have not just moved to a new space to encourage such movement.

INVENT A GAME

In a small rectangle with an end line, the 2 with the ball could have 3 'lives' or attacks against '1', who has to defend hard because outnumbered, guarding the goal line.

GROUP PRACTICES AND SMALL-SIDED GAMES

1 '3 lives', half pitch, hoop-ball produces lots of goals because of the 2 separate target hoops. Defenders cannot crowd round as when there is only one goal target. Ask children to decide on how to re-start after a goal, the one main rule, and any ways to limit either attack or defence for fairness and to keep game moving.

2 The passive '1' works hard to keep in front of the player with the ball, forcing the receiver to move to one side for the pass.

3 In 1-versus-1, at a line, invent a game, limiting length of line to about 3 metres, and agree some form of limit on each player.

Lesson Plan – 30–45 minutes

WARM-UP AND FOOTWORK PRACTICES - 4–6 minutes

1 Run and jump over lines and carry on running. In a long jump, reach well forward with front leg. In a high jump, which is slower, reach up with the leading knee.

2 Free-and-caught. 6 chasers wearing bands try to catch others who then stand still, hands on head, until freed by a touch on the elbow from an uncaught player.

SKILLS PRACTICES: WITH SKIPPING ROPES - 8–12 minutes

Individual practices

1 Practise slow, 'double beat' skipping on the spot. Jump twice for every turn of the rope. Hands turn very slowly and easily.

2 Practise quicker, '1 beat' skipping where rope turns with every jump on the spot.

3 Now practise a favourite way of skipping and travelling.

Partner practices

1 Follow your leader who will show you a sequence that includes something on the spot and something on the move.

2 Can you copy and move in unison, trying to mirror each other?

INVENT A SKILLS PRACTICE FOR 2 SKIPPERS - 3–5 minutes

Can you and your partner, both skipping to keep active and warm, invent a skipping practice which has very obvious variety? (For example, one skips on the spot, turning anti-clockwise, while the other skips in a clockwise circle around him.)

GROUP PRACTICES AND SMALL-SIDED GAMES - 15–22 minutes

1 Skipping rope between 2 partners. Can you and your partner invent ways to skip together using 1 rope only? One can hold rope for both. Each can hold an end of the rope.

2 Large ball, hoops and skittles, 4 v 4. Skittle-ball with skittles in 4 corner hoops, giving attackers a choice of goals to aim at. Space out in attack. Keep them guessing with fake passes.

3 Foam ball among 4, 2 v 2 heading ball across half area. Score by heading ball passed by partner over opponents' goal line. Defenders keep 'in line' to impede attackers. Use bounce passes under arms of defender.

Lesson Notes • 4–5 Lessons Development

Lesson's main emphases

a The NC requirement to work safely with others, particularly as they plan, organise, refine and play their own games.

b Enjoying an interesting, almost non-stop lesson with its varied apparatus and activities, making us feel alive ('Life effervescing within me') and refreshed for our return to the classroom. Nothing else we do in a school day brings us closer together with others than the partner and group activities and games that we do in these lessons.

Equipment 30 skipping ropes; 1 large ball; 4 hoops and skittles; 2 foam balls.

TEACHING POINTS

Footwork practices

1 In the long jump you can see your front foot reaching out in front of you. In the high jump you can only see your leading knee reaching up in front of you.

2 Keep changing the 6 chasers and encourage the chasers to space themselves out, 2 to each third of the netball court.

Individual practices

1 'Double beat' slow motion skipping is a jump as you clear the rope, and a little bounce of feet as rope passes slowly overhead. '1 and; 2 and; 3 and;' where '1' is the jump and the 'and' is the little bounce.

2 In '1 beat' skipping you jump on every count. '1; 2; 3' with a much quicker action of wrists and hands needed.

3 A favourite way of skipping should be one you can continue.

Partner practices

1 In follow-the-leader, keep about 3 metres behind leader to avoid swinging rope over partner's head! Staying back also helps the observer to have a better look at the leader's leg actions.

2 'Moving in unison' can be on the spot or on the move.

INVENT A SKILLS PRACTICE

The variety requested can be produced, by using different actions, going in different directions, varying speeds, on the spot and moving.

GROUP PRACTICES AND SMALL-SIDED GAMES

Remember to demonstrate the varied ideas for partner skipping with 1 rope. This will extend and develop the class repertoire (and the teacher's repertoire) in this lively activity.

2 In skittle-ball, encourage 2 of the team to play forward as target players for the rear court bringers of the ball to pass to. Good 'in line', vigorous, chasing defending should be praised, and an excellent team can be used for a demonstration.

3 In heading-ball in half area, emphasise that a player on opponents' line can pass back to running partner for good header or head large foam ball passed forward to him for shot at goal.

Lesson Plan – 30–45 minutes

WARM-UP AND FOOTWORK PRACTICES - 4–6 minutes

1 Follow your leader who includes some hurdling actions over a line and some scissors jumping, swinging leg up and over a line.

2 Stand beside a partner, spaced well away from all other couples. On my signal, one races to touch all 4 outside lines and back to touch partner who does the same thing. Go!

SKILL PRACTICES: WITH SMALL BALLS - 8–12 minutes

Individual practices

1 While walking, throw, clap hands, catch in both hands at eye level.

2 Throw low, throw medium, throw quite high and catch with both hands.

3 Roll ball away from you, run after it, drop down to field with fielding hand and opposite foot forward, ball at good hand side.

Partner practices

1 Stand facing each other about 3 metres apart, hands forward ready and feet apart. Throw low (knee), throw medium (waist), and throw high (shoulders).

2 10 metres apart. A rolls ball towards B who runs forward, then crouches to pick ball up and and throw back to A. Change places after 4-6 practices.

INVENT A SKILLS PRACTICE OR SIMPLE GAME - 3–5 minutes

Can you and your partner, with 1 ball, invent a practice or little game to improve and develop your throwing and catching in a very small area? (For example, see how many sets of low, medium and high catches you can make while your partner runs to touch the 4 sides of your third of the netball court.)

GROUP PRACTICES AND SMALL-SIDED GAMES - 15–22 minutes

1 3s, 1 ball and 1 cone.
A bowls to B who bats ball a short distance forward. A fields ball and throws to stumper C. C then rolls ball back to A. Rotate often.

2 Long skipping ropes.
Teams of 5 skipping practices. Plan the best time to come into and leave the swinging long rope. Aim to have all 3 in skipping.

3 Quoits, 1 v 1.
Rope 'net' at head height, tied between netball posts. If quoit lands on partner's side a point is scored. What is your main rule?

Lesson Notes • 4–5 Lessons Development

Lesson's main emphases

a The NC requirement to make judgements of performance and suggest ways of improving.

b Concentrating on the less physical, less active net and striking/fielding games which are appropriate in warmer weather.

Equipment 30 small balls; 2 long skipping ropes; 5 quoits and high rope 'net'.

TEACHING POINTS

Footwork practices

1 In follow-the-leader, emphasise 'Lead your partner into good spaces for your lively jumping.' In hurdling, run straight at the line. In scissors jumping, approach at an angle to the line which nearer leg swings over.

2 In sprinting to touch all 4 side lines, the quick thinkers will run to 2 diagonally opposite corners, touching the 2 lines that meet in those corners!

Individual practices

1 Clapping puts the hands in a good catching position, cupped near eye level in front of you, where you can see the ball well.

2 The low, medium and high throws for catching practice are all quite low to stop silly high throws which are never caught. 'Low' is waist high; 'medium' is chest high; 'high' is head high only.

3 To field a ball correctly, run and crouch while running beside it, facing the way the ball is rolling. The other ways of running sideways or trying to get past and ahead of it are too slow and awkward.

Partner practices

1 In this stationary throwing and catching practice at different heights, the main points are 'Hands both forward ready. One foot in front of the other for balance. Close your cupped hands round the ball to stop it bouncing out again.'

2 In running in to field a rolling ball to throw back, crouch with a turn, feet wide with throwing arm side back. Pick up, swing arm back and throw.

INVENT A SKILLS PRACTICE OR SIMPLE GAME

In addition to the example game, an aiming practice, throwing at a line between you to count direct hits, develops throwing and catching competitively.

GROUP PRACTICES AND SMALL-SIDED GAMES

1 3s, bowling; batting with hand for greater control; fielding; stumping – restrict these to a very small space, at most half of the group's third of the netball court.

2 You come into the long rope as it hits the ground, swinging away from you. You come out of the rope left as it starts to swing right. With beginners, a low swing to waist height is used.

3 Throw quoit with 1 hand, catch with 1 or 2. The serve should be made at least 3 metres from the 'net'.

Lesson Plan – 30–45 minutes

WARM-UP AND FOOTWORK PRACTICES - 4–6 minutes

1 Run to all parts of the playground, emphasising good lift of leading knee to lengthen your strides.

2 Now emphasise strong, powerful straightening behind you of the driving leg.

3 With a partner, count how many 2-footed long jumps from a standing start your pair needs to cross from side line to opposite side line. Each one jumps from partner's landing spot.

SKILL PRACTICES: SHORT-TENNIS RACKETS AND BALLS - 8–12 minutes

Individual practices

1 Walk, gently hitting ball up a very short distance.

2 Continue, and can you change the hand position each time, from forehand to backhand to forehand to backhand?

3 Walk, gently hitting ball up and forward to bounce in front. Run to recover. Repeat.

Partner practices

1 Throw to bounce up for easy forehand return for partner to catch. Striker tries to hit ball from side-on position. Change over every 6 practices. What is your best score out of 6?

2 Using hands, rackets or a mixture of the 2, stand side on to your partner and see how long a rally you can make together.

INVENT A SKILLS PRACTICE OR SIMPLE GAME - 3–5 minutes

With 1 or 2 rackets and balls, can you and your partner invent a game or practice to improve and develop your sending and receiving of the ball? (For example, one stands still, hitting ball up, letting it bounce, hitting it up, while the partner hits it up only and changes from forehand to backhand each time, slowly walking in a circle round the stationary partner. Keep going until one partner's rally breaks down.)

GROUP PRACTICES AND SMALL-SIDED GAMES - 15–22 minutes

1 Short-tennis with a partner.
Play over low rope 'net' tied to chairs or netball posts. Co-operate to learn and improve forehand stroke.

2 Non-stop-cricket in 4s.
Bowler, batter, fielder, wicketkeeper decide on how out and how to score. Play in small area. (n.b. Hit out of small area is 'out').

3 Athletic activities.
Measured, standing long jump. Hurdling practice over canes on low cones. Throw small ball to partner, hitting target line.

Lesson Notes • 4–5 Lessons Development

Lesson's main emphases

a The NC requirements to improve the skills of sending and receiving a ball in net, striking/fielding games, and playing simplified versions of recognised games.

b Athletic activities to practise and develop basic actions in running, throwing and jumping.

c Appreciating that our good habits of practising quietly and thoughtfully, plus being asked often to look at demonstrations and suggest ways of improving, have helped to make us become better, more confident and more versatile performers.

Equipment 30 short-tennis rackets and small balls; long rope as 'net'; 2 bats, small balls and 2 sets of wickets or 2 cones; 3 canes, 6 low cones.

TEACHING POINTS

Footwork practices

1 Stride length is increased by a higher lift of knee and thigh.

2 Increased power comes from a stronger push by the driving foot.

3 In the partner, standing long jumps across the court, the jumper swings arms high above head, swings arms behind back and bends knees ready, then drives forward with legs and swings arms forward to help. Partner stands with toes in line with jumping partner's toes, ready to do the next jump.

Individual practices

1 In hitting ball up, hold racket at upper chest height, and hit ball up to about head height only.

2 Explain 'forehand and backhand' by showing palm and knuckles side of hand alternately uppermost. Wrist twists quickly to make the changes.

3 In the walking and hitting up practice, 'gently' means using the wrist, not the elbow or shoulder, to move the racket.

Partner practices

1 In partner bowling and batting, tell bowler to throw 'low and slow' to partner's forehand side, to bounce to mid-chest level.

2 'Side on to partner' at moment of strike means that racket is at right angles to partner for a straight hit back.

INVENT A SKILLS PRACTICE OR SIMPLE GAME

One partner, watched by other, could try tiny forehand and backhand strokes over a line on the playground, shuttling feet from side to side. When rally breaks down, other partner can start. Whose is the best rally?

GROUP PRACTICES AND SMALL-SIDED GAMES

1 The short tennis with a partner can be played with hand, racket or combination, if play with the racket is too difficult for both.

2 In non-stop-cricket, insist 'ball must stay in your small area.'

3 Place a metre stick parallel with the jump in the standing long jump, and draw the take-off line with chalk. Place low cone hurdles far enough apart to allow 3 steps in between. 'Over, 1, 2, 3, over.'

Lesson Plan – 30–45 minutes

WARM-UP AND FOOTWORK PRACTICES - 4–6 minutes

Jog round the outside of the marked area (netball court or courts) which we will call the 'track' of about 90 metres. Keep a steady pace for 1 minute, and count your laps and part laps completed. Back in class we can work out how far you jogged, easily, in a minute. Next lesson, you might travel a bit further. Off you go!

SKILL PRACTICES: BAT SHAPES AND SMALL BALLS - 8–12 minutes

Individual practices

1 Walk about with your ball balanced on the bat as in an egg and spoon race.

2 Change to gentle batting upwards using your wrist only. No big elbow or shoulder movements. What is your best score?

3 Throw ball up with hand, let it bounce on the ground, bat it up with bat and catch it with 1 hand. Repeat.

Partner practices

Partner A strikes ball from hand to partner B who catches it at various heights and speeds. Have 6 each, then change. What is your team's best score out of 12 attempts?

GROUP PRACTICES AND SMALL-SIDED GAMES - 18–27 minutes

1 Tip-and-run-cricket in groups of 5.
In small area. 1 bowler, 2 batters, 1 wicketkeeper, 1 fielder. The group decide how 'out', how to score, how and when to rotate positions. Bowler tries to make the batter play as he then has to run, giving the chance to catch or run out.

2 Hand-tennis, 1 v 1, over low rope 'net'.
Children decide how to start games, how to score, when ball is out of play, and when to change ends, if at all.

3 Athletic activities.

a Shuttle relays, 2 teams of 4 or 5.

b Bean bag putting from a line.

c Standing high jump over low cane held by partner.

Lesson Notes • 4–5 Lessons Development

a The NC requirements to improve the skills of sending, striking and receiving a ball in net and striking/fielding games.

b Understanding that action, doing, performing is the main thing in any physical education lesson, so we keep quiet until asked for comments, respond quickly and get on with producing action.

c Appreciating that good sporting behaviour makes such a big contribution to our enjoyment of the final part of the lesson.

Equipment 30 bats and small balls; long rope for 'net'; 2 sets of wickets or cones; 5 canes; 10 bean bags.

TEACHING POINTS

Footwork practices
Jogging is done with arms hanging loosely at sides and little lifting in the heels. It should be as easy as quick walking. Feel your own repeating rhythm: 'jog, 2, 3, 4; jog, 2, 3, 4.'

Individual practices

1 Balance ball on racket held in front of you at waist height, using wrist to control the rolling ball on the racket.

2 Gentle batting up to no more than head height, using a small wrist action, not a big elbow or shoulder hit.

3 Judge how high and far ahead to hit ball to let it bounce once before batting it up. This is a good example of 'a longer and increasingly complex sequence of movement' involving a throw, a strike and a catch.

Partner practices
Partner hitting for a catch starts off easily, aiming straight at partner. With progress your catching partner can be made to move to one side or other, forward or slightly back, for a variety of situations such as we experience in a game. Main coaching points are 'Hands both forward, ready to catch. Move early to be stationary when catching. Watch ball right into hands.'

GROUP PRACTICES AND SMALL-SIDED GAMES

1 Tip-and-run-cricket will need a space at least as big as a third of the netball court. Any big hits must be penalised by making batter 'out' if ball goes over any of the surrounding paint lines.

2 In competitive hand-tennis, suggest a 5-point game, then on to a new game, possibly with a change of ends if wind, sun or slope is an advantage to either player.

3 In shuttle relay, A to B to C to D to E to change ends. Have best of 3 races, then they all go on to practise bean bag putting as a whole group activity from a line. In 'putting', the bag is held next to your neck and pushed forward, not taken back and thrown. In the standing high jump, the cane will be held low, at knee height by your partner. Jump from 2 feet to 2 feet.

Lesson Plan – 30–45 minutes

WARM-UP AND FOOTWORK PRACTICES - 4–6 minutes

1 Run quietly and well, visiting every part of the playground 'classroom'. If I shut my eyes I should not be able to hear you.

2 Now add in some neat long jumps, springy high jumps and hurdling over the lines. Which is your take-off foot in long and high jumps, and which is your leading leg in hurdling?

3 Shuttle relays with class divided into teams of 4, with 2 players stationed at each side of the netball court. 'As' race across court to touch the outstretched hand of the waiting 'Bs'. The 'Bs' then race to touch the waiting 'Cs', while the 'As' stay at the opposite end of the line behind the 'Ds'. The race ends when your team is back in its starting place, each one having raced twice.

GROUP PRACTICES IN 4s: BAT SHAPE AND SMALL BALL - 8–9 minutes

Bowler (Bo) bowls an easy ball to batter (B) who aims ball back to bowler or across to fielder (F). Once or twice the batter lets the ball go through to wicketkeeper (Wk) to give him practice. Change round often on teacher's signal.

GROUP PRACTICES AND SMALL-SIDED GAMES - 18–30 minutes

1 Non-stop-cricket in groups of 4.
Batter must run round cone after a hit. Groups decide how to score and how to be 'out'.

2 Short-tennis, partners, rope 'net'.
You choose. Play with your partner to make a long rally or play against your partner. If the latter, decide how to start and how to score. How many points in each game? (5 is a good number.)

3 Tunnel-ball-rounders, 4 or 5 v 4 or 5.
Batting team all follow the striker to score by passing 1, 2, 3 or 4 cones before fielding team pass the ball through the tunnel of legs to end person who calls 'Stop!' Each batter has 1 strike, then teams change places.

Lesson Notes • 4–5 Lessons Development

Lesson's main emphases

a The NC requirements to play small-sided versions of recognised games and to understand the common skills and principles in net and striking/fielding games.

b Being trusted to get on with the 3 games, sensibly and quietly, without arguments about whether or not somebody scored. Our teacher lets us decide some of our own rules.

How to score, how to re-start after a score, how much space we may use, and the 1 main rule are all decisions in which we have shared.

Equipment 8 bat shapes and small balls; 2 sets of wickets or 2 cones; 10 short-tennis rackets and 5 balls; 4 cones and 1 small ball.

TEACHING POINTS

Footwork practices

1 After watching a group of silent runners, the observers can be asked to reflect on 'why are these runners so quiet?' The answers should include 'They are running with a good lift in the knees and the heels. They place their feet down gently. They are light and springy.'

2 The take-off or jumping foot in high and long jumps is not always the same one. They probably have not been aware of which they use for jumping or of which leads over the imaginary hurdle.

3 In the shuttle relays, ask for 'right hands to touch right hands' before outgoing runner starts to move. Race ends when last runner is standing at end of own line. Encourage a sprint start position with legs half bent for an explosive start on being touched.

GROUP PRACTICE IN 4s

Ask bowler to try to bowl on a 'good length' where the ball bounces about 1 metre in front of the batter for an easy hit with the bat. Encourage the 3 non-batters to stand, ready, hands both forward towards the batter so that they are able to react quickly if the ball comes their way.

GROUP PRACTICES AND SMALL-SIDED GAMES

1 After the batter is 'out', i.e. bowled, caught or run out, all 4 players move round clockwise, Bo to F to B to Wk to Bo. Batter is also 'out' if ball leaves agreed area. This stops big hits. If unbeatable batter comes along, the teacher should ask for 'all change!' after fair share of time.

2 Depending on level of skill, the pairs may play co-operatively or competitively. A good way to start each rally is to drop the ball beside you to bounce up for an easy forehand stroke.

3 In tunnel-ball-rounders, the ball must be kept in the rectangle of the third of the netball court. Batting is by hand. Each cone passed gains 1 more point for the running batting team.

Lesson Plan – 30–45 minutes

WARM-UP AND FOOTWORK PRACTICES - 4–6 minutes

1 Run freely, using the whole area, keeping clear of others and not following anyone. When I call 'stop!' be in a space by yourself. Stop! (Repeat).

2 All-against-all-tag, using two-thirds of netball court. Count the number that you tag and count how often you are tagged.

SKILL PRACTICES: WITH SMALL BALLS - 8–12 minutes

Individual practices

1 Walk or jog slowly, throwing and catching with both hands at eye level.

2 Can you walk forward bouncing the ball on to the ground with the fingertips of 1 hand? Have a try with right and left hands.

Partner practices

1 Throw for your partner to catch, standing 3 metres apart. Receiving partner should have hands forward as a target.

2 Can you show me other ways in which you can send the ball to your partner, standing or on the move?

INVENT A GAME OR GAMES PRACTICE IN 2s - 3–5 minutes

Can you invent a throwing and catching practice or game where one partner remains on the spot while the other partner moves? (e.g. player with ball counts his throws and catches while partner races to touch a line and come back to starting place next to partner. Change over and see who made more catches.)

GROUP PRACTICES AND SMALL-SIDED GAMES - 15–22 minutes

1 Small ball each.
Practise many ways of throwing and catching. One hand to same, one to opposite, 1 to 2, 2 to 1, at different heights, still and on the move.

2 Bench-ball.
Pass to team-mate on bench to score. Change bench-catcher often, particularly in cold weather. Decide on our main rule and how to re-start after a goal.

3 Skipping rope each.
With feet together can you skip forwards, backwards and sideways? Now can you travel forward, skipping with a walking or running action?

Lesson Notes • 4–5 Lessons Development

Lesson's main emphases

a The NC general requirements to respond readily to instructions, be physically active and work safely alone and with others.

b Pupil co-operation to enable the lesson to flow, almost non-stop, from running start to 3 groups ending, to give enough time for each of the 3 groups, which is the climax and main part of the lesson. 'Dead spots' when nothing is happening because of noise, slow responses or bad behaviour should not be tolerated.

Equipment 30 small balls; 1 large ball; 10 skipping ropes.

TEACHING POINTS

Footwork practices

1 Emphasise that the first running practice is to re-establish space awareness in the class, while moving about within the netball court playground 'classroom'. The year's games programme starts with lively action, concerned with safety and immediate responses, setting the standard for all future lessons.

2 In the tag game, emphasise 'Touch gently to catch someone. No hard, dangerous pushing which could lead to broken bones.'

Individual practices

1 Let the arms recoil on catching with fingers folding round the ball. They should be looking closely at the ball throughout.

2 In bouncing, use wrist action with no movement in elbow or shoulder. A slight bending in the knees helps the dribbler to be down nearer the ball and in better control of it.

Partner practices

1 With a partner, show thrower where you want the ball by holding hands forward at upper chest height for a throw you can see and catch easily. Throw is helped by a preliminary swing back of the throwing arm, then the reach forward and aiming throw.

2 Other ways to send? Kick, head, bat, roll, bounce, side by side throwing, rugby style, with both hands.

INVENT A GAME

If the class is unused to inventing a game, give them one to try until they become used to this short part of the lesson, where we want them to become more thoughtful, independent and appreciative of the necessity for rules, fairness and sharing.

GROUP PRACTICES AND SMALL-SIDED GAMES

1 September is still warm enough, usually, for a last practice of small ball skills that are associated with summer's fielding/striking games.

2 In bench-ball, only the bench-catcher is allowed to stand on the rectangular 'bench', marked with chalk. 4 or 5 a side play in one third of the netball court.

3 Skipping, when kept going, is excellent for 'sustaining energetic activity' and a first class leg muscles exercise.

Lesson Plan – 30–45 minutes

WARM-UP AND FOOTWORK PRACTICES - 4–6 minutes

1 Run quietly and try to feel a lifting in your heels, knees, arms, chest and head.

2 10-points-tag. All have 10 points to start with. Lose 1 point every time you are tagged.

SKILL PRACTICES: WITH LARGE BALLS - 8–12 minutes

Individual practices

1 Can you throw the ball above your head a short distance, jump and catch at full stretch, and land well balanced?

2 Dribble by hand using fingertips. Try left and right hands.

Partner practices

1 Throw above partner's head for a stretched jump and catch above head.

2 Pass to partner, 3 metres away; 2-handed chest pass; move sideways and forwards to a new space to receive pass from partner. Receive, pass, move, receive.

INVENT A GAME OR GAMES PRACTICE IN 2s - 3–5 minutes

Using part of a line as a target or goal, can you invent a game that involves sending the ball towards it in some way?

GROUP PRACTICES AND SMALL-SIDED GAMES - 15–22 minutes

1 Large ball between 2.
Practise freely sending the ball to your partner on the spot or moving, e.g. throw and catch, kick, head, volley, running rugby fashion, etc.

2 Skittle-ball, with 2 target skittles in each hoop. Score by knocking skittle down. No-one may stand inside the hoop.

3 Team passing large ball.
2 v 1 or 2 v 2 where 3 good passes to team-mate equal 1 goal. Encourage 'pass and run to a new space', 'short passes at about 3 metres', and include bounce, 2-handed, chest and 1-handed shoulder passes.

Lesson Notes • 4–5 Lessons Development

Lesson's main emphases

a The NC requirements to improve the skills of sending, receiving and travelling with a ball, to make appropriate decisions quickly and to plan responses.

b Much running in the warm-up, the skills practices and in all 3 games. We also run smartly to each new part of the lesson, responding quickly to commands to save time and to keep warm.

Equipment 30 large balls; 2 hoops; 4 skittles.

TEACHING POINTS

Footwork practices

1 The 'run quietly' start needs an explanation. 'Feel your heels, knees, arms, chest and head lifting.'

2 In 10-points-tag, emphasise that you touch 'gently, with no hard pushing lest someone falls and breaks a bone'. Stop game every 12 seconds to maintain control, calm them down, and to check on 'who are the best dodgers, caught only 2 or 3 times? Which best catchers caught 5 or more?'

Individual practices

1 Much linking of skills into 'increasingly complex sequences' here with the throw, jump to catch, and balanced landing.

2 In dribbling by left or right hand, the challenge to develop is 'can you change the speed, direction and height of your dribble?'

Partner practices

1 Partners stand next to each other for the vertical throw up for a jump up to catch at full height and stretch before landing well balanced on both feet. Catching partner should wait until ball starts to descend, then spring up to meet it.

2 A pass to partner and run to space to receive pass can be expanded by adding a fake pass before the real thing.

INVENT A GAME

Sending by reckless, hard kicking is the least satisfactory, and usually someone has to be stopped from doing it. Send by heading, batting, bouncing, easy throwing after a fake, or even by dribbling over the line by hand or foot.

GROUP PRACTICES AND SMALL-SIDED GAMES

1 Send the ball 3 metres to your partner to allow easy receiving and lots of repetitions. Send in front of a travelling partner when side by side. Send into the space ahead of a partner who is facing you and moving sideways.

2 In skittle-ball, 'Pass and run forward to help.' 'Run into a space if you want to be passed to. Don't stand, shouting for it.' A diamond shape attack is good for advancing ball. One at rear keeps an eye on own goal. One well ahead is target person. 2 in mid-court advance ball and themselves.

3 Stop the '2s' from standing miles apart and throwing over the heads of the others. Insist on '3 metres apart passing.'

Lesson Plan – 30–45 minutes

WARM-UP AND FOOTWORK PRACTICES - 4–6 minutes

1 Run well and quietly without following anyone. Show me slow running when near others or in a corner, and sprint running when there is plenty of space.

2 Tag, where 6 chasers can touch you if you are running about within the lines. You can 'hide' or take refuge on the lines. When caught, take a band and help the chasers.

SKILLS PRACTICES: WITH HOCKEY STICKS AND BALLS - 8–12 minutes

Individual practices

1 Run, with right hand carrying stick in the middle like a suitcase, flat side to left and head of stick forward.

2 On 'Change!' place left hand at the top of your stick, leaving right hand where it is. Carry in front, head of stick near ground, ready to receive ball.

3 Run with stick in both hands with its head almost touching ground and in front of you. Flat side is forward and slightly to the right. Gently push ball ahead of you with many little touches, feeling how easy it is to send ball forwards.

INVENT A PRACTICE - 3–5 minutes

Can you invent a practice, travelling with the ball, using the lines in some way.

(Consider using direction changes, zig-zags, etc.)

GROUP PRACTICES AND SMALL-SIDED GAMES - 15–22 minutes

1 Hockey stick and ball each.
Walk around with ball glued to stick. Can you jog or run? Now run around, ball glued to stick and trying to turn little circles. Emphasise stick in constant contact with ball and angled to the ground.

2 Mini-basketball, netball apparatus.
Netball apparatus in 3 metres from end so that ball is not continually going out of court.

Encourage 'pass and move' to advance ball, but basketball dribbling allowed. 1 point for near miss, hitting hoop, 2 points when ball goes through ring.

3 Large ball between 2.
Hand, foot and heading tennis, sending ball to partner over chalk line 'net'. How long a rally can you make? Invent a simple 1 v 1 game with one main, fair rule.

Lesson Notes • 4–5 Lessons Development

Lesson's main emphases

a The NC requirements to sustain energetic activity, understand what happens to our bodies during exercise, and plan, perform and reflect on their own games and practices.

b Becoming and staying warm by doing all the activities 'on the move'. Using our legs so strongly and continuously warms us up easily and we know that only wet weather will stop us going outside to enjoy our lively, varied and exciting games lessons.

Equipment 30 hockey sticks and small balls; 6 large balls.

TEACHING POINTS

Footwork practices

1 Running along straight lines so as not to follow others should now be a feature of the class running. In the anti-clockwise, curving running seen in many primary schools, all follow each other.

2 If anyone is non-adventurous in tag, lingering on the lines to avoid being caught, the teacher must call out 'All move!' at regular 5-second intervals.

Individual practices

1 The controlled carry of the stick by the right side prevents dangerous swinging of the stick and easily transfers to the push position with both hands in front of you.

2 On 'Change!' the change to a push stroke hold in front is immediate and neat.

3 Emphasise how dangerous a hockey stick can be if swung wildly behind or in front of you. Stick is placed behind ball which is pushed away carefully. There is no noise of stick hitting ball and no backswing as a preparation for a hit.

INVENT A GAME

They can be asked to 'feel' how the stick is held firmly by the left hand and allowed to rotate in the looser grip of the right hand. This allows rotation of the head of the stick to move the ball from side to side or forward and back.

GROUP PRACTICES AND SMALL-SIDED GAMES

1 Bean bags or skittles spread around the third of the netball court provide obstacles to dribble round. Teacher can check control by calling 'Stop!' to see how quickly they can bring ball to a standstill using the stick.

2 In mini-basketball, dribbling by hand is allowed. However, passing is always a quicker way to advance the ball, and dribbling should be discouraged when a team-mate is in a space, free to receive a pass. Encourage lots of shooting by awarding 1 point for a near miss, when the ball hits the ring but does not go through the hoop.

3 Playing across a third of the netball court gives lots of little courts for 1 versus 1 games over chalk line drawn as a 'net'. Use hand, foot or head, or, by agreement, a combination, for an enjoyable game where good rallies are possible. Decide how many points in a game – 5 is a good number – then change ends.

Lesson Plan – 30–45 minutes

WARM-UP AND FOOTWORK PRACTICES - 4–6 minutes

1 Run, emphasising good 'straight ahead' position of head, shoulders, arms and legs.
2 Dodge and mark in 2s. Marker chases dodger. On command 'Stop!' see who is the winner – dodger who can't be touched by partner, or marker who can still reach to touch dodging partner. Change duties and repeat.

SKILLS PRACTICES: WITH RUGBY OR LARGE BALLS - 8–12 minutes

Individual practices

1 Run, carrying ball in both hands in front of you, letting it swing naturally from side to side.
2 Throw ball above head height a short distance; jump to catch it at full stretch; grab it in to your chest with both hands.

Partner practices

Jog side by side, passing ball just in front of partner for easy, two-handed catch. Change sides often to practise passing to both left and right.

INVENT A SKILLS PRACTICE IN 2s - 3–5 minutes

Invent a simple chasing and dodging game with 1 rugby ball between 2 players (e.g. one with ball chases after partner to try to touch him on hips with ball held in both hands).

GROUP PRACTICES AND SMALL-SIDED GAMES - 15–22 minutes

1 Rugby-touch.
When touched, release ball or pass to team-mate. Score when ball placed on ground behind opponents' end line. Think of ways to increase scoring chances (e.g. have a catcher on line).
2 Ground-football.
Score by arriving on opponents' end line with ball under control under foot, or pass to team-mate near end line. Encourage 'pass often, dribble seldom.'

3 2 v 2 hockey across half pitch.
You score by placing ball on opponents' goal line. Push pass: stick on ground behind ball and push with strong, right hand action.

Lesson Notes • 4–5 Lessons Development

Lesson's main emphases

a The NC requirements to understand and play small-sided versions of recognised games, to work vigorously to develop suppleness, strength and stamina, and to exercise the heart and lungs strongly.

b Being guided by those children who, when asked to comment, say that a games lesson appeals to them when 'it is fun to play; is always going; is exciting; no-one is left doing nothing; there is lots of action; the rules prevent quarrels, let the game run smoothly, let all have a turn and prevent rough, foul play.'

Equipment 30 large or rugby balls; 1 large or medium flattish round ball; 10 hockey sticks and 2 small balls.

TEACHING POINTS

Footwork practices

1 'Straight ahead' running practice to make children aware of their arms, shoulders and feet, parts which often deviate from the straight ahead and twist inefficiently from side to side.

2 On command 'Stop!' insist on an instant stop to check winner. If either player takes one step after game is stopped, the wrong result happens. Insist on good dodging, not fast sprinting away.

Individual practices

1 Only in rugby games are we allowed to run carrying the ball. Practise the run and carry, with hands spread round the ball and arms swinging easily from side to side.

2 The 'grab in' to chest with both hands is a good habit to practise in a game where possession is everything.

Partner practices

Partner passing is often described as 'sympathetic' by rugby coaches, meaning that my aim and force must be just right and just ahead of my partner for an easy, well-placed and well-timed catch.

INVENT A GAME OR SKILLS PRACTICE

If trying the 1 versus 1 game suggested, insist on a very small area to help chaser. They could play end to end rugby-touch across part of a third of the netball court. When touched, ball must be put on ground for opponent.

GROUP PRACTICES AND SMALL-SIDED GAMES

1 The touching of an opponent in rugby-touch must be gentle. 'No hard pushing allowed. It's dangerous.' Ask catchers to try to take the pass near to the passer and on the move to advance quickly.

2 Ground-football with a softish ball that does not roll away. Some limits on the defenders will produce a calmer game. A 'no tackling' rule is a suggestion to give attackers more confidence.

3 2 versus 2, half pitch hockey needs an agreed main rule and some limits on the defenders to help game flow. Such limits might include defenders being 'passive' and not allowed to tackle.

Lesson Plan – 30–45 minutes

WARM-UP AND FOOTWORK PRACTICES - 4–6 minutes

1 Run freely over whole netball court. To avoid others coming towards you, use a little side step: one foot goes straight to the side, putting you on a new line but in the same direction.

2 Chain-tag. 3 or 4 couples start as chasers, When caught, join the chain that tagged you, When 4 in chain, split into 2 pairs and continue chasing. Last caught wins.

SKILLS PRACTICES: WITH LARGE BALLS - 8–12 minutes

Individual practices

1 Dribble using different surfaces of both feet, keeping ball close.

2 Gently toss ball up to hit you on the head, then catch it. Use forehead and keep eyes open.

Partner practices

Shadow dribbling, 1 ball between 2, front person dribbling, other following behind. Change over after 6 touches.

INVENT A GAME OR SKILLS PRACTICE IN 2s - 3–5 minutes

Can you invent a simple game with a part of a line, 1 ball between 2? (e.g. heading to see how many consecutive headers; throw up to self to head past partner on line.)

GROUP PRACTICES AND SMALL-SIDED GAMES - 15–22 minutes

1 1 large ball among 4.
3 v 1 where '1' tries to win ball from 3 players who are inter-passing, football fashion. Decide a rule to give '1' a fair chance to win ball.

2 Heading-ball, foam ball, 4 or 5 a side.
Score by heading pass from team-mate over the opponents' end line. (n.b. 2 people must be involved in every goal.)

3 Change-bench-ball, 4 or 5 aside.
One passes to team-mate on chalk bench to score, then changes places with him.

Lesson Notes • 4–5 Lessons Development

Lesson's main emphases

a The NC requirements to explore and understand the common skills and principles, including attack and defence, in invasion games, and to play fairly, compete honestly and demonstrate good sporting behaviour.

b 'What you don't use, you lose.' In this lesson we are vigorously using the legs throughout. By exercising legs and heart muscle so strongly, we develop their strength and assist in their normal, desirable growth.

Equipment 30 large balls; 1 large foam ball.

TEACHING POINTS

Footwork practices

1 In the side step there is no direction change, just a change of line to a parallel one.

2 In chain-tag, emphasise 'Gentle touch to catch someone. No hard pushing or shoving.' Dodgers are encouraged to use good dodges such as direction and speed changes, and head, foot and shoulder fakes, rather than high speed running away.

Individual practices

1 In football dribbling, test class with an occasional 'Stop!' to see how quickly they bring ball under foot, still and under control.

2 In heading, feel the upper body and legs being active and coming into the action so that the ball is struck firmly by the forehead.

Partner practices

Shadow dribbling tests the dribbler's ability to repeat a short sequence, and tests the following observer's ability to recognise and copy the actions exactly.

INVENT A GAME OR SKILLS PRACTICE IN 2s

Games involving travelling with the ball to take it just over the line to score have the advantage that the ball is not continually wandering away, as when you score by sending it across the line.

GROUP PRACTICES AND SMALL-SIDED GAMES

1 In 3 versus 1, passing and screening, football fashion, a large flattish ball is recommended because it is easier to keep it in the limited area. For example, allow the passers 1 touch only, before they have to pass, to give the '1' a chance.

2 A target player on opponents' line can head a pass made, or catch and pass back to a running team-mate who shoots.

3 Player leaving chalk 'bench' should pass to a team-mate on court, then leave bench to make way for the one who made the scoring throw to come on to bench. A game of quick reactions. Keep awake!

Lesson Plan – 30–45 minutes

WARM-UP AND FOOTWORK PRACTICES - 5–7 minutes

1 Run beside partner, keeping together at same speed.

2 Now A changes speed over a very short distance to lose B in a sprint dodge. Change over dodgers.

3 Couples-tag. 3 couples start as chasers. When one of the pair touches a dodger, the caught dodger changes place with the chaser who touched him to form a new chasing couple.

SKILLS PRACTICES: WITH HOCKEY STICKS AND BALLS - 7–10 minutes

Individual practices

1 Walk with ball 'glued' to open side of stick. When you see a space about 2-3 metres ahead, push pass the ball into this space. Run after ball and repeat.

2 Indian dribble (turning stick up and down). Hold flat side of stick against ball with stick head pointing up, to right of ball. Now point head down and transfer to other, left hand side of ball. Move ball left and right with stick head pointing up and down.

3 Walk, moving ball from left to right to left in a curving formation around bean bags, cones, quoits, etc.

INVENT A HOCKEY PRACTICE IN 2s - 3–5 minutes

Can you invent a simple practice that we might all enjoy which keeps you both moving and uses and improves dribbling and pushing?

GROUP PRACTICES AND SMALL-SIDED GAMES - 15–23 minutes

1 Hockey games, half pitch, 2 v 2, 3 'lives'. Attackers score by push passing ball through goal, and have 3 lives. When they lose possession 3 times, attackers become defenders.

2 Free-netball, 4 or 5 a side.
No limitations on who can score or where you can go. No dribbling. To advance ball, run forward into space, particularly after passing.

3 Handball, 4 or 5 a side.
Goal when ball thrown between posts from outside 6 metre shooting circle. Decide rule to keep game moving, e.g. you must shoot after 3 passes.

Lesson Notes • 4–5 Lessons Development

Lesson's main emphases

a The NC requirements to improve the skills of sending, receiving and travelling with a ball, and to play small-sided versions of recognised games.

b Recognising that vigorous physical exercise, particularly in the fresh air, makes you fitter, is good for your heart, and makes you look and feel better. In winter, when we spend most of our time indoors, these lessons become even more important for young, growing children.

Equipment 30 hockey sticks and small balls; 2 large balls.

TEACHING POINTS

Footwork practices

1 Partners, side by side running, is an exercise in co-operation to maintain a steady, unchanging running rhythm together.

2 The sprint dodge practice shows the partners how easily a sudden, unexpected sprint can lose an opponent, to free the sprinter, for example, to receive a pass or shoot.

3 Encourage the dodgers to use good footwork rather than high speed running away to evade chasers. Direction changes, sprint dodges, and head and shoulder fakes should all be tried. Ask the 3 or 4 starting chasing couples to space themselves out over the thirds of the netball court.

Individual practices

1 In dribbling, the ball is in front of you, being pushed ahead by a series of gentle taps. To give ball a gentle push ahead, turn body slightly to face right, place stick behind ball, now between feet, and push without a sound as ball is hit.

2 In Indian, zig-zag dribbling, emphasise the dominance of the upper left hand in turning stick, and the sleeve-like right hand allowing ball to rotate both ways.

3 Use this left hand turning of the stick to dribble the ball up to, in between and around the scattered obstacles.

INVENT A HOCKEY PRACTICE IN 2s

For example, partners stand about 10 metres apart, one on a side line, other ready with ball. One with ball responds to signals of watching partner as he advances to partner's line. Agree a set of signals: dribble straight; dribble zig-zag; push ahead a short distance; push to me.

GROUP PRACTICES AND SMALL-SIDED GAMES

1 Half pitch, '3 lives' games allow both defenders and attackers to concentrate on one thing at a time. Teams should agree one main rule, how to re-start and how to limit opponents.

2 In free-netball, encourage shooting by giving 1 point for a near miss when ball hits hoop but does not go through. Some limit on where defenders and attackers may go will open up the game.

3 Aim for 'fast break' to opponents' end when your team gains possession, and have a target player to whom to try and pass.

Lesson Plan – 30–45 minutes

WARM-UP AND FOOTWORK PRACTICES - 4–6 minutes

1 Run, jump, land in 2 counts. Count '1' is, back foot, which must not move. With heel of back foot up and toes into ground, turn round or pivot other foot on '2'. Let front foot find a space. Repeat.

2 Free-and-caught. If caught by 1 of the 6 chasers in coloured bands, stand still, with hands on top of head. Others can free you by touching your elbows. Change chasers frequently.

SKILLS PRACTICES: WITH RUGBY BALLS OR LARGE BALLS - 6–8 minutes

Partner practices

1 All pairs in a third of netball court. Try to make a short pass of 2-3 metres, rugby fashion, to your partner. Pass at varied heights and speeds to avoid others around you, and according to the situation.

2 Shuttle pick up and place in 4s. A picks up ball from hoop, runs to put it in opposite hoop and stays at back of opposite line. B repeats to other side, and so on.

DEVELOP A WHOLE CLASS GAME WHERE HALF HAVE A BALL - 4–6 minutes

If touched by one without ball, put yours down for another to pick up. What other rules could develop this game? (e.g. ball-carrier may touch another with ball then have 2 rugby balls if quick enough to pick up his when placed on ground.)

GROUP PRACTICES AND SMALL-SIDED GAMES - 16–25 minutes

1 Rugby-touch, 4 or 5 a side.
Score by placing ball behind opponents' end line. If touched you must pass ball. After score, opponents throw ball from behind their goal line. Stress 'Run forward to gain ground until touched.'

2 Ground-football, 4 or 5 a side; large, flattish ball.
Keep ball below knee height at all times.

Score by placing foot on ball on opponents' goal line. Stress 'Receive ball, look for team-mate in a space, pass, then follow to help.'

3 Playground-hockey, 4 or 5 a side.
Score by placing stick on ball on opponents' goal line. For more open game, tell left and right side forwards or defenders to stay on their own sides of the court.

Lesson Notes • 4–5 Lesson Development

Lesson's main emphases

a The NC requirement to work safely, alone and with others, and to plan, perform and reflect.

b A strong sense of 'togetherness' within the class from the group chasing game; skills practices with a partner, then in lines of 4; a whole class chasing and dodging game where we are invited to invent some developments; and finally 3 small-sided versions of popular games where we feel strongly the sense of being in a team.

Equipment 15 rugby or large balls; 1 flattish large ball; 10 hockey sticks and 1 playground hockey ball.

TEACHING POINTS

Footwork practices

1 A 2-count stop when receiving ball on the move applies in netball and in basketball. The front foot which landed second may be moved to let you see around you or to take you and ball away from a defender. This action on a still rear foot is called 'pivoting'.

2 In free-and-caught, ask the 6 chasers to space out, with 2 covering each third of the netball court. Have more chasers if the 'freers' keep winning easily.

Partner practices

1 All of class in a third of the court, trying to interpass in 2s, requires much care, self-control and a good awareness of all around you. In rugby, you are allowed to run with the ball, which helps because you have more time.

2 Shuttle pick up from, or run and score in a hoop. This is a sprint pick up and score practice, involving you only.

DEVELOP A WHOLE CLASS GAME

In a lesson with a high level of social activity, a whole class 'invents and develops a game started and suggested by the teacher'. This should provide some good ideas, fun and excitement.

GROUP PRACTICES AND SMALL-SIDED GAMES

1 In rugby-touch, insist on gentle touching and no hard, dangerous pushing. With a good class, we can say 'no forward passing allowed in the opponents' half, but you may pass forward to advance ball to the halfway line.'

2 Ground-football needs 1 rule to help keep game open, by limiting attackers or defenders in some way. For example, '2 touches only in attack. Defenders may shadow, but must not tackle.'

3 Restrictions on defenders and attackers, as suggested, aim to keep game open with all spaced out better and more room to pass.

Lesson Plan – 30–45 r

WARM-UP AND FOOTWORK PRACTICES - 4–6 minutes

1 Follow your leader. Can you include some hurdling across the lines and some scissors jumps with nearer leg swinging up and over the line?

2 Cross court sprint relays in 2s, starting side by side at centre of court. One races te side line and back to touch partner who races to touch his side line and sprints back. Make 8 touches. Go!

SKILLS PRACTICES: WITH BATS AND BALLS AND SKIPPING ROPES - 8–12 minutes

Individual practices

Bat and ball

1 Walk, striking ball up, letting it bounce, striking it up.

2 Walk, batting ball down on to ground, making it rise to waist height.

Ropes

1 Skip on the move with feet together or one after the other.

2 Can you skip, travelling forward, backward and sideways?

Partner practices

Bat and ball

1 3 metres apart, one throws with gentle bounce for partner to strike back.

2 A strikes with own hand to B who catches at various heights.

Ropes

1 Can you follow your leader and build up to mirroring each other in your actions?

2 1 rope between 2. Show me ways in which 2 can skip.

GROUP PRACTICES AND SMALL-SIDED GAMES - 18–27 minutes

1 Skipping rope each with a partner. Show your partner some of your favourite ways to skip.

2 Non-stop-cricket, 1 ball, 1 bat among 4 or 5. Batter must run round post after hitting ball. Change duties often.

3 Mini-basketball with netball posts, 4 or 5 a side.
For more open game, ask left and right forwards and guards to keep to own side of court. Score 1 point for near miss and 2 for shot through basket. Decide on rule to game keep moving, e.g. no dribbling in own half. Pass and run forward to help!

Lesson Notes • 4–5 Lessons Development

Lesson's main emphases

a The NC general requirements to develop skill by exploring and making up activities, and to practise, improve and repeat longer sequences of movement.

b Remembering that our lessons take account of the time of year with very lively lessons in mid-winter, full of almost non-stop, running activities and games to make and keep us warm. This means trying to cover most of the less lively net/ball and striking/fielding practices and games from April onwards.

Equipment 16 small bat shapes and 16 small balls; 16 skipping ropes; 2 sets wickets or cones; 1 large ball.

TEACHING POINTS

Footwork practices

1 and **2** Many athletic activities – running, jumping and throwing – are being performed in every games lesson. We concentrate on their 'athletic-ness' more obviously from April on. 'Over, 1, 2, 3, over' in hurdling as we clear the imaginary hurdle on 'over', then take 3 steps between our hurdles on '1, 2, 3'. We help children discover their natural leading leg in hurdling, their swinging up leg in scissors jumping, and how to sprint off quickly from a semi-crouched start position in the relays.

Skills practices

Bat and ball and skipping practices are done individually then with a partner, with the same equipment, before changing to the other item of equipment for individual then partner practices. The very physical skipping contrasts well with the less vigorous bat and ball practices. Half the class are working with each of the 2 implements typically associated with the warmer weather of spring, summer and early autumn.

GROUP PRACTICES AND SMALL-SIDED GAMES

1 With good performers, skipping with a partner can progress to 2 skipping with 1 rope, to expand the class repertoire of skipping ideas and to practise 'sustained energetic activity', as required in the NC. Partners alternating to give non-stop skipping is also worth trying.

2 Non-stop-cricket is even more 'non-stop' when good bowling makes the batter hit the ball which means the batter has got to run. While the batter is running, all are involved in fielding, backing up the wicket or trying to give ball to bowler who bowls, whether or not the batter is at the wicket. Poor bowling, when the batter does not have to hit the ball, means no action for anyone.

3 In mini-basketball, where we can apply the 2-count footwork rule met and practised last month, encourage lots of shooting by giving 1 point for a near miss when the ball hits the hoop, and 2 points when the ball goes through the hoop. Bring posts in 2 metres from end line so that a missed shot stays in play.

Lesson Plan – 30–45 minutes

WARM-UP AND FOOTWORK PRACTICES - 4–6 minutes

1 Stay in one third of the netball court, space out sensibly and find out how many **(a)** long hops **(b)** bounding steps and **(c)** jumps from 2 feet to 2 feet you need to take across your third from line to line.

2 Now run round the whole netball court, jogging one third, sprinting the middle third, jogging the end third. Turn back and repeat.

SKILLS PRACTICES: WITH SHORT-TENNIS RACKETS, BALLS AND HOOPS - 8–12 minutes

Individual practices
Racket and ball

1 Walk, bouncing ball up on face of racket.

2 Walk, hitting it up, letting it bounce, hitting it up. Soft hits.

Hoop

1 Show me how you can use the hoop on the ground.

2 What can you do with the hoop, using 1 or 2 hands?

Partner practices
Short-tennis

1 One throws gently underarm to partner's forehand. Partner does forehand hit back to be caught by bowler.

2 Make little rallies to each other, emphasising 'side on' position.

Hoop

1 Bowl to partner while standing or running.

2 Show your partner a favourite way to skip with or balance on hoop.

GROUP PRACTICES AND SMALL-SIDED GAMES - 18–27 minutes

1 Hoop each.
Can you make up sequence that includes 3 different ways to use your hoop, e.g. throw up and catch, walk bowling, skip on the spot in hoop?

2 Short-tennis in 2s.
Throw over rope 'net' (long rope tied between netball posts) for forehand return to partner.
A hoop on bowler's side can be target for return strike.

3 Tunnel-ball-rounders, 4 or 5 a side.
Batting team follow striker to score by reaching 1, 2, 3, 4 cones before fielding team pass ball back through tunnel of legs to end person who calls 'Stop!' Each batter has 1 strike then teams change places.

Lesson Notes • 4–5 Lessons Development

Lesson's main emphases

a The NC requirement to improve the skills of sending, receiving and travelling with a ball in net games.

b Enjoying the variety within summer term games lessons. In the winter, to keep warm, the games played are nearly all invasion games. In summer we enjoy several versions of racket/net and batting/fielding games; practices with skipping ropes and hoops; and the athletic activities of running, jumping, throwing, hurdling and relays. There should be something for everyone to enjoy.

Equipment 16 short-tennis rackets and balls; 16 hoops.

TEACHING POINTS

Footwork practices

1 The long hop, the bounding step and the long jump to land on 2 feet are practices which relate to the triple jump. Self-testing across the third of the court will let some of the class learn that they are particularly dynamic as jumpers.

2 Jog, sprint, jog practices can be made more interesting by asking class to count how few sprinting strides they need to cross the middle third. Demonstrate with excellent striders whose thighs are high, and who stride rapidly and long.

Skills practices

1 Practise the individual and partner versions of each piece of equipment before changing to the individual and partner versions of the other one. Hoop on ground activities can include balancing round on feet or feet and hands; hopscotch in and out, as you go round; jumps across; run and jump into; cartwheel in and out. Hoop in hand activities can include skipping; throwing and catching; throwing with backspin; bowling.

2 Emphasise the importance of being 'side on' to partner in racket games so that racket can be at right angles to partner for an accurate straight return. Help partner in learning stages by aiming for partner's forehand side. Try to be stationary at time of hit.

GROUP PRACTICES AND SMALL-SIDED GAMES

1 Plan a hoop sequence to include 3 varied hoop activities. Aim for a contrast somewhere. For example, 1 action could be very vigorous, as in skipping; 1 on the move as in easy bowling; and 1 slow, where you balance walk round the hoop on the ground.

2 In short-tennis over low rope 'net', one throws good length to target hoop or chalk circle. The other with racket returns from a side on to partner position. To encourage care and accuracy the teacher can ask 'What is your best score in good hits for an easy catch before your practice breaks down?'

3 Limit distance ball is allowed to be hit in tunnel-ball-rounders to give fielders a chance to make their tunnel quickly and say 'Stop!' before the batters go all the way round and score 4 points. 'Keep the ball inside this third where we are playing.'

Lesson Plan – 30–45 minutes

WARM-UP AND FOOTWORK PRACTICES - 4–6 minutes

1 Run freely, following no-one and hurdling over lines. Which is your leading leg in hurdling?

2 Stand at an angle to a line about 3 steps from it. Can you take a 3-step approach and show me a scissors jump over the line? Start by stepping on to the foot that is your take-off foot.

SKILLS PRACTICES: WITH SMALL BALLS - 8–12 minutes

Partner practices

1 Across court, from side line to side line, practise the throwing action from a side on starting position.

2 Now stand closer, about 5 metres apart, with a line mid-way between you. Throw to your partner by way of a bounce on the target line.

3 Stand closer, about 3 metres apart, and throw low (mid shin) medium (waist) and high (head) to give your partner practice in receiving balls coming at varying heights.

INVENT A GAME OR PRACTICE IN 4s - 3–5 minutes

Can you invent a game using 1 small ball to develop throwing and catching? For example, 3 versus 1 in circle formation, with '1' in circle.

GROUP PRACTICES AND SMALL-SIDED GAMES - 15–22 minutes

1 Tip-and-run-cricket.
Batsmen must run to other end when ball is hit. Change duties often if others are slow to get batsmen out.

2 Hand-tennis, short-tennis or quoits.
Rope 'net' tied between netball posts. 1 v 1. What is your main rule? How many points before changing ends?

3 Timed team relay.
Each team member touches 2 lines and passes baton to next in line. Times of both teams taken several times to record improvement by better turning at ends and baton receipt.

Lesson Notes • 4–5 Lessons Development

Lesson's main emphases

a The NC requirements to explore and understand common skills and principles in net and striking/fielding games, to make appropriate decisions quickly and to plan responses.

b A varied content with the athletic activities of running, jumping and relays; striking/fielding skills; and net and striking/fielding games.

Those interested in testing themselves in running fast, jumping high throwing, catching, batting, bowling, fielding, and/or controlling a racket, have plenty to interest them here.

Equipment 15 small balls; set of wickets or pair of cones; rope 'net' and 10 short-tennis rackets or 5 quoits; 3 relay batons.

TEACHING POINTS

Footwork practices

1 Leading leg in hurdles swings straight up and down. Trailing, following leg bends and lifts round sideways and down to clear hurdle. Action is to run, almost unimpeded, over the low obstacles.

2 In scissors jumps the foot further from the line being crossed is the jumping, pushing foot. The leg nearer to the line swings up and over the imaginary high jump bar.

Partner practices

1 Throwing about 10 metres across court, start with straight arm behind you in side-on position. Throw by bending and stretching arm with hand coming over shoulder.

2 5 metres apart, with a target line between you, you will still throw overarm to make the ball bounce up well for your partner.

3 3 metres apart only, throw everything underarm with a straight arm action.

INVENT A GAME OR PRACTICE

The invented game or practice with 1 small ball among 4 should include either a variety of unpredicted angles and speeds at which the ball comes to the catcher, or some form of opposition to impede the thrower.

GROUP PRACTICES AND SMALL-SIDED GAMES

1 In tip-and-run-cricket, try to make the receiving batter play at the ball so that both batters must run to change ends. This gives all fielders action and the chance of a run out or a catch.

2 Play a level of net game which is appropriate for the class: quoits is the easiest, short-tennis with rackets the hardest.

3 Techniques to speed up the relay include: taking baton while moving forward; jumping into a turn at each line; jumping into a crouched springing position at each turn; rapid driving steps.

Lesson Plan – 30–45 minutes

WARM-UP AND FOOTWORK PRACTICES - 4–6 minutes

1 Run to all parts of the playground alternating between jogging and sprinting, emphasising **(a)** the straightening of the driving leg behind and **(b)** the good lift of the leading thigh.

2 With a partner, check how many standing broad jumps your pair needs to travel from side line to side line of netball court. Each starts from previous person's landing spot.

SKILLS PRACTICES: WITH SMALL BALLS - 8–12 minutes

Partner practices

1 Stand 10 metres apart. A rolls ball to B who runs forward, crouches to pick up and return to partner. Change duties.

2 Stand one behind the other. Front partner runs after ball, rolled past him or her, gently, stoops to pick up and return to partner. Change places after 6.

3 Stand about 2 metres apart and practise low, medium and high catches. How many can you catch without dropping any?

INVENT A GAME OR PRACTICE IN 4s - 3–5 minutes

Can you invent a game with 1 ball, emphasising fielding and catching? For example, 3 versus 1 rounders, where fielders have to make 3 good catches before batter goes round agreed 'diamond' to get batter 'out'.

GROUP PRACTICES AND SMALL-SIDED GAMES - 15–22 minutes

1 Cricket in pairs.
Each pair of batters to receive 6 balls, then all change duties by rotating.

2 Short-tennis, 2 versus 2.
Rope tied between netball posts. Agree a main rule. When will you change ends?

3 Athletics circuit.
Individual, timed 50 metres sprint. Hurdling over canes on cones. Standing long jump.

Lesson Notes • 4–5 Lessons Development

Lesson's main emphases

a The NC requirement (in athletic activities) to measure and compare results of own performances.

b Hoping that the class will remember their games lessons with great pleasure, 'an essential by-product of every good physical education occasion', and feel inspired to say 'We believe our lessons have been good for us in several ways. We have learned an enormous amount from our teacher and from one another. We are very pleased with and proud of our achievements and our skilfulness. Our class has helped us to get on well together because we have all helped or been helped by others many times. Fresh air and vigorous exercise are good for us, make us look and feel better, and inspire a calmness afterwards.'

Equipment 15 small balls; rope 'net' and 10 short-tennis rackets; set of wickets or pair of cones and 2 cricket bats; stop watch; 4 canes resting on 8 cones; 1 metre stick.

TEACHING POINTS

Footwork practices

1 If running rhythm is the same, a lifting of the leading thigh to give a longer stride speeds up the running.

2 In standing broad jumps, stand feet apart, toes turned in; swing arms up, down behind with knees bent; throw arms forward and jump.

Partner practices

1 To field a ball coming towards you, run in and turn as you bend down to put shoulder of throwing arm back. Ball is picked up near front foot and taken back to throwing position.

2 In fielding a ball rolling past you, run beside ball facing same direction, drop to pick up with nearer hand. Take 1 step into a side on position to put arm behind you into throw position.

3 Standing 2 metres from your partner in a catching practice, have both hands forward in a 'ready' position. Hands are cupped with fingers forward, thumbs out to sides. Cup closes round ball to stop it rebounding out again.

INVENT A GAME OR PRACTICE IN 4s

Emphasise that ball must stay in agreed, very limited area, which will probably be half of the third in which the group are playing.

GROUP PRACTICES AND SMALL-SIDED GAMES

1 A group of 8 is the ideal in pairs cricket, with batters having an over (6 balls) in which to score, then all rotating. Agree ways to be 'out'.

2 In short-tennis, agree the serving method, the scoring system and how many points in a game before changing ends.

3 Circulate in the athletic activities practices: be timed over 50 metres sprint; then you time the next sprinter; have several hurdles practices, trying to lead with same leg each time; then have several standing long jumps, with metre stick for distances.

Lesson Plan – 30–45 minutes

WARM-UP AND FOOTWORK PRACTICES - 4–6 minutes

1 Show me your best running, quiet and not following anyone. Can you visit all parts of our playground 'classroom' – sides, ends, middle and corners?

2 Keep running, and when I call 'Stop!' let me see who is first and last, standing perfectly still and balanced on tiptoes on a line. Stop! Repeat.

SKILLS PRACTICES: WITH SMALL BALLS - 8–12 minutes

Individual practices

1 Walk or jog, throwing ball from one hand to the other.

2 Walk, throwing ball up, clap hands, catch with both hands.

3 Juggle ball to keep it bouncing up and down, using hands, feet, thighs, head, etc.

Keep your best score.

Partner practices

1 Stand close, about 2 metres apart, and throw to each other. Each move back 1 large step and repeat. Move back, repeat. After 4 or 5 moves, start coming in again.

2 Stand 3-4 metres apart. One throws straight to partner who returns it with bounce half way. Change over after 6.

INVENT A GAME OR PRACTICE IN 2s - 3–5 minutes

Can you and your partner invent a game or practice with 1 small ball, throwing, catching or aiming? You can use part of a line if you wish, and no more than 1 third of the netball court.

(e.g. aiming practice at a line between you, starting 1 metre back from the line. Move back 1 step each time to see what is the limit of your accurate aiming.)

GROUP PRACTICES AND SMALL-SIDED GAMES - 15–22 minutes

1 Small ball between 2.
Dribbling ball by hand or foot, screening ball from pursuing partner. Decide on 1 rule to give pursuer a fair chance.

2 Hand-tennis, 2 with 2, rope 'net' tied between netball posts. See how long you can keep rally going over rope 'net'.

3 Competition in pairs, rotating clockwise, 3 shots each.
Netball, hockey, football and basketball shooting.

Lesson Notes • 4–5 Lessons Development

Lesson's main emphases

a The NC general requirement to respond readily to instructions, and to be physically active.

b Re-establishing the good habits and traditions of: good, safe and unselfish spacing with no uncalled-for talking; wholehearted participation with all contributing to the 'scene of busy activity', essential and obvious in all good lessons.

Equipment 30 small balls; long rope 'net' tied between 2 netball posts; 4 cones for goals; 2 hockey sticks; 2 large balls for football and basketball shooting.

TEACHING POINTS

Footwork practices

1 Pursue the elusive 'correct', quiet, easy running style with its lifting of heels, knees, arms, shoulders and head. Encourage running along straight lines, not the whole class following each other anti-clockwise as is common in primary schools.

2 The first-to-stop-on-a-line game is a way of training the class to be listening while working, as well as providing for the 'quick decision-making' needs within the NC.

Individual practices

1 In controlling the small ball, throwing and catching, the main point is to watch the ball closely all the time, catch it in a sensible position near eye level, and let the body parts concerned 'feel' how much effort is needed.

Too much force in throwing, batting and kicking is a common fault.

2 The hand clap places both hands in a good place and shape for a catch, near eye level where you can see ball well.

3 Allow 1 bounce between hits with the varied body parts. You need to 'keep on your toes' to move quickly to the next bouncing place, to be balanced, ready.

Partner practices

1 2-5 metres apart, partners should be throwing underarm, aiming at each other's hands reaching out to where they want the throw to go. Thrower follows through after sending the ball. Catcher lets hands 'give' after the catch.

2 The throw to bounce ball about 1 metre in front of partner starts from above shoulder.

INVENT A GAME OR GAMES PRACTICE

The example suggested can be co-operative, with pair keeping best score of consecutive hits, or competitive, trying to beat partner's number of hits.

GROUP PRACTICES AND SMALL-SIDED GAMES

1 The 1 versus 1 dribbling to screen the ball is competitive. Come to an agreement on the size of the 'pitch' to give chaser a chance, and 1 main rule for fairness.

2 In hand-tennis, emphasise 'side on to your partner' when you hit the ball at ideally just below shoulder height.

3 Careful, well placed shots in hockey and football, rather than over-hard shots that send the ball out of court and play.

Lesson Plan – 30–45 minutes

WARM-UP AND FOOTWORK PRACTICES - 4–6 minutes

1 Follow your leader, who will show you a sequence of 2 or 3 lively leg actions. Can you work together to repeat the actions in unison?

2 Half of the class with coloured bands tucked into back of shorts. All chase to collect and retain as many bands as possible.

SKILLS PRACTICES: WITH LARGE BALLS - 8–12 minutes

1 About 3 metres apart, practise passing to your partner's chest and then running into a new space to receive the return pass. Use 2-handed, chest, bounce and overhead passes.

2 Run side by side, interpass rugby fashion.

3 Shadow dribbling with foot. Change after 6 touches. Following partner notes the actions being shown and changes places with leader to try to repeat the sequence.

INVENT A GAME OR PRACTICE - 3–5 minutes

Can you invent a game for 4 players and 1 ball, using 1 or more of the 3 ball skills above? (e.g. 3 versus 1, where the '3' may keep the ball by using chest passes when a partner is available, or football dribbling when no partner is available.)

GROUP PRACTICES AND SMALL-SIDED GAMES - 15–22 minutes

1 2 v 2 passing large ball.
3 passes = 1 goal. Encourage short passes to partner who should have moved into a space.

2 Floor-football, 4 or 5 a side.
To score, arrive on opponents' goal line, ball under foot. Keep ball below knee height. Receive, look for team-mate, pass, move to new space to help. Decide ways to make game more 'open', e.g. 2 players in front half, 2 in rear.

3 Free-netball.
No positions or limits to who may shoot. Passing to a partner who has moved, unmarked, into new space. 'Pass and follow your pass. Stop shouting for a pass. Move to a good space to be ready to receive a pass.'

Lesson Notes • 4–5 Lessons Development

Lesson's main emphases

a The NC requirements to improve the skills of sending, receiving and travelling with a ball, and to make appropriate decisions quickly and plan their responses.

b Remembering that with the approach of colder weather, the habit of quiet work, immediate responses and near non-stop activity must be insisted upon so that all keep warm, and all parts of an enjoyable and varied lesson can be covered.

Equipment 15 large balls; 15 coloured bands; 1 flattish large ball for the floor-football; 1 set netball apparatus.

TEACHING POINTS

Footwork practices

1 In follow-the-leader, emphasise that leader must lead partner into good spaces, visiting all parts of the playground, preferably travelling along straight lines. 3 actions would be a challenging sequence to observe and copy.

2 In coloured-band-chase, let us be adventurous and do more chasing after others' bands than hiding to retain own band.

Skills practices

1 3 metres apart, 'Pass and move sideways into a space. Give ball and go. Pass, move, signalling with leading hand, receive' until these become habitual actions over a short distance.

2 Only 1-2 metres apart in side by side, rugby style, passing and catching. Turn the upper body and pass ball with both hands just ahead of partner for him to run on to.

3 Shadow dribbling, follow leader who peels off to end of line after a short sequence, using changes of feet or direction.

INVENT A GAME OR PRACTICE

1 ball among 4 to create an activity, competitive or co-operative, to develop and improve any of the 3 skills already practised. If a group has no idea, suggest the 3 versus 1 sample practice.

GROUP PRACTICES AND SMALL-SIDED GAMES

1 In 2 versus 2, team passing, defending pair can be passive (not trying to grab ball) if passers are being unsuccessful. Whether passive or highly active, 1 defender must confront the ball-carrier, keeping between him and the intended receiver. This forces the receiver to move quickly to find a space not blocked by the ball-handler's defender.

2 Softish football stays in playing area better than a hard bouncer, giving more action and less waiting about. Scoring is difficult and the defending team has a big advantage. Limits may need to be put on the defenders (no tackling in opponents' half, for example).

3 In netball, encourage shooting with a point for a near miss, hitting ring, and 2 points for a correct score. Emphasise that the passer is expected to move 2-3 metres into a space, to be available to receive the next pass.

Lesson Plan – 30–45 minutes

WARM-UP AND FOOTWORK PRACTICES - 4–6 minutes

1 Run, changing direction often. Pushing hard with 1 foot to go other way.

2 Teacher's-space-tag. Try to cross middle third of netball court guarded by teacher and 4 helpers in coloured bands without being caught. Crossing untouched earns you 1 point. (Teacher checks best score and changes helpers frequently.)

SKILLS PRACTICES: WITH HOCKEY STICKS AND BALLS - 8–12 minutes

Individual practices

1 Revise running with stick in right hand carry position. On 'Change!' bring left hand to top of stick, stick down to just above ground. On next 'Change!' return stick to 1 hand in suitcase position at right side.

2 Indian dribble side to side, along a line, round chalk marks, or round cones or quoits. Hold flat side of stick against right side of ball, stick head pointing up. Now point head down and transfer to other, left hand side of ball. Move ball left and right with stick head pointing up and down.

Partner practice

Dribble about 4 metres to line between you. Push to partner who receives and repeats. Run back to own line after passing.

INVENT A GAME OR SKILLS PRACTICE - 3–5 minutes

Invent a game in 2s with 1 ball and part of line, using dribble and/or gentle push pass. (e.g. stationary partner passes ball to running partner, who moves to left and right to receive and return. Aim at space into which running partner is moving.)

GROUP PRACTICES AND SMALL-SIDED GAMES - 15–22 minutes

1 2 v 2 hockey across half of area.
Attacking pair interpass to place ball on opponents' line. Opponents may only intercept a pass. Push pass gently. No tackling. When opponent confronts you, you must pass to partner.

2 Bench-ball, 4 or 5 a side.
Goal scored when catcher on chalk 'bench' receives good throw. Change catcher often, particularly in cold weather. Encourage 'pass and move to receive a pass.'

3 Heading-ball, large foam ball, 4 or 5 a side. Goal scored when attacker heads ball over opponents' line. No running with ball. Pass and run forward. When near line expect pass to forehead for shot at goal. After a goal, ball thrown in from end line by team scored against.

Lesson Notes • 4–5 Lessons Development

Lesson's main emphases

a The NC requirements to explore and understand the common skills and principles, including attack and defence, of invasion games, to sustain energetic activity and show understanding of what is happening to their bodies when they are exercising.

b In really cold weather keep the discussion, which ideally follows every demonstration, until back in the classroom. A class trained to expect questions in the warm after being outside will watch more intently, remember and, of course, learn, which is the whole point.

Equipment 30 hockey sticks and small balls; 1 large ball and 1 large foam ball; playground chalk for marking the 'bench'.

TEACHING POINTS

Footwork practices

1 Practise direction changes at lines, with right foot, for example, stopping you then pushing off to the left.

2 In teacher's-space-tag, emphasise careful running and dodging, looking out for others. Use good dodges, not dangerous fast sprints, to avoid being caught. Stop the game every 12 seconds to keep careful control, calm them all down, and bring in new chasers.

Individual practices

1 Running, carrying stick at right side, is a good exercise in 'sustaining energetic activity' as well as a good teaching point, practising the efficient, safe way to run with the stick when not playing the ball.

2 In side to side dribbling, strong left hand grip turns the stick which rotates inside the sleeve of the more loosely held right hand. 'Point of stick up, point of stick down. To left, to right.'

Partner practice

In the push, emphasise that the stick is placed behind the ball then pushed, with no sound of stick on ball, not hit with a big, dangerous, preliminary backswing.

INVENT A GAME

If the less creative are having difficulty in devising and agreeing a practice, and are standing, becoming cold, they should have the example activity given to them to do.

GROUP PRACTICES AND SMALL-SIDED GAMES

1 In hockey, dribble to advance the ball until confronted by an opponent when you must pass the ball, ideally into a space for partner to run in to. Players may attack side by side or one ahead of the other.

2 In bench-ball, only the catcher may stand on the 'bench'. After a goal, the team scored against throw in from the end line. Bench-catcher is encouraged to move from side to side along the bench to assist throwers find him, unmarked, still on the bench.

3 In heading-ball, 2 players are needed to make a goal. You may not throw the ball up and head it yourself.

Lesson Plan – 30–45 minutes

WARM-UP AND FOOTWORK PRACTICES - 4–6 minutes

1 Run round the whole netball court once, then run a third, hop a third, and leap a third to one end. Repeat.

2 Dodge and mark in 2s. Marker shadows dodger. On 'Stop!' both must stop immediately to see who is the winner – dodger clear or marker still within touching distance. Change duties.

SKILLS PRACTICES: WITH RUGBY BALLS OR LARGE BALLS - 8–12 minutes

Group practices in 3s with 1 ball

1 Passing weave. A passes to B and goes to B's position. B runs to centre with ball, passes to C, then goes to C's position as C runs into centre to pass to A. Receive; run in and pass to opposite side; run to outside.

2 2 v 1, team passing. 2 passers try to make groups of 4 passes which equal a goal. '2s' keep about 3 metres apart only to give '1' a chance.

INVENT A GAME OR SKILLS PRACTICE - 3–5 minutes

Invent a game in 3s with 1 ball and part of line in small area of playground. Use dodging and passing. (e.g. passing pair try to touch third person with ball. When touched, you become one of chasing pair who must pass and not run with ball.)

GROUP PRACTICES AND SMALL-SIDED GAMES - 15–22 minutes

1 Rugby-touch, 4 or 5 a side.
Place ball on opponents' line to score. After score, opponents throw in ball from behind their line. With ball, run forward and straight. Pass if touched. Increase scoring chances with target player on line for passes.

2 Mini-basketball, 4 or 5 a side, netball apparatus.
Left and right side forwards and defenders keep to own sides of court for more open game. You may dribble, but passing is quicker. In attack, a diamond shape with target player near opponents' goal is a useful tactic.

3 Playground-hockey, 4 or 5 a side.
Score by placing ball on opponents' goal line. Left and right side attackers and defenders keep to own side of court so more room to move and pass. Push pass only. No hitting or swinging stick behind or in front.

Lesson Notes • 4–5 Lessons Development

Lesson's main emphases

a The NC requirement to play small-sided and simplified versions of recognised games.

b Taking a reasonable level of individual and partner skill for granted now that we are half way through Year 5 of the NC, and moving on to a higher, team level of thinking and performing. 'Watch this team' or 'Watch this group' should now be heard as often as 'Watch this individual' or 'Watch this pair.' The team, the game, the offence, the defence, the tactics, the rules and the scoring systems are all now to be emphasised more as we set and demand higher standards and levels of expectation during these primary school years of enthusiastic pursuit of skilfulness and achievement.

Equipment 10 large or rugby balls; netball apparatus and 1 large ball; 10 hockey sticks and a playground-hockey ball.

TEACHING POINTS

Footwork practices

1 Whole class start behind an end line. All run round the outside of the court and back to starting line, from which they then progress down court with running, then hopping, then long stride leaping. Repeat, starting from opposite end line.

2 In dodge-and-mark, emphasise 'Use good dodges, direction and speed changes, and fakes with head, foot or shoulder to dodge away, not high speed sprinting which can cause bumps and accidents and gives no practise in either dodging or marking.'

Skills practices

1 In 3-player passing-weave, ball starts at centre, from where it is thrown to an outside person who runs, carrying ball in to centre, for next pass out to opposite side. After each pass you follow to the place where you passed and all 3 players will be moving, almost nonstop, as they weave round the figure 8.

2 2 versus 1, where '2s' may not run with ball, and work hard to move into spaces to which passes can be made. Pass across 2-3 metres only, since long throws mean the '1' in the middle has no chance to make an interception.

INVENT A GAME

Another example might be for the '1' in a 2 versus 1 game to try to touch the ball, then change places with the one who had the ball becoming one of the ball passing players.

GROUP PRACTICES AND SMALL-SIDED GAMES

1 In rugby-touch, the 'tackle' has to be made by both hands of tackler touching the runner's hips. This is harder to achieve than the previous touch of hand on person, helps the attacking team and leads to more scoring if runners will keep on running.

2 In mini-basketball, aim for a '1 on 1' marking situation, where each knows his opponent to mark or dodge away from.

3 In playground-hockey, restrict player movement in an agreed way to allow more open play. Outlaw and make big fuss against hitting.

Lesson Plan – 30–45 minutes

WARM-UP AND FOOTWORK PRACTICES - 4–6 minutes

1 In your running, practise side steps and direction changes to avoid others coming towards you.

2 1 versus 1, across court, line to line, dodging and marking, with dodger using good footwork and fakes. Change duties.

SKILLS PRACTICES: WITH LARGE BALLS - 8–12 minutes

Partner practices

1 2-hand pass from shoulder over running partner's head for a jump and catch, about 3 metres away. Run to space to jump to catch.

2 Juggle ball with foot, thigh or head. Single, controlled bouncing between you both.

3 1 versus 1, dribbling with foot to screen ball from pursuing partner.

INVENT A GAME - 3–5 minutes

Can you invent a 1 versus 1 game, using the throwing, juggling or screening practised above?

(e.g. football-tennis over a line 'net'.)

GROUP PRACTICES AND SMALL-SIDED GAMES - 15–22 minutes

1 Team passing, 4 or 5 a side, 1 large ball. Pass to team-mate in a space and not too far from you, ideally about 3 metres. Grab ball into stomach on receipt. 4 good passes = 1 goal. Vary passes to include chest, bounce and overhead passes.

2 Free-netball, 4 or 5 a side. No limits to area or who may shoot. No dribbling. Pass and move forward for return pass. 1 point for near miss, hitting hoop. 2 points for goal, through hoop. If overcrowding around ball, discuss solutions (e.g. at least 1 to stay in own half).

3 Floor-football, 4 or 5 a side, slightly flat ball. Score by arriving on opponents' goal line, ball under foot. Keep ball below knee height. Defenders stay in own half, attackers in opponents' half, so less overcrowding. To encourage passing play, 2 passes may be made before opponents can tackle.

Lesson Notes • 4–5 Lessons Development

Lesson's main emphases

a The NC requirements to plan, practise, improve and refine performance, including within their own created games with their rules and scoring systems.

b Remembering that mid-winter and dark evenings probably mean that the lifestyle of the majority of our girls and boys is now at its least physical, most inactive and sedentary, and mostly indoors.

This lively lesson, out in the fresh air, with its chasing game warm-up, varied co-operative and competitive skills practices, 'invent a game' and varied small-sided team games, aims to inspire the action, play, fun and friendly competition that is particularly lacking in January.

Equipment 15 large balls; netball apparatus; 1 flattish big or medium sized ball for football.

TEACHING POINTS

Footwork practices

1 The side steps and direction change practices could be done in two-thirds or one-third of the netball court so that you would continually be dodging others coming towards you.

2 In 1 versus 1, across court, line to line, dodge-and-mark, ask the dodgers to move fairly slowly and try to beat the defender with a sudden clever dodge or direction change, never a sprint past them.

Partner practices

1 Runner moves when thrower signals readiness by bringing ball up to throwing position. Runner can also signal by pointing 1 arm to side chosen.

2 You can juggle to a pattern. 'Me, me, me; you, you, you' or 'Me, you; me, you.'

3 In screening the ball in football, try to keep your back towards the attacker with ball remote from attacker's side.

GROUP PRACTICES AND SMALL-SIDED GAMES

1 In team passing, the goal is to make sets of 4 passes, without loss. Good dodging is essential to find a good space in which to receive the ball. Faking, as if to pass one way then passing a different way, should be tried here. Defenders should mark a player each and be a 'big' nuisance by spreading arms and legs wide to prevent passing or receiving.

2 In free-netball, good spacing can be imposed by limiting some players' movements, for example to own half of court, or defenders must be passive, allowing passes to be made without interference in own half of the court.

3 Flattish ball helps the floor-football by rolling away less often.

Lesson Plan – 30–45 minutes

WARM-UP AND FOOTWORK PRACTICES - 4–6 minutes

1 In your running, emphasise 'straight ahead' action of head, legs, arms and shoulders.

2 Tag, where the 6 starting chasers in coloured bands can catch you if you are running about within the lines. You can take refuge and be safe on a line. When caught take a coloured band and become a chaser. Be good sports and don't hide for too long on a line.

SKILLS PRACTICES: WITH HOCKEY STICKS AND BALLS - 8–12 minutes

Partner practices

1 Push pass, 5 or 6 metres apart, and move to a new position to receive your next pass. Emphasise:

a feet sideways to direction of push and shoulder width apart

b ball between feet and level with front foot

c stick placed behind ball and pushed, no sound of stick on ball

d stick kept low at end of stroke.

2 Side by side, dribble slowly forward. On signal 'Push!' stop dribbling, push gently ahead of partner who now continues dribbling slowly and carefully, waiting for signal to 'Push!'

GROUP PRACTICES AND SMALL-SIDED GAMES - 15–22 minutes

1 Hockey tackling, a third of group without a ball.
Those with a ball dribble in area trying to avoid tackles by those without a ball. Tell class about 'Obstruction rule': dribbler must not shield ball with body or turn to place body between ball and opponents. Keep feet facing the way you are going when tackler approaches.

2 Rugby-touch, 4 or 5 a side.
Score by placing ball down on opponents' line. When touched you must pass ball. You may pass forward in own half, but only sideways or backwards in opponents' half. Run straight and fast until touched, to gain ground.

3 Change-bench-ball, 4 or 5 a side, with chalk 'bench'.
Goal is scored when you pass ball to team-mate on 'bench' then run to bench to change places with him. He must pass ball to team-mate on court before leaving bench. Challenge teams to agree rule to speed up play, e.g. only 1 pass is allowed in own half.

Lesson Notes • 4–5 Lessons Development

Lesson's main emphases

a The NC general requirement to improve skills such as sending, receiving and travelling with a ball in invasion games.

b Working individually in the warm-up, in pairs in the partner practices, in 4s (or 5s) in the games, to try to make this lesson almost non-stop. With the almost continuous action ensuring that no-one is cold, and with 3 varied games as the lesson's climax, it is hoped that there is something for everyone to look forward to, to enjoy while participating, and to reflect on with great pleasure.

Equipment 30 hockey sticks and 15 small balls; 1 rugby ball; 1 large ball; chalk for marking the 'benches'.

TEACHING POINTS

Footwork practices

1 Much running is spoiled by arms and shoulders twisting instead of pointing straight ahead. If you run along a line, your hands should remain parallel to the line, not cross it, as often happens.

2 If class stay on lines too long, becoming cold and not giving chasers a chance, the teacher should call 'All move!'

Partner practices

1 Emphasise that the push pass is literally a silent push with stick starting behind and touching ball. There must be no dangerous hitting with wild backswings of the stick.

2 In the change from dribbling to pushing the player has to move side on to the ball to make the push pass to the partner.

GROUP PRACTICES AND SMALL-SIDED GAMES

1 In the introduction to tackling in hockey, one third of the class are allowed to try to 'steal' a ball by contacting the ball and trying to take it away. Those with the ball may not 'screen' it as you may do in football, but they can try to push ball past the would-be attacker and run round him.

2 In new-image-rugby we must now pass the ball sideways or backwards in the opponents' half of the court. If the ball is passed forwards in the opponents' half, a 2-person scrum is formed. The ball is put in to the scrum by a player of the non-infringing team whose scrum team-mate is the one who hooks it back into play.

3 In cold weather particularly, change over the bench-catcher often. Encourage the catcher to be lively, on the move continuously, trying to position well for a variety of chest, overhead and bounce catches, moving from end to end of the 'bench'.

Lesson Plan – 30–45 minutes

WARM-UP AND FOOTWORK PRACTICES - 4–6 minutes

1 Running, using 2 thirds of netball court, slowly when near others, more quickly when space allows. Emphasise short rapid strides, forward body lean and explosive arm action in sprinting.

2 Third of class in each third of court. Sprint to touch 4 sides of third, back to start. Run in a straight line, not in a circle. Repeat 2 or 3 times, with class final for regular winners in each group.

SKILLS PRACTICES: WITH RUGBY BALLS OR LARGE BALLS - 8–12 minutes

1 Triangle pass, 5 metres apart, 1 ball. A passes to B and runs to B's place as B passes to C and runs to C's place as C carries ball to what was A's place to re-start drill.

2 Lines of 3 running up and down court passing to each other along the line. Change middle person over often.

INVENT A GAME OR SKILLS PRACTICE - 3–5 minutes

Invent a running, passing practice in 3s with 1 ball. (e.g. lines of 3 run forward. Middle person with ball passes to one side then runs behind that person who becomes new middle. He now passes and runs behind to other side.)

GROUP PRACTICES AND SMALL-SIDED GAMES - 15–22 minutes

1 Rugby-touch, 4 or 5 a side.
Ball may be passed forward in own half, but only sideways or backwards in opponents' half. Stress 'run fast and straight until touched' to gain ground. Team-mates must back up the player with the ball.

2 Playground-hockey, 4 or 5 a side.
Place ball on opponents' line to score. 2-touch hockey: receive on '1', find team-mate moving to space for pass on '2'. Defenders stay in own half for space. 1 rule to keep game moving, e.g. no dribbling in own half. Pass only.

3 Heading-ball, large foam ball, 4 or 5 a side.
After pass from team-mate, head ball over opponents' goal line to score. No running with ball. Pass and run forward to advance ball for pass to a forehead when near opponents' line. A target person there can head or pass back.

Lesson Notes • 4–5 Lessons Development

Lesson's main emphases

a The NC requirements to explore and understand the common skills and principles, including attack and defence, of invasion games, and to play fairly, compete honestly and demonstrate good sporting behaviour.

b Remembering, as we come to the end of the winter games programme, with its emphasis on the lively, running or invasion games, that teachers should be on the look out for, and be warm in their praise for the many signs of achievement, improvement and success being enjoyed by so many children after about 6 months of working and practising hard. While these little games played in the small area of 1 third of a netball court might seem diminutive to the teacher, to the child who proudly says 'I have just scored my first ever try in rugby' the occasion is most important and memorable, and needs to be seen to be appreciated.

Equipment 10 rugby or large balls; 10 hockey sticks and 1 ball; 1 large foam ball.

TEACHING POINTS

Footwork practices

1 As primary school children become older we can ask them to work harder at more things for longer, and we keep the running going longer without stopping, plus asking them to be aware of spaces and to include short sprints in good style when space permits.

2 After the full warm-up and 2 or 3 sets of sprints we can ask them to reflect on how their bodies are feeling after the strong leg activity. 'Breathing deeply; feeling hot; whole body feels alive; slightly puffed out; feel wide awake, etc.'

Skills practices

'Sympathetic' is the expression often used of the way we pass to another to ensure a carefully aimed pass is sent at just the right speed and height for the runner to run on to. Turn your upper body right round towards the catcher.

INVENT A GAME

Aim for continuous, whole court activity, with each group keeping very close, always aware of and never impeding other groups. Because we may run with the ball in this practice, it should be easy for Year 5 to refine it.

GROUP PRACTICES AND SMALL-SIDED GAMES

1 In new-image-rugby, a 2-person scrum follows a pass forward in the opponents' half. Non-offending team player puts ball at far foot of scrumming player in his team who is the only one allowed to hook it back.

2 In playground-hockey, encourage children to make up rules to help keep this difficut game moving without all encircling the ball 'like bees round a honey pot'. 'No tackling! One defender only may confront and the player must pass' is a good suggestion.

3 Heading-ball attackers can try 'Plan 1 – get ball to head of target player for a header' or 'Plan 2 – get ball to target player who passes back to team-mate running in for a shot.'

Lesson Plan – 30–45 minutes

WARM-UP AND FOOTWORK PRACTICES - 4–6 minutes

1 Run and jump long or high, and continue running. In your long jump swing your leading foot well forward. In your upward jump swing your leading knee high up in front.

2 Free-and-caught. If caught by a chaser in coloured band, stand still, hands on head. Others can 'free' you by touching you on the elbow. Change chasers often.

SKILLS PRACTICES: WITH LARGE BALLS - 8–12 minutes

Individual practices
Keep ball above head, throwing, catching, volleying. To volley, cup hands, palms clear of ball. 2 thumbs and index fingers make a triangle through which you sight ball. Elbows slightly bent, knees bent. Strike and follow through on to toes.

Partner practices
2 metres apart only. Volley high and low to make partner move back, forward and from side to side.

INVENT A GAME OR GAMES PRACTICE IN 2s - 3–5 minutes

Can you create a little game or practice to help you improve your volleying skills, sharing 1 ball? (e.g. each in turn tries for a long rally, volleying ball straight up above head. Watching partner keeps count.)

GROUP PRACTICES AND SMALL-SIDED GAMES - 15–22 minutes

1 Volleyball, 1 ball between 2, rope 'net' between netball posts.
Throw up to self and volley to partner. How long a rally can you make? No 1-handers but you may volley up to 3 times on your side before sending it to your partner.

2 Long skipping ropes.
Group skipping side to side, low or overhead, depending on ability and numbers. Work out best way to learn long rope skipping. When do you enter rope?

3 4-player rounders, 2 games.
Children to decide on scoring, how out, number of balls bowled per batter.

Lesson Notes • 4–5 Lessons Development

Lesson's main emphases

a The NC requirement to plan, perform and refine their own games and practices, working safely alone and with others.

b Understanding that net and striking/fielding games are less active and vigorous than the invasion games. With young learners these games can be static and inactive, and they should never be taught outdoors in cold winter weather. From April till July, during warmer weather, the emphasis is on teaching skills, small group practices and games of net and striking/fielding games.

Since many of the NC requirements for athletic activities are also being pursued during summer months, it is essential that the children are trained to listen, respond, practise and work well and enthusiastically to cover as much work as possible. It is equally essential that schools totally reject the very common practice of 15-a-side rounders, often with the teacher bowling and 30 children spending an entire lesson learning nothing, practising nothing, hardly moving, and satisfying nothing within the NC.

15-a-side rounders, the commonly seen 'game' within summer term physical education, is the antithesis of all that good physical education stands for. It is neither physical nor educational and should be banned as a waste of precious time.

Equipment 20 large balls; 3 long skipping ropes; 2 playbats and small balls and cones for rounders; long rope as 'net' for the volleyball.

GROUP PRACTICES AND SMALL-SIDED GAMES

1 Co-operative volleying practice over rope 'net' tied above head height of teacher. Emphasise the power that comes from the straightening of legs, elbows and the wrist flick follow through. Move early, receiving, to place body under ball in the settled down ready position with high arms ready. Aim ball above head of partner when you volley for an easy return.

2 Groups of 4 or 5 with a long skipping rope. Come in when rope hits ground and is swinging away from you. Come out to left when rope swings to your right. With beginners, let the rope swing low from side to side only, not overhead.

3 Limit area where ball may travel to that third of netball court. 6 turns for each batter, then all change round, seems a fair way to ensure that all experience all the activities.

Lesson Plan – 30–45 minutes

WARM-UP AND FOOTWORK PRACTICES - 4–6 minutes

1 Run and hurdle over lines in playground. Which is your leading leg in hurdling?

2 2s, sprint relay. Start back to back at centre of court with partner. On signal, one runs to nearer side line and back to touch partner who runs to line at his side. Who can touch 10 lines first?

SKILLS PRACTICES: WITH SMALL BALLS, BATS AND BALLS - 8–12 minutes

Partner practices

Small balls

1 Aim at a line between you and count your good hits.

2 Stand close, throwing and catching underarm. Move a little further apart, and note the point when you start to throw over-arm. Then start moving closer again.

Bat and ball

1 Balance ball on your bat; hit it up 3 times; then hit it to partner to see if he can catch it dead on bat; then repeat. Balance; strike up for 3; hit to partner.

2 8 metres apart, one strikes ball along ground for partner to run to field.

INVENT A GAME - 3–5 minutes

Can you invent a game for 4 players with 1 bat and 1 ball, lines making a corner and a limited area? (Batter in corner strikes ball from own hand and calls name of the person who has to try to make a good catch. If successful, catcher takes bat.)

GROUP PRACTICES AND SMALL-SIDED GAMES - 15–22 minutes

1 'Newcombe', 2 with 2, rope 'net' tied between netball posts.
Throw ball over net to serve. Receiver catches in volley position before returning over net. How long a rally can your 4 make?

2 Non-stop-cricket in 4s, 2 games.
Batter runs around skittle and back. Bowler may bowl at wicket even if batter not there. Change duties often.

3 Follow-the-leader, choice of small or large balls, bat and ball, skipping rope, quoits or bean bags. Follow leader at about 2 metres and aim to develop a matching sequence in unison. Can leader include 3 different actions?

Lesson Notes • 4–5 Lessons Development

Lesson's main emphases

a The NC requirements to practise, adapt, improve and repeat longer and increasingly complex sequences of movement, and to improve the skills of sending and receiving a ball in striking/fielding games.

b Putting the class in the picture, as always, about the contents of this lesson. 'The lesson this month includes athletic activity practices – running, hurdling, relays, throwing; striking/fielding games skills practices and game of non-stop-cricket; net games practices in the game of Newcombe; and the opportunity to 'develop your own games practices' with 1 bat and ball among 4 of you, and the follow-the-leader with a choice of equipment. The lesson is filled with variety and I hope that you all find something to enjoy very much. I also hope that you will all work hard, quietly and enthusiastically because we have a lot to do.'

Equipment 15 bats and small balls; 5 large balls and long rope 'net' for Newcombe, cones or wickets for cricket, small and large balls, bats, ropes, bean bags, quoits for follow-the-leader.

TEACHING POINTS

Footwork practices

1 In hurdling, leading leg goes up and down straight. Following leg trails to side, round and over imaginary hurdle. If it came straight through it would hit the hurdle.

2 For fair play's sake, all must run and touch the line before racing back to touch partner. Look out for and rebuke any who cheat by failing to touch the line, or who run off before the hand touch from partner.

Partner practices

1 Small ball practices to develop aiming, throwing, catching, and the judgement of height, speed and distance vital in striking/fielding games.

2 In the bat and ball practices we are practising good timing and judgement of direction, force in sending a ball in striking/fielding games, and fielding a ball rolling towards you.

INVENT A GAME

The invented game or activity can be non-competitive, simply being practised to improve a difficult skill or, more likely, it will be competitive in a very limited court area, where the main consideration is to provide activity for all.

GROUP PRACTICES AND SMALL-SIDED GAMES

1 Newcombe is volleyball with the simplified skill of momentarily receiving the ball in the volley position before sending it.

2 Bowl straight in non-stop-cricket to force the batter to play and then run. This makes the game more lively with all active: fielding, backing up, waiting for return throw for runout or to bowl again.

3 In follow-the-leader, plan for a 3 part, varied sequence. Can you repeat your little pattern together?

Lesson Plan – 30–45 minutes

WARM-UP AND FOOTWORK PRACTICES - 4–6 minutes

1 Run beside a partner, keeping together at same speed. Feel a good cruising rhythm that you can continue easily.

2 Now, by yourself, can you show me a 3-step approach and a scissors jump over 1 of the many lines on the playground? 1, 2, 3 and swing up inside leg over the imaginary bar.

SKILLS PRACTICES: WITH SHORT-TENNIS RACKETS AND BALLS AND HOOPS - 8–12 minutes

Individual practices
Short-tennis

1 Walk with ball balanced on racket, strike it up, catch it dead.

2 Practise forehand and backhand strokes, side to side, over line.

Hoops

1 Can you spin the hoop on wrist, ankle or waist or on the ground to make it come back to you?

2 Try skipping with 1 or 2 hands on the hoop.

Partner practices
Short-tennis

1 Partner throws for partner to hit back.

2 How long a rally of forehand hits can you make over a line 'net'?

Hoops

1 Can you bowl the hoop about 3 metres to your partner?

2 Can you and your partner make up a skipping routine together or alternately?

GROUP PRACTICES AND SMALL-SIDED GAMES - 15–22 minutes

1 Short-tennis, 1 with 1.
Working with, not against your partner, how long a rally can you make? Serve by dropping ball and hitting it over net.

2 Tunnel-ball-rounders, 4 or 5 a side.
Batting team all follow leader round diamond, scoring 1 point for every cone passed before fielders pass ball through legs to end of tunnel and shout 'Stop!'

3 Newcombe or quoits, over rope 'net' tied between netball posts.
Point is scored when ball or quoit lands on opponents' court or fails to clear net. Let children decide on a fair way to serve and when to change ends.

Lesson Notes • 4–5 Lessons Development

Lesson's main emphases

a The NC requirements to develop an understanding of and play small-sided versions of recognised games, and to improve sending and receiving skills in net games.

b Allocating a full 6 or 9 minutes at least to each of the 3 games of the final, most important part of the lesson for a satisfactory climax.

Equipment 15 short-tennis rackets and balls; 15 hoops; long rope 'net' tied between netball posts for quoits or newcombe; 5 quoits or 5 large balls for net games.

TEACHING POINTS

Footwork practices

1 In side by side running together, runner on the inside steps short on turns because outer partner's arc is greater. Try to 'feel' your steady cruising speed, running in unison.

2 Scissors jumping is slow and springy with the last, jumping stride a heel, ball, toes rocking up action. Bent leading knee and both arms swing up into the action.

Individual practices
Short tennis

1 To catch a ball 'dead', go up to meet it early, then let racket 'give' to catch ball without a rebound.

2 Shuffle side to side, playing gentle forehand and backhand shots up and over the line.

Hoops

1 Spin hoop on the spot. Now try throwing it away with back spin to make it come back.

2 Low swing from side to side with 1 hand is a good way to start skipping with a hoop before the difficult overhead swings.

Partner practices
Short-tennis

1 Encourage a side on to partner position when striking, so racket easily faces intended direction of hit. From ready position facing partner, turn to one side or other. Take racket well back, ready to hit ball at top of bounce when opposite you.

2 Rally gently at about 5 metres from the line, trying to hit ball to about 2 metres in front of partner.

Hoops

1 Hold top of hoop steady with non-bowling hand. Bowl it by pulling with a flat hand on top of hoop.

2 The skipping routine can include skipping with hoop flat on ground.

GROUP PRACTICES AND SMALL-SIDED GAMES

1 In co-operative short-tennis, aim to land ball just short of partner's forehand to make the return easy, leading to long rallies. Take racket back early and turn for a 'side on' hit.

2 In tunnel-ball-rounders, the ball is struck by hand forwards and must remain within the third of the netball court. Fielding player who receives ball stands and lets team-mates form a tunnel behind him. Last one in tunnel calls 'Stop!'

3 Competitive quoits or newcombe, where 5-point games are played before changing ends. Much decision-making by children about rules and scoring systems should be encouraged.

Lesson Plan – 30–45 minutes

WARM-UP AND FOOTWORK PRACTICES - 4–6 minutes

1 With a partner, 2 metres apart, one behind the other, run avoiding other couples, at rhythm set by leader. On 'Change!' following runner sprints to take lead, 2 metres in front, and tries to repeat rhythm set by partner. Repeat 'Change!' often.

2 Pairs standing high jump with 2-footed take-off and landing. Partner notes how high you have jumped, e.g. to partner's knees, hips, etc.

SKILLS PRACTICES: WITH LARGE BALLS - 8–12 minutes

Partner practices

1 Two metres apart, make volley passes. 2 thumbs and index fingers make a triangle through which you sight ball. Elbows and knees are slightly bent, and you strike and follow through smoothly on to toes.

2 Five metres apart, throw to partner who catches it momentarily as in newcombe or volleys it straight back as in volleyball.

INVENT A GAME OR PRACTICE IN 2s - 3–5 minutes

Can you create a little game or practice to help you improve your volleying skills, sharing 1 ball? (e.g. each in turn tries for a long rally, volleying ball straight up above head, watching partner keeps count.)

GROUP PRACTICES AND SMALL-SIDED GAMES - 15–22 minutes

1 Volleyball, 2 v 2, over rope 'net'.
Serve with volley push from behind line. 3 volleys allowed on 1 side. No 1-handers. You score while you are serving.

2 Short-tennis, 2 v 2, over chalk 'net'.
Teams decide on a fair system of serving, how many points in a game before changing ends, and 1 main rule.

3 Tip-and-run-cricket.
Rotate when a batter is caught, bowled, stumped or run out.

Lesson Notes • 4–5 Lessons Development

Lesson's main emphases

a The NC requirements to play small-sided versions of recognised games, and to make judgements of performance and suggest ways to improve.

b A hoped for end of year reflection (worth pursuing as much as end of lesson or end of demonstration reflection) that would produce the following encouraging comments: 'We have looked forward to and enjoyed our Year 5 games lessons. They are good fun and we believe that the vigorous exercise in the fresh air is good for us. We have learned an enormous amount from our teacher and from one another. We are pleased with and proud of our achievements and our skilfulness.

We have always felt refreshed, wide awake and calm after our games lessons, and we think that this helps our classroom work.'

Equipment 15 large balls; long rope 'net' tied between netball posts; 10 short-tennis rackets and 3 balls; 1 kwik cricket set.

TEACHING POINTS

Footwork practices

1 Each partner can set his own repeating rhythm and see if he can remember it second and third time round after running at partner's speed in between.

2 Standing high jump can also be done over a garden cane held low by kneeling partner. Jumper prepares with a swing of arms above head; arms swing down behind back and knees bend; arms swing up and jump is made. 2 feet to 2 feet.

Partner practices

1 Cupped hands for volley. Use finger and thumb tips, never the flat palm of hand. Aim high enough for ball to be above partner who plays it above and slightly in front of head.

2 Ball thrown must be high enough for partner to be under, and to play at above head height.

INVENT A GAME

One can volley up high for receiving partner to let bounce, then catch and throw for another high return. Rallying, using the volley only, is very difficult and soon breaks down.

GROUP PRACTICES AND SMALL-SIDED GAMES

1 Competitive volleyball, 2 versus 2, starts to look like 'proper' volleyball with its service start, its 3 strikes allowed on each side, and its scoring only while you are the serving team. The children should be allowed some decision making such as: **(a)** how many points make a win? **(b)** how to serve easily so that all are able to do it? **(c)** what scaling down of rules is reasonable if game is not flowing smoothly because skill level is not good enough?

2 In competitive short-tennis, let class decide the 1 main rule, ways to score, and any ways to help longer rallies.

3 In tip-and-run-cricket with 2 batters, bowl straight to force batters to change ends and keep game alive and interesting.

Lesson Plan – 30–45 minutes

WARM-UP AND FOOTWORK PRACTICES - 4–6 minutes

1 Run quietly and well, tall and relaxed, keeping away from all others. When I call 'Stop!' check to see that you are not near anyone. Keep looking for spaces and running into them.

2 Free-and-caught. 6 chasers wearing coloured bands try to touch and catch others who then stand still with both hands on top of head. Those caught can be freed by others not caught touching them on the elbow.

SKILLS PRACTICES: WITH LARGE BALLS - 8–12 minutes

Partner practices

1 Revise chest, bounce and overhead passing at 3 metres apart and move into a new space for the return pass.

2 Shadow dribble as in basketball. Changes of hand, speed, height for variety.

3 Juggle with hand, foot, head or thigh to strike ball upwards, and allow 1 bounce only between touches. What is your best score?

INVENT A GAME OR PRACTICE IN 2s - 3–5 minutes

Can you invent a game with 1 ball and 3-4 metres of a line? Include dodging, travelling with ball. (e.g. in rugby, basketball or football fashion, can 1 player score by placing ball on line guarded by the other player?)

GROUP PRACTICES AND SMALL-SIDED GAMES - 15–22 minutes

1 Dribbling-tag, large ball each.
Dribble basketball fashion, ball in control. Touch others to score. Think of a rule to make game more interesting.

2 Bench-ball, 4 or 5 a side.
Pass to team-mate on chalk 'bench' to score. No-one else may go on bench. Change bench-catcher often, particularly on cold days.

3 2 half-pitch games of ground level football, large, flattish ball among 4.
B v C v D, trying to score past A, the goalkeeper. Scorer becomes goalkeeper. At least 2 dribbling touches before shooting.

Lesson Notes • 4–5 Lessons Development

Lesson's main emphases

a Improving the skills of sending, receiving and travelling with a ball in invasion games.

b Ensuring that September is used to re-establish the traditions which are essential for a successful and enjoyable games programme – working quietly, but vigorously; responding to instructions immediately; and unselfishly sharing space.

Equipment 15 large balls; 2 flattish balls for football and 4 cones for goals; playground chalk to mark 'bench'.

TEACHING POINTS

Footwork practices

1 Insist on silent running in good style with heels and knees lifting. Run along straight lines, not in a circle all following each other. 'Stop!' is an exercise in gaining an immediate response. Praise the quick responders and rebuke others who need to smarten up.

2 In free-and-caught, stop the game every 12 seconds or so, to establish control and check the success of the chasers. Insist on 'gentle touches only when catching, with no dangerous pushing.'

Partner practices

1 The teacher has the right to expect the skills of passing, catching and dribbling to be done well after several years of being practised. 'Court circulation' and the way the children move after passing now become the main teaching points. We move to find a space to receive a return pass. We move to take a pass on the move when it is passed to one side or ahead of us. We move away from the action sometimes to leave more room for others in our team to do things, unhindered by those standing around.

2 With a well spread hand, use your wrist, not elbow or shoulder, as the moving part to bounce the ball. Crouch slightly, down nearer the ball, with bent knees for closer control but a straight back to be able to see around you.

3 Ball is being sent by many body parts, with 1 bounce in between. Player must keep 'on toes' to be able to move quickly to be nicely balanced for next strike up.

INVENT A GAME OR PRACTICE

Both need to agree the nature of the game; how to score fairly; how and where to re-start after a goal; when to change roles; and the 1 main rule to make the game fair.

GROUP PRACTICES AND SMALL-SIDED GAMES

1 In dribbling-tag, use low dribbling stance with hips and knees well bent, back straight, head up. To add interest, rule that a player on a line is 'safe', but must keep dribbling.

2 In bench-ball, where lots of opponents may be crowding in front of catcher, encourage chest, bounce and overhead passes, with good fakes to mislead the marking opponents.

3 Careful, not too hard, low shots at goal, so ball not forever being lost. All think of ways to give player with ball more time and space.

Lesson Plan – 30–45 minutes

WARM-UP AND FOOTWORK PRACTICES - 4–6 minutes

1 Run, jump, land, 1, 2. Do not move back foot which landed first. Pivot on it, with moving front foot looking for a space. Then run, jump, land, 1, 2, pivot, again.

2 Long-line-tag. Start with 4 couples as chasers with hands joined. When caught by a couple, join the line and continue chasing. Last caught is winner.

SKILLS PRACTICES: WITH LARGE BALLS - 8–12 minutes

Partner practices

1 Throw to partner who runs, jumps to catch ball above head, lands one foot in front of other, 1, 2, then pivots on rear foot and throws high pass to partner now running to jump to receive return pass.

2 Stand 2 metres apart, throw for partner to head back for you to catch. Eyes on ball, use forehead. Place one foot in front of the other for good balance. Change after 6 headers.

INVENT A GAME OR PRACTICE IN 2s - 3–5 minutes

Invent a game with 1 ball and part (3-4 metres) of a line. Throw, catch and/or head.

(e.g. heading-tennis over the line, with or against your partner.)

GROUP PRACTICES AND SMALL-SIDED GAMES - 15–22 minutes

1 Mini-basketball, netball apparatus, 4 or 5 a side.
Dribbling permitted but 'pass and run' for more open, exciting game. 1 point for near miss if ball hits basket, 2 for a score. Apparatus in 2 metres from end line so ball not always going 'out' after a shot.

2 Heading-ball, 4 or 5 a side, large foam ball. Score if ball headed over opponents' end line after pass from team-mate. Good attack tactic to have 1 player near opponents' line for easy pass back to team-mate running forward for header at goal.

3 Hockey, 2 a side, half-pitch, '3 lives' games. Attackers start from centre and try to outwit and score against defenders. When a team has won or intercepted ball 3 times (lives), teams change places and duties.

Lesson Notes • 4–5 Lessons Development

Lesson's main emphases

a The NC requirements to understand and play small-sided versions of recognised games, and to make appropriate decisions quickly and plan their responses.

b Remembering that the most important and climactic part of the lesson is the last part, the group practices and small-sided games. To ensure that this part is never cut short, leading to 3 very short, therefore frustrating games, the teacher needs to be aware that the command to 'Begin!' the games must be given at least 15 or 22 minutes (short or long lesson) before the command 'Stop everyone!', when equipment is collected and the lesson ended. This tradition is as important as those emphasised in the last lesson.

Equipment 15 large balls; 1 large foam ball; 10 hockey sticks and 2 balls.

TEACHING POINTS

Footwork practices

1 Pivoting round on your rear foot is allowed in netball and basketball. Jump and land, calling out '1, 2' as each foot lands. The one to land first is fixed as the pivot foot. Rotate on the ball of this foot with heel lifted. Front foot does the moving, 'looking' for a partner to pass to. A pivot can also be used as a fake to evade a close marking opponent.

2 Start with 2 or 3 quartets as chasers, possibly with 1 working in each third of the court.

Partner practices

1 The point of pivoting, to land legally and to be mobile on the spot, will become obvious in the partner practice which emphasises that Year 6 games players are expected to be mobile before and after receiving passes.

2 In the heading practice, 'Keep your eyes open and aim your header at your partner's hands.' Eyes shut and passively letting ball hit forehead are the usual faults.

INVENT A GAME OR GAMES PRACTICE

The line can be the goal an attacker has to throw, roll, kick, bounce, carry or head the ball across.

The line can also be a net for heading/football-tennis over.

GROUP PRACTICES AND SMALL-SIDED GAMES

1 Ask players to shape the game when they are attacking. Opponents should be marking '1 on 1', and a diamond shape, for example, makes an open formation and easier passing, particularly if the rear court guard and their markers have to stay in 1 half.

2 With a diamond attacking formation in heading-ball, the target player at front of diamond can head for goal, or catch and pivot to look for a running team-mate to whom to pass.

3 One hockey rule which might help to make game more enjoyable is 'No tackling by defender. Confront the player with the ball and they must pass it.' Goal can be a hit between cones 3 metres apart.

Lesson Plan – 30–45 minutes

WARM-UP AND FOOTWORK PRACTICES - 4–6 minutes

1 Free running over whole court. Jog or sprint as space permits. To sprint, increase heel and knee lift, forward lean of body. Use short, rapid arm movements.

2 Couples-tag. 3 couples start as chasers, hands joined. When one of couple touches a dodger, the dodger and that chaser change places.

SKILLS PRACTICES: WITH HOCKEY STICK AND BALLS - 8–12 minutes

Partner practices

1 Shadow dribbling: leader makes 6 touches of ball then swaps with following partner who repeats leader's sequence. Gentle taps, stick near ground in front of player.

2 Push pass across 4 or 5 metres. Watch approaching ball carefully. Note to which side partner is running into a space. Receive ball, pass to partner's new position, then move for return pass into good open space.

INVENT A GAME OR PRACTICE IN 2s - 3–5 minutes

Invent a practice with 1 ball to develop dribbling and/or passing and receiving. (e.g. 10 metres apart, one dribbles ball up to and round partner and returns to starting place. Ball pushed to partner who repeats. Coach each other for improvement.)

GROUP PRACTICES AND SMALL-SIDED GAMES - 15–22 minutes

1 Hockey, 2 v 2, 2 games.
Dribblers or passers aim to arrive on, or pass ball to partner to finish on opponents' goal line, ball in control under stick.

2 Junior-netball, 4 or 5 a side, all may score.
Left and right side defenders and attackers keep to own sides of court for 'open' game and better visibility for marking when opponent has ball.

3 New-image-rugby, 4 or 5 a side, 4-person scrums.
Place ball down on opponents' goal line to score. If touched on hips by opponent's 2 hands, pass forward in own half, sideways or backwards in opponents'. Run fast and straight with ball.

Lesson Notes • 4–5 Lessons Development

Lesson's main emphases

a The NC requirements to explore and understand common skills and principles, including attack and defence in invasion games, and to play fairly, compete honestly and demonstrate good sporting behaviour.

b Knowing and sticking to team positions and marking an opponent closely. These are the 2 greatest contributors to making our games start to look more advanced and expert. The 'bees all round the honey pot' situation, typical of games in a small area, can only be changed when forwards, centres and defenders understand their positions and try to operate in those areas, instead of all chasing after the ball, all the time. If your opponent marks and stays with you, when your team has possession, you can take him away from the action to give team-mates more space.

Equipment 30 hockey sticks and small balls; 1 large ball; 1 rugby ball.

TEACHING POINTS

Footwork practices

1 As they warm up, running freely, using the whole area, it is a good idea to stop the class occasionally, ask them all to stand in a space as far away from others as possible, and observe the vast number of open spaces which you hope they will strive to create in their games. Only good positioning and pulling defenders into the shape you wish, can produce this.

Partner practices

1 Dribbling should now include reverse stick work, toe down and flat surface to right, as well as normal toe-up dribbling, face of stick to left. Stick turn created by left hand turning the stick inside loose, sleeve-like, right hand grip.

2 The push, made by placing stick next to ball and pushing, makes no sound and follows through low in front. Stick never goes behind you where it might strike someone.

INVENT A GAME OR PRACTICE

One partner gives the other a commentary of dribbling actions: 'straight; zig-zag to left and right; then short push forward to dribble round me; now pass to me for my turn.'

GROUP PRACTICES AND SMALL-SIDED GAMES

1 In 2 versus 2 hockey across half of one third of the court, encourage children to agree rules to help game flow more smoothly, e.g. defenders do not tackle, they confront to make attacker pass, and might stay in own half to help attack.

2 In netball, 'pivot often to look for running partner; to stop, nicely in balance; to fake marking opponent to go wrong way.'

3 In new-image-rugby we can go on to a 4-person scrum after a forward pass in opponents' half. 'Scrum half' places ball for team-mate in scrum to hook back. Rest of scrum passive.

Lesson Plan – 30–45 minutes

WARM-UP AND FOOTWORK PRACTICES - 4–6 minutes

1 All run to end of court then return using 'boxer's shuffle' sideways, backwards to starting line, to practise defensive footwork. Feet apart, hips low, weight forward.

2 Dodge and mark across court, 1 versus 1, side line to side line. Marker moving backwards tries to stop partner running past him to cross the side line. Keep rotating duties.

SKILLS PRACTICES: WITH RUGBY BALLS OR LARGE BALLS - 8–12 minutes

Small group practices

1 4s, 1 ball, half or third of court. Move, interpass to team-mate running to receive. Use corners and do not always move when others running into spaces.

2 3 versus 1 in small area, team passing. 3 passes = a goal. Change '1' often. Stress 'pass and move': having passed, move into a space, ready to receive.

INVENT A GAME OR PRACTICE IN 4s - 3–5 minutes

Invent a game to develop passing, catching, running into spaces. (e.g. in a square facing inwards, 6 metres apart, A passes to B, follows ball to touch B's corner and back to own place. B passes to C, follows and returns, etc.)

GROUP PRACTICES AND SMALL-SIDED GAMES - 15–22 minutes

1 New-image-rugby, 4/5 a side, 4-person scrums, line-outs.
Place ball down over opponents' line to score. Pass when hip tackled by opponent's 2 hands. Forward pass in own half, sideways or backwards only in opponents'. Agree positions to shape and space team.

2 Floor-football, 4/5 a side with flattish ball.
Arrive on opponents' end line, ball under foot, to score. Ball below knee height.
Left/right attackers or defenders on own sides of court so that it is easy to see who to work against or to mark. Receive; find team-mate; pass; move.

3 Change-bench-ball, 4/5 a side.
Goal when team-mate on bench catches your pass and throws to another on court before leaving bench. You become new bench-catcher. Vary passes to bench-catcher. Fakes mislead opponents.

Lesson Notes • 4–5 Lessons Development

Lesson's main emphases

a The NC requirement to plan and make up their own games, and to practise, refine and improve performance.

b Emphasising the '1 on 1' marking as an important feature of our lesson to make the physical demands even greater, help to maintain mid-winter warmth, and make the games start to look more like end of Key Stage 2 standard – understanding offence and defence; using simple tactics; understanding roles as team members.

Equipment 8 large or rugby balls; 1 flattish large ball for football; 1 large ball and playground chalk for drawing 'benches' in bench-ball.

TEACHING POINTS

Footwork practices

1 Class can mirror teacher in the 'boxer's shuffle', defensive footwork practice, moving backwards against an imaginary opponent.

2 In 1 versus 1, across court, dodge-and-mark to practise defensive footwork, ask attackers not to sprint past defenders. They should use careful, varied dodges, changing speed or direction and using head, foot and shoulder fakes.

Skills practices

1 Only pass to a moving player with a well aimed pass ahead of him. Others can help by keeping out of the way and leaving space for the running player.

2 To give the '1' a chance, there is no running with the ball, as is normal in rugby.

INVENT A GAME OR PRACTICE

The main feature to practise is the running into spaces. If running to receive a pass, the space can be in front, behind or to either side of you, particularly if it follows a successful dummy or fake, deceptive move to take your opponent another way.

GROUP PRACTICES AND SMALL-SIDED GAMES

1 In new-image-rugby, we now have 4-person scrums when ball is wrongly passed forward in opponents' half, and 4-person lineouts when ball goes over a side line. Non-offending team put ball in and only they are allowed to play the ball.

2 Floor-football is spoiled by all players wanting the ball and all being in a tiny area, usually with no possibility of open play or good passing movements. Enlist suggestions of class to make game more open and enjoyable by limiting some players to certain parts of the court. If defenders stay in own half; if defenders do not tackle team in its own half; if attackers have 1 'free' pass that is not intercepted, for example, the game will improve for everyone.

3 Change-bench-ball demands quick decision making by the scoring team. Defending team have to decide 'Who am I marking now?'

Lesson Plan – 30–45 minutes

WARM-UP AND FOOTWORK PRACTICES - 4–6 minutes

1 Run round quietly with tall, relaxed action, and practise side steps or changes of direction to avoid others coming straight towards you.

2 Chain-tag. 3 or 4 couples are chasers. When caught, join the chain. When it grows to 4, split into 2 chains and continue to chase. Last one caught wins.

SKILLS PRACTICES: WITH LARGE BALL - 6–10 minutes

Partner practices

1 3 metres apart, show me 2-handed chest and bounce passes to your partner after making a fake pass in other direction. Move to new space for return pass.

2 Follow-the-leader, football dribbling for 6 touches. Vary feet, speed, direction, parts of feet. Following partner observes, remembers sequence and repeats it on 'Change!'

INVENT A GAME OR PRACTICE IN 4s - 4–6 minutes

Can your 4 invent a game or practice to develop hand or foot control with 2 balls? (e.g. while 2 count their rapid passes at 3 metres apart, the other 2 dribble round them, 1 at a time. Change duties and see which pair makes more passes.)

GROUP PRACTICES AND SMALL-SIDED GAMES - 16–23 minutes

1 Floor-football, 4 or 5 a side with flattish ball. Score by arriving, ball in control, on opponents' goal line. Ball below knee height. 2 defenders stay in own half. Left/right side attackers and defenders play on own sides for 'open' play. 'Pass often, move to new space to help.'

2 Mini-basketball, 4 or 5 a side, netball apparatus.
1 target player stays near opponents' basket when his team has ball, to receive pass for easy shot at goal or pass back to team-mate in position to shoot. Agree how to restart after goal and whether to allow dribbling.

3 Playground-hockey, 4 or 5 a side, push pass only.
Scoring push in front half of opponents' court only. No hitting. Shape team into left and right side attackers and defenders for better spacing. Agree 1 rule to help game, e.g. 1 v 1 only.

Lesson's main emphases

The NC places a very big emphasis on planning, performing and reflecting in physical education. The doing or performing, particularly in cold January, should be uppermost in the teacher's intentions anyway. The planning is straightforward and should be being asked for continually throughout the lesson. The challenging words 'Can you ... ?' or 'Show me...' call for planning to answer the tasks. For example 'Can you plan to include changes of feet, speed or direction in your dribbling sequence where your partner is following?' and 'In attack in your 3 games, can you plan to move into a space every time you have passed the ball?' Team-mates with the ball then know that at least 1 of their team is going to try hard to be available for the next pass. Other team-mates can help by keeping out of the way and pulling their defender out of the way.

Reflection/evaluation, usually after a demonstration by an individual, a pair or a group, is not so easy in mid-winter when we want to keep inactive, stationary moments to an absolute minimum. To enable almost non-stop activity from beginning to climactic busy, exciting end of the lesson, it is recommended that we ask for very few comments immediately after the demonstration and continue the reflecting in class after the lesson.

Teacher questioning while the activities are continuing might inspire all to reflect more while working. For example 'While you are defending in your 3 games, can you feel where your body weight should be while you are 'boxer's shuffling' backwards?' (Weight should be forward on balls of feet, not back.)

Reflection leads to planning and adapting in a more focused way and should lead to better, more efficient and correct performing.

The teacher should be planning to keep the class active for the maximum number of minutes out of the 30 or 45 so that when the children reflect on their January games lesson, they are agreed that they performed almost non-stop, kept warm and had 3 good length games to finish with.

Equipment 15 large balls; 10 hockey sticks and 1 ball.

GROUP PRACTICES AND SMALL-SIDED GAMES

1 The difficulty in controlling the lively ball and evading the very close marking opponents makes the game difficult for the attacking team. If necessary, for a more enjoyable attacking game, place limits on the defenders. For example, no tackling in a team's own half; or allow 1 unhindered pass before you may tackle; or only 1 defender ever allowed to tackle 1 attacker.

2 If necessary, for a more flowing, enjoyable attacking game, leave the target player unmarked to encourage a quick advance of the ball, with minimum dribbling or delay, to the opponents' end of the court. The target player, with his back to the basket, must be encouraged to keep moving into good spaces to receive a chest, bounce or overhead pass.

3 In hockey, encourage the attackers to shape the game with some keeping well away, to provide space. Insist on defenders marking own opponents (i.e. being shaped and spread out by attackers).

Lesson Plan – 30–45 minutes

WARM-UP AND FOOTWORK PRACTICES - 4–6 minutes

1 Follow-the-leader, trying to include at least 3 different leg activities you can practise, improve and perform together.

2 Dodge-and-mark in 2s. On 'Stop!' both freeze. Dodger clear of marker's reach or marker able to touch dodger wins. Change duties.

SKILLS PRACTICES: WITH HOCKEY STICKS AND BALLS - 6–8 minutes

Partner practices

1 Shadow dribble, both with ball. Leader does easy left and harder right turn where feet move ahead of ball so it is behind as you overtake it.

2 Right side dodge. Practise dribbling up to your partner who is facing you. Push ball past non-stick side of partner, run past partner by going to own left. Practice 6 times and change.

INVENT A GAME - 4–6 minutes

Invent a 2 v 2 game to develop dribbling and dodging, in half of third of court, e.g. '3 lives', half pitch game. Attacking pair have ball. Defenders, 1 on goal line, 1 on court, try to steal ball three times. Score by arriving on line, ball in control under stick. Change over.

GROUP PRACTICES AND SMALL-SIDED GAMES - 16–25 minutes

1 Playground-hockey, 4 or 5 a side.
In own half quick pass to team-mate to clear ball from near own goal. In opponents' half outwit opponents with right side dodge or good dribble. Scoring pass from within opponents' half only.

2 New-image-rugby, 4 or 5 aside, 4-person scrums.
Score by placing ball down behind opponents' goal line. Pass when touched on hips by opponents' 2 hands. No forward passing.
    Fakes to fool opponents. In 4-person scrum, scrum half puts ball by right foot of far team-mate, the only one who may hook ball back.

3 Free-netball, 4 or 5 a side with no scoring restrictions.
Forwards and defenders all mark opponent with ball. When team-mate has ball, dodge to lose marker long enough to receive pass. Think of ways to score in addition to netball ring, e.g. target hoops at ends.

Lesson Notes • 4–5 Lessons Development

Lesson's main emphases

a The NC requirements to sustain energetic activity and show understanding of what is happening to their bodies while exercising, and to explore and understand common skills and principles, including attack and defence, in invasion games.

b Emphasising that the lesson is full of examples of players being in close proximity to other players, dodging, shadowing and marking. In our games let us try the fast break as an attacking tactic, to travel from one end to the other at full speed before the opposing defenders. 'Get there fastest with the mostest!' is an American expression for a main tactic from the world of professional basketball.

It is essential for the whole team to be thinking 'fast break' so that when they suddenly steal the ball or it is their throw in after a goal, the ball is passed rapidly down court to fast breaking players, all looking for a pass in an open space. 3 such passes can send the ball to the opposite end before the opponents, running backwards, arrive there.

At the moment of a 'change of possession', when team A steal or intercept the ball from team B, all team A members are unmarked because team B had been trying to get away from team A. At that moment, team A should take advantage of not being marked to 'fast break!' before team B pick up and mark their opponents again.

During the 'fast break' learning period, the class can be asked to co-operate in helping to produce good fast breaks by being quite passive in defence during the first few seconds of an attempted fast break, possibly allowing 2 or 3 passes to advance unimpeded.

Players knowing their respective positions – left or right side attack or defence, or centre – is essential to good fast breaking progress down the court. Good '1 on 1' marking is equally important so that the game is being shaped by the attacking players to allow room for good individual attacking to be practised.

Equipment 30 hockey sticks and 15 small balls; 1 rugby ball; 1 large ball and netball apparatus.

GROUP PRACTICES AND SMALL-SIDED GAMES

1 Team with ball thinks 'minimum dribbling in own half; much first time passing to 'break' quickly; shape game in opponents' half to create spaces for easy passing or individual dribble to score.'

2 In new-image-rugby, a 4-person scrum is awarded to the non-offending team after a forward pass anywhere now. Ball thrown in to foot of far team-mate in scrum, the only player allowed to strike the ball back from scrum.

3 Occasionally, in this and the other 2 games, the teacher should call 'Stop!' to check that defenders are marking their own opponents and that attackers are trying to shape the game.

Lesson Plan – 30–45 minutes

WARM-UP AND FOOTWORK PRACTICES - 4–6 minutes

1 Steady run beside partner. Now 'sprint dodge' ahead for a moment, then slow down to side by side run again. Repeat. Change duties.

2 10-points tag. All start with 10 points. Lose 1 each time touched. Teacher checks who has most points left and who caught most.

SKILLS PRACTICES: WITH RUGBY BALLS OR LARGE BALLS - 8–12 minutes

Small group practices

1 4s, file pass and follow, rugby passing. A passes to B and runs to end of opposite line, B to C, then runs to end of opposite line. How many passes by your team in 30 seconds?

2 4s, pick up, put down. One picks ball up on line, runs to put it down after 3 metres, then runs to opposite end. Others in turn pick same ball up and put down after 3 metres.

INVENT A SKILLS PRACTICE IN 4s - 3–5 minutes

Invent a run, pass, touch down practice with 2 balls. (e.g. run pass to partner in small part of third of court. On 'Change!', all balls touched down, find new partner and ball, start again.)

GROUP PRACTICES AND SMALL-SIDED GAMES - 15–22 minutes

1 New-image-rugby, 4 or 5 a side.
Score by placing ball down over opponents' line. Re-start with back pass at centre. No forward passing. Pass after 2-hand touch on hips by opponent. Devise extra ways to score, e.g. target hoops at corners to bounce ball in.

2 Handball, 4 or 5 a side.
Score by throwing ball from outside goal semi-circle into goal. Goalkeeper only allowed in scoring area. Challenge teams to suggest other ways to score, e.g. knock down a goal skittle.

3 2 versus 2, half pitch, '3 lives' games.
Choice of football, netball, basketball, hockey, rugby-touch or heading-ball. After defenders make 3 scores or interceptions change over duties.

Lesson Notes • 4–5 Lessons Development

Lesson's main emphases

a The NC requirement to understand, make up and play small-sided versions of recognised competitive games.

b Encouraging the class to think beyond the limited, traditional ways of scoring in running/invasion games so that the games become more exciting, scoring increases and more children go home saying 'I scored today!' For example, 1 point might be awarded in rugby for a score in a hoop. 2 points can be scored by a traditional try. In handball, 2 points for a ball through the goal, 1 point for a ball bounced into a hoop, also in the scoring area. 1 point for a near miss, hitting ring in netball or basketball, 2 points for a shot passing through the hoop.

Equipment 8 rugby or large balls; 1 large ball for handball; and large balls, hockey sticks and balls for the choice of games in 2 versus 2, 3 'lives' games; netball apparatus.

TEACHING POINTS

Footwork practices

1 A sprint dodge is a sudden and excellent way to shake free of a close marking opponent, momentarily, to receive a pass.

2 In 10-points-tag, ask class to plan ways of dodging others, and to recognise what they (or other impressive dodgers) are doing. Sprint dodges; head, foot and shoulder fakes; direction changes.

Skills practices

1 4s, file pass and follow, should build up to a pass each second. 'And 1, and 2,...' where 'And' is the pass, and the number is the run by passer.

2 The pick up, put down relay, practising gathering and the act of scoring, is played across a 12 metre area. Remember to score by a 2-hand touch down on top of the ball, not a throw down.

INVENT A SKILLS PRACTICE

For example, 3 pass 1 ball, dodging fourth with own ball with which he tries to touch a ball-handler. When he succeeds, both balls are touched down on ground. Caught player picks up a ball to become new chaser, and 1 of the other 3 picks up other to re-start.

GROUP PRACTICES AND SMALL-SIDED GAMES

1 A re-start with pass back at centre after rugby try means no forward passing henceforth. 4-person scrum after a pass forward, and 4-person line-out after the ball goes out of play over a side line. For both, non-offending team throws in and plays the ball.

2 A scoring area for handball is marked by chalk on a 3-4 metre radius. Only the goalkeeper may stand in this area.

3 For the 2 versus 2, '3 lives' games, the class may choose amicably their favourite game to be played in half of the area.

Lesson Plan – 30–45 minutes

WARM-UP AND FOOTWORK PRACTICES - 4–6 minutes

1 Alternate jogging and sprinting. In your short sprints emphasise the straightening of the rear driving leg for power and the good lifting of the leading thigh for distance.

2 Teacher's-space-tag. Can you cross from one side to the other of the area being 'guarded' by the teacher and 4 helpers with coloured bands, without being touched, to score a point? Helpers are changed over often and best scores for crossings are checked and praised.

SKILLS PRACTICES: WITH SHORT-TENNIS RACKETS AND BALLS - 8–12 minutes

Partner practices

1 One bowls gently underarm for partner to strike back for a catch by the bowler, using backhand and forehand strokes, standing side on to partner or where net would be. Change after 8 hits.

2 Racket each. Try to keep a rally going and return to readiness position, with both hands, after every stroke, i.e. face partner with racket head held in front of body with its edge towards partner. Can you rally up to 8? Stand at least 12 metres apart, ideally with a line 'net' between you.

GROUP PRACTICES AND SMALL-SIDED GAMES - 18–27 minutes

1 Short-tennis, teams of 4 or 5.
Hit ball over net and run to back of own line. What is team's best score in a rally?

2 Rounders, 4 or 5 a side, 3 catches.
Batting team follow striker to score 1-4, depending on number of bases passed before fielders make 3 catches and shout 'Stop!'

3 2 v 2, side to side games.
Choice of netball, floor-football, hockey, rugby-touch.

Lesson Notes • 4–5 Lessons Development

Lesson's main emphases

a The NC requirements to make judgements of performance and suggest ways to improve.

b From now on, with the arrival of better weather, giving greater emphasis to reflection and evaluation during lessons, after demonstrations by individuals, pairs or groups. During the winter, such moments should have been few and very short to avoid loss of warmth. Even now, particularly in the 30 minute lesson, the teacher should warn the demonstrators that they will be performing to show a certain feature of the work, so that they are standing ready for an immediate start.

Take about 40 seconds to cover the following: 'Stop everyone! Watch how Thomas and Sarah are rallying well in short-tennis. Tell me, after the demonstration, why they are being so successful and making long rallies', then the observation, the small sample of answers, and 'Thank you for the excellent demonstration and answers. Now continue and try to use some of the features that were praised.' At the start of each new set of lessons we should put the class 'in the picture' regarding the lesson's main aims and content. It seems a good idea, also, to put them in the picture regarding the value of the demonstrations, spoken reflection and evaluation. But it must not be allowed to monopolise the lesson, as often is the case.

Equipment 30 short-tennis rackets and balls; 4 cones as bases in rounders; large balls; hockey sticks and balls; netball apparatus for choice of 2 versus 2 games across thirds of the netball court.

GROUP PRACTICES AND SMALL-SIDED GAMES

1 Short-tennis net is paint line on playgound, low, long rope tied between netball posts, or long rope tied between chairs. A target circle of chalk on each side, about 5 metres from the net, helps the striker to aim at a point where the receiver is hoping the ball will come. Encourage 'Help your receiver by hitting to the forehand side.'

2 In 3-catch-rounders the ball must be kept within the third of the netball court or long, wild hitting will ruin the game. The 3 catches must be made among 3 different players of the fielding side. Batting team's score is determined by number of cones passed by the whole team, with a maximum of 4, but teams might suggest another system. For example, the striker alone might be allowed to continue running to gain extra team points.

3 A choice of 4 games for 2 versus 2 in a smallish rectangle. The 2 (or same) games chosen would each be played in half of the third used for this practice. The players would stay with their choice of game for 1 lesson, but would be allowed to change the following week, or the pairings could be changed from week to week for variety.

Lesson Plan – 30–45 minutes

WARM-UP AND FOOTWORK PRACTICES - 4–6 minutes

1 Run and jump high and run and jump long over the lines on our playground. Find out which foot you push off with in a high jump and in a long jump. It's not always the same one.

2 Partner watches height of your standing high jump over a line or cane held by partner. Feet slightly apart, swing arms up, down behind, then spring up strongly from both feet. Pull knees up for maximum height.

SKILLS PRACTICES: WITH SMALL BALLS - 8–12 minutes

Partner practices

1 At different distances throw and catch underarm and overarm. At what distance apart do you change from one to the other?

2 Across the netball court, practise bowling underarm or overarm to each other. Aim to make ball bounce a 'good length' (about 1 metre) in front of partner.

3 Backstop rolls ball for fielder to run, pick up and throw firmly just above wicket or cone height to the stationary wicketkeeper or backstop. Change over after 6 practices.

INVENT A SKILLS PRACTICE IN 2s - 3–5 minutes

Invent a practice to develop throwing, catching, fielding, wicketkeeping. (e.g. batter uses hand to strike ball at target line 'wicket', then runs to bowler's mark and back if he hits ball gently past fielders. Players decide on how batter can be 'out'.)

GROUP PRACTICES AND SMALL-SIDED GAMES - 15–22 minutes

1 Stoolball in 4s, half court, 2 groups.
After 5 bowls all rotate round 1 position (batter, bowler, backstop, fielder). Batter runs to bowler's end to score a run.

2 Volleyball, 2 v 2 over high rope 'net' between posts.
Long rally volleying, both hands. 3 volleys each side. Groups can decide how to re-start after a rally.

3 Skipping rope each or long rope, team skipping.
Quick, 1-beat action; 1 skip per rope turn. Slower, 2-beat action; 2 skips per turn. With long rope, work out best way to enter, start skipping, and leave it.

Lesson Notes • 4–5 Lessons Development

Lesson's main emphases

a The NC requirements to improve the skills of sending, receiving and striking the ball in net and striking/fielding games, and to plan, perform and reflect, for example on their own created games.

b Recognising and valuing the variety that has always been a feature of these playground games lessons. There is variety in the lesson plan itself – warm-up, skills practices, invent a game or practice, and 3 varied games. Over the year as a whole there is good variety, with the change to net and striking/fielding games and athletic activities during the summer term. We want all our children to enjoy their games lessons, to remember them with pleasure because they were interesting, challenging, exciting and varied, meaning that there was always at least some part of each lesson that they really enjoyed.

Such enjoyment and good memories, while at school, are a main incentive to continuing to participate as adults in some forms of physical activity.

Equipment 15 small balls; 1 set of stoolball apparatus; 1 long rope 'net' tied high between netball apparatus and 2 large balls for volleyball; 10 skipping ropes and 2 long skipping ropes.

TEACHING POINTS

Footwork practices

1 Be aware of your take-off foot in high and long jumps. Use the scissors high jump, swinging non-jumping foot over an imaginary bar, and landing on it first. In long jumps, with a long straight leg reaching out in front of you, land gently on both feet.

2 The 2-foot take-off, after a long swing back of both arms and a preparatory knee bend, is an explosive spring up to land on both feet. Partner judges 'As high as my waist: Well done.'

Skills practices

The 3 practices – throwing and catching; bowling; fielding, then throwing to wicketkeeper – all lend themselves to continuous practice if teacher ensures that the distances apart are sensible and not too wide.

GROUP PRACTICES AND SMALL-SIDED GAMES

1 Stoolball is a cross between rounders and cricket. The bowl to batter is like rounders and the running between the posts is like cricket. Ways to be 'out' are like cricket, and the class can agree 1 main rule and suggest ways to be 'out' to keep all fielders on their toes.

2 In volleyball, aim to volley high enough each time to lift ball above partner for a good return volley. It is co-operative, trying for a long rally together. With beginners, 1 bounce on the ground might be allowed, to be followed by striking the ball above own or another's head for the next volley.

3 In long rope, team skipping, 'Can 2 or 3 of you come in to, then leave the rope, after skipping together as a group?'

Lesson Plan – 30–45 minutes

WARM-UP AND FOOTWORK PRACTICES - 4–6 minutes

1 The outside measurement of the netball court is approximately 90 metres. Run at a comfortable speed for a minute and let me see how many circuits and metres you can do, compared with your own estimate.

2 2s, standing broad jump from a side line. Your partner will mark your distance. Try 3 jumps and use **(a)** toes turned in slightly at start, **(b)** a strong backward, then forward arm swing and **(c)** a long, low stretch out o:f body in flight.

SKILLS PRACTICES: WITH LARGE BALLS - 8–12 minutes

Group of 3 players:

1 Volley pass and follow your pass.

2 2 balls on move. Can you pressurise middle person?

3 If you have a wall, can you keep ball going, volleying to rebound to yourself?

GROUP PRACTICES AND SMALL-SIDED GAMES - 18–27 minutes

1 Volleyball or newcombe, 2 a side at high 'net' rope between netball posts.
In newcombe, receiver may catch and hold ball for a moment before 2-hand return over net. Ball may be interpassed on same side 3 times before being sent over net. No 1-handed play allowed.

2 Circular-cricket.
1 bowler, 2 batters, 1 wicketkeeper, 4 fielders. Rotate to new position every 5 or 6 balls.

3 2 v 2 over line 'net', hand-tennis, short-tennis, or quoits.
Serve from own rear line. Play 4-point game and then change sides. Encourage players to communicate with partners to cover front and rear of own court and to decide who will return a ball between them. Winning or losing couples can compete.

Lesson Notes • 4–5 Lessons Development

Lesson's main emphases

a The NC requirements to improve the skills of sending and receiving a ball in net and striking/fielding games, and to practise, adapt, improve and repeat longer and increasingly complex sequences of movement.

b A stepping back by the teacher, as the class come to the end of Key Stage 2 and primary school, to observe and reflect on:

1 Is there an atmosphere of quiet but busy, purposeful activity with all physically and wholeheartedly active, and demonstrating a pleasing level of skilfulness and versatility?

2 Is there an impression of independence and understanding with the class able to organise itself in a co-operative way, without the teacher always needing to step in to get something started?

3 Is there an impression of good sporting behaviour and making allowances for team-mates of different (lesser) abilities? Are all children given their turn and helped to take part?

4 Is everything that is happening good, safe practice? Are the class sensibly dressed, having changed for the lesson, and without jewellery? Is there a total lack of any form of anti-social, selfish or dangerous behaviour?

5 Is there an obvious impression of children at play, thoroughly enjoying themselves and having great fun together?

Equipment 10 large balls; 1 set of Kwik cricket; 10 short-tennis rackets and 3 balls; quoits as alternative choice for 2 versus 2 games.

TEACHING POINTS

Skills practices

Volleying is difficult and if some children are finding it impossible to do well, let them have 1 bounce in between volleys. After the bounce, the ball can be played up to a partner with a 'dig' with front of forearms. Hands are clasped, arms are low and straight with front of forearms used to hit the ball up with a long, smooth swing, helped by a stretching of the knees.

GROUP PRACTICES AND SMALL-SIDED GAMES

1 If the skill level is low, play newcombe, where you may hold ball momentarily on fingertips, before bending and stretching the arms to send it on its way. If skill level is average, they can try, co-operatively, to make a long rally. If skill level is very good, they can play 2 versus 2 competitively.

2 If there are 2 netball courts, one can be used for the circular-cricket so that a 20 metres wicket can be used and a bigger playing area.

3 Over the low 'net', playing a competitive 2 versus 2 game, their ability level should help decide which game they will play – the easiest quoits, the fairly easy hand-tennis, or the more difficult short-tennis with rackets.

Lesson Plan – 30–45 minutes

WARM-UP AND FOOTWORK PRACTICES - 4–5 minutes

1 Run anti-clockwise around netball court, then jog end third, sprint middle third, jog end third. Turn and repeat. Count the number of foot strikes needed to take you across the middle third and try to reduce this number by better knee lift and stronger rear leg action.

2 2s, side line sprint relay. Stand side by side down centre of court. Race on signal to touch nearer side line with foot; turn and race back to touch partner's hand. Teacher calls 'make six hand touches. Go!'

SKILLS PRACTICES: WITH SHORT-TENNIS RACKET AND BALLS - 6–10 minutes

Partner practices

1 One bowls underarm to batting partner about 4 metres away, who strikes it back, forehand, to bowler. Change over after 8 practices. Which couple can make the most catches before dropping one?

2 Have a competition with your partner, alternating striking ball up a short distance using forehand and backhand grips, i.e. palm facing up, then knuckles facing up.

GROUP PRACTICES AND SMALL-SIDED GAMES - 10–30 minutes

1 Short-tennis, 2 v 2.
Drop on end line, serve with a forehand hit. Change sides after a 4-point game. Ask teams to suggest fair ways to serve to start and restart games, e.g. by drop and hit from behind own line to person diagonally opposite.

2 Tip-and-run-cricket, 4 or 5 a side.
Challenge cricketers to agree a way to keep game moving so that no outstanding batter keeps 1 team at wicket, e.g. batters help to field before and after being 'in'.

3 Volleyball, 4 a side over high rope 'net' between netball posts.
Allow 3 volleys on each side of net. Score while serving. Team rotates round after a loss of service. Challenge volleyers to agree a 'friendly' rule to help game keep moving, e.g. 1 bounce allowed on each side.

Lesson Notes • 4–5 Lessons Development

Lesson's main emphases

a The Performing. Are skilfulness and ability evident in the neat, efficient, controlled, poised and adaptable way the skills are being used? Are the children versatile and successful performers?

b The Planning. Are their performances well organised, clearly focused and successful because they are 'seeing' ahead to guide them to be in the right place to do the right action, at the right time?

c The Reflecting/Evaluating. Following a performance, can they demonstrate that they are careful, accurate observers who can recognise main features; express pleasure about certain aspects; identify contrasting actions; and make good judgements as they suggest areas for improvement, at all times using language that is appropriate?

Equipment 30 short-tennis rackets and balls; 1 Kwik cricket set; high rope 'net' tied between netball posts and 2 large balls for volleyball; low, long rope 'net' between chairs for tennis.

TEACHING POINTS

Footwork practices

1 A better knee lift action and longer stride takes you to the line quicker if rhythm of running stays the same.

2 The relay can be speeded up by runner jumping to turn and face partner at line; by partner crouching at start for a quicker take off; by both using short, rapid strides.

Partner practices

1 The signal for the bowler to serve ball to batter is the batter taking racket from ready position in both hands back to start of forehand hit position, body turned side on to bowler. Ball is aimed to bounce up on forehand side between chest and shoulder.

2 Each has a ball and counts own score, hitting ball straight up and down, with racket face turning each time.

GROUP PRACTICES AND SMALL-SIDED GAMES

1 In short-tennis, the non-server can stand at the 'net' to cover the return of service, as a simple tactic.

2 Play tip-and-run-cricket on a second netball court if there is one, with the outside lines the ball's limit.

3 If a 1 bounce suggestion is made, it helps to remind the players to 'dig' the ball up after the bounce if it is too low to volley. The dig would be extra to the 3 volleys allowed to each team before ball must be played over the net.

Lesson Plan – 30–45 minutes

WARM-UP AND FOOTWORK PRACTICES - 4–6 minutes

1 Run, jump and land in 2 counts, nicely balanced. Pivot on rear foot and let front foot find a new space, then carry on running through that space into next jump and land '1, 2'.

2 2s, standing one behind other, facing same way down centre of court. Dodger at front sprints to a side line and stops suddenly. This sudden stop should free the dodger of the marker who has continued on for a step or 2. Change duties.

SKILLS PRACTICES: WITH LARGE BALLS - 8–12 minutes

Group practices with 1 ball among 4

1 File pass and follow using chest passes. A passes to B and runs to end of opposite line. B passes to C and runs to end of line, etc

2 Team passing using a variety of chest, bounce and overhead passes to 3 other team-mates. Pass, ideally, to a partner who has just run into a space. Passer should then move into a space to be available.

INVENT A GAME OR PRACTICE IN 4s - 3–5 minutes

Can your 4 invent a game or practice to develop passing, catching and moving into spaces? Use 1 ball and a limited area, half of third of the netball court. (e.g. team number themselves 1 to 4. One with ball passes to number he calls and the receiver must take ball running into a space. New player with ball immediately calls next number. Those not called stand still or keep away from the action.)

GROUP PRACTICES AND SMALL-SIDED GAMES - 15–22 minutes

1 2 v 2, end line touch, '3 lives', half pitch games. Attackers try to place ball on defenders' end line. Pass if touched. After 3 'lives', i.e. interceptions or goals, change duties.

2 Partner shooting practice, 1 v 1. Netball, football, basketball and hockey. 3 shots each then rotate to next goal.

3 Rugby ball and end line catch, 4 or 5 a side. Goal scored when ball thrown to team-mate on end line. Pass to team-mate is only pass allowed forward.

Lesson Notes • 4–5 Lessons Development

Lesson's main emphases

September's lesson, as always, will be used to re-establish the high standards of behaviour, instant responses, careful spacing and wholehearted participation which are essential for the successful and enjoyable progression of the year's learning programme.

Equipment 8 large balls; cones for goals for football and hockey shooting practices; 4 hockey sticks and 2 balls; 1 rugby ball.

TEACHING POINTS

Footwork practices

1 Revision of running, jumping, landing and pivoting to emphasise the 'pivot on back foot' rule. Front foot moves, 'looking' for a partner or a space'.

2 Sprint dodge frees you to receive a pass while your marking opponent continues on past you after your sudden, unexpected stop.

Skills practices

1 File passing and following practice aims to make the act of running after every pass almost subconscious. In invasion games, the one who receives the ball has the right to expect the passer, at least, to move to be available.

2 In team passing in 4s, practise passing, receiving after running into a space, and sometimes keeping out of the way by standing still. The space you run in to can be to either side, behind and in front of you. A good group should be asked to demonstrate 'court circulation' which includes those 3 features, as well as the 3 types of passing.

INVENT A SKILLS PRACTICE

By now pupils should quickly come up with an idea, a main rule to keep game moving with all having turns, and a scoring system fair to both groups in a game such as 3 v 1.

GROUP PRACTICES AND SMALL-SIDED GAMES

While the teacher has the right to expect high standards of the children, the children have the right to be given the full share of lesson time for the 3 games; the high point of their lesson.

1 '3 lives', half pitch games are good because you concentrate completely and continuously on attacking or defending. The main tactic for attackers is to pass to running partner when one is touched and has to pass. The main tactic for defenders is to mark 'in line' between attacker and goal line, preventing progress.

2 In netball and basketball, one shoots while partner watches. In football and hockey, goalkeeping partner uses 'careful, low, not too fast, well aimed shots'.

3 The end-line target player can stay there throughout, or teams can agree to throw to any team-mate on opponents' goal line, or an end-line player can have 1 turn at catching before vacating line for another to come on.

Lesson Plan – 30–45 minutes

WARM-UP AND FOOTWORK PRACTICES - 4–6 minutes

1 Run, hockey stick carried like a suitcase in right hand only, flat side to left, head of stick forward. On 'Both hands!' add left hand at top grip. Carry stick in front, head near ground.

2 Walk round practising the head up, head down position of stick head where left hand turns the stick which rotates within right hand grip.

SKILLS PRACTICES: WITH HOCKEY STICK AND BALL - 8–12 minutes

Partner practices

1 Follow-the-leader, 1 ball between 2. Indian dribble, flat side against right side of ball, stick head up, then left side of ball, head down. Zig-zag dribble, left hand turning stick, right hand supporting. Change over after 10 touches.

2 Third of class in each third of court, half with ball to dribble. All against all. Those with ball dribble to keep possession, those without try to win one.

INVENT A WHOLE CLASS GAME WHERE HALF HAVE A BALL - 3–5 minutes

Dribblers try to keep ball from those without one. Can you invent rules to make the game more interesting? (e.g. those with ball may 'hide' on a line from tacklers.)

GROUP PRACTICES AND SMALL-SIDED GAMES - 15–22 minutes

1 Playground-hockey, 4 or 5 a side.
Push pass only, no hitting. Score pass from opponents' half only. After goal, restart with pass back at centre. Defenders stay in own half for more open game. Agree main rule to prevent scrums round ball, e.g. 1 defender only may tackle.

2 Heading-ball, 4 or 5 a side with large foam ball. Goal if ball headed over opponents' end line after pass from team-mate. Target player on opponents' end line can receive pass to head or catch and throw to team-mate running forward for header. If goal line area crowded, agree rule, e.g. 2 attackers remain in own half.

3 Mini-basketball, 4 or 5 a side.
Full court, 1 on 1 marking. Encourage attacking team to space well by keeping to left and right side positions. 1 target attack player for easy shot at basket or for pass back to team-mate running in to shoot.

Lesson Notes • 4–5 Lessons Development

Lesson's main emphases

a The NC requirement to understand how well they and others have achieved what they set out to do.

b Putting the pupils 'in the picture' regarding what is expected of them this year. First and foremost we want almost non-stop action, to create and maintain warmth for maximum enjoyment of the lessons, particularly in winter, and for maximum improvement. We want signs of planning and focused activity with an emphasis on teams planning tactics so that games are no longer the 'free for alls' of earlier years. A variety of roles experience is now a requirement to replace the 'bees round a honey pot'/everyone chasing the ball impression of younger classes' games.

After demonstrations, we want to hear children expressing pleasure at admirable features; identifying the main points of good practice; sometimes contrasting 2 methods of answering a challenge; and suggesting ways in which the demonstrators (and their observers) might improve.

'In other words, children, your progress is being assessed under the 3 main headings of performing, planning and appreciating. The main heading, of course, is the performing. Let's go!'

Equipment 30 hockey sticks and 15 balls; 2 large balls.

TEACHING POINTS

Partner practices

1 In follow-the-leader, zig-zag dribbling, part of the practice can be along a line, crossing and criss-crossing it.

2 In all against all, stealing to dribble, no-one with a ball may screen the ball from a challenger. You must continue to face them.

GROUP PRACTICES AND SMALL-SIDED GAMES

Teams should agree team positions at start of games and either keep those positions for 1 week or rotate, for variety, from game to game, e.g. left attack to centre to right attack to right guard to left guard. Keeping positions is a good idea to save time on changing games. A target attack player who advances quickly to opponents' goal line when his team has possession, is a good tactic for all aware of 'Plan 1' – advance ball to the target player who can a) score, b) pass back to a running team-mate or c) pass back to safety to a guard keeping good position at the rear.

1 In hockey, aim for a less crowded game by limiting defenders to own half and to 1 side of the area, i.e. left and right defence stay to left and right sides of court.

2 Heading-ball requires 2 players to make a goal – the one who passes the ball and the one who heads it. A pass to a running player is the aim, because it is unexpected and more powerful than a header by a stationary player.

3 Full court, 1 on 1 marking demands strong, vigorous leg action from everyone. Because defenders stay with the attackers, the attacking team can shape the game as they wish.

Lesson Plan – 30–45 minutes

WARM-UP AND FOOTWORK PRACTICES - 4–6 minutes

1 Show me your best running, relaxed and quiet and with good lifting of heels, knees, head and arms. Do not follow anyone.

2 Dodge and mark across court, dodger outwitting defender with good changes of speed and direction, to reach opposite line.

SKILLS PRACTICES: 1 LARGE BALL AMONG 3 - 8–10 minutes

1 3-player weave with 2-handed chest pass. B, A, C. A passes to B and runs to B's place. B receives ball, takes 1 or 2 bounces into centre and passes to C. C receives, bounces into centre and passes to A.

2 2 v 1 passing. 2s interpass, including fakes. Always run to a space after passing, ready to receive the next pass. 3 good passes = 1 goal. Change duties often.

INVENT A GAME OR PRACTICE IN 3s - 3–5 minutes

Invent a practice for passing, receiving and running into spaces. Use 1 ball, part of line if necessary, in about half of a third of court. (e.g. 2 versus 1 passing where '1' marks person without ball so he must make successful dodge to be free to receive next pass.)

GROUP PRACTICES AND SMALL-SIDED GAMES - 15–23 minutes

1 Change-benchball, 4 or 5 a side.
To score, one on court passes to team-mate on chalk 'bench', then changes places after catcher has passed ball back to another team-mate on court. Use fakes and varied passes.

2 Floor-football, 4 or 5 a side, flattish ball.
Score by arriving, ball under control, on opponents' end line. Keep ball below knee height. Agree 1:2:1 diamond or 2:2 square attacking shape to encourage an open game, supported by 'Receive, look, pass, then move to help.'

3 Junior-netball, 4 or 5 a side.
In marking opponent, keep between him and your own goal. Tight marking 'in line' makes it hard for attacking team to move forward into good shooting or receiving position.

Lesson Notes • 4–5 Lessons Development

Lesson's main emphases

a The NC requirements to explore a variety of small-sided, competitive team games, and to devise and adapt tactics and strategies.

b Inspiring a particularly physical lesson with its running, plus dodge-and-mark, warm-up; continuous running, passing weave and 2 versus 1, passing, running, chasing skills practices; an 'invent a game' idea designed to make players run and dodge to become free; and 3 games which should be full of running by offenders and by 1 on 1, close marking defenders.

If one main aim of physical education is to inspire vigorous, wholehearted and almost non-stop action to compensate for the inactive, sedentary lifestyles of the majority of our children nowadays, this lesson can do just that, particularly if the 3 linking parts to the lesson are carried out smartly.

Equipment 10 large balls; 1 flattish ball for football; set of netball apparatus; chalk to mark 2 'benches'.

TEACHING POINTS

Footwork practices

1 At Year 7 level, keep the running going non-stop for about 2 minutes, teaching while the action is going on.

2 Explain that we will be using close, 1 on 1 marking in our games today, and defenders aim to keep 'in line' between attacking player and where they want to go. Defenders stay low, feet apart, 'boxer's shuffling' backwards and to the side, never crossing feet or bringing feet together. Weight is forward.

Skills practices

1 At its best, the 3-player weave is a continuous figure 8 pattern, with all 3 weaving. Pass is very short, almost a little hand-off. 'Move in, receive, bounce, recover, pass, move out.'

2 Practise faking with head, shoulder or 1 foot, and see which influences the '1' the most. Reflect on which succeeded, and remember it for future use.

GROUP PRACTICES AND SMALL-SIDED GAMES

1 Keep wide awake in change-bench-ball. One who made the pass goes on to bench. One on bench passes to a team-mate before leaving bench. Defenders have to pick up a new opponent if own one goes on to bench. To practise skill of the weave above, allow 1 bounce, then you must pass.

2 In floor-football, ask players to decide how to limit player movement to help make game more open. For example, 1 or 2 defenders must stay in own half.

3 Encourage shooting by scoring 1 point for a near miss that hits ring, and 2 for a proper goal going through the hoop.

Lesson Plan – 30–45 minutes

WARM-UP AND FOOTWORK PRACTICES - 4–6 minutes

1 Run freely over netball court, side steps to avoid others. In a crowded area, run slowly, faster when space permits.

2 Dodge-and-mark. Dodgers try to lose partner with sudden sprint, stop or direction change. On 'Stop!' all freeze. Is dodger clear or within reach of marker? Change duties.

SKILLS PRACTICES: WITH RUGBY BALLS OR LARGE BALLS - 6–10 minutes

Partner practices
Third of class in each third of netball court, 1 ball between 2.

1 Run and pass to partner, varying passes to avoid other couples near you.

2 On 'Change!' one with ball puts it down. All try to pick up nearest ball, find new partner and interpass again.

INVENT A GAME OR GAMES PRACTICE - 4–6 minutes

Half of group in your third of court have ball to start with. Invent chasing game using dodging and 2 hands on hips tackle. (e.g. 1 player calls '1!', '2' etc. every 10 seconds.

Each game, score if you keep ball, i.e. were not tackled and had to give it up, or if you gained one.)

GROUP PRACTICES AND SMALL-SIDED GAMES - 16–23 minutes

1 Playground, new-image-rugby, 4 or 5 a side. Score by placing ball on ground behind opponents' goal line. If touched on hips by opponent's 2 hands, pass. After score, re-start with pass back at centre. Back passes only. If forward pass, form 4-person scrum. 4-person line-out if ball over side line.

2 Playground-hockey, 4 or 5 a side. Shooting area is restricted to end third marked by chalk line, i.e. no long hits. Restart after goal with push pass back at centre. Passing is quicker than dribbling. Look, pass, move forward for next pass.

3 Mini-basketball, 4 or 5 a side. Mark opponent all over court. Keep 'in line' between opponent and own basket. In attack, shape game 1:2:1: 1 defender, 2 forwards moving about to receive passes, 1 target player near their basket to shoot or pass back to advancing player.

Lesson Notes • 4–5 Lessons Development

Lesson's main emphases

a The NC requirements to extend the skills and principles learned in earlier years to develop techniques, tactics and strategies; and to work vigorously to develop strength and stamina, and to exercise the heart and lungs strongly.

b Developing quick reactions by: side stepping to avoid others and reacting quickly to dodging partner in the warm-up and footwork practices; reacting to others near you and to 'Change!' in the skills practices; quick dodges to avoid being tackled in the 'invent a game'; and 3 games where we will emphasise 'Plan 2' today, that is the fast break to react at high speed as a team when you suddenly gain possession.

The whole team must be 'fast break conscious' and never hold up play when our team, who were defending, suddenly become the attackers after an interception or a 'steal'. The target player or centre sprints to the opponents' line, the 2 forwards advance down own sides and the defender follows play. Person with ball should pass it forward at speed, then follow at speed to help.

Equipment 15 large or rugby balls; 10 hockey sticks and 1 ball; 1 set netball apparatus.

TEACHING POINTS

Footwork practices

1 It's December. Keep the running and side stepping going non-stop for 2 minutes, and do the teaching, coaching and praising while the action is happening.

2 Limit dodgers to evading partners by changing direction or speed, stopping suddenly, or faking one way and going the other. Fast sprinting not allowed. It's dangerous in a crowded area.

Partner practices

1 Much use of peripheral vision is needed in the running and passing where all are weaving in and out of one another. Aim pass just ahead of running partner for him to run on to.

2 Find a new ball and a new partner and see if your couple is first to get started, running and passing again.

GROUP PRACTICES AND SMALL-SIDED GAMES

All start by standing in team positions (centre, forwards or guards), marking own opponent. Teacher asks 'Will you all point to the opponent you are marking. When that team has the ball, you must defend vigorously between your opponent and your own goal line' and 'When your team suddenly steals or intercepts the ball, all think 'Fast break' and advance ball to your centre or forwards, before opponents race back.'

1 In the rugby, encourage 'Run straight to gain

ground until 'tackled', then pass to someone running, not too far behind you, to try to advance the ball again.'

2 In hockey, score by arriving on end line with ball under control or by passing to someone at the end line. As in the other 2 games, the attackers shape their positions to create space.

3 In basketball, remember that a pass travels quicker than a dribbled ball. Minimum dribbling, maximum passing and following.

Lesson Plan – 30–45 minutes

WARM-UP AND FOOTWORK PRACTICES - 4–6 minutes

1 Move backwards, using 'boxer's shuffle', feet always apart, knees and hips bent in low dodging position. Small, quick movements across and backwards on court. Sprint back to start line and repeat.

2 10-points-tag where all start with 10 points. A point is lost each time someone touches you. Use good footwork to avoid being caught. Teacher checks best remaining score.

SKILLS PRACTICES: WITH LARGE BALLS - 6–10 minutes

Partner practice

1 Third of class in each third of netball court, half with ball at foot, dribbling to stay in the third and to shield ball from those without.

2 3-4 metres apart, passing with foot and moving, using 1 touch to stop and receive ball, gentle touch to push it forward towards space partner has moved into, and a third touch to pass to partner. Having passed, move to a new space for partner's return pass.

3 Football-tennis with partner, using line as 'net'. Allow ball to bounce once only on each side. Can you control ball with foot instep and forehead?

GROUP PRACTICES AND SMALL-SIDED GAMES - 20–29 minutes

1 Football, 2 v 2 against 2 goalkeepers.
Couples must make 1 pass at least before shooting. Gentle shots, please. Others waiting their turn to rotate with above 6 can have ball each and see how many consecutive headers they can make. After successful shot, scorers change places with the 2 goalkeepers.

2 New-image-rugby, 4 or 5 a side.
2-hand touch on hips = a tackle. Pass backwards only. If ball thrown forward, opponent throws it into 4-person scrum, 2 from each side. Only throwing-in side may heel it back. If ball goes over side line, non-offending team throws it into 4-person line-out.

3 Handball, 4 or 5 a side.
Shoot from inside opponents' half only, but outside goal semi-circle, where goalkeeper only allowed. Defending team mark 1 on 1, very tightly, to block opponents' view of goal, making it hard to pass, catch, shoot.

Lesson Notes • 4–5 Lessons Development

Lesson's main emphases

a The NC requirements to play a variety of small-sided versions of recognised games, and to play fairly, compete honestly and demonstrate good sporting behaviour.

b Emphasising that cold January is an ideal time to have a lesson concerned with being thoughtful, quiet, safety conscious, unselfishly trying to bring everyone into a full share of the lesson, particularly the 3 games, and noticing and complimenting those deemed to be 'fair play' exponents.

After the lesson, back in class, the teacher should make a point of praising those pupils who demonstrated those very good personal qualities sometimes lacking in gifted, but greedy, selfish sportspersons.

Equipment 15 large balls; 1 rugby ball; chalk for drawing semi-circles round goal in handball.

TEACHING POINTS

Footwork practices

1 The 'boxer's shuffle', defensive footwork practice, going backwards down the court, is best done against the teacher, advancing and moving side to side as well as gradually forwards. The class keep 'in line' between the teacher and the end line.

2 In 10-points-tag, encourage class to chase as keenly as they are trying to keep their points. 'Who was a good dodger and still has 10 points? And who was adventurous and caught at least 4?'

Partner practices

1 The dribbling practice can be enlivened by the teacher occasionally calling 'Change!', a signal to leave the ball you are dribbling and go chasing after another one.

2 The partner passing and moving practice which starts off with 3 touches per person can be made more challenging with a good group by changing to 2 touches, and then to 1 touch only, each time. Receivers must quickly place themselves ready, well balanced, to send the ball straight back to their partner.

3 In football-tennis over a line, you may play with your partner, making long rallies, or against your partner to make points, depending on your ability and choice.

GROUP PRACTICES AND SMALL-SIDED GAMES

'Children, as well as enjoying 3 exciting games today, I want you to think about who are the best players in helping others to be fully involved, hard working and unselfish and an example to us with their good sporting behaviour.'

1 In this football game, we have 1 of the few occasions when we shoot through a goal. Usually we arrive on the line with the ball under control. Therefore 'Gentle, low, well-aimed shots, please.'

2 Because of difficulty of placing 2 hands on 2 hips to tackle, encourage 'Run fast and straight to gain ground, and try out your best dodges and fake passes to mislead your opponent.'

3 Limit scoring throws to 'below waist height only' so that ball does not leave the playground or strike players' faces.

Lesson Plan – 30–45 minutes

WARM-UP AND FOOTWORK PRACTICES - 4–6 minutes

1 Run, jump and land in 2 counts, pivot on rear foot. Front foot finds space to run through. Then sprint and stop suddenly to evade imaginary opponent. Sprint again into run, jump, land, pivot, etc.

2 Couples-tag. 3 couples start as chasers, hands joined. When one of the couples catches a dodger, the dodger changes places with the catcher to form a new chasing pair. Winner is last person caught.

SKILLS PRACTICES: WITH HOCKEY STICKS AND BALLS - 8–12 minutes

Small group practices

1 Files of 4, pass and follow. A passes to B and runs to end of opposite line. B passes to C and runs to end of opposite line. How many passes can you make in 1 minute?

2 3 versus 1, interpassing in an area no bigger than half of a third of a netball court to give '1' a chance. Change duties often.

INVENT A GAME OR GAMES PRACTICE IN 3s - 3–5 minutes

With 1 ball in limited area, invent a practice for passing and moving skills. (e.g. start in a triangle, 7 metres apart. 1 passes to 2, runs to touch 2's corner then back to own, while 2 passes to 3 and runs to touch 3's corner, etc.)

GROUP PRACTICES AND SMALL-SIDED GAMES - 15–22 minutes

1 Playground-hockey, 4 or 5 a side.
End third marked by chalk is shooting area. After goal, re-start at centre with pass back. '2 touch' game: catch on '1', look for team-mate in a space, pass on '2', run to new space to be ready.

2 Mini-basketball, 4 or 5 a side, 1 on 1, full court. In defence, keep between opponent and own basket to hinder dribbling, good moves, receiving or shots. In attack, advance ball fast to centre target player for shot or return pass.

3 Floor-football, 4 or 5 a side, flattish ball. Score by arriving on opponents' line, ball in control under foot. 2 defenders in own half cover each other and quickly advance ball to forwards spaced out in opponents' half.

Lesson Notes • 4–5 Lessons Development

Lesson's main emphases

The games now should be looking less frantic, slower and more careful, open and deliberate, with:

a some players keeping out of the action to give others space

b a target player, or centre, in an advanced position with his back towards the opponents' goal line, moving all the time to be free to receive a pass

c left and right side forwards and defenders generally playing on those sides of the court where others expect them to be, for an attacking pass to a forward or a back, safety pass to a defender

d close marking, 1 on 1 defence in all games to make passing catching, dribbling, shooting and moving generally difficult

e an awareness of the fast break as the best way to advance the ball, before the opponents gather themselves, after a sudden change of possession

f the passer, at least, always running to look for a space, in which to receive the next pass

g 4 or 5 attacking players understanding that they can shape their game and make the opponents mirror that shape. Well spaced attackers can create opportunities for combining to pass and advance the ball by keeping away from one another – unlike so much of the play among younger children, all shouting for the ball and surrounding the ball-handler.

Equipment 30 hockey sticks and 10 balls; 1 large ball; 1 flattish ball for football; 4 cones for goals in hockey.

TEACHING POINTS

Footwork practices

1 By now they should have their own, well practised jump and land action that gives them the same pivoting foot each time.

2 The 3 starting couples can keep to a third each as chasers, covering the whole space efficiently, in a well planned way.

Skills practices

1 File pass and follow, give and go, trains a player to pass, then move to a new position. A careful, silent push of stick placed behind ball, not hit, must be insisted on. A long backswing of stick and a long, high, dangerous follow through must never be allowed.

2 To make the practice realistic of the game situation, ask the chasing '1' to confront the ball-holder each time. Those with the ball should be reminded that 'screening' the ball (putting your own body between ball and opponent) is not allowed in hockey.

GROUP PRACTICES AND SMALL-SIDED GAMES

1 In playground-hockey, score through a 3-metre-wide goal marked by cones. In cold weather, change goalkeeper often. If game is not open and flowing, challenge teams to decide on a rule that helps. For example, no tackling allowed. Defenders may only confront an attacker who then must pass, or no tackling a player in own half.

2 'No dribbling in own half' is a good rule in basketball, particularly for fast breaks. A pass is quicker than a dribble. In attack, focus on centre playing near post. He can shoot, pass back to a running player, or take guard out of way to leave space for a team-mate to come in for a shot.

3 To increase scoring chances in football, a goal might be scored by a pass to a team-mate, anywhere on the opponents' goal line.

Lesson Plan – 30–45 minutes

WARM-UP AND FOOTWORK PRACTICES - 4–6 minutes

1 Run in steady rhythm beside partner. On turns, one takes shorter steps, the other longer to move in an arc.

2 Side by side running. One makes short sprint dodge away from partner, then slows to side again. Change to let partner practise.

SKILLS PRACTICES: WITH RUGBY BALLS OR LARGE BALLS - 8–12 minutes

Group practices in 8s

1 A and B with balls run to give them to opposite players, C and D, then stay at back of that line. Avoid bumping in middle. C and D carry ball back to next person opposite.

2 Same formation but ball placed on ground by first runner. When opposite team-mate touched, he runs in, bends down, one foot in front of other, to pick up ball and give it to opposite person who runs in to put it down.

INVENT A GAME IN 8s - 3–5 minutes

Invent a running, dodging game to improve reactions. (e.g. in half of third of netball court, 4 have a ball. Those without try to win one by touching ball-carrier on both hips. Every 10 seconds, 1 player calls 'Change!'. Aim now is to get rid of ball by touching someone with it.)

GROUP PRACTICES AND SMALL-SIDED GAMES - 15–22 minutes

1 New-image-rugby, 4 or 5 a side.
Pass backwards only. If forwards, form 4-person scrum, 2 from each side. Only throwing in, non-offending team may heel it back. After score re-start at centre. 'Run straight till tackled, then pass to near, running team-mate.'

2 Heading-ball, 4 or 5 a side, using large foam ball.
Goal when ball headed over opponents' goal line after pass by team-mate for a header. In attack, put 1 target player near opponents' goal line to receive passes to head or pass back to team-mate running for header.

3 Playground-hockey, 4 or 5 a side.
Scoring shot only from inside end third marked by chalk. After goal, restart at centre with pass back. Emphasise 'Pass is quicker than dribble for advancing ball. 'Receive it; look for a team-mate; pass; run forward to a space.

Lesson Notes • 4–5 Lessons Development

Lesson's main emphases

The NC requirement to understand how well they and others have achieved what they set out to do, appreciating strengths and weaknesses.

October's lesson included putting the class 'in the picture' regarding the 3 main headings when progress in physical education is being considered. They are performing, planning and evaluating/reflecting, with the doing or performing the most important. We want children to demonstrate physical competence and versatility, and we want them to become observant, thoughtful and good learners.

As we come to the last, wholly invasion games centred lesson of the year, it is a good time to ask the class to reflect on the skills, knowledge and understanding which they feel they have achieved so far. They can also be asked to assess the quality of the attitudes being displayed, generally, in their games lessons.

Equipment 8 rugby or large balls; 1 large foam ball for heading-ball; 10 hockey sticks and 1 ball.

TEACHING POINTS

Footwork practices

1 Keep the steady, repeating rhythm of the easy, 'cruising speed' running going for 1 to 2 minutes. It is a pleasant partner activity and an excellent exercise for stimulating heart and lungs.

2 The sudden acceleration in the unexpected, short sprint dodge frees the dodger momentarily to receive a pass in a game.

Skills practices

1 In the run-and-pass drill, ball can be handed to receiver's outstretched hands. Awareness of other runner crossing in front of you is good practice for quick reactions.

2 Focus on the press down with both hands as in try scoring, and the run, turn, swoop down, quick pick-up to retrieve.

INVENT A GAME

'Quick reactions' are the teacher's main requirements for this practice.

GROUP PRACTICES AND SMALL-SIDED GAMES

1 In rugby, the close, hand-off pass practised in 8s can be used to someone running across behind you in a scissors movement. This move can also be a fake pass with the ball-handler pretending to pass to the runner crossing behind,

2 The close, scissors-like pass can be used in heading-ball to a player cutting close to the

person with the ball, who almost places the it against the running team-mate's forehead.

3 In hockey, contrast the short pass back to a close team-mate in rugby and heading-ball with long, through passes to a well spaced team-mate.

Lesson Plan – 30–45 minutes

WARM-UP AND FOOTWORK PRACTICES - 4–6 minutes

1 Run and long jump over the lines, emphasising the straight front leg reaching forward. Now run and jump high emphasising the high knee lift of the leading leg.

2 2s standing at one side line do a standing broad jump alternately across the court. See how many jumps your pair needs to cross to the other side.

SKILLS PRACTICES: WITH SMALL BALLS AND STOOLBALL BATS - 8–12 minutes

Partner practice

1 Batting partner strikes to catching partner at various height and speeds, to left and right. Fielder with hands forward in the catching position should move early and try to be stationary, eyes on the ball, at the time of catching.

Group practice in 4s

2 Bowler, batter, backstop and fielder. Gentle underarm bowling for easy batting back to bowler or fielder and occasionally to backstop when batter lets it go through. Rotate often.

INVENT A GAME IN 4s - 3–5 minutes

Can your 4 invent a game with bat, ball, corner of third of netball court and perhaps a cone or hoop?

(e.g. decide rules, scoring, when 'out', and how to rotate duties.)

GROUP PRACTICES AND SMALL-SIDED GAMES - 15–22 minutes

1 Change-bench-ball, 4 or 5 a side.
Goal scored by passing to team-mate on chalk bench. Passer changes places with bench-mate, who throws ball to a team-mate on court. Use bounce, chest, overhead and fake passes.

2 Stoolball, 4 or 5 a side.
Posts about 12 metres apart, bowling line midway. 2 batters score as in cricket. Each of team fielding bowls a 6 ball over. Bowl underarm, without bounce, at stool or post.

3 Short-tennis, 2 groups of 4 or 5.
Ball is hit carefully over net line and hitter runs to end of opposite team line. How long a rally can your group make?

Lesson Notes • 4–5 Lessons Development

Lesson's main emphases

a The NC requirements to explore a variety of small-sided versions of recognised games; and to increase their range of skill, adapting and refining performance.

b Informing the pupils that the lessons followed during April to July concentrate on net/wall and striking/fielding games and athletic activities. Point out that the variety within each lesson is provided to give enjoyment to as many as possible, and that the variety provided by the changing seasons also aims to make the programme as interesting and informative as possible.

Equipment 15 small bat shapes and 15 small balls; 1 set of stoolball apparatus; 10 short-tennis rackets and 2 balls; 1 large ball for bench-ball, and chalk for marking the benches.

TEACHING POINTS

Footwork practices

1 'Notice how you can see your leading foot at the end of your straight leg in the long jump action. In your bounding, springing high jump action, notice how you can see only the bent knee of your leading leg.'

2 In the standing broad jump, start with feet slightly apart, toes turned in. Swing arms strongly above head, then down behind back along with a knees bend. Spring strongly forward with arms reaching ahead, and try to pull legs from stretch in flight to a good bend on landing.

Partner practices

1 Batter and fielder stand 4 metres apart. This practice emphasises the unpredictable heights, speeds, and angles at which the ball comes to you in striking/fielding games. 'Be ready!' with hands forward. Watching ball all the way and trying to be stationary at the time of catching are the important points.

2 In the group practice of bowling, batting and fielding, the batter should let about 1 ball in 4 go through to the backstop to give him practice. Rotate every eighth ball.

GROUP PRACTICES AND SMALL-SIDED GAMES

Inform class of the varied nature of the 3 games types represented.

1 Invasion games like bench-ball and our traditional winter games are full of action, chasing and being chased, with opponents beside you in the same area, making scoring difficult. These vigorous, running games are the only ones appropriate in cold weather.

2 Striking/fielding games like stoolball, cricket and rounders are less active, have difficult skills and pit 1 or 2 batters against all the rest who are trying to get them out in a variety of ways. Because of their potential inactivity, these games are only played during late spring, summer and early autumn.

3 In net games like short-tennis, teams are in separate areas and teamwork is simple. They can be played enjoyably by 2 players. These games which can be static and not very vigorous are more suitable for warmer weather from April until September.

Lesson Plan – 30–45 minutes

WARM-UP AND FOOTWORK PRACTICES - 4–6 minutes

1 Follow your leader who will try to include 3 different actions, e.g. hurdling, hopping, long jumping. Can you build up to repeating your sequence in unison?

2 Stand one behind the other at centre of court forming a long line. Front person sprints to touch side line, sprints back to touch opposite side line, runs in and touches partner's hand as signal to do same. Make 6 touches, 'Go!'.

SKILLS PRACTICES: WITH SMALL BALLS - 8–12 minutes

Partner practices

1 Throwing to a partner, 2-3 metres apart. Throw at medium height (waist), higher (chest), higher (head). Can you do this walking around?

2 Face partner at 3 metres. Throw low (shins), medium (waist), and higher (head).

3 Can you bowl ball to partner and spin it between index and long fingers?

GROUP PRACTICES AND SMALL-SIDED GAMES - 18–27 minutes

1 3-catch-rounders, 4 or 5 a side.
Batting team runs behind hitter and round bases, scoring 1 point for each base passed before fielders make 3 catches and shout 'Stop!' Each batter has 1 innings only, then teams change duties.

2 Newcombe, 2 or 3 a side, high rope 'net' tied between netball posts.
In this simplified form of volleyball, server throws ball over net. Receiver may catch and hold ball momentarily before 2-hand return over net. Ball may be interpassed on same side 3 times before sending it over net. No one-handed play is allowed.

3 Non-stop-cricket in 4s or 5s in half of area. On touching the ball, batter must run round cone while fielders try to get him out, even by bowling when he is not at wicket.

Lesson Notes • 4–5 Lessons Development

Lesson's main emphases

a The NC requirements to understand how well they and others have achieved what they set out to do, appreciating strengths and limitations; and to suggest ways to improve quality and degree of difficulty of performance.

b Reflecting and evaluating within the lesson, which was difficult to carry out in cold, winter lessons when we wanted almost non-stop action to keep warm. Such reflection is easier now in warmer weather, but still needs to be carried out quickly, with the demonstrators warned to be ready. 'Stop! Let us all watch a couple of balls being bowled in non-stop-cricket. Notice how the fielders have hands forward ready to pounce on the ball and to return it quickly to the bowler or wicketkeeper. Tell me where a good length ball should bounce in front of the batter.' Demonstration and the follow-up answers should take no more than 45 seconds.

Equipment 15 small balls; 2 large balls for newcombe and a high rope 'net' between netball posts; 1 Kwik cricket set.

TEACHING POINTS

Footwork practices

1 In the follow-the-leader sequence, the class can be asked to check on which foot they use in take-offs in long and high jumps and hurdling.

2 In the touch-2-side-lines relay, greater speed can be produced by a jumping turn at each line into a crouch for the sprint back; by being crouched for the hand touch; and by using small, rapid strides for quick starts.

Partner practices

1 Catching throws below chest height is done with fingers pointing down, thumbs out. Catching throws above chest height is done with fingertips pointing upwards, thumbs in.

2 In standing, catching at short distances, have 1 foot forward for balance as you reach forward and down, and have hands well forward, ready to move.

3 Spinning can be practised on the spot, throwing the twisting ball straight up, and watching it come down vertically, then spin off to one side. If overarm bowling is a problem, let them bowl underarm which also makes the spinning easier.

GROUP PRACTICES AND SMALL-SIDED GAMES

In all 3 games, ask for suggestions to 'keep games moving, involve everyone, be fair.'

1 If possible, use different netball court for 3-catch-rounders. Limit distance ball may be hit to outside lines of court. Fielders must involve 3 different catchers. Batters use hand or bat.

2 Because ball may be caught momentarily (making game easier) before return over net or pass to partner, allow no bounces. 2-hand (fingertips) contact, even for catches. Agree main rule, scoring method, length of game.

3 A good length circle can be drawn in chalk to help bowlers aim at a spot where the batter will have difficulty in playing.

Lesson Plan – 30–45 minutes

WARM-UP AND FOOTWORK PRACTICES - 3 minutes

With your partner, jog round the outside of the netball court which is a 'track' of about 90 metres. Keep a steady pace for a minute and count your laps and part laps to work out how far you ran in your minute. Next lesson you might travel a little bit further.

SKILLS PRACTICES: WITH LARGE BALLS - 6–10 minutes

Partner practices

1 Volleyball dig pass to partner. Contact is made with forearms. Hands placed one on other, thumb and arms straight with elbows close and inner part of forearms forward and held low at all times. Use dig when ball is too low to volley. Long smooth swing of arms is helped by the bending and stretching of legs. Dig; let bounce; dig; let bounce.

2 One throws ball up just above head height, volleys to partner who allows ball to bounce, then digs it above partner's head for return volley. Change duties after 5 or 6 practices.

GROUP PRACTICES AND SMALL-SIDED GAMES - 21–32 minutes

1 Stoolball, 4 or 5 a side.
Posts, about 12 metres apart, bowling line midway. 2 batters score by changing ends as in cricket and can be 'out' as in cricket. Fielders rotate after every 6 ball over. Ball bowled, no bounce, at stool or post.

2 Choice of 2 v 2 volleyball, newcombe or quoits over high rope 'net'.
2 partners volleying to each other over 'net'. 3 interpasses allowed before returning ball.

3 Short-tennis, 1 v 1.
In 2s, over a 'net'. Either compete against each other or try to sustain rallies as long as possible.

Lesson Notes • 4–5 Lessons Development

Lesson's main emphases

a The NC requirements to develop tactics and to observe the etiquette and rules/laws specific to each game.

b Hoping that a 'healthy and enjoyable lifestyle' might now be becoming a way of life for many of the pupils, inspired in the beginning by their intense enjoyment of their physical education lessons.

All staff involved in teaching physical education, from Key Stage 1 upwards, need to be believers in the D.E.S. Assessment of Performance Unit's statement: 'Motor development, which forms an integral part of the individual's total development, contributes to the quality of life, to the development of personal and interpersonal skills and often significantly influences the choice of lifestyle. The individual's regard for and attitude towards his physical self, especially at primary school stage, is important to the development of self-image and to the value you give yourself.'

Equipment 15 large balls; 1 long rope 'net' tied between netball posts; stoolball apparatus; 10 short-tennis rackets and 5 balls.

TEACHING POINTS

Footwork practices
Class will be able to monitor how their easy, steady jogging (arms and heels fairly low) becomes easier and goes further, week by week. They will be interested to know that this simple stimulation of the heart beat, practised for 20 minutes 3 times per week, would compensate for the inactive, sedentary lifestyles typical of the majority of children today. They may wish not to be included among those now deemed to be 'sick at heart' by researchers at Exeter University studying the health and lifestyles of hundreds of children.

Partner practices
1 'Digging' is as easy as volleying is difficult. In games at the end of a lesson, allow 1 bounce for dig up to nearby partner for him to volley.

2 In pairs, one can throw ball above own head and volley to partner, who digs up above partner for a return volley. This adds good variety to last game in the lesson.

GROUP PRACTICES AND SMALL-SIDED GAMES

More than half of the lesson time has been allocated for the 6 teams to prove that they are sufficiently independent now to organise their 3 games amicably and sensibly As the teacher visits each group in turn, he should ask 'What is your main rule? How are you scoring? How are you ensuring that everyone is fully involved?'

Lesson Plan – 30–45 minutes

WARM-UP AND FOOTWORK PRACTICES - 4–6 minutes

1 Advance down court in lines of 5 or 6 across, walking first third of netball court, jogging through middle third and then sprinting to race to cross the end of court line where teacher will call out names of winners. Finish fast! Don't slow down at end of line.

2 Relay race with 3 in a team. A runs to touch B's hand at line. B runs to touch C's hand at line. C runs to end line and turns back to touch B who runs to touch A who runs to end line which was also the start line, where teacher calls out the winning trio.

SKILLS PRACTICES: WITH SHORT-TENNIS RACKETS AND BALLS - 6–9 minutes

Partner practices

1 Serve by dropping ball and doing forehand hit. See how long a rally you and your partner can make using the full width of the court.

2 Now can you serve a forehand to partner who volleys? Volleying is when the ball is struck before it bounces. It is a 'punch' shot without a follow through. Remember to return to the ready position each time between strokes. Racket is held in front of body with the edge towards your partner. Change duties after about 8 practices.

GROUP PRACTICES AND SMALL-SIDED GAMES - 20–30 minutes

1 Short-tennis, 2 v 2, 5-point games.
Change ends after 5-point games. Serve by dropping on end line, then striking.

2 Partners-cricket.
Couples rotate every 8 balls (2 short overs).

3 Volleyball, 5 a side.
Volleying over high rope 'net' tied between netball apparatus. Rotate positions regularly.

Lesson Notes • 4–5 Lessons Development

Lesson's main emphases

The NC requirement to select and combine skills and apply them accurately and appropriately in increasingly demanding situations.

As we come to the final, forty-fourth lesson of the Middle School games programme, it is hoped that the majority of the class will confirm 'We have thoroughly enjoyed our playground games lessons. All year round we have looked forward to them because they are good fun, interesting and varied. We have learned an enormous amount from our teacher and from one another. We are very pleased with and proud of our achievements and our skilfulness which our bodies seem to retain.

The lessons have helped our class to get on well together as we have all been helped or helped others many times. We have been well praised by our teacher and thanked for our quiet, non-stop, enthusiastic way of working. There has never been a serious accident in spite of all the activity in quite a small space. We believe that exercise in the fresh air is good for you and we have always felt refreshed, wide awake and calm after these lessons. This has helped our classroom work.'

Equipment 30 short-tennis rackets and 15 balls; 1 set of Kwik cricket; 1 long rope 'net' tied between netball posts and 1 large ball for volleyball; 1 long rope, short-tennis 'net' tied between chairs.

GROUP PRACTICES AND SMALL-SIDED GAMES

As last month the games are allocated more than half of the lesson time. As last month the class is entrusted to be independent and to organise itself, possibly with a different 'leader' as they come to each game. The 12-15 changes of game during the 4-5 weeks duration of the lesson provide plenty of opportunity for everyone to experience the variety of roles appropriate from this age onwards.

Officiating is one of the roles to be included, and 1 player from each side could have the responsibility for calling out infringements when they are caused by his own team. As last month the teacher, moving from game to game, will ask: 'What is your main agreed rule? How are you scoring? How are you ensuring that the game keeps going and involves everyone fairly?'

Index